Empire and Environment

Empire and Environment

Ecological Ruin in the Transpacific

Edited by
Jeffrey Santa Ana
Heidi Amin-Hong
Rina Garcia Chua
and Zhou Xiaojing

University of Michigan Press
Ann Arbor

Published in the United States of America by the
University of Michigan Press
Manufactured in the United States of America
Printed on acid-free paper
First published October 2022

A CIP catalog record for this book is available from the British Library.

Library of Congress Control Number: 2022025002
LC record available at https://lccn.loc.gov/2022025002
Ebook LC record available at https://lccn.loc.gov/2022025003

ISBN 978-0-472-07493-8 (hardcover : alk. paper)
ISBN 978-0-472-05493-0 (paper : alk. paper)
ISBN 978-0-472-90299-6 (open access ebook)

https://doi.org/10.3998/mpub.11580516

An electronic version of this book is freely available, thanks to the support of libraries working
with Knowledge Unlatched (KU). KU is a collaborative initiative designed to make high quality
books Open Access for the public good. More information about the initiative and links to the
Open Access version can be found at www.knowledgeunlatched.org.

The University of Michigan Press's open access publishing program is made possible thanks
to additional funding from the University of Michigan Office of the Provost and the generous
support of contributing libraries.

Cover illustration: Joy Enomoto, *The Spill*, acrylic, paint pen, salt, and molasses on cardboard,
by permission of the artist.

CONTENTS

Part II. Militarized Environments

Part III. Decolonizing the Transpacific: Settler Colonialism and Indigenous Resistance

Part IV. Climate Justice and Ecological Futurities

Digital materials related to this title can be found on
the Fulcrum platform via the following citable URL:
https://doi.org/10.3998/mpub.11580516

ACKNOWLEDGMENTS

This book volume began as a panel at the Association for the Study of Literature and Environment (ASLE) Conference held in Detroit, Michigan on June 20–24, 2017. The panel consisted of the volume's editors, whose work engages with the environmental humanities and ecocriticism, specifically the environmental legacies and degradation of empires in their former colonies in the transpacific region. Thus, we thank ASLE for bringing the four of us together, and for facilitating spaces where this collaborative work was able to develop and flourish from that fateful meeting in Detroit to field trips, manuscript workshops, and subsequent panels at the ASLE Conference held at UC Davis on June 26–30, 2019. We appreciate ASLE and the UC Davis English department for providing time and meeting space for a manuscript workshop. This gathering was transformative for the coeditors and for the contributors who were able to attend, and enabled us to strengthen the volume's focus on literary and aesthetic responses to ecological destruction.

We are especially grateful to Sara Jo Cohen at the University of Michigan Press. Sara's sustained commitment to our project from the start of its publication at the press was an indispensable source of assurance. We are grateful for her and her colleagues' professionalism, and very much appreciate their continuing dedication to publishing in American studies and transpacific studies. We give thanks to the anonymous reviewers who read the manuscript with care and dedication, providing generative feedback at a critical stage of the project. The book benefits from the funding and support of Knowledge Unlatched and Open Access; Stony Brook University's Faculty of the Arts, Humanities, and Social Sciences (FAHSS); Davidson College's Faculty Research Grant; and University of the Pacific's Faculty Research Grant.

Our gratitude also goes to Joy Enomoto, designer of the cover image, "The Spill," which evokes one of the worst marine disasters in recent Hawaiian history, when in 2013 a Matson container leaked 226,000 gallons of molasses into Honolulu harbor, killing thousands of fish. We are honored that Enomoto created "The Spill" to capture the themes of this anthology.

Jeffrey Santa Ana expresses warm and heartfelt thanks to his coeditors Heidi Amin-Hong, Rina Garcia Chua, and Zhou Xiaojing. I am most fortunate to have them as friends and colleagues. This book exists because of their unwavering effort and dedication to bring it to fruition.

Heidi Amin-Hong is deeply thankful for Jeffrey Santa Ana, Rina Garcia Chua, and Zhou Xiaojing, who have been dream collaborators in every sense. I learned so much from you all and am so grateful to call you friends, colleagues, and co-conspirators. I also appreciate the many colleagues and friends at the University of Southern California, Davidson College, and the University of Santa Barbara who have seen this project at various stages of completion. I am grateful to my faculty mentors at USC, Viet Thanh Nguyen, Aimee Bahng, John Carlos Rowe, Nayan Shah, and Neetu Khanna, who have been unwavering in their support for this work. At Davidson, I am grateful to Fuji Lozada for his crucial support in funding this project. I also would like to thank my writing group, Keva Bui, Athia Choudhury, Huan He, and Sam Ikehara—I would be completely lost without you all. My parents, Jinlin and Bill, have taught me so much about this precious world that we live in. To Mac and Kubo, my constant and loving companions, you guide my scholarship and dreams in more ways than you know. Many other colleagues, mentors, family members, and friends too numerous to name here have shaped my work through their conversations, insight, and support.

Rina Garcia Chua expresses her deep gratitude for her colleagues and friends in Canada and in the Philippines, especially to her professors in the University of British Columbia Okanagan (Greg Garrard, Daniel Keyes, Nancy Holmes, and George Grinell) and to her professors in De La Salle University–Manila (Charlie Samuya Veric, Marjorie Evasco, Robert Baytan, Shirley Lua, and Dinah Roma) who have been critical and supportive of my ideas as a young scholar before and while I completed the work for this book. I am also very thankful to my coeditors, Jeffrey Santa Ana, Heidi Amin-Hong, and Zhou Xiaojing, for their support, encouragement, and friendship. I also have deep gratitude for my collaborators from ASLE, ASLE-ASEAN, and ALECC (Association of Literature, Environment, and Culture in Canada) for contributing in one way or another to the development of this project, specifically Amy McIntyre, Laura Barbas-Rhoden, Astrida Neimanis, Joni Adamson, Kiu-Wai Chiu, Chitra Sankaran, and many more wonderful people who have orbited my space. I feel lucky to be able to live and study on the unceded and traditional territories of the Syilx Okanagan Nations, where I was settled in as a migrant while I was working on this project. Most of all, I am thankful for my family in the Philippines—my parents Benjamin and Regina (+), sisters Ria and Karren, and daughter Stella—for being touchstones in the pursuit of my career.

Zhou Xiaojing is indebted to the coeditors Jeffrey Santa Ana, Heidi Amin-Hong, and Rina Garcia Chua and to the contributors. I am grateful to Jeffrey for inviting me to present on the panel he organized for the ASLE conference in 2017. The opportunity to meet with Jeffrey and the other panelists, Heidi and Rina, enabled me to explore with them the possibility of an anthology on Asian American environmental literature or ecocriticism, which I had long wished to see in print. The result was beyond what I had imagined. The panelists became a dream team of coeditors who have been extremely conscientious and a great pleasure to work with at every stage of our collaboration, which nurtured our friendship and generated exciting new ideas for further critical investigation in different areas. This experience also characterizes my interactions with our contributors, whose intellectual rigor and deep commitment to environmental justice inspires me, and whose gracious collegiality moves me. I am especially grateful to the poets, Kathy Jetñil-Kijiner and Craig Santos Perez, whose work galvanizes, nourishes, and compels me to engage scholarship and teaching as a form of activism.

The editors are in deep gratitude to the contributors of *Empire and Environment* who have eagerly worked with us throughout the editing and completion of this project. This book would never have been possible without each and every one of you.

FOREWORD

Out of the Ruins

Macarena Gómez-Barris

How can we begin to chronicle the ecological ruination of the Pacific and Transpacific? What radiates outward to reveal the extent of the catastrophe? The editors and authors of *Empire and Environment* offer profound analytics, poetics, and tools toward understanding the historical and contemporary dynamics of the relationship between capitalism, empire, and our planet in crisis. A geography that is both land and sea, in perpetual ruin and repair, the Transpacific connects the Pacific, the world's largest ocean, to Indigenous territories. It also links the Americas to Asia, Australia, and the Pacific Islands, including Hawai'i, Guam, the Philippines, and Easter Island or Rapa Nui. It is a space of Afro-diasporic memory, as the work of Arturo Escobar with African-descended communities in the northwest Pacific coast of South America (chiefly Colombia) remembers, lest we forget.[1]

The Pacific Ocean was the route of Australian and Spanish conquest and encounter, especially during the seventeenth and eighteenth centuries. Colonial ships that brought genocidal and extractive ruination to Indigenous worlds and the environs. The authors of this volume place emphasis on the Pacific as a theater of war after World War II, during the rise of the U.S. empire. And, we might add, the Pacific Ocean is not a garbage patch. It biodynamically devours and expels these memories of war, these hauntings and traces of the colonial/imperial divide. Through these enlightening chapters, we are better able to account for the imprint of transpacific colonial and imperial militarism. Its deep, violent, and continuous imprint. For how this all shows up in the land and in bodies, in the human and more than human sites of ruination that will take thousands of lifetimes to dissipate. This is more lifetimes than we might have in front of us or behind us.

The Rapa Nui remember. Histories connected to the Polynesian archipelago and now tied to their Chilean colonizer. Their island territories ruined by
the imposition of sheep monoculture. Unlike a Western linear time-scape,
the past lies in front and the future is found over the shoulder. In the current
predicament of acute and intensifying climate and environmental catastrophe, how do we also look back as much as we look forward? The "colonial
Anthropocene" is a term that is meant not to endlessly proliferate concepts
but to modify and specify. It references the more than five-hundred-year
period of "human"-led environmental catastrophe that emerges from coloniality. The disaster that comes from asymmetrical power relations and racial
extractive practices. Marking the something that is often missing. Marking
the fact that we can measure environmental impact through ice cores that
correlate with the rise of global capitalism. Marking that it is racialized and
Indigenous spaces that are continually immiserated by colonial environmental impact.

What is the memory of ruination? As Lisa Yoneyama attended to more
than twenty years ago in her brilliant book *Hiroshima Traces*, imperialism
must be considered within a complex relay of power where nations often
co-opt, erase, or elide devastating events toward the construction of social
and political consensus.[2] Yoneyama traces empire not only within Japanese
and Chinese expansion imaginaries but also in relation to U.S. imperial violence. Its afterlives, its suspended memory, its fatal elisions. In addition to the
many obstructed narratives about the U.S. nuclear bombing of Hiroshima
and Nagasaki is the oblivion of the deep impact of radiation on Japanese bodies and on land. Not just bodies. Not just land. Not just then. But ongoing.
Persistent. Continuous.

With my friend and collaborator Professor Akiko Naono, I had the privilege of visiting Hiroshima and the complex of memorials that compose its
peace park. I had recently completed fieldwork in the peace parks of Chile,
where concentration camps were used to torture, maim, and murder young
activists in the early 1970s. At the time, these had been reconverted into
haunted spaces of witness. Yet none of this had prepared me for the terror
within the testimonials of Hiroshima survivors. The unfathomable surviv-
ance of targeted, radiating elimination. The soil remembers. We remember.
And so do the sinews.

Akiko Naono was my fearless guide. She had already spent the better
part of more than a decade interviewing the remaining Habaksha survivors
who directly experienced the nuclear catastrophe. And then the long after-

math of the event, the environmental³ nightmare that dramatically changed the course of millions of lives. There were powerful and humbling moments about visiting the site, especially being with Akiko, who herself is a third-generation survivor. An embodied and living archive of transpacific imperial and ecological ruination. But the children's poems, drawings, and testimonies were perhaps the most impactful to me.

One online poem stands out to me now:

"It hurts, hurts!"
"Hot! Water!"
"Help! Mother!"
"I don't want to die . . ."
"How could this have happened to me?"
"My son, where are you?"
"I am sorry I cannot save you."
Each of those who perished as well as those who survived,
all cried out from the depths of their hearts.⁴

All cried out from the depths of their hearts. In this moment of heightened racial anxiety in the public domain and of ongoing environmental disaster, expulsion, and mourning, how do we live with the mother's call, "I cannot save you"? There is no singularity here but instead the invocation of the singular plural. We cannot save you. The mothers who could not save their children from the imperial U.S. "mistake." From the weapons of nuclear destruction that threaten all human and nonhuman life. From the pharmaceutical and agricultural greed that diminishes rainforest biodiversity. From the impact of military testing and chemical warfare in Vieques, Vietnam, El Salvador, Guam, and Hawaiʻi. This is why looking at transpacific solidarities matters so much right now. Solidarities such as with the Rapa Nui, Kanaka Maoli, and Chamorro peoples, who have witnessed the devastating collapse of their cultivated Native ecologies upon delicate archipelagos.

I think too of all the mothers who bear witness in the Atacama Desert, searching for remains of their disappeared and missing loved ones near the northern Chilean Pacific. This transpacific otherwise that refuses closure and catalogues their disappeared as environmental and imperial calamity. And the now disappeared ocean and marine life that has been almost entirely eviscerated by the large ships of transpacific corporations. The netted loss not an aberration but an ongoing and permanent war against the Earth and its peoples that continues unabated. Mostly unreversed. Our inboxes and newsfeeds full every day with mounting tragedy. They accelerate and we must refuse.

What this volume allows is a context to consider the terror upon us, its accumulation, but also how to think beyond the colonial and imperial divide. Chapters that frame ecological ruination for us through a broad understanding of what a transpacific episteme could be and is. Not just as geographical space, bounded by the outlines of a colonial map, but also as a powerful way to counter-narrate a history of decimation. A route to potential futures. Against histories of the normative nation-state. A way to inscribe, undo, remake.

We might take courage from the Japanese anti-nuclear movement. Mothers who could not save their children. Mothers and grandmothers who think beyond their singularity into the plural, into the future. And from the women in Juarez who challenge the state's impunity of feminicide. From our own nonseparation from feminicide, genocide, and ecocide. How is Mexico the transpacific, you ask? How is it not? Those bodies that traverse maps and create counter-maps with so much always on the line. I once took a class of MFA art students to Tijuana, and we stood before the place where the rusting border fence melted into the Pacific Ocean. Could one swim around it? Would this be a transpacific act of refusal?

The Pacific. That wild and enormous container of cultural memory. The authors have given us so much with this exceptional volume that crosses between spaces and boundaries, dissolving without dissolution into the trans, into the sea. There is no one method of study here for imagining and acting upon a decolonial inhabitance. Yet with these powerful intellectual voices and chapters, we may think about how to return, resurge, remember. The traces of Hiroshima. The radiation. The hurt. The water. To act upon a vision of decolonial inhabitance. Out of these ruins.

Notes

1. See Arturo Escobar, *Territories of Difference: Place, Movements, Life, Redes* (Duke UP, 2008).

2. See Lisa Yoneyama, *Hiroshima Traces: Time, Space, and the Dialectics of Memory* (U of California P, 1999).

3. See Akiko Naono, "Embracing the Dead in the Bomb's Shadow: Journey through the Hiroshima Memoryscape," vols. 1–2, PhD diss., University of California, Santa Cruz, 2002.

4. See "Cries of the Soul" poetry collection, Hiroshima Peace Memorial Museum website, http://hpmmuseum.jp/modules/exhibition/index.php?action=CornerView&corner_id=31&lang=eng (accessed 23 Sept. 2021).

INTRODUCTION

Confronting Ecological Ruination in the Transpacific

Jeffrey Santa Ana, Heidi Amin-Hong, Rina Garcia Chua, and Zhou Xiaojing

Empire and Environment underscores the interrelation of colonialism, racial and extractive capitalism, and environmental destruction as an imperial formation in the transpacific. The collection draws its rationale from the imbrication of imperialism and global environmental crisis, but its inspiration is from the ecological work of activists, artists, and intellectuals in the countries, nations, and lands across and within the Pacific Ocean that make up the transpacific region. The entanglement of empire and ecological destruction is, however, frequently absent in discussions of anthropogenic climate change, extinction, and other evident manifestations of human-caused environmental crises. Although the Pacific Islands and its inhabitants have been hypervisible in climate change narratives, critiques of colonialism and empire are problematically lacking in these popular representations. Craig Santos Perez points out that Indigenous Pacific Islanders have been depicted "as harbingers of climate change ('canaries in the coal mine'), drowning victims ('polar bears on melting glaciers'), and environmental sages ('carriers of traditional ecological wisdom')." To be sure, these popular representations have raised awareness about the existential climate threats that Pacific Islanders face in their homelands. Yet, as Perez further contends, these representations often traffic in "imperialist nostalgia," defined by Renato Rosaldo as "the feeling that emerges when 'agents of colonialism long for the very forms of life they intentionally altered or destroyed'" (qtd. in Perez). Perez emphasizes that representations of climate change's devastating impacts on Pacific Island regions and nations "need to become more attuned to how Pacific Islanders are feeling the precarity and urgency of climate change." This feeling of profound loss critically registers histories of imperialist militarism, foreign incursion, and colonial occupation that have rendered Indigenous Pacific Islanders especially vulnerable to climate change.[1] In accord with Perez, we submit that any critique of climate change's ruinous impacts on the environment in the transpacific region must also emphasize and reckon with *empire* in both its historical contexts and its ongoing (neo-imperial and neocolonial) manifestations.[2] In discussions of human-caused environmental crises, colonialism and imperialism must be understood not only in historical contexts but as *ongoing* ideologies and state practices executed through destructive ecological transformations and consequences that exert power, dominance, and oppression (Katz-Rosene and Paterson).

In turn, this volume takes up the "transpacific" not only as a geographical region but also as an analytic that provides a guide for countering and remaking the legacies of imperial ruination across the Pacific and its diasporas. Our approach to the transpacific extends Janet Hoskins and Viet Thanh Nguyen's concept of the region as both an "imperial fantasy" and a "contact zone" for coalitional possibilities. In expanding the boundaries of the transpacific to engage frictions, intimacies, and coalitions across the Asia-Pacific and the Americas, this volume articulates a transpacific environmental ethic that is preoccupied with empire and settler colonialism's impact on the planet. While its geographical and epistemological reach is expansive, *Empire and Environment* engages decolonial perspectives that are attuned to historical and cultural specificity. Its chapters show how Asian North American, Asian diasporic, and Indigenous Pacific Island cultural expressions critique a dehistoricized and universalized sense of place, attachment, and belonging for Asian-descent people and Indigenous Pacific Islanders in the Anthropocene epoch—when, in the words of Anna Tsing et al., human beings "have become the major force determining the continuing livability of the earth," changing its climate and environment catastrophically for both humans and nonhumans for millennia to come (G1). Erin Suzuki reveals that much recent scholarship around the concept of the Anthropocene has drawn attention to the entanglements of "human" and "natural" history, resulting in the generalization of human activity as the dominant influence on climate in our present historical moment (49).[3] This universalizing of Anthropocene discourses overlooks the fact that the accumulation of greenhouse gases causing global warming are historically and primarily the result of imperialist-based consumer capitalist economies of rich nations. The master narrative represents climate change as a planetary emergency of the modern era, but one that myopically envisages this emergency as an existential threat to the normative social relations of the Global North's affluent postindustrial societies. As Suzuki asserts, "Postcolonial and Indigenous studies critics have objected to the universalizing tendency of this discourse, pointing out that the causes and effects of human-induced climate change have never been experienced in the same ways or at the same time, and, indeed, for many communities— particularly Indigenous and minoritized communities and people living in the global South—such apocalyptic and genocidal events, in the form of colonial projects, have already occurred" (49–50).

In their cultural works, Asian-descent and Indigenous Pacific Islander writers and artists envision Earth's global environmental crisis to critically implicate the destructive consequences of imperialism in the Anthropocene epoch. Their remarkable expressions of imagination give voice to and honor those who live in the transpacific region and confront the ecological ruination deriving from settler colonialism, military imperialism, and neoliberal capitalist expansion. In drawing attention to the ways in which so-called developed societies of the Global North have accumulated power and profit to become a major force determining Earth's livability, Asian-descent and Indigenous Pacific writers and artists express a decolonial perspective that brings the vast scale of the Anthropocene's global environmental crisis within the realm of understanding this epoch's provenance in colonial powers. Their works position us to comprehend concerns of environmental justice that follow from the environmental violence wrought by the material and historical forces of Western empires: the Global North's resource extractions, technologies for militarism and war, pollution and degradation of physical environments, petrocapitalism, and the ruinous commodification and commercialization of the natural world.

Confronting Climate Change and Imperialism in the Transpacific

It is said these changes are caused by the foul smoke from

the white behinds of the big and rich nations of the world.
I'm still paddling my oars until now. My boat is not motorized.
I dislike the noise the motor makes and I've nothing to pay for gas.
Many in our fishing community are like me. And because our daily

catch has dwindled, we keep asking where are the mackerels?
Sheepheads? Jarbuas? Slipmouths? Gobies? Halfbeaks and sharks?
Fishes among the corals? Parrotfish? *Danggit*? Poisonous blowfish?
We see the sea slowly eating up our small island. . . . (Evasco 28)

In the poem "Krutsay" by the Filipina writer Marjorie Evasco, a seafarer in the Visayas mourns the disturbing loss of marine life in the local waters where he struggles to make a living as a fisherman, while his home, like many others on the Pacific Islands, is on the verge of being swallowed by the rising sea. As the typhoons get stronger, both flooding and destroying his village, he notices "our catch getting less and less. The living / body of the sea seems thinner and our usual fishing grounds are / dying" (28). The speaker's lamentation registers the losses suffered and endured by poor farmers and rural laborers in Southeast Asia under climate change—losses directly attributable to the "big and rich nations" of the Global North that pollute Earth with increased levels of climate-warming carbon dioxide and other greenhouse gas emissions. And yet, as the agents of the most significant of geological impacts that have pushed Earth into the Anthropocene, the fossil fuel industry of the Global North's rich nations refuses to shoulder responsibility for atmospheric concentrations and emissions from carbon-intensive technologies, putting the Philippines and other Southeast Asian island nations especially at risk of runaway rates of climate change.

Fossil fuel companies headquartered in North America and Europe are subsidized by the Global North's federal governments through tax breaks, low-interest loans, and investments in petroleum extraction. After decades of spending millions to promote misinformation and spread doubt about anthropogenic climate change, oil companies are now profiting from "greenwashing"—marketing campaigns that depict their industry as environmentally friendly and social justice oriented. Environmental studies scholars show how the fossil fuel industry is appropriating discourses of climate activism and social justice movements (in particular, Black Lives Matter and Me Too) to delay efforts to curb fossil fuel emissions (Westervelt). Engaging in "discourses of delay" and "wokewashing" to signal their advocacy for ecological sustainability and social justice causes, oil companies headquartered in North America and Europe such as ExxonMobil, Chevron, BP, and Shell are concurrently and surreptitiously continuing to downplay the urgency of the climate crisis. While claiming solidarity with racial justice, women's rights, and marginalized people's movements in their ad campaigns, oil companies simultaneously argue that poor and marginalized communities' dependence on fossil fuel energy overrides their concerns about pollution and climate change (Westervelt). To be sure, Evasco's poem in the voice of a seafarer confronts anthropogenic climate change from both an Indigenous and a poor person's perspective, which exposes the greed of the Global North's fossil fuel industry as a culprit of global warming. But the poem also registers the unrecognized losses and displacements of the working poor and their livelihoods, who are often the casualties of the endeavor for global economic growth that many former colonies and developing countries strive for. The poem's listing of fish that have disappeared from the seas surrounding the seafarer's island catalogues these losses and displacements, calling into question the rich nations that disavow their role as agents of anthropogenic climate change.

Filipina diasporic writer Gina Apostol's journalistic writing about Super Typhoon Yolanda offers another compelling decolonial expression that confronts ecological ruination in direct association with past and present colonial powers. Yolanda struck the Philippines on 8 November 2013, and caused catastrophic damage and unfathomable loss of life. Writing for the *New York Times* on 14 November 2013, six days after Yolanda (known internationally as Haiyan) blasted through Tacloban City in the Visayan islands of the central Philippines, Apostol invoked the history and memory of U.S. imperialism in her response to Yolanda's massive destruction of lives and environment. A disastrous consequence of anthropogenic climate change, Yolanda's devastating impact on human life and environment in Visayas is not unprecedented, Apostol explains:

> Tacloban is my city. I grew up directly facing the Pacific Ocean, on the Philippines' eastern shore, which takes the brunt of the yearly monsoons. Geography and history provide the textbook nickname of Leyte and Samar, the provinces hardest hit by Haiyan: "The Typhoon Path." . . . The island of Leyte has always attracted opportunists. . . . In a 1901 revolutionary battle in Balangiga, a historic town that Haiyan has devoured, Filipinos raided the American garrison—but Tacloban remained pacifist. Gen. Jacob H. Smith, who ordered his troops to make the island "a howling wilderness" and was later court-martialed for the butchery of Balangiga, held firm sway in Tacloban. Tacloban's dubious hero worship and its attachment to colonial powers persists. Gen. Douglas MacArthur's statue, celebrating his bronze khakis wading onto Red Beach in 1944, is still the crowning glory of the city's parks—MacArthur

remains untoppled. This history of surrender to awesome forces marks my city's story.

The Visayan islands of Samar and Leyte were a primary site of violence and destruction by imperialist occupation and militarism during the Philippine-American War (1899–1902) and World War II, when the Philippines was a commonwealth of the United States (1935–46) and Japan's Imperial Army brutally occupied the country (1942–45). For Apostol, who was born and grew up in Tacloban City, where Yolanda inflicted the most devastation, the vast ruin caused by the superstorm must be understood in the historical context of Western imperialist plunder, conquest, and war in Southeast Asia. Yolanda's thirteen-foot (four-meter) storm surge that swept through Tacloban's streets, destroying the city's airport, and the lethal flying debris that filled the city's air from the typhoon's 195 mile per hour battering winds have precedent, Apostol contends, in the militarist and genocidal actions of General Jacob H. Smith, who ordered the killing of every Filipino male over ten years old to make Samar island "a howling wilderness." This is an incident historians call the Balangiga Massacre, one of the ugliest moments in the history of U.S. militarism and imperialist violence in Southeast Asia.[4] It is one particularly gruesome historical example of American militarist incursion and destruction in the transpacific that demonstrates the lie of the United States as a benevolent "savior" and protector of the Philippines.[5]

Typhoon Yolanda and other extreme weather events attributable to global warming are exacting immense devastation and loss of life in the Philippines, largely in consequence of the Western world's fossil fuel–burning war technologies that exploit and destroy the environment. From the nineteenth to mid-twentieth centuries, the West's innovations in weaponry for military dominance in the transpacific were contingent on maintaining control of the fossil fuel–based capitalist economy. As Amitav Ghosh points out, Western capitalist trade and industry would not have thrived "without access to military and political power" (109). The West's exertion of imperial rule through military dominance in the transpacific was meant to prevent the colonized region from developing its own carbon-intensive technologies. By creating "the conditions in which Western capital could prevail over indigenous commerce" (109), imperial rule ensured that a fossil fuel capitalist economy on which the West's power and wealth were based could not take hold and be imitated in the countries, nations, and lands across and within the transpacific region.

It was not until the major Western empires had been dismantled in the mid-twentieth century that formerly colonized countries in Asia began to develop their own carbon economies and expand fossil fuel industries. In the period of decolonization during the mid-twentieth century, large Asian economies (particularly those of China and India) began to develop rapidly through fossil fuels, especially coal consumption, and construct and maintain military and political powers of their own, which greatly accelerated greenhouse gas emissions that contribute to climate change. China's and India's recent and alarming surge in greenhouse gas emissions, particularly methane, is a result of rapid industrialization and the relentless drive for economic growth in the period of decolonization.[6] To supply the immense consumption demands of their own growing populations, China and India have sought rapid economic growth through product and resource-intensive manufacturing industries (Hackett). China, in particular, is the world's largest product manufacturer, accounting for 28 percent of global manufacturing output in 2018 (Richter).[7] The postindustrial rich countries of the Global North, however, make up one-quarter of the world's population and consume 80 percent of all resources ("Dimensions of Need"). Thus, private companies and businesses in the Global North are able to accumulate larger profits by outsourcing the production of goods and services to industrializing nations such as China, India, Singapore, the Philippines, and more recently Vietnam, where there is an abundance of lower-wage workers available and manufacturers operate under a much more permissive regulatory environment (Bajpai). To put it simply, the private sector of the Global North has *outsourced* to mainland Asian economies both the production of consumer goods and the resultant emission of carbon dioxide and methane greenhouse gas pollutants.

Undoubtedly, carbon-based capitalism has been the foundation for industrialism and modernization in the period of decolonization for Asia, and this is why Ghosh argues "that the continent of Asia is conceptually critical to every aspect of global warming: its causes, its philosophical and historical implications, and the possibility of a global response to it" (87). However, Asia's centrality to global warming and anthropogenic climate change must be understood as the historical outcome of Western imperialist incursion. If Asia's recent and precipitous industrialization has contributed significantly to the period of accelerated human-driven climate change (Chakrabarty 381–82), this is because Asian nations have rushed to achieve economic growth through carbon-intensive technologies in a global capitalist economy, established by Western empires that brutally enforced economic exploitation, hardship, and privation in its colonies.[8] Ghosh conclusively underscores that histories of imperialism in the transpacific are inextricable from the advent of the carbon-intensive capitalist economy and its globalization, which constitutes the basis for human-induced climate change in the Anthropocene (149).

In the case of the Philippines, to comprehend what *human-induced* means in terms of anthropogenic climate change requires an understanding that climate change has a long history in Western imperialism and militarism's dependence on carbon-based energy for war and resource extraction. Furthermore, the recent history of global capitalist development is inextricable from the Philippines' colonial past. For example, the predatory lending practices of global institutions such as the International Monetary Fund and the World Bank put formally colonized poor countries hundreds of billions of dollars in debt for structural adjustment policies (Huggan and Tiffin 31). These capitalist development schemes reinforce a trade system that relies on fossil fuels and environmentally destructive resource extraction, forcing poor countries to pay back loans at exorbitant interest rates that bleed funding from projects to address poverty, agricultural facilities, and the ability to adapt to the catastrophic weather events of climate change.

Apostol further suggests, "It is easier, after all, to blame nature for the thousands of dead rather than on the choices we make . . . of our continuing pillage of forests, of our clinging to Western allies that spurn our demands for a forceful response to climate change." While the devastating effects of climate change in the Philippines are cast as "natural disasters," this characterization ignores the historical forces of imperialism and present-day global capitalism that have led to "choices" that "pillage" the environment and create unlivable conditions for Indigenous populations. Apostol critiques the dependence of the Philippines and the formerly colonized countries in the transpacific region on *neocolonial* relationships with rich nations, who tout fossil fuel development and resource extraction as the only way to achieve economic equality, while simultaneously making transpacific environments more vulnerable to catastrophe. Postcolonial ecocritics have critiqued these development schemes that corporations from rich nations of the Global North execute in poor countries. Implementing environmentally destructive capitalist policies as "economic schemes of modernization and progress" (DeLoughrey and Handley 19), wealthy nations of the Global North deny their continued colonial plunder and exploitation of the Global South. While fossil fuel–based corporations peddle capitalist development as a global model for growth and equality, they contribute disproportionately to global warming and simultaneously refuse to redress damages from rising sea levels, droughts, powerful storms, and other adverse impacts of climate change. Apostol articulates a decolonial perspective when she refers to the worsening poverty, inequality, and environmental degradation caused by capitalist development schemes in the Philippines and reminds us of the country's embedment within and continuing attachment to past and present colonial powers.

Decolonial Perspectives on the Anthropocene

Dear Matafele Peinam,

I want to tell you about that lagoon
that lucid, sleepy lagoon
lounging against the sunrise

Men say that one day
that lagoon will devour you

They say it will gnaw at the shoreline
chew at the roots of your breadfruit trees
gulp down rows of your seawalls
and crunch your island's shattered bones (Jetñil-Kijiner 70)

As Marshallese poet Kathy Jetñil-Kijiner explains in her work, the ruinous impacts of climate change that disproportionately affect women and girls of color need to be understood in the historical context of colonial violence in the Pacific, as well as ongoing neocolonial forms of resource extraction and consumption that primarily benefit rich countries of the Global North. In her poem "Dear Matafele Peinam," which she read at the opening ceremony of the 2014 United Nations Climate Summit in New York, Jetñil-Kijiner both identifies and defies in gendered terms the extractive capitalism of global corporations that has accelerated greenhouse gas emissions, leading to global warming and sea level rise as existential threats to the Marshallese people: "no greedy whale of a company sharking through political seas / no backwater bullying of businesses with broken morals / no blindfolded bureaucracies gonna push / this mother ocean over / the edge / no one's drowning baby / no one's moving / no one's losing / their homeland / no one's gonna become / a climate change refugee" (71). While Jetñil-Kijiner's assurances to her daughter evoke the form of a comforting lullaby, they also delineate the impetus for Indigenous solidarity and resistance with other people—such as victims of "typhoon Haiyan in the Philippines"—to "fight" against corporate greed and systemic neglect.

Engaging ecological relations as they are influenced, determined, and put into crisis by the ongoing depredations of imperialism and racial capitalism, *Empire and Environment* resonates especially with the decolonial perspectives of Indigenous Pacific Islander, Asian diasporic, and Asian North American artists, writers, intellectuals, and scholars. Their environmental knowledge underscores and contests the extractive capitalism of settler colonialism underpinning the global environmental crisis that defines the Anthropocene epoch. As they reveal how extractive capitalism has accelerated toxic pollution in oceans and greenhouse gas emissions that cause sea level rise and threaten coastal life, the work of Indigenous Pacific Islander, Asian diasporic, and Asian North American writers and activists contests *ecocide*, defined by Macarena Gómez-Barris as "the massive death of ecosystems by global climate change and extractive capitalism" (141, n16). Gómez-Barris calls into question the definition of "Anthropocene" through a general term of "humanity" that is detached from "histories of racial thought and settler colonialism." The universal term of "humanity" hides the fact that "colonial capitalism has been the main catastrophic event that has gobbled up the planet's resources, discursively constructing racialized bodies within geographies of difference, systematically destroying through dispossession, enslavement, and then producing the planet as a corporate bio-territory" (Gómez-Barris 4). Indigenous Pacific Islander writers have also critiqued the lasting environmental impact of U.S. military occupation in the Pacific, drawing fundamental connections between militarization, the destruction of land and wildlife, and the erosion of Indigenous ways of life. Studies show that the U.S. military is one of the largest polluters in history, with greenhouse gas emissions exceeding that of 140 countries ("U.S. Military Consumes"). As Gómez-Barris contends, Indigenous thinkers offer a "multidimensional way of relating to the land that works to decolonize the Anthropocene by creating another relation to the planetary" (62–63).[9] This alternative environmental knowledge allows us to imagine a different set of relations to land and water that do not depend on domination and extraction. Reimagining our relations to land and water entails breaking away from anthropocentric terms such as "humans" versus "animals" and "culture" versus "nature." We draw on Indigenous concepts of kinship with other beings, animate or inanimate, in other words, the "more-than-human," to refute hierarchical binary categories that serve to justify conquest, colonization, exploitation, and even massacre of those defined as "nonhuman" or less "human."

Situated within and across the geographical scope of the transpacific, our work also acknowledges the collaborations and productive tensions between Asian diasporic and Pacific Islander racial formations and sociocultural movements. Transpacific studies as an emerging framework risks reproducing the erasure of the Pacific Islands evident in previous Cold War configurations of the Asia-Pacific, or "accounting for Pacific Islands as transit and meeting places, in which the trope of movement originates externally" (Lyons and Tengan 550). Instead, Paul Lyons and Ty P. Kāwika Tengan's coedited special issue "Pacific Currents" centers a complex range of Native Pacific perspectives on decolonizing the Pacific and preserving the well-being of Pacific peoples and natural environments. Erin Suzuki and Aimee Bahng urge transpacific studies to acknowledge the "epistemological and historical distinctions that have differently shaped Indigenous and migrant relationships to the Pacific" in order to understand Asian diasporic and Pacific Islander epistemologies relationally (Suzuki and Bahng). In *Ocean Passages*, Suzuki expands on this argument to center the Pacific Islands and Indigenous Pacific communities in discursive and geographical formulations of the transpacific. Keith Camacho, Vicente Diaz, and Evyn Le Espiritu Gandhi have shaped work at the junction of Native Pacific and American ethnic studies, examining the convergence of Indigenous, migrant, and refugee histories "in ways that prefigure contemporary possibilities for coalition" (Lyons and Tengan 554).

In the Native Hawaiian context, Kanaka Maoli scholar Haunani Kay-Trask reveals that the Native Hawaiian connection to land and nation is born from a genealogical understanding of place. In Native Hawaiian genealogy, Trask explains, "Papahanaumoku, 'earth mother,' mated with Wakea, 'sky father,' from whence came our islands, or *moku*" (59). This genealogical approach to the environment understands the earth, sky, islands, and taro as kin to human beings, which creates a reciprocal relationship of care with the land. Trask emphasizes that this Indigenous knowledge of kinship and stewardship is "not unique to Hawaiians" but shared across other Indigenous cultures. Anishinaabe writer and scholar James Sinclair Niigaanwewidam avows Trask, saying that Indigenous acts of creation are "an ongoing commitment to tie our world together and contribute to it via the methods we've been given in this life and the next" (208). As we formulate practices of resistance against both colonization and environmental degradation, this anthology draws from Indigenous knowledges to shape a relationship to the land that is rooted in care and reciprocity rather than extraction. Our approach heeds calls to decolonize the transpacific and to engage Native Pacific studies' foundational contributions to ecological interconnectedness and decolonial resistance.

For women of the Marshall Islands and other Pacific Island nations, demanding action against climate change is no different from fighting colonialism and injustice—the "backwater bullying of businesses with broken morals," as Jetñil-Kijiner puts it—because the U.S. military, which historically has caused immense ruination in the transpacific, consumes fossil fuels in order to maintain and preserve an imperialist North American political power whose global dominance depends on the petroleum industry. Dr. Hilda Heine, president of the Marshall Islands, has also exposed the disastrous ecological impacts of the petroleum industry's extractive activities over all regions of the world. The petroleum industry's global processes of environmental exploitation and ruin is a continuation of the U.S. empire's devastating impact on the Pacific after World War II. The U.S. military's nuclear testing in the Pacific wreaked havoc on the environment and on people's bodies, most devastatingly on the health of women and girls. As Heine elaborates, "The women of the Marshall Islands and the Pacific have been fighting colonialism and injustice for a long time. . . . The tragic reality of gender and climate is that women, especially women of color, are disproportionately affected by the impacts of climate change, but are far less likely to be empowered to cope because they have fewer resources such as power and access to finance and technology." U.S. oil consumption and dependency is an imperial project whose bearing on Pacific Islanders is deeply gendered.[10] Women and girls not only endure "the heaviest burden of climate change's impacts" but are also leaders in movements against the petroleum industry's destruction of the environment despite being "threatened with harassment and violence" for their protests (Heine). Marshallese women and girls "continue to speak up to defend our waters, our trees, our soil, and our atmosphere," Heine contends. "They have proven to be the most effective agents of change." To be sure, both Heine and Jetñil-Kijiner attest to the gendered reality of climate change for Indigenous Pacific Islanders. However, ongoing processes of ruination caused by the petroleum industry have also *racialized* destructive effects. These gendered and racialized consequences of climate change likewise may be understood as ecological ruination caused by multinational corporate power that profits through racial capitalism from the earth's destruction.

Building on Cedric Robinson's incisive critique of racial capitalism as the racialization of "the social structures emerging from capitalism," we understand racial capitalism also as the organization of labor, economic exploitation, and abstraction along racial lines (2). As capitalism was inherently racialized, the ruinous effects of capital also became distributed across racial lines, constituting physical spaces and embodied experiences as part of its destruction. To understand this power's effect on Indigenous Pacific Islander lives is to recognize that the petroleum industry and the military forces that maintain its power deposit ruin "in the disabled, racialized spaces of colonial histories past and present" (Stoler, *Duress* 359). Embodying ruination brought upon them by the imperial formation of U.S. militarism and U.S.-based multinational corporations, Marshallese women voice the injuries to which this ruination gives rise.

In this manner, gender and race in the imperial and colonial contexts of anthropogenic climate change clearly "inflect how ruination is embodied and who bears the debris" (Stoler, *Duress* 359). Here, Ann Laura Stoler's concept of imperial debris not only enables us to comprehend the racialized and gendered consequences of climate change's impacts on the lives of Indigenous Pacific Islanders but also places these consequences in a critical framework of empire and environment that compels us to see the relevance of militarism and multinational corporate power as dominant human activities in global ecological ruination. The collection engages with Stoler's concept of ruination by focusing on the materiality of colonialism's destructive environmental impacts, calling critical attention to "the toxic corrosions and violent accruals of colonial aftermaths, the durable forms on which they bear on the material environment and on people's minds" (Stoler, "'The Rot Remains'" 2). *Empire and Environment* expands on the critical framework of imperial debris by moving beyond the remains of the colonial "rot" that continues in previously colonized countries, to where and how colonial ruination begins with the production of colonial knowledge about "nature." It also extends the concept and temporality of "ecologies of remains" by investigating how new forms of socio-ecological ruination, local resistance, and environmental activism start with the expansion of global capitalism, with the dumping of toxic, plastic wastes by existing and emergent empires (22). It highlights the fact that attritional and often invisible violence of ecological damage entangled with the subjugation, dispossession, and exploitation of Indigenous people and degradation of Indigenous communities and cultures structure the very logic and systemic operations of imperial regimes.

By understanding how climate change's disastrous impacts are further evident as the violent accrual of extractive racial capitalist power, we are accordingly *confronting ecological ruination* by revealing this power as an imperial formation—one of many colonial stories stemming from racialized histories of empire in the transpacific region (e.g., the U.S. military's nuclear weapons testing in the Marshall Islands after World War II) and extending into the present as oil dependency (e.g., the petroleum industry's bankrolling of climate science denial in order to maintain a capitalist culture of hyper-extracting and overconsuming fossil fuels, while downplaying and preventing us from grasping this culture's ecocidal degradation of the natural world and Earth's systems: the dire consequences of biodiversity loss, extinction, and genocide of Indigenous people in the transpacific and throughout the Global South).

As Heine and Jetñil-Kijiner oblige us to recognize and understand, Indigenous Pacific Islanders who are losing their homes, lives, and cultural traditions from sea-level rise and cyclones embody the ruination of racial capitalism and empire. In the U.S. context, oil dependency has led to genocidal wars and forced migrations, creating displaced populations in the Pacific as well as the Middle East, South America, Africa, and Europe, most recently and evidently in Ukraine. The ecocidal violence of global climate change in the transpacific is in large part the result of an imperial carbon-intensive capitalist industry and militarism that profit from the violence of forced alienation of humans from the natural world (animals, plants, organisms, lands, and seas) and also of humans (colonizers, white settlers, and men) from other humans (Indigenous peoples, subaltern populations, and women). Such racialized and gendered hierarchical divides, as Gómez-Barris points out, underlie both extractive capitalism and colonialism whose "civilizational projects" constructed the Global South "as a region of plunder, discovery, raw resources, taming, classification, and racist adventures" (3). Until colonial ruination of the constructed Global South is addressed in a way that builds on a foundation of coalition with Native Pacific Islanders and other Indigenous ethnic groups who are directly affected, these systemic issues will persist.

Empire, Environment, and the Americas
in a Transpacific Context

> Dear presidents of the nine Amazonian countries and to all world leaders that
> share responsibility for the plundering of our rainforest,
>
> My name is Nemonte Nenquimo. I am a Waorani woman, a mother, and
> a leader of my people. The Amazon rainforest is my home. I am writing you
> this letter because the fires are raging still. Because the corporations are spill-
> ing oil in our rivers. Because the miners are stealing gold (as they have been
> for 500 years), and leaving behind open pits and toxins. Because the land
> grabbers are cutting down primary forest so that the cattle can graze, planta-
> tions can be grown and the white man can eat. Because our elders are dying
> from coronavirus, while you are planning your next moves to cut up our lands
> to stimulate an economy that has never benefited us. Because, as Indigenous
> peoples, we are fighting to protect what we love—our way of life, our rivers,
> the animals, our forests, life on Earth—and it's time that you listened to us.
>
> —Waorani leader Nemonte Nenquimo, *The Guardian*, 12 October 2020

Nemonte Nenquimo, an Indigenous leader and environmental activist from
the Ecuadorean Amazon, recently garnered international acclaim for her
work to protect Indigenous lands from resource extraction. In 2019, Nenquimo and fellow members of the Waorani Indigenous group were the plain-
tiffs in a lawsuit against the Ecuadorean government, which had plans to put
Waorani territory up for sale to foreign petrol companies. The lawsuit culminated in a ruling to protect half a million acres of Waorani ancestral lands in
the Amazon rainforest from oil drilling. Nenquimo asserted, "We fought in
court so that no one can enter our territory for petrol. We want to save our
territory and our jungles. They are our children's heritage."

The Waorani people's struggle to protect their territory from resource
extraction is a compelling example of women-led Indigenous environmental
justice and activism in the Global South. In the Americas, Indigenous environmental activists are fighting against multinational industries that seek
revenue from oil drilling and mining in the Amazon, resource extraction and
infrastructure projects that alienate and displace Indigenous people from
their ancestral lands. By emphasizing that "land grabbers are cutting down
primary forest so that the cattle can graze, plantations can be grown and the

white man can eat," Nenquimo's pointed comment lays bare the historical "weight and persistence of white settler colonial control over Indigenous territories" (Gómez-Barris 85). The racialized terms of extraction in histories of white settler colonialism continue in the present with the neocolonial development schemes of federal governments in partnership with a multinational private sector that pursues economic growth through oil drilling, mining, and clear-cutting in South American forest regions that make up Indigenous peoples' territories.

In the twenty-first century, racial capitalism and its extractive logics have shifted to adapt to new global forms of economic dominance and exploitation. In particular, China's emergent domination in the global economy depends on alliances with postcolonial governments in Asia, Africa, and South America, which produces environmentally exploitative relationships that complicate the relationship between Asia/the Asian diaspora and Indigenous peoples outside of the transpacific. While Nenquimo's activism points to the persistence of white settler control over Indigenous lands, the case study of Chinese investments in Brazil evidences the intersection of white colonial dominance with Asian global capital. Thus, a transpacific perspective becomes necessary for critiquing both the endurance of white colonial structures of extraction and the emergence of neo-imperial and extractive Asian economies.

Seeking revenue from investments and development schemes to resolve food security problems *and* to assert global superpower status, China has pursued "non-interference" policies with its South American trade partners. With the objective of prioritizing economic growth, China's non-intervention principles of conducting business with South American governments have emboldened right-wing populist leaders, notably Brazil's Jair Bolsonaro, to trample on Indigenous people's rights over their traditional lands and natural resources. Since becoming Brazil's thirty-eighth president in 2018, Bolsonaro and his administration have worked to erode protections for Indigenous land to make it easier for non-Indigenous Brazilians to carry out extractive economic activity in the Amazon. Bolsonaro has tried to shift authority over Indigenous land demarcation away from environmental and social justice agencies, whose mission is to safeguard Indigenous rights, and toward the Ministry of Agriculture, which has a vested interest in expanding development (Chemnick). Bolsonaro has also taken steps to prevent the designation of any new land for Indigenous use and control. The dispossession of Indigenous communities of their land opened more Native habitats for devastating destruction by extractive capitalism. A study by the National Academy of

Sciences estimates that the Bolsonaro government's refusal to grant Indigenous communities control of new territories may have resulted in an extra 1.5 million hectares of deforestation per year (Chemnick). Yet such violation of Indigenous people's rights and violence against the more-than-human are at once justified and disavowed by a settler colonial view of Native people as obstacles to "progress" and their land as "vacant" for development. Bolsonaro's colonial viewpoint at the heart of his Amazon development policy is predicated on the settler colonial "representational evacuation" of Indigenous spaces in South America (Gómez-Barris 84). Native peoples are perceived as an obstacle to the wealth accumulation sought in the development of primary forest habitats for cattle ranching and oil production. As Gómez-Barris contends, this extractive view shows how the whiteness of land development, even under the guise of environmental conservation and preservation, reduces majority Indigenous regions in South America to a "representation of *terra nullius*. . . . Whiteness fluctuates, but is unified in its 'magisterial view,' as a visual entitlement that symbolically appropriates land as patterns of racialization that reproduce material inequalities" (85). It should therefore be understood how the environmental justice struggles of the Waorani and other Indigenous peoples in the Americas are activist labors against the Global North's racial capitalist destruction of the environment and the exploitation of Indigenous people and their territories. The forced alienation and displacement of Native peoples from their ancestral lands are the consequences of imperialist resource extractions (i.e., the incursion of fossil fuel corporate capitalism and the extraction and production of petroleum on Indigenous territories) and the alliance of federal governments with the private sector to clear-cut rainforests for cattle production.

As the largest importer of Brazilian soy and beef, China and its state-owned companies are Bolsonaro's principal investors in his Amazon policy. Driven by its growing demand for commodities and energy resources as well as the political desire to assert its status as the world's economic superpower,[11] China has turned to Brazil and other South American countries as a trade partner, investor, lender, and geopolitical ally. From 2007 to 2018, China invested an estimated $58 billion in Brazil in areas like oil, minerals, soy, electricity, infrastructure, and technology. In 2019, China pledged to invest $100 billion in Brazilian infrastructure and agribusiness projects. Chief among these are Brazil's plans to build a railway in the Amazon that would run parallel to the region's 2,800-mile-long highway used to transport timber, petroleum, cattle, soy, and other agricultural and energy resource products (Southerland). Implementing the expansion of unregulated extractive activity on Native ancestral lands, the presence of China as a trade partner and investor in South America is accelerating the destruction of the Amazon rainforest, the world's largest tropical rainforest, and seriously threatening Indigenous territories where isolated and uncontacted Native groups make their homes. As its multibillion-dollar investments in Brazilian extraction projects indicates, China is striving to meet the immense consumption demands of its growing population through rapid industrialization not only by manufacturing low-cost consumer goods and construction resources for the Global North but also by investing in trade and infrastructure projects in the Americas and throughout the Global South. "Countries in Africa, Asia, and Latin America," reports Krishnadev Calamur in *The Atlantic*, "have a hard time securing international financing because of poor governance, corruption, and their economic policies. But China goes to them, builds desperately needed roads, railways, and ports, and uses these new facilities to transport raw material to feed its growing economy and population. China is an attractive investor not only because it has a policy of non-interference in the domestic affairs of its partner countries but because its projects are completed at a speed that developing nations are unused to. More importantly, perhaps, it offers to finance these projects on easy terms."

Much of the reason for China's investments in extraction projects in poor countries of the Global South stems from a global food security problem. As the adverse effects of climate change, environmental pollution, and extraction of major natural resources continue to impact China's food production, the scope of its food security problem increasingly grows. According to Kai Cui and Sharon P. Shoemaker in *Nature*, "China feeds 20% of the world's population on 7% of the world's farmlands. To accomplish this feat, China paid a heavy price. China's excessive and inefficient use of chemical fertilizers, increasing 3-fold in the past three decades, efficiencies averaging at 32% compared to the world average of 55%, has contributed to its current harmful state of environmental pollution." Moreover, China's recent political and economic tensions with the United States, intensified under President Donald Trump's trade war, have exacerbated China's food security problem. These tensions, which are further enflamed with the spread and worsening conditions of infectious diseases among China's population of 1.4 billion, have compelled Chinese state-owned enterprises to broaden investments in South American extraction projects encouraging food production.[12]

Under Bolsonaro's polices that favor multinational beef industries, "cattle ranching is now the single-largest driver of Amazon deforestation, accounting for 80 percent of the current rate. Amazon Brazil is home to approximately 200 million head of cattle, and is the largest exporter in the world, supplying about one quarter of the global market. . . . Approximately 450,000 square kilometers of deforested Amazon in Brazil are now in cattle pasture. Cattle ranching and soy cultivation are often linked as soy replaces cattle pasture, pushing farmers farther into the Amazon" (Pearce). The immense deforestation for cattle ranching that is happening under Bolsonaro has led to an unprecedented scale of habitat destruction and biodiversity loss in the Amazon. In July 2019, for instance, Amazon wildfires burned over 7,200 square miles of Brazilian rainforest, "an aggregated area nearly the size of New Jersey" (Borunda). The fires released a massive amount of greenhouse gases and noxious contaminants, notably the discharge of 228 megatonnes of carbon dioxide, the highest emission from Amazon fires since 2010. The wildfire winds carried carbon monoxide, a pollutant that is toxic at high levels, beyond South America's coastlines (Borunda).

Consequently, China's attempts to resolve its food security problem by investing in South American extraction projects should be understood as *underwriting* the racial capitalist exploitation of majority Indigenous regions in the Amazon. The economic partnerships between Chinese state-owned enterprises and South American governments are subsidizing neocolonial development schemes that bring about vast environmental destruction (e.g., the ecocidal acceleration of biodiversity loss in the continent's forest habitats and marine ecosystems) and the genocidal undermining of Indigenous people's rights to control their own territories and resources.[13] Accordingly, "the racial logics of South American states," in which African and Indigenous populations were historically subordinated, "are expanded through new forms of extractive capitalism," as Gómez-Barris notes in her argument that modes of racial capitalism are both preserved and ongoing in the Global South (xvii). The Bolsonaro government's racially exploitative and environmentally destructive trade deals with China exemplify how the ongoing depredations of settler colonialism and racial capitalism that are infused in the tide of ecological ruination sweeping the transpacific have their scope and reach in the Americas.

Racial Capitalism and the Environment

Racial capitalism is central to alienation in imperialist resource extractions (e.g., fossil fuel capitalism and the extraction and consumption of petroleum) and militarized environments. The alienation caused by racial capitalism is a characteristic feature of the Anthropocene: the relation between capitalism's devastation of the environment and the collaborative survival of humans and the nonhuman (or the more-than-human) within multispecies landscapes, the prerequisite for continuing life on Earth. Addressing catastrophic climate change, biodiversity loss and extinction, pollution of landscapes and oceans, and other conditions of human-induced environmental devastation, each of this collection's chapters makes central to the book's artistic and scholarly imagination the critical depiction of a divide between humans and the nonhuman natural world. The divide is, as both Anna Tsing and Elizabeth DeLoughrey maintain,[14] a hierarchical binary through which humans pursue profit at the expense of Earth's ecosystems and, correspondingly, rationalize themselves as alienated masters over other humans as well as over nonhuman and more-than-human living things. Situated in histories of colonialism and its afterlife, *Empire and Environment* shows how racial capitalism is intrinsic to understanding alienation in the Anthropocene, which has been exacerbated by the military-industrial complex of industrialized rich nations, whose racially violent consequences are evident in the forced separations and dichotomies between humans (colonizers and white settlers) and other humans (Indigenous people, subaltern populations, and impoverished migrants), as well as between humans and the natural world (animals, plants, organisms, lands, and seas).

Through their framework of empire and environment, the collection's chapters foreground the Global North's political power as an imperial force that Indigenous and Asian-descent people in the transpacific must confront and overcome as they face climate change's catastrophic impacts. Their framework articulates a trenchant critical perspective on the urgent conditions of ecological ruination and reclamation transforming life across the transpacific region today. Their framework characterizes, furthermore, a primary feature in decolonial and ecocritical dialogue: to demonstrate that "the environment stands as a nonhuman witness to the violent process of colonialism" (DeLoughrey and Handley 8) and to document ecologically ruinous imperial powers as what Dipesh Chakrabarty describes as "geological agents" with "invented technologies that are on a scale large enough to have an impact on the planet itself" ("The Climate" 207).

Empire and Environment builds upon and extends existing interdisciplinary scholarship in the fields of ethnic studies and the environmental humanities to address these issues with an emphasis on the decolonial critical perspective.

Our collection is aligned with scholarship in ethnic studies that charts new understandings of racial formation, settler colonialism, and ecology. Leilani Nishime and Kim D. Hester Williams's *Racial Ecologies* as well as Sarah Wald et al.'s collection *Latinx Environmentalisms* are examples of works that trace both the racialized impact of environmental destruction and the tradition of communities of color engaging in ecological analysis. Expanding on these efforts, our collection reframes the contributions of Asian American, Asian diasporic, and Pacific Islander scholarship to environmental studies broadly conceived. We turn to the transpacific as a geographical region and ideological imaginary that have been shaped by multiple imperial and militaristic powers, which have produced unsustainable conditions for humans and nonhumans alike.

Though their scholarship has not been traditionally situated within environmental studies, Asian North American scholars and writers have long been concerned with place and the role of Asian labor—as railroad workers, farmers, and miners—in shaping North American landscapes.[15] For Asian diasporic populations who migrate or are forcibly displaced from their homelands, narratives of environmental attachment become intertwined with the construction of new social and political identities. Asian American approaches to environmental studies and ecocriticism necessitate an engagement with the intersectionality of race, labor, and place.[16] Anita Mannur and Casey Kuhajda point out that many contemporary works of Asian American literature directly engage place and environmental degradation as forces shaping racialized and classed experiences (3). The role of Asian labor, when considered in relation to the exploited labor of Black and Indigenous workers in constructing America, further illuminates the workings of racial capitalism and its extractive effect on land and racialized peoples. Narratives of "pristine nature" and "westward-moving pioneers" have always been racial constructions that uphold the white colonial nation-state (Hayashi). Asian American studies scholars have pointed out the ways in which Asianness is deliberately positioned as oppositional to these ideals, associated not with natural purity but with contamination and categorized as robotic or less human.[17] Rather than reclaiming these problematic notions of purity, Asian American scholars and activists have championed movements for environmental justice across the United States and transnationally to build communities of resistance against pollution and toxic exposure along racial lines.[18] The organization Asian Pacific Environmental Network, based in east Oakland, California, mobilizes Asian immigrant and refugee communities against industrial pollution and envisions sustainable alternatives to extractive economies (Asian Pacific Environmental Network). Such work requires the ability to *imagine otherwise* in order to bring forth new ways of sustainable living that enable communities of color to thrive.[19] Addressing Gómez-Barris's critical objective to refuse the ecocidal terms of capitalist extraction and create multidimensional ways of relating to the land, the chapters in *Empire and Environment* enable the "creation of emergent alternatives" that envision environmental justice for Indigenous Pacific Island and Asian diasporic communities (4). Our work as cultural studies scholars and writers in this volume complements the work of environmental justice movements to not only restore clean air and water to communities of color but also envision a new world order that does not depend on destructive cycles of consumption and extraction.

Specifying empire and global capitalist development as the driving forces of the Anthropocene, *Empire and Environment* investigates the ways in which Indigenous Pacific Islander, Asian diasporic, and Asian North American cultural expressions confront the environmental violence and ecological ruination caused by colonialism and the expansions of imperial power. It explores how formal and aesthetic experimentation in these works foregrounds living within spaces of ruination. It inquires, furthermore, how Indigenous theoretical and cultural works broaden our understandings of imperialist violence to consider ruination of the environment and nonhuman life alongside human life. The collection also poses urgent questions: How do Indigenous and postcolonial peoples in the transpacific resist colonization and strive for recovery from socioecological degradation resulting from colonial plunders and U.S. military operations? In what ways can Indigenous Pacific Islander and Asian North American studies contribute to the critical perspectives of the environmental humanities? These questions seek to highlight marginalized Indigenous and postcolonial peoples' agency for exposing, negotiating, and resisting the persistent ecological destruction by imperial and (neo)colonial empires. In so doing, they help broaden the possibilities of intervention in the accelerated damage to the earth, while confronting the impact of past and present empire building on global ecological systems.

Each chapter makes an indispensable contribution to the environmental humanities by expanding its scope to include critical conversations about histories of imperialism, colonialism, militarism, racialization, and capitalist development in the transpacific region. The chapters are organized into four parts according to particular themes. Each part begins with a poem by Craig Santos Perez, an Indigenous Chamoru (Chamorro) writer from Guåhan

(Guam), thus highlighting Indigenous Pacific voice, creativity, resistance, and activism in disrupting the Anthropocene. Authored by an international range of scholars from North America, Australia, Asia, and the Pacific Islands who specialize in the environmental humanities, the chapters take a postcolonial ecocritical approach to explore environmental violence and recovery in recent Asian North American and Indigenous Pacific Islander cultural expressions. In part 1, "(Framing) Postcolonial Ecocritical Approaches to the Asia-Pacific," contributors establish a range of theoretical and methodological approaches to analyzing ecological themes in cultural works from the transpacific region. The chapters in this section frame new analytics in the study of empire and environment that compel the fields of Asian American studies, Asian studies, and transpacific studies to attend to global ecological predicaments. In his reading of Han Ong's *The Disinherited*, Jeffrey Santa Ana proposes a "transpacific queer ecologies" to understand the exploited and subjugated bodies of child prostitutes, Indigenous people, and the working poor as incarnations of imperial debris in the Philippines. Kathleen Gutierrez's chapter on the colonial intellectual history of *cycas wadei* reconsiders the biological and epistemological labor of colonial botany as enactments of imperial and ecological violence within and beyond the Philippines. Chitra Sankaran's chapter on South Indian goddess films introduces new approaches to ecofeminism that consider the complexities of gender and environmental consciousness in rural India. Finally, John Charles Ryan's reading of Papua New Guinean (PNG) poetry published before 1975 considers PNG writers' adaptation of oral traditions as a critical tool to narrativize environmental and cultural destruction as linked. The chapters by Santa Ana, Gutierrez, Sankaran, and Ryan all offer new approaches to understanding the intersections of environment, gender and sexuality, race, and class in studies of empire in the transpacific region.

In part 2, "Militarized Environments," the contributors examine militarization as the violent enforcement/maintenance of colonial, political, and economic rule, which has devastating consequences on bodies and environments across the Pacific. Emily Cheng's chapter examines water and palm trees as tropes in Vietnamese American narratives that "tell" of the lasting violence of American military intervention in the present-day lives of Vietnamese refugee populations in the United States. Analyzing Vietnamese environmental art alongside Bao Ninh's *The Sorrow of War*, Heidi Amin-Hong's chapter situates the degradation of Vietnamese waterscapes within a longer history of U.S. militarism and East Asian sub-imperialism as manifest in transnational capitalism. In her chapter, Zhou Xiaojing traces the ecological ruination by the U.S. empire in Guam and the Marshall Islands through readings of Craig Santos Perez's and Kathy Jetñil-Kijiner's ecopoems, which document, critique, and counter the painful legacies of U.S. nuclear testing and militarized expansion in the Pacific Islands.

The chapters in part 3, "Decolonizing the Transpacific: Settler Colonialism and Indigenous Resistance," reckon with the possibility of a decolonized transpacific through critiques of ongoing settler colonialism and a turn to Indigenous perspectives and epistemologies. Rebecca H. Hogue's chapter mobilizes Kanaka Maoli (Native Hawaiian) narratives of birth and genealogy to contest U.S. military occupation in the struggle to demilitarize the Pōhakuloa Training Area, which is located on sacred and ceded lands. Rina Garcia Chua's chapter explores the critical concept of "disentrancing" as a way to draw attention to the complicit role of white settlers and Filipino postcolonial subjects in the dispossession of Aboriginal peoples. Ti-Han Chang offers in her chapter literary perspectives from Taiwanese and Aboriginal writers that confront Japanese colonial and Taiwanese nationalist regimes' degradation of water environments.

The fourth and final part, "Climate Justice and Ecological Futurities," speculates on future possibilities of surviving ecological destruction. Amy Lee's chapter reads Asian American climate fiction that adopts a global perspective to construct a racially conscious climate aesthetics that maps a terrain of climate justice activism. Emalani Case's chapter discusses the chant "Nā Kūkulu," by her cousin Pua Case, as an opportunity to investigate the current rise at Mauna Kea, the highest mountain in Hawaiʻi, which is a deeply sacred place revered in Native Hawaiian traditions. For the kiaʻi mauna (protectors of the Mauna Kea), uttering the chant together has become a powerful expression of resistance against the construction of a Thirty Meter Telescope near the sacred mountain's summit. In his chapter, Chad Shomura follows plastic debris across the beaches of Hawaiʻi to the Great Pacific Garbage Patch to investigate how artists imagine the possibilities of plastic as an archive for neocolonial consumption and an aesthetic medium that brings humanity into intimate relation with the earth. *Empire and Environment*'s focus on processes of colonialism, racial capitalism, international development, and the centralization and transference of power connects these processes to the places in which Asian diasporic and Indigenous Pacific peoples in the transpacific live and make their home, while simultaneously recognizing that the recuperation of place, environment, and resources is a key part of the process of thriving and liberation.

Notes

1. In their study of colonialism and climate change on islands of the Caribbean and Southwestern Indian Ocean, Kristina Douglass and Jago Cooper assert that histories of colonization and imperialist resource extraction forced islanders to move away from building homes that traditionally were more resilient to tropical storms. Moreover, Europeans destroyed the forests and other land resources for monoculture agriculture to wrest profit from their colonies. The Indigenous people living in these former colonies today inhabit poorer land that evinces the ecological ruins of "reduced water retention and increased soil erosion," making them even more vulnerable to the impacts of climate change (Douglass and Cooper).

2. Alfred Crosby has argued that imperialists and colonizers have produced systemic environmental consequences (i.e., "environmental terrorism") that intensify and exploit unjust social relations and power inequities across and between societies and states. See Crosby for discussion of the ecological dimensions of settler-colonial violence and genocidal campaigns against Indigenous people.

3. By referring to Elizabeth DeLoughrey's concept of "tidalectics" as an oceanic mode of understanding time and space, Suzuki further explains how Indigenous Pacific Islanders' oceanic approach to temporality can "decenter the assumptions of human exceptionalism that remain embedded in many discourses of the Anthropocene" (50).

4. The Balangiga Massacre was an incident that happened during the Philippine-American War. It refers to an attack on the United States Ninth Infantry allegedly by Filipino insurgents in the town of Balangiga, Samar, on 28 September 1901. Of the seventy-four men in the U.S. contingent, forty-eight died and twenty-two were severely wounded. Of the Filipino insurgents who attacked the U.S. infantry, twenty-eight died and twenty-two were wounded. See Delmendo.

5. As Paul A. Kramer reveals in his study of U.S. colonial rule in the Philippines, President William McKinley and U.S. military commanders attempted to conceal their intentions for empire building in the Philippines by announcing "'in the most public manner' that the Americans had come 'not as invaders or conquerors, but as friends, to protect the natives in their homes, in their employments, and in their personal and religious rights . . . by proving to them that the mission of the United States is one of benevolent assimilation, substituting the mild sway of justice and right for arbitrary rule'" (110).

6. Methane is one of the most potent greenhouse gases. It warms the planet by thirty times as much as carbon dioxide. A recent article in *Yale Environment 360* reports that methane has been responsible for about a fifth of global warming, and it has more than doubled in the atmosphere in the past 250 years (Pearce).

7. China has become the world's leading manufacturer of industrial goods, including iron and steel; aluminum; coal; armaments; textiles and apparel; petroleum; cement; fertilizer; food processing; automobiles and other transportation equipment (rail cars, ships, and aircraft); consumer products (footwear, toys, and electronics); and telecommunications and digital technology ("China Manufacturing").

8. Asia's rapid industrialization in the period of decolonization simultaneously with the Great Acceleration compels Ghosh to provocatively ask, "Could it be that imperialism actually delayed the onset of the climate crisis by retarding the expansion of Asian and African economies? Is it possible that if the major twentieth-century empires had been

dismantled earlier, then the landmark figure of 350 parts per million of carbon dioxide in the atmosphere would have been crossed long before it actually was?" (110).

9. To emphasize the decolonial critical purposes of this book, we refer to an account of decolonizing the Anthropocene offered by Gómez-Barris. To be sure, "the term 'Anthropocene,' which has been used by Western geologists and climatologists to term the period of human intervention from 1610 forward, now popularly identifies the crisis of future life on the planet. . . . Yet we use the term too generally, addressing 'humanity' as a whole without understanding histories of racial thought and settler colonialism that are imposed upon categorizations of biodiversity, spaces where the biotechnologies of capitalism accelerate" (4).

10. Elizabeth DeLoughrey asserts that "masculinized trajectories of nomadic subjects and capital attain their mobility by invoking feminized flows, fluidity, and circulation, while the feminine (as an organizing concept) and women (as subjects) are profoundly localized" (*Roots and Routes* 5). It is also important to note that women who either are forced to stay or stay on their island homelands by choice are imposed upon by masculine narratives as beacons of hope or purveyors of localized knowledges. These women are oftentimes stripped of their agentic roles in explorative narratives, which erases and diminishes their crucial contributions to these kinds of discourses.

11. China's multibillion-dollar investments in Asian, African, and South American extraction projects prompted the *New York Times* to refer to China as the "world's new colonial power." China's geopolitical rise in the Global South under President Xi Jinping's leadership has enabled state-owned Chinese companies to build up enormous holdings in poor, resource-rich countries in Asia, Africa, and South America (Larmer).

12. According to economist Scott B. MacDonald, the year 2020 was not good for China. "The economy suffered a 6.8 percent economic contraction in Q1, followed by a 3.2 percent rebound (anemic by Chinese standards) in Q2. Relations with the United States remain tense and complicated. On top of that, heavy rains have caused massive flooding that has wiped away billions of dollars of value in China, washing up factories, homes and agricultural land in a frothy tide of destruction. This last is important. While China supports over 20 percent of the world's population, it has a little over 12 percent of its arable land (according to the World Bank). Heavy rains and floods are bad enough; add in an African Swine Fever resurgence in some parts of southern China and the question of food security gains some traction as something to watch" (MacDonald).

13. Another recent case of China's environmentally destructive extraction practices in the Americas are the Chinese fishing fleets that plundered the waters around Ecuador's Galápagos Islands between 13 July and 13 August 2020. An analysis conducted by the marine conservation group Oceana accuses the Chinese fleets of engaging in unsustainable fishing practices that damage Ecuador's marine-protected areas and threaten the region's local economy that depends on revenue from tourists who visit the Galápagos Marine Reserve, a UNESCO World Heritage site covering more than 133,000 square kilometers around the archipelago (Cranor). According to the analysis, during the one-month period, "99% of the visible fishing activity off the Galápagos was by Chinese-flagged vessels. . . . The massive and ongoing fishing effort of this fleet threatens both ecological balance and livelihoods" (Cranor).

14. See Tsing, *The Mushroom at the End of the World* and DeLoughrey, *Allegories of the Anthropocene*.

15. See Hayashi; Chiang; and Sze, "Asian American."

16. See Fitzsimmons et al.; and Mannur and Kuhajda.

17. See Shah; Lye; and Niu et al.

18. See Sze, *Noxious New York*; Chiang, *A Village Called Versailles*; and Asian Pacific Environmental Network, "Our History."

19. We borrow the phrase "imagine otherwise" from Kandice Chuh, *Imagine Otherwise*.

Works Cited

Apostol, Gina. "Survival, Surrender, Oblivion." *New York Times*, 14 Nov. 2013, www.nytimes.com/2013/11/15/opinion/surrender-oblivion-survival.html. Accessed 9 Jan. 2017.

Asian Pacific Environmental Network. "Our History." *APEN*, https://apen4ej.org/our-hist ory/. Accessed 31 Mar. 2021.

Bajpai, Prableen. "Why China Is the World's Factory." *Investopedia*, 13 Feb. 2020, www.investopedia.com/articles/investing/102214/why-china-worlds-factory.asp. Accessed 17 Jan. 2021.

Borunda, Alejandra. "See How Much of the Amazon Is Burning, How It Compares to Other." *National Geographic*, 29 Aug. 2019, www.nationalgeographic.com/environm ent/2019/08/amazon-fires-cause-deforestation-graphic-map/. Accessed 15 Jan. 2021.

Calamur, Krishnadev. "What's the Price of China's Influence in Latin America?" *The Atlantic*, 3 Feb. 2018, www.theatlantic.com/international/archive/2018/02/rex-in-latam/55 2197/. Accessed 17 Jan. 2021.

Chakrabarty, Dipesh. "The Climate of History: Four Theses." *Critical Inquiry*, vol. 35, Winter 2009, 197–222.

Chakrabarty, Dipesh. "Humanities in the Anthropocene: The Crisis of an Enduring Kantian Fable." *New Literary History*, vol. 47, no. 2–3, 2016, 377–97.

Chemnick, Jean. "Amazon Deforestation Falls Where Land Is Under Indigenous Control." *Scientific American*, 11 Aug. 2020, www.scientificamerican.com/article/amazon-defor estation-falls-where-land-is-under-indigenous-control/. Accessed 15 Jan. 2021.

Chiang, Connie Y. "Imprisoned Nature: Toward an Environmental History of the World War II Japanese American Incarceration." *Environmental History*, vol. 15, April 2010, 236–67.

"China Manufacturing." *Encyclopedia Britannica*, www.britannica.com/place/China/Man ufacturing. Accessed 17 Jan. 2021.

Chuh, Kandice. *Imagine Otherwise: On Asian Americanist Cultural Critique*. Duke UP, 2003.

Cranor, Dustin. "New Oceana Analysis Finds 300 Chinese Vessels Pillaging the Galapagos for Squid." *Oceana*, 16 Sept. 2020, https://usa.oceana.org/press-releases/new-oceana-analysis-finds-300-chinese-vessels-pillaging-galapagos-squid. Accessed 15 Jan. 2021.

Crosby, Alfred W. *Ecological Imperialism: The Biological Expansion of Europe, 900–1900*. Cambridge UP, 1986.

Cui, Kai, and Sharon P. Shoemaker. "A Look at Food Security in China." *Nature*, vol. 2, no. 4, 20 Feb. 2018, www.nature.com/articles/s41538-018-0012-x. Accessed 17 Jan. 2021.

Delmendo, Sharon. *The Star-Entangled Banner: One-Hundred Years of America in the Philippines*. Rutgers UP, 2004.

DeLoughrey, Elizabeth M. *Allegories of the Anthropocene*. Duke UP, 2019.

DeLoughrey, Elizabeth M. *Roots and Routes: Navigating Caribbean and Pacific Island Literature*. U of Hawaii P, 2007.

DeLoughrey, Elizabeth M., and George B. Handley. "Toward an Aesthetics of the Earth." *Postcolonial Ecologies: Literatures of the Environment*, edited by Elizabeth DeLoughrey and George B. Handley. Oxford UP, 2011, 3–39.

"Dimensions of Need—Sharing the World's Resources." *Food and Agricultural Organization of the United Nations*, www.fao.org/3/u8480e/U8480E0x.htm. Accessed 17 Jan. 2021.

Douglass, Kristina, and Jago Cooper. "Archaeology, Environmental Justice, and Climate Change on Islands of the Caribbean Southwestern Indian Ocean." *Proceedings of the National Academy of Sciences of the United States of America*, 14 Apr. 2020, www.pnas.org/content/117/15/8254. Accessed 10 Sept. 2021.

Evasco, Marjorie. "Krutsay." *AGAM: Filipino Narratives on Uncertainty and Climate Change*, edited by Renato Redentor Constantino. Institute for Climate and Sustainable Cities, 2014, 27–29.

Fitzsimmons, Lorna, et al. *Asian American Literature and the Environment*, edited by Lorna Fitzsimmons, Youngsuk Chae, and Bella Adams. Routledge, 2015.

Ghosh, Amitav. *The Great Derangement: Climate Change and the Unthinkable*. U of Chicago P, 2016.

Gómez-Barris, Macarena. *The Extractive Zone: Social Ecologies and Decolonial Perspectives*. Duke UP, 2017.

Hackett, Conrad. "Which 7 Countries Hold Half the World's Population?" *Pew Research Center*, 11 July 2018, www.pewresearch.org/fact-tank/2018/07/11/world-population-day/. Accessed 14 Jan. 2021.

Hayashi, Robert. "Environment." *Keywords for Asian American Studies*, https://keywords.nyupress.org/asian-american-studies/essay/environment/. Accessed 13 Mar. 2021.

Heine, Hilda. "Global Climate Action Must Be Gender Equal." *The Guardian*, 15 Nov. 2017, www.theguardian.com/environment/2017/nov/15/global-climate-action-must-be-gender-equal. Accessed 28 Feb. 2019.

Hoskins, Janet, and Viet Thanh Nguyen. *Transpacific Studies: Framing an Emerging Field*. U of Hawai'i P, 2014.

Huggan, Graham, and Helen Tiffin. *Postcolonial Ecocriticism: Literature, Animals, Environment*. 2nd ed., Routledge, 2010.

Jetñil-Kijiner, Kathy. "Dear Matafele Peinem." *Iep Jaltok: Poems from a Marshallese Daughter*. U of Arizona P, 2017, 70–73.

Katz-Rosene, Ryan M., and Matthew Paterson. "Imperialism and Environment." *The Palgrave Encyclopedia of Imperialism and Anti-Imperialism*. Palgrave, 25 July 2019, https://link.springer.com/referenceworkentry/10.1007%2F978-3-319-91206-6_129-2. Accessed 12 Sept. 2021.

Kramer, Paul A. *The Blood of Government: Race, Empire, the United States, and the Philippines.* U of North Carolina P, 2006.

Larmer, Brook. "Is China the World's New Colonial Power?" *New York Times*, 2 May 2017, www.nytimes.com/2017/05/02/magazine/is-china-the-worlds-new-colonial-power.html. Accessed 17 Jan. 2021.

Lye, Colleen. *America's Asia: Racial Form and American Literature, 1893–1945.* Princeton UP, 2005.

Lyons, Paul, and Ty P. Kāwika Tengan. "Introduction: Pacific Currents." *American Quarterly*, vol. 67, no. 3, 2015, 545–74.

MacDonald, Scott B. "China, Food Security, and Geopolitics." *The Diplomat*, 30 Sept. 2020, https://thediplomat.com/2020/09/china-food-security-and-geopolitics/. Accessed 17 Jan. 2021.

Mannur, Anita, and Casey Kuhajda. "Asian American Ecocriticism." *Oxford Research Encyclopedia of Literature.* Oxford UP, 28 Aug. 2019, https://doi.org/10.1093/acrefore/9780190201098.013.769

Nenquimo, Nemonte. "This Is My Message to the Western World—Your Civilisation Is Killing Life on Earth." *The Guardian*, 12 Oct. 2020, www.theguardian.com/commentisfree/2020/oct/12/western-worldyour-civilisation-killing-life-on-earth-indigenous-amazon-planet. Accessed 15 Jan. 2021.

Niigaanwewidam, James Sinclaire. "The Power of Dirty Waters: Indigenous Poetics." *Indigenous Poetics in Canada*, edited by Neal McLeod. Wilfrid Laurier UP, 2015, 203–15.

Nishime, Leilani, and Kim D. Hester Williams. *Racial Ecologies.* U of Washington P, 2018.

Niu, Greta, et al. "Technologizing Orientalism: An Introduction." *Techno-Orientalism: Imagining Asia in Speculative Fiction, History, and Media*, edited by Greta Niu, David Roh, and Betsy Huang. Rutgers UP, 2015, 1–20.

Pearce, Fred. "The Methane Riddle: What Is Causing the Rise in Emissions?" *Yale Environment 360*, Yale School for the Environment, 25 Oct. 2016, e360.yale.edu/feature/methane_riddle_what_is_causing_the_rise_in_emissions/3047/. Accessed 9 Jan. 2017.

Perez, Craig Santos. "Thinking (and Feeling) with Anthropocene (Pacific) Islands." *Dialogues in Human Geography*, 21 May 2021, https://journals.sagepub.com/doi/abs/10.1177/20438206211017453. Accessed 12 Sept. 2021.

Richter, Felix. "China Is the World's Manufacturing Superpower." *Statista*, 18 Feb. 2020, https://www.statista.com/chart/20858/top-10-countries-by-share-of-global-manufacturing-output/. Accessed 12 Jan. 2021.

Robinson, Cedric J. *Black Marxism: The Making of the Black Radical Tradition.* 2nd ed., U of North Carolina P, 2000.

Shah, Nayan. *Contagious Divides: Epidemics and Race in San Francisco's Chinatown.* U of California P, 2001.

Southerland, Dan. "Brazil: Cutting Trees for China Threatens Amazon Rain Forest." *Radio Free Asia*, 5 Apr. 2020, www.rfa.org/english/commentaries/china-amazon-04052020115654.html. Accessed 17 Jan. 2021.

Stoler, Ann Laura. *Duress: Imperial Durabilities in Our Times.* Duke UP, 2016.

Stoler, Ann Laura. "'The Rot Remains': From Ruins to Ruination." *Imperial Debris: On Ruins and Ruination.* Duke UP, 2013, 1–35.

Suzuki, Erin. *Ocean Passages: Navigating Pacific Islander and Asian American Literatures.* Temple UP, 2021.

Suzuki, Erin, and Aimee Bahng. "The Transpacific Subject in Asian American Literature." *Oxford Encyclopedia of Asian American Literature and Culture*, edited by Josephine Lee. Oxford UP, 30 Jan. 2020. *Oxford Research Encyclopedias*, https://doi.org/10.1093/acrefore/9780190201098.013.877. Accessed 8 Sept. 2021.

Sze, Julie. "Asian American, Immigrant and Refugee Environmental Justice Activism Under Neoliberal Urbanism." *Asian American Law Journal*, vol. 18, 2011, 5–23.

Sze, Julie. *Noxious New York.* MIT Press, 2006.

Trask, Haunani-Kay. *From a Native Daughter: Colonialism and Sovereignty in* Hawai'i. Rev. ed., U of Hawai'i P, 1999, 59.

Tsing, Anna Lowenhaupt. *The Mushroom at the End of the World: On the Possibility of Life in Capitalist Ruins.* Princeton UP, 2015.

Tsing, Anna Lowenhaupt, et al. "Haunted Landscapes of the Anthropocene." *Arts of Living on a Damaged Planet*, edited by Anna Tsing, Heather Swanson, Elaine Gan, and Nils Bubandt. U of Minnesota P, 2017, G1–G14.

"U.S. Military Consumes More Hydrocarbons than Most Countries—Massive Hidden Impact on Climate." *ScienceDaily*, www.sciencedaily.com/releases/2019/06/190620100005.htm. Accessed 13 Mar. 2021.

A Village Called Versailles. Directed by S. Leo Chiang. New Day Films, 2009.

Wald, Sarah D., David J. Vásquez, Priscilla Solis Ybarra, and Sarah Jaquette Ray, editors. *Latinx Environmentalisms: Place, Justice, and the Decolonial.* Temple UP, 2019.

Westervelt, Amy. "Big Oil's 'Wokewashing' Is the New Climate Science Denialism." *The Guardian*, 9 Sept. 2021, www.theguardian.com/environment/2021/sep/09/big-oil-delay-tactics-new-climate-science-denial. Accessed 16 Sept. 2021.

PART I

(Framing) Postcolonial Ecocritical Approaches to the Asia-Pacific

Excerpt from "Family Trees"
Craig Santos Perez

~

Before we enter i halom tano': deep jungle
    dad asks permission
of i taotaomo'na: *the spirits* who dwell
    within. He closes his eyes
& says, "ekungok": *listen.*

~

As we walk, he names
    each tree, each elder:
"Niyok, Lemmai, Ifit, Yoga', Nunu,"
who has provided us
    clothes and tools,
canoes and shelter,
    food and åmot.

"When you take," he says,
    "Take with gratitude,
& never more than
    what you need."

~

When we reach the fence,
    he tells me how the military
uprooted trees with bulldozers,
     paved i tano with concrete,
planted toxic chemicals
    & ordnances.

He translates "eminent domain,"
    as "theft": to turn a place
of abundance into a base
for destruction.

Barbed
wire spreads
like invasive
vines
whose only flowers
are cancerous
tumors
that bloom
on every branch
of our family
tree.

Today, the military invites us
    to collect plants and trees
within areas of Litekyan*
    slated to be cleared
for the construction of a live
firing range complex.

Fill out appropriate forms
    and wait 14 business days
for background and security check. If
    we receive *their* permission,
they'll escort us to mark and claim

what trees we want delivered
      after removal.

They call this "benevolence,"

            yet why

does it feel   like a cruel

      reaping?

Litekyan (Ritidian) is an ancestral Chamorro village in northern Guam. The US first classified Litekyan as a restricted military site, and then as a wildlife preserve covering 371 acres of coral reefs and 832 acres of terrestrial habitats. Litekyan is home to many endangered species and archaeological remains. Today, the US military is turning Litekyan into a live firing range complex.

            ∼

dad never showed me the endangered
      hayun lågu: *fire tree*

      the last
struggling to survive   in Litekyan—
                  its only home.

"Don't worry," the military says.
"We'll build a fence around the tree."

      They call this "mitigation,"

yet why
does it feel like the disturbed   edge

      of extinction?

"Litekyan" translates as "to stir," or "a stirring place," referring to waters off the coast hanom hanom hanom

~

Ekungok, ancient whispers rouse the jungle
   Listen, oceanic waves stir against rocks

  Ekungok, i taotao'mona call us to rise
     Listen, i tronkon Yoga' calls us to stand tall

Ekungok, i tronkon Lemmai calls to spread our arms wide
   Listen, i tronkon Nunu calls to link our hands

   Ekungok, i tronkon Ifit calls us to be firm
 Listen, i tronkon Niyok calls us to never break

Ekungok, i halom tano' calls us to surround
  i hayun lågu and chant: "We are the seeds

of the last fire tree. We are the seeds of the last
   fire tree. We are the seeds of the last fire tree!

   Ahe'! No! We do not give you permission."

Transpacific Queer Ecologies

Ecological Ruin, Imperialist Nostalgia, and
Indigenous Erasure in Han Ong's The Disinherited

Jeffrey Santa Ana

Focusing on the ecological ruin that is enmeshed with forces of imperialism and colonialism as portrayed in Han Ong's gay-themed novel *The Disinherited*, this chapter aims to contribute a decolonial transpacific perspective to the field of queer ecologies. By "decolonial transpacific," I refer to recent criticism from scholars of Pacific studies and decolonial theory who have critiqued the transpacific as a term in Asian American studies that has not fully attended "to the epistemological and historical distinctions that have differently shaped Indigenous and migrant relationships to the Pacific" (Suzuki and Bahng 2). As Erin Suzuki and Aimee Bahng contend, the transpacific should function as a decolonial term to reveal and assess the ongoing harms produced by settler epistemologies of possessive liberal humanism.[1] This decolonial critical focus seeks "to avoid the elisions and erasures of historical, cultural, and political difference engendered by militarist and capitalist rendering of the [Pacific] region as a homogenous space of transit and exchange" (Suzuki and Bahng 12). By examining *The Disinherited* within the emerging field of transpacific queer ecologies, I aim to advance decolonial theory's engagements with ecocriticism, memory studies, queer studies, and Pacific studies. Through a decolonial transpacific perspective, the chapter shows how Ong's queer "outsider" point of view critiques the exploitation of the working poor in association with Indigenous subjugation and environmental ruin. In this manner, Ong's queer critical perspective reveals the historical amnesia about empire implied by the colonial suppression and erasure of indigeneity in the Philippines.

According to Catriona Mortimer-Sandilands and Bruce Erickson in their landmark volume *Queer Ecologies*, the undertaking of queer ecologies is "to probe the intersections of sex and nature with an eye to developing a sexual politics that more clearly includes considerations of the natural world and its biosocial constitution, and an environmental politics that demonstrates an understanding of the ways in which sexual relations organize and influence both the material world of nature and our perceptions, experiences, and constitutions of that world" (5). Indigenous Pacific Islander and Asian diasporic writers and artists who identify as LGBTQ and who incorporate a queer ecological imagination in their work not only express in varying degrees a decolonial perspective that is grounded in a deeper relation to the land, to the ocean, and to the more-than-human natural world but also articulate this perspective by bringing into focus intersections of sex and nature in ways that disrupt binaries of human and nonhuman relations that have been implemented and maintained through histories of settler colonialism, racial capitalism, and the inequities of an unsustainable empire.[2] As LGBTQ Indigenous Pacific Islander and Asian diasporic writers show in their work, the histories of displacement, exploitation, and dispossession that form the substrate of racial capitalism and settler colonialism pivot on a dichotomy of human and nonhuman relations that is implemented and enforced through heteronormative and heteropatriarchal nature relations.

In their work, LGBTQ Pacific Islander and Asian diasporic writers express a decolonial perspective of queer ecologies that envisions Earth's global environmental crisis and implicates the destructive forces of empire in ecological ruination. Their remarkable expressions of imagination give voice to those who live in the Pacific region and confront the environmental degradation deriving from settler colonialism and racial capitalism. Accordingly, these writers express a decolonial critique that brings the vast scale of ecological ruination within the realm of understanding this ruination's provenance in colonial powers. These writers critique, moreover, an environmentally destructive, heteronormative, and patriarchal concept of separation between humans and nature *and* between colonizers and colonized. This is a heteropatriarchal binary deriving in colonialism on which the oppression of queer nonwhite and Indigenous sexualities and racial capitalist mechanisms of colonial power that extract profit from environmental destruction are premised.

In *The Disinherited*, the gay Filipino American playwright and fiction writer Han Ong implies a decolonial critique of Indigenous subjugation and suppression that correlates with ecological ruin in the Philippines. Ong reveals how extractive colonial powers employ an environmentally and racially destructive colonial binary (i.e., humans/nature and Western colonizer/colonized Indigenous) that is most evidently realized by the exploitation of the working poor and the neocolonial development of both rural and urban physical environments. This colonial binary is discernable in the novel's portrayal of poor people, who are associated with or implied as Indigenous. Ong critiques Indigenous subjugation among Filipinx people who have internalized the racial oppression of indigeneity as a result of colonization.[3] In this sense, he makes connections between the material and cultural dimensions of environmental issues by employing a decolonial transpacific perspective to expose and confront an imperialist nostalgia that entails the colonial erasure of indigeneity in the Philippines. His novel shows, in particular, how the imperialist nostalgia of a metropolitan Filipinx elite enables the continuation of extractive colonial powers that exploit both the Indigenous working poor and the physical environment. In the final analysis, *The Disinherited* cynically suggests that even those of the wealthy elite who naively seek to absolve themselves from profiting by the ruination and subjugation of the poor, the Indigenous, and the environment only end up furthering their complicity with the brutality of extractive colonial powers.

Imperialist Nostalgia, Environmental Destruction, and Queer Ecological Critique

Han Ong was born in 1968 in Manila, in the Philippines. In 1984, he left his country of origin to migrate to the United States with his family. Although much of his work concerns the Philippines and the lives of Filipinx people in the diaspora, Ong has never returned to the Philippines since leaving it when he was sixteen. In interviews, when asked about his perspective as an immigrant and a queer writer in relation to the Philippines and the United States, Ong has replied, "I've written enough now to figure out I have a recurring tendency, which is that a lot of my characters are outsiders. It comes from being an outsider twice over—my queerness and my ethnicity. . . . I'm not particularly fond of looking back, though. It's like running a race looking over your shoulder" (Ong, Interview by Regina Marier). In his comment, Ong refuses the nostalgia for the Philippine homeland of his childhood that other Filipinx immigrants in the United States express feeling for their native land when it was under the dictatorial rule of Ferdinand Marcos (1965–86) and in the years following Marcos's removal by the People Power Revolution, a decade during which new government leaders attempted to restore democracy in the Philippines, which had been severely vitiated, if not outright destroyed, by the Marcos dictatorship's corruption, extravagance, and brutality. Ong reveals that his anti-nostalgic feeling—the fact that he is not "fond of looking back"—is premised on his being both a queer person and a nonwhite immigrant in the United States, a country that occupied the Philippines as an imperialist force first by establishing settlements during the Spanish colonial period (1565–1898) and then by ruling the country as a colonizer for forty-eight years (1898–1946). In the decades following U.S. colonial rule, the Philippines withstood, and today continues to endure, the aftermath of this colonization as well as neocolonial authoritarian violence (i.e., under the dictatorship of President Rodrigo Roa Duterte, which this chapter will discuss further in a later section).

In the context of U.S. colonialism and Ong's refusing a nostalgia for his country of origin, it seems pertinent to raise the question: Can we understand his anti-nostalgic feeling for the Philippines as a queer of color to be a critique—a critical negation from his gay nonwhite immigrant perspective—of imperialist nostalgia? Renato Rosaldo has written trenchantly on the affective condition of imperialist nostalgia. In his essay "Imperialist Nostalgia," Rosaldo contends that this condition "revolves around a paradox: a person kills somebody and then mourns his or her victim. In more attenuated form, someone deliberately alters a form of life and then regrets that things have not remained as they were prior to his or her intervention" (108). Of particular interest is how imperialist nostalgia involves mourning and regret about the ruination of nature and the environment. "At one remove," Rosaldo explains, "people destroy their environment and then worship nature. In any of its versions, imperialist nostalgia uses a pose of 'innocent yearning' both to capture people's imaginations and to conceal its complicity with often brutal domination" (108). According to Rosaldo, what is especially mourned through "a pose of 'innocent yearning'" in imperialist nostalgia is an apparently lost pristine natural environment and the native inhabitants who once lived and thrived uncorrupted in this environment.

Ann Laura Stoler has also written trenchantly on imperialist nostalgia. In *Imperial Debris*, a study of the physical and environmental devastations caused by imperialist powers in the regions and countries these powers have colonized, Stoler insists, "But in thinking about 'ruins of empire,' [*Imperial*

Debris] works explicitly against the melancholic gaze to reposition the present in the wider structures of vulnerability, damage, and refusal that imperial formations sustain. Nor is [imperial debris] the wistful gaze of imperial nostalgia to which we turn" ("'The Rot Remains,'" 9). In their critical negation of imperialist nostalgia, Ong, Rosaldo, and Stoler articulate a countering move against the allure of a *false* nostalgia for eras of empire and the periods before and immediately following colonization. Imperialist nostalgia is, in other words, a sham sentiment because it is predicated on longing for a lost natural world and native people who have been devastated by the ecological ruination of colonialism, but the sentiment does not recognize imperialism as the cause of this devastation. The feeling is artificial and dishonest because it denies not only the involvement of imperialism as the cause of environmental destruction but also the fact that native people and their communities continue to exist in the aftermath of empire, albeit they have been adversely affected and transformed by the ecologically destructive impacts of colonization.

When Ong reveals that he's "not particularly fond of looking back" to his childhood and adolescence in the Philippines, he asserts his "outsider" point of view as both queer and a nonwhite immigrant as a critical perspective premised on anti-nostalgia. He's confronting, in other words, ecological ruination and imperialist nostalgia by *refusing* the denial of imperialism as a primary cause of environmental devastation and the abject poverty of the majority poor in the Philippines. Through an anti-nostalgic standpoint, Ong resolutely rejects any yearning for a time when he was growing up in Manila in the decades of the twentieth century following U.S. imperialist occupation and colonization of the Philippines. Further, when Rosaldo and Stoler explain how their respective critical positions against imperialist nostalgia refute a mood of wistfulness that makes devastation and abjection under colonial domination appear innocent and pure, they likewise assert a critical perspective that makes visible the ecological ruination of empire in order to confront and challenge a false nostalgia that would blind us to the horrors of empire that have caused immense physical destruction and, in the present, continue to injure, kill, and destroy in regions and countries that have been colonized.

In the burgeoning field of postcolonial ecocriticism, scholars also assert a critical perspective that underscores colonialism's destructive impact on physical environments and the natural world. As Graham Huggan and Helen Tiffin contend, postcolonial ecocriticism brings "postcolonial and ecological issues together as a means of challenging continuing imperialist modes of social and environmental dominance" (2). Postcolonial ecocriticism challenges destructive forces of imperialism through its critical attention not only to environmental ruin in the aftermath of colonization but also to current processes of ruination that continue in the present under conditions of *neocolonialism*. However, postcolonial ecocriticism has yet to handle adequately a queer "outsider" and an anti-nostalgic perspective like Han Ong's. And while postcolonial ecocriticism makes central to its analysis a focus on natural landscapes and nonhuman organisms that have been devastated by colonial powers, it has not sufficiently turned its critical gaze on the lives of colonized humans in places such as slums in megacities,[4] in human-made urban surroundings that are decidedly not the rustic and rural locations that ecocriticism traditionally privileges and esteems appropriate for critique. As Rosaldo and Stoler make clear, ruined physical environments cannot be understood apart from the impoverishment and destroyed lives of colonized humans. Indeed, the ruination of human bodies is both a material embodiment of colonial ecological destruction and a metaphor for the scarred landscapes, polluted places, and exploited and devastated organisms that Rosaldo and Stoler contend are the rotting remains of empire.

In *The Disinherited*, Ong turns his sardonic critical gaze on the slums of Manila and the millions of desperate poor, some of whom are Indigenous people dispossessed of their tribal lands,[5] who live in these densely populated urban areas. Undoubtedly, Manila's slums and the subjugation of poor and Indigenous people in the novel can be understood in Rosaldo's and Stoler's terms as the rot that remains from imperialist incursions and continuing modes of colonialism in the Philippines. To be sure, Ong in his novel focuses his criticism on the sexual exploitation of children who live in Manila's slums. His incisive depiction of a male child prostitute who is exploited by Western gay men is a decolonial critique that implicates the colonial legacies of economic deprivation, racism, and Western white privilege in "the contemporary (and historical) hypersexualization of Filipinos, including children, in a globalized tourist economy" (Nubla 238). Yet because Ong depicts through his anti-nostalgic queer "outsider" perspective the exploited body of the child prostitute in direct association with the pollution and ruination of physical environments, this child prostitute in his novel, who Ong suggests has Indigenous origins, can be understood as an incarnation of ecological ruination, the material embodiment of neocolonial environmental devastation evident in the slums of Manila and the city's fraught poverty, which are categorically signs of environmental ruin as well as the geographical displacement of Indigenous people.

Ong critiques environmental ruin, human impoverishment, and neocolonial capitalist development in his novel—in particular, the sexual exploitation of Filipinx children in a globalized tourist economy. Through a third-person omniscient point of view, he both sympathetically depicts and mocks his novel's protagonist, Roger Caracera, a heterosexual Filipino expat living and working as an adjunct college writing instructor in New York City. In 1997, Roger returns to his native Philippines to bury his father, the corrupt head of a patriarchal sugar dynasty in the Philippines. Roger loathes his family's ill-gotten wealth and has tried for many years to detach himself from their reach and influence. Accordingly, his prominent family in Manila consider him to be a deadbeat and a black sheep because he's been in the United States estranged from his relatives since adolescence, when his father sent him to California to finish high school. At forty-four, Roger returns to the Philippines for the first time since leaving his birthplace as a teenager. While attending his father's funeral in Manila, he not only observes the extreme separation between rich and poor in this megacity, which makes him feel disgust for his family's aristocratic status, but also beholds an immense population living in slums, which makes him feel shame for his family's ostentatious displays of wealth amid the city's vast deprivation.

Roger's disgust and shame for his family and their illicit wealth portray him sympathetically as a protagonist with a moral conscience. And curiously, he expresses this moral conscience through anti-nostalgic feelings—his shame and disgust—that also characterize his deliberate failure to recall with any affection the home place of his childhood. Roger's anti-nostalgia, in other words, can be understood as his *disremembering*—a willful "break with the past and a betrayal of the 'duty to remember'" (McGrattan 60)—the place of his origins when he returns to the Philippines and feels revulsion for his family's opulence while witnessing pervasive ecological ruination: teeming urban slums, omnipresent pollution of land and waterways, a massive population of working and exploited poor, and other disturbing material signs of what Stoler calls the "imperial debris" of colonial aftermaths. Imperial debris is what colonized people are left with after colonialism's "degradation of environment" and "the psychic weight of colonial processes that entangle people, soil, and things" (Stoler, "'The Rot Remains'" 10).

For Ong in his novel, imperial debris is manifest not only in the Philippines' "poverty all around" (3) but also in Roger's inheritance of $500,000 from his father, who states in his will that he bequests this money to Roger because he believes his son is ill-equipped "to deal with the business of life"

(45). For the father, such business is primarily about the accumulation of wealth acquired by industrious forebears who managed the sugar dynasty for the benefit of the family. But for Roger, the business is an industry of colonial capitalism, an "empire [that] had been built on sugar" (3), whose profits made from the exploitation of Indigenous itinerant laborers and environmental degradation during and in the decades after U.S. colonialism are utterly repulsive and reprehensible. Roger's disgust makes him view this inheritance as tainted with "abuses visited on the [plantations'] overworked, underpaid laborers" (67). Because he wants no part in his family's immorality and yearns to be innocent of their classism and corruption, Roger seeks to give away the unfortunate inheritance as a form of reparation to the Indigenous laborers and working poor his family exploited on their sugar plantations. Therefore, his anti-nostalgia is connected to reparations insofar as he wants to get rid of his inheritance "to forget who he was and where he'd come from" (129). He is only interested in cutting ties with his family and disremembering his country of origin. Hence, reparations for Roger means giving away his inheritance not as a measure to redress gross and systemic violations of the working poor's human rights—not as restitution to the Indigenous laborers his family have exploited in their empire of sugar. Rather, he wants to give away the money to ease his own conscience by erasing his filial ties to a history of colonization and imperialism in his native country. He thinks that if he can bestow his inheritance onto the working poor as a sort of debt payoff, he can cleanse himself of this colonial history and expunge from his memory the existence of the exploited poor, the marginalization and dispossession of Indigenous people, and the displeasing rotting remains of empire they embody.

Confronting the Erasure of Indigeneity through a Decolonial Transpacific Perspective

Roger's anti-nostalgia and his willful disremembering of his birthplace can be understood as Ong's queer "outsider" critique of both ecological ruin and imperialist nostalgia in the Philippines, revealed in a Western globalized tourist economy that has relied on the selling of poor women and children for prostitution as a direct result of neocolonial development following U.S. colonization in the mid-twentieth century. As the novel's omniscient narrator with a "queer outsider" perspective, Ong, to be sure, *validates* Roger's anti-nostalgic feelings of disgust and shame for his family's wealth and for the imperial debris that has been produced by Western exploitation. Yet Ong also *satirizes* Roger's attempts to enact disremembering and repudiating his birthplace—his endeavor to detach himself from his family's reach and influence—while he is in the Philippines. After the funeral, Roger despairs at being given the inheritance by his father not only because he believes it's illicit money but also because the bequest makes it harder for him to disremember his birthplace and cut ties with his family. His most determined attempt to give away his inheritance centers on a poor boy named Pitik Sindit, who works nightly as a gay prostitute in a seedy strip club and lives with his mother in their dilapidated shack in a Manila slum. During the day, Pitik attends middle school and is bullied by classmates for his shyness, sensitivity, and perceived femininity:

> They did ridicule him, with a passion, or like a vocation, or simply by animal instinct, smelling out his weakness like vultures drawn to carrion. . . . They put their hands to their foreheads and their chests in a pantomime of feminine bereavement, like penitent churchwomen whom they had seen, having internalized this country's sinfulness, to clutch at their weakened bodies. (193)

The bullying is also racially motivated. Neighbors believe that Pitik's physiognomy and physical features bear Indian ancestry: They "sniffed at the strain of Indian blood they claimed to see so strongly in his complexion, making them spit out poisonously, 'Bumbay', every time he drew near" (194).[6] Pitik's dark brown skin and curly black hair also suggest Indigenous origins. Moreover, his surname, Sindit, does not resemble the adopted Spanish colonial surnames of his classmates and neighbors. Rather, it appears to derive from one of the Philippines' Indigenous ethnolinguistic groups, such as the Igorot and Negrito people of Luzon.

Internalizing the oppression of indigeneity as a result of colonization, Pitik perceives his racially disparaged bodily features in association with his mother's poverty in Manila society. He fantasizes about a rich white heterosexual American man who can rescue him from his life of abjection and take him away to the United States:

> He would be granted an ascension. . . . into heaven—living in a house, dressed in clothes and being driven in cars and eating food that, being American, would have the natural cellophane of superiority over them [his classmates and neighbors]; objects that were the living embodiment of English, which

acquisition meant that native-born handicaps like poverty and brown skin were being improved upon, overcome. (199)[7]

Anticipating the day when he will meet his romanticized white savior, Pitik endeavors to be "beautiful not just in the eyes of the men but, most importantly, in his own eyes. That was what he was saving his money for. Because to be beautiful—every day he felt himself inching closer—he had to have things like creams and gels and shampoos. His skin had to be softer, whiter, his hair less kinky" (199–200). For Pitik, relief from his life of abjection in Manila's slums requires that he subdue his Indigenous features by lightening his "native" complexion and delaying the onset of male sexual maturity: "By the application of his creams and by trying to avoid or minimize hard labor, like lifting the five-gallon containers to and from the communal pump for his and his mother's daily water (which they paid a laborer to do), he had managed to keep his boyish (girlish) figure, retarding the onset of roughness and musculature" (199–200). As a light-skinned mestizo living in New York, Roger Caracera fits Pitik's colonial race romance to a T. When Pitik first notices Roger following him on the street, he imagines this Western foreign man as a masculine Hollywood idol resembling the movie icon Cary Grant (204). The two meet in the strip club, which eventually enables Roger to disburse his inheritance to Pitik by taking him away from his work as a prostitute and moving him and his mother to a condominium in an upscale Manila suburb. Unfortunately, Pitik mistakes Roger's intentions and falls in love with him, believing that Roger will love him in return and bring him to North America, where he will be taken care of for the rest of his life. Roger, however, returns to New York alone, abandoning Pitik once he has given him his inheritance.

As Ong ultimately suggests through his narrative's "queer outsider" point of view, the exploited bodies of children and the working poor are, indeed, an incarnation of imperial debris, an environmental metaphor for Manila's desperate poverty that should also be understood as ecological ruination wholly attributable to a globalized prostitution industry that has prospered through neocolonial development. The disremembering of place and the witnessing of imperial debris in the novel hence articulate a queer outsider perspective within a decolonial concept of queer ecologies that critiques the political dynamics of capitalism and nationhood—a heteropatriarchal dynamics that has defined masculinist and fascist dictatorships in the Philippines from Ferdinand Marcos, who was president of the country in the mid-twentieth century (1965–86), to the Philippines' current authoritarian macho dictator, President Rodrigo Roa Duterte (2016–present).[8]

However, because Ong wrote *The Disinherited* twelve years before Duterte became president, I suggest that a decolonial transpacific perspective
enables us to see how Ong's novel challenges continuing imperialist modes
of social dominance and environmental ruin that are *traceable* to neocolonial capitalist development schemes under Marcos and his fascist regime.
These are murderous schemes against the poor that continue under Duterte,
whom former U.S. president Donald Trump praised for his so-called drug
war. According to a 2019 report from the UN Human Rights Office, Duterte's "drug war" has resulted in over 8,660 extrajudicial killings linked to the
Philippines' national police and sanctioned by the national government (Ratcliffe).[9] It should also be noted that the war against the poor implemented
under Duterte's authoritarian regime has led to an undeclared war against
Indigenous people in the Philippines. Duterte's government has signed off
on environmentally disastrous but profitable mining, agribusiness, hydroelectric, and infrastructure projects on Indigenous ancestral lands, and when
Indigenous leaders protest and stand in the way, they risk being labeled as
"terrorists" on official lists and treated as such. According to reports from
environmental journalists in the Philippines, "In 2019, 212 environmental
defenders were killed worldwide, the worst tally since the NGO Global Witness started keeping track in 2012. Of those, 43 were killed in the Philippines.
Duterte's government has seemingly turned a blind eye to this violence, and
sometimes even tacitly encouraged it" (Lomax).

As Neferti Tadiar contends, Marcos attempted to effect modernization
and create a "New Society" in the Philippines that was predicated on a heteropatriarchal concept of dictatorship, in conjunction with the demands of
a globalized and neocolonial capitalist economy. Marcos's implementation
of martial law, according to Tadiar, created the conditions for a hospitality
industry in the Philippines that was largely based on the sexual exploitation
of women and children. "The hegemonic 'strong man' regime of Marcos engineered a 'prostitution' economy of the nation and the 'feminization' of Philippine labour" (Tadiar 23). With Marcos and his cronies manning the nation,
"modernization and militarism went hand in hand in restructuring the economy" as a tourist and hospitality industry that "relied on a predominately
female" and infantilized labor force (52). The selling of women and children
for prostitution was a direct result of Marcos's restructured economy. Tadiar
further explains that the

> boom of the "sex industry" is only the necessary consequence of the "devel-
> opment" of a larger hospitality industry, that is, one that hosts the capital and

arms of touring men and multinationals. In fact, the establishment of the Ministry of Tourism in 1973 was a key achievement of the Marcos State in its revitalized efforts to transform the nation into a lucrative business beginning with the declaration of martial law. . . . With the military imposition of stability in an otherwise crisis-ridden country, the number of hotels and tourists, multinationals and investors increased rapidly. Martial law was not, however, merely the whim of a dictator in pursuit of power (although that was undoubtedly at work as well), but part of the engineering of a new economic order necessary to meet the intensified demands of global capitalism. (50–51)

To show further how a queer outsider position within a decolonial concept of queer ecologies critiques poverty and prostitution in Ong's novel, I want to turn once again to Ong's comment in an interview he gave in *The Advocate* in 2004, the year he published *The Disinherited*. Based on his marginalized position both as a queer person and as a racialized Filipino immigrant from a country formerly colonized by the United States, Ong openly articulates an anti-nostalgic perspective in his view of the Philippines from his place of being an "outsider twice over" in the United States. "I'm not particularly fond of looking back," he divulges, because "it's like running a race looking over your shoulder" (Ong, Interview by Regina Marier). Clearly, Ong feels no idealistic longing for his country of origin. His lack of sentiment and fondness for the Philippines is striking but understandable, considering that he also felt like an outsider when he was a child growing up in Manila because of his Chinese ethnicity and his queerness. In this regard, he resembles to some extent his novel's fictional protagonist, Roger Caracera. Both are intensely anti-nostalgic in their view of the Philippines. To be sure, it would seem that Ong's anti-nostalgia for the Philippines would characterize the sardonic tone of his novel's third-person narration because its omniscient and satirical point of view is limited nearly entirely to Roger's anti-nostalgic perspective, which is deeply scathing of the Western exploitation of the Philippines and those affluent Filipinx elites, such as his aristocratic family in Manila, who have acquired their wealth from this exploitation. Yet it would be a mistake to confuse Ong's queer outsider position entirely with his protagonist's anti-nostalgic perspective, because Ong's characterization of Roger and his morally righteous denunciation of his family is clearly satirical. Moreover, in other interviews, Ong has denied creating his protagonist as a direct resemblance to himself. "I hope I'm not anything like him!" Ong exclaimed when asked how much of Roger is based on his own life (Ong, Interview by Terry Hong, "Returning"). He explained,

> Part of the writing process is how willing you are to spend time in the company of someone you don't totally identify with. I spent two years with these people, and some of them are definitely not companionable. Writing about them has to be worth overcoming a certain discomfort because the story is compelling and worth being committed to the page. I was able to spend two years with Roger. I think his criticisms of the Philippines, as well as his realization of the Western exploitation of places like the Philippines, are very valid. He is ultimately very clear about that, and I think that's admirable.

Based on these additional comments from Ong, we can understand that Ong's anti-nostalgia for his upbringing in the Philippines, which characterizes his queer outsider identity *and* his decolonial perspective, infuses his novel's third-person narration in which the narrator, arguably Ong himself, adheres closely but also satirically to Roger's anti-nostalgic outlook. This decolonial queer narrative position is an intensely critical one that contradicts "the wistful gaze of imperial nostalgia." An anti-nostalgic outlook that militates against the "melancholic gaze" is central to Stoler's concept of imperial debris: "the wider structures of vulnerability, damage, and refusal that imperial formations sustain" ("'The Rot Remains'" 9). The anti-nostalgia in both Ong's and his novel's queer perspectives further expresses a transpacific queer ecologies that makes visible the evidence of imperial debris as environmental devastation in the Philippines. Accordingly, we can understand that for Ong, a queer postcolonial subject in the Filipinx diaspora, his anti-nostalgia is primarily a feature of his queerness and his ethnicity. In this regard, the "outsider" position of his novel's protagonist, Roger Caracera, and his disremembering the home place of his childhood in the Philippines suggest Ong's own queer anti-nostalgia, a decolonial perspective that brings into focus and is borne from the ecological ruination wrought by colonialism and neocolonial development.

When Roger returns to the Philippines to attend his father's funeral and fails to remember the familial "place" of his childhood there, his disremembering is a way for him to affirm being an outsider. In doing so, he can detach himself from a country that is the site of traumatic childhood memories and the abuses of a national government and police that maintain a ruthless class system to uphold an aristocratic class, whose wealth is largely dependent on resource imperialism and the exploitation of the working poor. The slums of Manila and the ruined natural landscapes of rural areas are ultimate signs of imperial debris in the novel, because these places of imperial debris are consequences of the upper class's exploitation of the poor.

Ong introduces Roger at the beginning of the novel by referring to the shame he feels for his family's spectacle of wealth during the funeral procession for his father, Jesus Caracera. Here, Roger's shame is an emotion that expresses his anti-nostalgia: his intense dislike of Manila and disdain for his family. By his shame, then, the novel depicts anti-nostalgia through environmental metaphors for witnessing imperial debris: the omnipresent poverty in Manila and the many onlookers who watch the funeral procession. These onlookers, some of whom are dispossessed Indigenous people but all of whom are poor, observe and take part in the funeral procession as a "vulgar display of wealth" (4). In effect, the Caracera family signify imperial debris insofar as they have accumulated their wealth and maintain their aristocratic status through exploitation of the poor and dispossession of Indigenous people:

> The sky was an uninterrupted sheet of aluminum. Below it lay an expanse of asphalt and concrete convecting the heat from the ground up. Some of the women in the procession, noticed Roger Caracera, perhaps due to poverty, though more likely and more disturbingly, with a sense of voluntary, punitive penitence, were marching barefoot. He felt *shamed* by the extravagance of their display—wailing, hitting their chests, making of the long trip to the cemetery a walk on hot coals. It was as if for them a hero, long missed and much needed, had finally returned and they were pouring out all the energies and hopes accumulated during a lifetime of waiting. . . . On their way to Quezon City's Kalayaan Cemetery, they attracted onlookers who were made equal parts reverent and resentful of such a vulgar display of wealth. The choosing of the cemetery, which was not where Jesus Caracera's father and grandfather were buried (they were in Negros, the province where the sugar business once thrived but which consideration no longer seemed apt for the succeeding generations), was also left to Mrs. Amador Caracera. . . . It was understood by the family, including the three children of Jesus Caracera, that she knew whereof she spoke. So Kalayaan it would be, the name meaning Freedom. In Manila, it was apparent that to attain freedom you had to have a shitload of money. (4–5)

As this beginning part of the novel suggests, the Caraceras both signify and preserve their aristocracy as a status that must be publicly performed—a spectacle of wealth that must be enacted—for the poor to consume, with the intended outcome of their accommodating and internalizing oppression and subjugation. Moreover, note the past conditional in this quote: "It was as if for them a hero long missed and much needed, had finally returned and they were pouring out all the energies and hopes accumulated during a lifetime of waiting." The past conditional here denotes not only the shame Roger feels for his family's wealth but also his disgust. As Roger sees the "onlookers" who come from Manila's majority poor watching the funeral procession, he views his family's performance of aristocracy and the spectators who consume this display of wealth and internalize their abjection from an external perspective, an outsider's critical position. Hence, it becomes clear that the *place* of home for Roger is not with the Caraceras in the Philippines, nor is it with the country's majority poor. He feels no reverence for his ancestry and origins. His antagonistic, anti-nostalgic position at the beginning of the novel suggests the opposite of belonging and a willful detachment from his country of origin.

Haunted by the Rot of Empire in Historical Amnesia

In the novel, disremembering place, specifically Roger's acute sensation of "place-disconnectedness" when he is in Manila, is weirdly contextualized in natural landscapes. Through strange and outlandish plant metaphors for forgetting origins and disconnecting from the place of origins, the novel naturalizes, satirizes, and queers Roger's willful detachment from his homeland. For Roger, this strange and queer naturalization of disremembering place is evident when his aunt Irene, the wife of his uncle Amador, tells him that she wants to throw a party for him to welcome him "home" to his birthplace and family. "You, Roger. To welcome you," Irene tells him. "To thank you for deciding to stay here in Manila and not going back so soon, like you initially planned to. This tells us . . . that you are willing to give the family a chance. Your past—it's all here. You're willing to consider that none of us are irrelevant to your life" (128). But Irene's words make Roger realize that he desperately seeks *dis*connection from his birthplace and family. While listening to Irene, he recalls a bizarre news story that he recently read in a Manila tabloid: "A young boy lost by his parents, a missionary couple, in the southern provinces of Mindanao in the late eighties and feared either dead or adopted by Communist mountain rebels had been recently discovered—alive in the interior jungle" (129). The child had survived "by hunting game and drinking from a forest lagoon and, more importantly, by being able to tell apart edible and poisonous plants (helped by a guidebook from his parents)" (129). For Roger, the most remarkable thing about this feral boy who apparently survived on his own in the jungle for more than a dozen years is that when he was finally discovered, "he had no idea how much time had elapsed and he grew to forget who he was and where he'd come from" (129). The boy had been able to avoid detection for years because he had "grown over his skin a layer of moss, in essence making him a green thing surrounded by many other green things. The moss had not embedded itself with roots but could be brushed off and the skin underneath cleaned, but a few days later, a new layer would be seen to start sprouting, as if the boy had taken a bath in green water" (129–30). The moss covering the feral boy's body signifies forgetting origins—"he grew to forget who he was and where he'd come from"—and, consequently, this moment of Roger's identification with the boy's disremembering his origins and nationality can be understood as an environmental metaphor for his deliberate betrayal of the "duty to remember" both his family and his own past.

> This was what Caracera felt had happened to him. . . . The humidity and the rains could partly explain this feeling. The rest he didn't know how to account for. There seemed over his skin a layer that was mosslike, but unlike the boy's, his was invisible. His movements were slowed, his speech robbed of the more complex vocabulary of his teacher self—moss on his tongue. And enshrouding his brain, a kind of mist or tropical vapor that would occasionally retreat and make clear a few mysteries of the country's sights and customs, but which he would only remember for that brief instant of clarity—a tease. (130)

As Ong suggests in this passage, his novel implies a decolonial and queer ecological imagination to critique Roger's attempt at *naturalizing* his forgetting the past: his peculiar sensation of disremembering place and origins through tropical rainforest imagery that is at once otherworldly and native. Here, it can be understood that Roger endeavors to forget his family and his past as a narrative affect of imperialist nostalgia[10]—an "invisible" mosslike feeling "enshrouding his brain"—as a way for him to establish his yearning to be innocent of his family's classism and corruption that dictate the colonial abjection and erasure of indigeneity. Admittedly, his empathic identification with the feral boy's disremembering his origins and nationality expresses his desire to naturalize imperialist nostalgia, his longing to be innocent of his own place in the rot of empire. However, because Roger desires to forget his implicit connection to the extractive colonial powers that have enabled his family's prosperity, which he is forced to claim as his inheritance, his intentional forgetting can only serve to remind him (as "a brief instant of clarity—a tease") of his family's wealth and the ruination of environment and dispossession of Indigenous people this affluence has caused. Roger's naturalization of imperialist nostalgia implies, in other words, the ruins of empire—the debris in the aftermath of Western colonization and neocolonial development, implemented through a prostitution economy and a globalized tourist industry that preys upon the poor and the marginalized (i.e., women, children, and Indigenous people).

The novel satirizes tourism in the Philippines when portraying Roger's trip to the island region of Negros, the place of his family's sugar plantations and where he intends to find the Indigenous laborers who worked for subsistence wages in his family's cane fields. It is here that his shame and disgust for his family's wealth especially register the novel's anti-nostalgic exposé of ruthless class division and ruinous neocolonial development of rural and urban environments.[11] As Ong reveals in this part of his novel, the exploitation of Indigenous laborers and the rural lands on which they work for meager earnings has enabled profit and power for a rich minority elite in Manila at the great cost of privation and dispossession for the majority working poor in the Philippines.

The shame that Roger feels for past injustices committed by the sugar empire against the plantations' Indigenous laborers compels him to search for these workers whom he believes his family has exploited. Yet when he arrives at the plantation looking for these workers to give them his inheritance, the only trace of them he finds is in some old photographs that hang on the walls of one of the plantation's buildings. This building has been turned into a museum. A Frenchwoman named Virginie has taken over the plantation and has converted its buildings and sceneries into a tourist attraction.

The museum had been started by Virginie and the locals as a gesture of civic pride as well as for the benefit of tourists. Inside, Virginie took her guests through a pasteboard-walled maze, stopping before each picture to explain in her accented English. . . . Here they were, stopped before this black-and-white picture: three sugarcane cutters regarding the camera with wide smiles, their eyes twinkling, as if their livelihoods required none of the heavy labor of lore. Around their necks were rags, which were not scarves but masks traditionally worn over their mouths to keep the insects that proliferated in the fields from getting in, and also over their ears and the sides of their faces to protect them from leaf cuts, and also their noses when the leaves that had been hacked off the canes became smoking bonfires. Virginie told them all this, shaking her head the whole time. It was only to oblige the photographer that the men had pulled down these rags. From this it could be assumed that the photograph had been taken for the Department of Tourism. (106–7)

It could be argued that these photos of the cane cutters, whose smiles for the Department of Tourism contradict and conceal the sheer misery of their labor, are meant by Virginie's curation to document racial capitalist mechanisms of colonial power that have extracted profit from the exploitation of Indigenous people and displacement from their territories in this island region. However, we need to recall that Ong's novel is a sardonic, anti-nostalgic exposé of *neo*colonialism in the Philippines. In this regard, he portrays Virginie and her liberal do-gooder intentions as especially worthy of mordant critique. Virginie, writes Ong, "had been with Médecins sans Frontières and had, after her itinerant group had departed for less hospitable and needier locations, stayed behind to fill a needed hole which few had wanted or thought to address: what were the deposed sugar workers to do to earn a living?" (105). Indeed, Virginie, who is both a Westerner and a foreigner, has taken over the defunct plantation apparently to preserve its history and to help the cane cutters, whose labor was no longer needed after the Philippines' sugar industry fell into decline, having been usurped by industries from Brazil, India, and China. When she explains to Roger that his plans to expend his inheritance to the cane cutters are futile, she *is* telling the truth, but it's also clear that she perceives Roger and the money he wants to give away as a threat to her own position as a leader of the villagers on the island.

She told [Roger] that any discussion would not find her deviating from what she'd already said. . . . She let her exasperation show on her face. First off, the descendants of the original workers . . . . who toiled the fields during the industry's prime, from roughly the turn of the century to the 1920s and '30s, had dispersed to other locations. They were itinerant by nature and went wherever the work was. The only descendants of those sugar workers remaining in the area were in the handful of graveyards scattered across the countryside. The only act of reparation these people needed was already being undertaken by Virginie. Every year, during All Soul's Day (which celebration she capitulated to as a symbol of goodwill), she paid local children to place sugar cubes on the earth above the graves. This was, of course, a borrowing from the Mexican tradition. (107)

As Ong thus portrays Virginie, she is a figure of settler *neo*colonialism, arriving at the abandoned former plantation as the villagers' self-appointed leader. The villagers are actually the region's native inhabitants but apparently bear no relation to the Indigenous cane cutters, whose racialized labor exploitation enabled profit and power for the Caracera family. Having started the museum with the locals "as a gesture of civic pride as well as for the benefit of tourists," Virginie and her tourist institution are a manifestation of imperialist nostalgia that she fabricates to conceal her own complicity in ongoing extractive colonial powers. The illusion of moral authority that she has invented for herself both as the sole purveyor of care and as a model of rectitude for the villagers is born of her desire to be innocent of their ruinous transformation into an impoverished people. Consequently, she vehemently disagrees with Roger's plans to give away his money to the villagers, revealing her condescending attitude of noblesse oblige but implicitly exposing her fears of losing moral authority over them.

> She painted a dark portrait of what the villagers would do with his [money]: The men abandoning families to go to Manila and take up with whores, finally being able to afford the easy life promulgated by the Filipino and American movies they saw. The women refurbishing their humble homes with imported appliances, the money run through at a clip. The children being rewarded for their stopgap schooling and poor ambitions with video games and shiny new TV sets. These people, said Virginie, need the discipline of industry, and to have the connection between money and hard work reinforced. (110)

Under the guise of her altruism, exemplified in her belief that she alone has authorized reparation for colonialism's ruination of the poor on the island, Virginie herself seeks power and profit through her purportedly morally righteous cause to keep the villagers *pure* of foreign and corruptive materialistic desires. Emphasizing that the locals "need the discipline of industry" and not handouts that would corrupt them with aspirations for "the easy life," Virginie entirely thwarts Roger's own reparation plans. Failing to give away his inheritance to the native inhabitants living nearby his family's defunct plantation, he returns to Manila and, ironically at one of the city's elite country clubs, is finally able to fulfill part of his plans. He is introduced to Donnie Osmond Magulay, a rising teenage tennis star from humble origins. Roger sponsors and coaches Donnie and eventually sends him to a tennis academy in the United States.

However, as I mentioned earlier, Roger's most determined attempt to expend his inheritance and extricate himself from his family's place in a brutal colonial legacy centers on the poor boy Pitik Sindit. Roger has learned that an earlier inheritance of $60,000 that he received from his reclusive uncle, Eustacio, was in fact diverted from its true beneficiary, Pitik Sindit. Exiled from the Caracera family because of his homosexuality, Eustacio initially represented for Roger "a kindred rebellious spirit" despite the fact that Roger identifies as heterosexual (Nubla 237). However, when he learns that Eustacio was not just homosexual but a pedophile, he is demoralized and disgusted especially because Pitik was just seven years old when Eustacio met him and began having sex with this child. Wanting to right the wrong of Eustacio's pedophilia and his family's refusal to pay out Eustacio's money to the child he sexually exploited, Roger tracks down Pitik to give him his inheritance. However, when Roger finds Pitik, who is now fifteen years old, he discovers that the boy is working as an erotic dancer and a prostitute named Blueboy in a strip club run by a transsexual who calls herself Madame Sonia. Roger enters the strip club one afternoon to find out more about Pitik and the work he performs. He sits among the strip club's audience of foreign white men who eagerly await Pitik's appearance as Blueboy. Madame Sonia has given to each of the men, including Roger, a child's plastic toy bucket. As they watch Blueboy strip and dance naked onstage, the men masturbate into their buckets, which Roger observes with revulsion. But he is most sickened when he sees Madame Sonia collect the buckets and pour their contents of the men's ejaculate onto Blueboy's rear end at the end of his performance: "The boy's body, it had occurred to him, had been used as a trash can, a dumping site" (155). In comparing Pitik's body to a trash can and dumping site for white Western pedophiles who come to the Philippines to have sex with child prostitutes, Roger witnesses, I would argue, imperial debris. For Pitik's exploited body that bears Indigenous features is an incarnation of imperial debris, an environmental metaphor for the slums of Manila, the city's desperate poverty, and the colonial abjection and erasure of indigeneity that can also be understood as an ultimate sign of ecological ruination.

This ruination is further evident in a conversation that Roger has with Madame Sonia after the show has ended and the men are leaving the club. Madame Sonia confronts Roger to ask him why he did not masturbate into the bucket she had given him. When she becomes suspicious about Roger's intentions, thinking he might be a competitor and want to steal Blueboy from her, she directs his attention to the sight of "the brown, barely flowing Pasig River" outside her club (155).

> Have you seen the river? asked Madame Sonia.
> Caracera looked. No, honestly he couldn't have said he'd seen it. He'd known it was there. Had been warned off it—by whom, he couldn't remember. The symbol of all that was wrong with the Philippines, a natural resource turned by the citizenry into a dumping ground. All the detritus of Manila life—corpses and condoms—floated by, serving as active reminders. Now, in the current, he could make out clusters of water lilies, their unseen roots so thick and tangled that it anchored them to the trash-congealed sediment of the river, rising: There were dead dogs, dead birds flowing slowly past. Perhaps his nose had already been stunned by the semen, because he couldn't smell anything. (155–56)

When Madame Sonia demands to know if Roger is in love with Pitik and will take him away from her, Roger says, "'I'm not in love'" (157). Madame Sonia angrily responds, "'You better not be . . . because Blueboy is my property! If you think you can love-love him away from me . . . ! He will end up in that river, just like all the trash in Manila, if he tries to go away!'" (157). Indeed, Roger does take Pitik away from Madame Sonia by giving him his inheritance. Ultimately, his quest to disburse his inheritance to Pitik exemplifies the novel's satirizing of modern Western tourism. For Roger, the tourist and tourism, especially white male pedophiles who come to the Philippines for its sex tourism and child prostitution industry, operate as the sign of his own fundamental disconnection from the place of his origins, as well as the most evident indication of ecological ruination in the Philippines. We can understand this ruination as the violent accrual of imperial debris, in Stoler's terms, that evidences "what people are 'left with': to what remains, to the aftershocks of empire, to the material and social afterlife of structures, sensibilities, and things" ("Imperial Debris" 194).

Forsaken by Roger, who returns to New York to resume his life far away from his family, Pitik is utterly bereft. He attempts to find Roger by appealing to his family in Manila. Yet Roger's patrician family are deeply offended by his behavior, and they become spiteful. Seeking vengeance for having been scandalized by Roger's disremembering and disrespecting them, they hire an assassin to murder Pitik when he comes to them pleading to be reunited with Roger. When in New York Roger learns of Pitik's death, he realizes that he will never be free of his family and that always he'll be haunted by his memory of this abused child, whose death at the rapacious hands of his family also means that Roger will forever be haunted by the "rot" of Western empire. His gesture of moral conscience to give away his inheritance cannot right the wrongs of his corrupt family, whose acquirement of wealth through the exploitation of the poor and abjection of indigeneity both reinforces and reenacts the colonizer's rule of the colonized within the intimate realms of Manila's slums, prostitution dens, and elite country clubs for the city's richest families. Most decisively for Roger, whose moral integrity turns out to be a sham, the novel suggests that Pitik is the real moral conscience "through the sleight of hand that positions Roger not as savior of his homeland but as one of the foreign exploiters" (Nubla 239).

Because Roger strives to give away his tainted inheritance as reparations in order to extricate himself from his family's guilt of exploiting and ruining the poor, his moral integrity as the assumed reason for why he wants to disremember his Philippine origins is a guise for imperialist nostalgia. His inherited wealth that he gives away to Pitik with the intent to wash his hands of both this child and his family only ends up furthering his complicity with the brutality of extractive colonial powers. In this manner, Roger's imperialist nostalgia really does revolve around a paradox: his act of reparation for the working poor and Indigenous people ends up killing an exploited and impoverished child, and then he mourns the death of this child. This paradox is evident at the end of the novel when Roger is home in New York and watches *Fiesta of the Damned*, a Hollywood blockbuster movie about the Philippine-American War that he saw being filmed when he was in the Philippines. Roger becomes profoundly disturbed to see a child in the film bearing an uncanny resemblance to the "dead boy" Pitik:

> Yet a few scenes later, in the undulations of the clear threads of heat, was another boy-creature who was (cut away from too quickly to be contradicted) the dead boy. Or rather, the dead boy's twin ... looking as if he'd never learned

how to smile in his entire life. The skin bronzed as a special distinguishment, but the eyes jaundiced and staring ahead, unblinking, to impart a message implacable and unscripted. . . . Still, afterward, as the credits rolled, that stare kept compelling itself into the foreground of Caracera's memory. (368)

This eerie image of an unsmiling child with "eyes dull in the manner of things vacated by hope" stares from the screen at Roger to destroy his assumed innocence evident in his imperialist nostalgia (369). Roger has given away his inheritance not only to dissociate himself from his corrupt family but also to evade the responsibility to recognize and educe the problem of immense death and destruction in the Philippines that has made the wealth of the U.S. empire. Hence, this final haunting moment in which the film's "boy-creature" confronts Roger to demand "correction for the huge injustice of his plight" is the novel's most unsettling moment of the paradox that is Roger's attempt to use reparations to disremember his origins and, by extension, appeal to historical amnesia.

In this sense, perhaps Roger can be understood to *embody* imperialist nostalgia because he wants to be innocent of the fact that his family is directly implicated in the exploitation and ruination of Indigenous people, the poor, and the environment. That he gives away his inheritance to Pitik and his mother for the sole purpose of disremembering the Philippines and divorcing himself from his avaricious family is really, in the final analysis, his yearning to be innocent of his place in the rot of empire. By granting his inheritance to Pitik so that he can willfully forget the Philippines and claim innocence, Roger causes the death and hence ultimate ruination of this child.

The Disinherited both reflects and documents the social reality of class society in the Philippines in the late twentieth century, the latter years of the half century following U.S. colonialism. Because the novel's queer outsider perspective confronts ecological ruin and imperialist nostalgia in its depiction of an exploited and ostracized queer child—whose exclusion, subjugation, and demise are premised on this child's implied indigeneity—the novel can, accordingly, be understood as a decolonial transpacific queer work that contests the historical amnesia of empire and the colonial erasure of indigeneity. By showing how this queer child commands not to be "forgotten"—demands unconditionally the justice of recognition and remembrance—Ong positions us to comprehend concerns of environmental *and* racial justice that follow from the ecological ruination instigated by imperialism and colonization.

Notes

Acknowledgments: This chapter began as a presentation at the Association for the Study of Literature and Environment conference at Wayne State University in Detroit, Michigan, 20–24 June 2017. I am deeply grateful to my coeditors, Heidi Amin-Hong, Rina Garcia Chua, and Xiaojing Zhou, who read my chapter and provided constructive advice.

1. Following Lisa Yoneyama's model for examining "decolonial genealogies of transpacific studies" and Lisa Lowe's argument about "liberal possessive humanism" as historically premised on "the coeval global processes of settler colonialism, slavery, and imported colonial labor," Suzuki and Bahng propose reconceptualizing the transpacific as a decolonial term to engage with Oceanic and Indigenous-centered epistemologies (1, 12). See Yoneyama 471; Lowe 20–21.

2. For more on the concept of decolonial queer ecologies, see Chwala.

3. For historical context on the colonial origins of racialization and the racial oppression of Indigenous people in the Philippines, see Kramer, especially 372–78; see also Gonzalez.

4. For an incisive inquiry into the slums of megacities such as Manila, see Davis.

5. According to Rey Ty, Spanish and American colonization of the Philippines enforced legislation that institutionalized racial distinctions and hierarchies among ethnic groups and Indigenous peoples throughout the archipelago: "Through laws, the tribal /minority/ indigenous communities were deprived of their right to their ancestral domains. Through so-called 'development' activities, they were dispossessed of the land they till for their livelihood. Their marginalization, dispossession and other forms of injustices continued long after colonial rule had gone."

6. In the Philippines, "Bumbay" is a racist term used for people with dark brown skin and who look like they are from India (Lacuata).

7. Pitik's fantasy of being rescued by a white American man has historical context in late nineteenth-century Anglophone "race romances," which are artifacts of U.S. imperialism in the Philippines. According to Nerissa Balce, these popular narratives are "inscribed with notions of white domesticity, female subjectivity, empire, and nation-building. . . . The romance narrative focused on the extraordinary actions and adventures of a heterosexual male hero who was a metaphor for the imperial nation or empire" (163).

8. As I finish writing this chapter, the 2022 Philippine presidential and vice presidential elections are three weeks away. Ferdinand Romualdez Marcos Jr., commonly referred to as Bongbong Marcos, is the son and namesake of the late Philippine dictator Ferdinand Marcos. Marcos Jr. is running for president and Sara Duterte, the daughter of Rodrigo Roa Duterte, is running for vice president. Marcos Jr. and Duterte hold a big lead in recent polls. According to *Rappler*, the Philippines' leading digital news and media company founded by Maria Ressa, if Marcos Jr. wins the presidency, he will concentrate "power in his office to authoritarian levels. He will be able to do so because President Rodrigo Duterte has already done so. He need only follow Mr. Duterte's rough-hewn template. . . . It is possible that we will see a burst of spectacular violence at the start of a Marcos Junior presidency, to strike fear in both the public and in public officials. . . . He will likely be able to do that in his first three years in office, in part by placing Marcos apologists and opportunistic mercenaries in charge of historical, cultural, and educational agencies. After that, he will have three more years to reshape the Philippines in his father's bloated image" (Nery).

9. The UN Human Rights Office report says it cannot confirm the number of extrajudicial killings during the anti-drugs crackdown without further investigation. However, it says government figures reveal that at least 8,663 people have been killed, but some estimates put the toll at triple that number. The report also "raises alarm over the vilification of dissent," adding that attacks against perceived critics are being increasingly institutionalized and normalized in ways that will be very difficult to reverse. Between 2015 and 2019, at least 248 human rights defenders, legal professionals, journalists, and trade unionists were killed in relation to their work (Ratcliffe).

10. See Heather Houser's *Ecosickness in Contemporary U.S. Fiction* for a study of the environment and human feeling in contemporary U.S. novels and memoirs. According to Houser, recent U.S. narratives that depict environmental change in relation to feelings of disgust, anxiety, and wonder show how these "narrative affects" organize the perception of ecological crisis to "establish the interdependence of vulnerable earth and soma and shape environmental investment" (81).

11. By "neocolonial development," I mean the attempt by wealthy privileged nations of the First World to benefit poor countries of the Third World with technical and financial assistance that subscribes to the First World's global capitalist growth model. As Graham Huggan and Helen Tiffin have pointed out, this form of strategic altruism is, on the surface, meant to close the gap between rich nations of the Global North (many of them former colonizers) and the underprivileged countries of the Global South (most of them former colonies of the Global North) (30). Yet the benefits of the First World's capitalist development practices, which are delivered to the Third World under the guise of assisted modernization by economic agencies such as the World Bank and the International Monetary Fund, are ultimately geared to the First World's own economic and political objectives to maintain the global capitalist market system (Huggan and Tiffin 31). Hence, this form of development that is meant "to address the persistence of poverty, environmental degradation and the violation of human freedom in the contemporary globalized world" continues to profit rich nations while spreading inequality among poor countries, but enabling the First World to champion its own "adherence to freedom, democracy and human rights" (31–32).

Works Cited

Balce, Nerissa S. *Body Parts of Empire: Visual Abjection, Filipino Images, and the American Archive*. U of Michigan P, 2016.

Chwala, Gregory Luke. "Ruins of Empire: Decolonial Queer Ecologies in Cliff's *No Telephone to Heaven*." *eTropic: electronic journal of studies in the Tropics*, vol. 8, no. 1, 30 May 2019, 141–56. https://doi.org/10.25120/etropic.18.1.2019.3690

Davis, Mike. *Planet of Slums*. Verso, 2005.

Gonzalez, Michael. "The Colonial Legacy of Racism among Filipinos." *Positively Filipino*, 29 June 2020, www.positivelyfilipino.com/magazine/the-colonial-legacy-of-racism-among-filipinos. Accessed 27 Sept. 2021.

Houser, Heather. *Ecosickness in Contemporary U.S. Fiction: Environment and Affect*. Columbia UP, 2016.

Huggan, Graham, and Helen Tiffin. *Postcolonial Ecocriticism: Literature, Animals, Environment*. 2nd ed., Routledge, 2015.

Kramer, Paul A. *The Blood of Government: Race, Empire, the United States, and the Philippines*. U of North Carolina P, 2006.

Lacuata, Rose Carmelle. "Why Pinoys Call Indians 'Bumbay'—and Other Indian Stereotypes." *ABS-CBN News*, 24 Jan. 2018, https://news.abs-cbn.com/focus/01/24/18/why-pinoys-call-indians-bumbayand-other-indian-stereotypes. Accessed 27 Sept. 2021.

Lomax, John Nova. "Philippines President Duterte Is Waging War against Environmental Activists." *Vice*, 15 Oct. 2020, www.vice.com/en/article/5dznx3/philippines-president-duterte-is-waging-war-against-environmental-activists. Accessed 5 Apr. 2021.

Lowe, Lisa. *The Intimacies of Four Continents*. Duke UP, 2015.

McGrattan, Cillian. *Memory, Politics, and Identity: Haunted by History*. Palgrave Macmillan, 2012.

Mortimer-Sandilands, Catriona, and Bruce Erickson. "A Genealogy of Queer Ecologies." *Queer Ecologies: Sex, Nature Politics, Desire*, edited by Catriona Mortimer-Sandilands and Bruce Erickson. Indiana UP, 2010, 1–47.

Nubla, Gladys. "Innocence and the Child of Sex Tourism in Filipino/American Literature and Culture." *Rocky Mountain Review*, vol. 63, no. 2, Fall 2009, 233–40.

Ong, Han. *The Disinherited*. Picador, 2005.

Ong, Han. Interview by Terry Hong. "Genius Han Ong: The Outsider American." *Bloomsbury Review*, vol. 25, no. 1, 2005, www.bloomsburyreview.com/Archives/2005/Han%20Ong.pdf. Accessed 23 Sept. 2021.

Ong, Han. Interview by Terry Hong. "Returning to the Real World after the MacArthur Grant." *Asian Week*, 10 Sept. 2004, www.smithsonianapa.org/bookdragon/the-disinherited-by-han-ong-author-interview-in-asianweek/. Accessed 20 Jan. 2019.

Ong, Han. Interview by Regina Marier. "Han Ong Returns: The Queer Literary Filipino Phenomenon Is Back with a Provocative New Novel." *The Advocate*, 23 November 2004, 94.

Ratcliffe, Rebecca. "Philippines War on Drugs May Have Killed Tens of Thousands, Says UN." *The Guardian*, 4 June 2020, www.theguardian.com/world/2020/jun/04/philippines-police-may-have-killed-tens-of-thousands-with-near-impunity-in-drug-war-un. Accessed 23 Jan. 2021.

Nery, John. "What We Can Expect from a Marcos Junior Presidency." *Rappler*, 2 March 2022, www.rappler.com/voices/thought-leaders/newsstand-what-can-people-expect-ferdinand-bongbong-marcos-jr-presidency/. Accessed 17 April 2022.

Rosaldo, Renato. "Imperialist Nostalgia." *Representations*, no. 26, Spring 1989, 107–22.

Stoler, Ann Laura. "Imperial Debris: Reflections on Ruins and Ruination." *Cultural* Anthropology, vol. 23, no. 2, 2008, 191–219.

Stoler, Ann Laura. "'The Rot Remains': From Ruins to Ruination." *Imperial Debris: On Ruins and Ruination*, edited by Ann Laura Stoler. Duke UP, 2013, 1–35.

Suzuki, Erin, and Aimee Bahng. "The Transpacific Subject in Asian American Literature." *Oxford Encyclopedia of Asian American Literature and Culture*, edited by Josephine Lee. Oxford UP, 30 Jan. 2020, 1–8. *Oxford Research Encyclopedias*, https://doi.org/10.1093/acrefore/9780190201098.013.877. Accessed 16 Sept. 2021.

Tadiar, Neferti Xina M. *Fantasy Production: Sexual Economies and Other Philippine Consequences of the New World Order*. Hong Kong UP, 2004.

Ty, Rey. "Indigenous Peoples in the Philippines: Continuing Struggle." *Focus*, vol. 62, December 2010, Asia-Pacific Human Rights Information Center, www.hurights.or.jp/archives/focus/section2/2010/12/indigenous-peoples-in-the-philippines-continuing-struggle.html. Accessed 27 Sept. 2021.

Yoneyama, Lisa. "Toward a Decolonial Genealogy of the Transpacific." *The Chinese Factor: Reorienting Global Imaginaries in American Studies*, edited by Chih-ming Wang and Yu-Fang Cho. Special Issue, *American Quarterly*, vol. 69, no. 3, September 2017, 471–82.

2

Cycas wadei and Enduring White Space

Kathleen Cruz Gutierrez

In 1931, U.S. botanist Elmer D. Merrill wrote his colleague, William Henry Brown, about the existence of a unique species of cycad, a seed plant resembling a palm. Collected on Culion Island in the province of Palawan in the western central region of the Philippine archipelago, the cycad differed from those observed in other tropical colonies. Merrill shared, "Among the plants sent in for identification from Culion is a very excellent fruiting specimen of the Cycas with narrow leaflets of which I collected sterile specimens in 1902; this is undoubtedly an undescribed species, and I have tentatively named it *Cycas herrei*" (Merrill to Brown, 10 August 1931). Merrill had first observed the species on an expedition to a site selected for the establishment of the Culion leper colony (founded in 1902) ("A New Philippine Species" 233). He deemed the cycad "a curious species" after comparing his scant material with similar specimens held at the Kew herbarium (*Enumeration* 1).

After notifying Brown in 1931, Merrill and Filipino botanist Eduardo Quisumbing scrutinized the plant and differentiated it from previous erroneous identifications ("A New Philippine Species" 235). In 1936, Merrill introduced the cycad to the international botany community in the *Philippine Journal of Science*. Though he had originally recommended naming it in honor of Albert W. C. T. Herre, an ichthyologist with the Philippine Bureau of Science, the species was named *Cycas wadei* after Herbert W. Wade, a pathologist and physician at the Culion leper colony from 1922 until Wade's death in 1968.

A Study of White Space

Upon surveying new colonial holdings, imperial administrations deployed botanists to catalog existing flora for intellectual and commercial aims. Mer-

Fig. 2.1. Image of live *Cycas wadei* specimen reviewed for the 1936 *Philippine Journal of Science*. Series 1, Series 3 (Oversized), Elmer D. Merrill Papers. Archives of the New York Botanical Garden, The Bronx, New York. 28 October 2019. Reproduction permission courtesy of the Archives of the New York Botanical Garden.

rill's careful accounting of the cycad's features—that he spotted a new species, collected it, and read it against extant Anglo-European publications on the plant—typified the botany conducted in the archipelago during its Spanish (1565–1898) and U.S. (1898–1945) colonial periods. Even Merrill's deliberation as to the cycad's Latin name illustrated imperial botany's standard patronage and creation of social capital.

Yet, the distinction between *Cycas herrei* and *Cycas wadei* was not arbitrary. The different names carry a dense narrative that entwines the history of colonial science in the Philippines, the local impact of global crisis, and the threatened disappearance of the Philippine cycad. For this chapter, I follow a single species and unearth the process behind its formal Latin naming to expose the deeply entrenched politics of colonial botany in the Philippines.[1] Routine cover letters to specimens sent between herbaria, personal communiqués, and scrawled notes upon which this chapter relies speak of institutional struggles, political intrigue, and pivotal worldwide moments as they unfolded in the archipelago. Within the very deliberation over the plant's determination as a new species—a history usually omitted from a finalized herbarium specimen—lie colonial conflict and decolonial aspirations. I, therefore, bring into relief the contexts absent from the white herbarium sheet holding *C. wadei* for intellectual study.

By tracking the Culion cycad's study, I expand art historian Daniela Bleichmar's concept of "white space," a pictorial language and approach common to European natural history that isolates portions of a biological specimen from their local context and presents them on a white page. In Bleichmar's reading of eighteenth-century Spanish imperial illustrations, such white space "deracinates naturalia, removing local plants and animals from their surroundings through a process of visual erasure that transforms them into decontextualized products that can circulate globally" (151). I build upon her analysis by arguing that for certain species, white space is not limited by intellectual endeavor during the colonial moment. It endures. By following *C. wadei* across time, I recontextualize a single species in the scientific milieu of the colonial Philippines and stress its increasing disappearance due to war, resource extraction, and land-use projects. In this sense, I observe the slow encroachment of white space beyond pictorial isolation and into complete loss. More than a striking conceptual tool, white space is an active process of erasure upon which the botanical study of a plant is predicated. The plant pressed and fastened upon a page is suspended, but white space continues even after the end of formal colonial rule.

I acknowledge, as well, Michael Mascarenhas's application of Elijah Anderson's concept of "white space" to science and technology studies (STS). As Anderson stresses, white spaces are marked not only by the overwhelming absence of Black people but also by subtle and overt manifestations of racism and social negotiations of status and stereotype (13–15.) Mascarenhas extends the term to STS and the "persistence of legacies of white male supremacy and Eurocentrism" within the field, as well as the "changing forms of racialization embedded in the construct of undone science" (154). In this sense, white space is the very place of investigation from which STS scholars have asked questions, conducted research, and produced knowledge. Some of the necessary political stakes of this piece point to such a lineage: white space is the place from which my interrogation begins and with which it must contend. The story of *C. wadei* reveals a historical dimension to Mascarenhas's conception of white space, particularly as local Filipino botanists challenged foreign-colonial dominance and politicking in Philippine intellectual institutions. Such a narrative resurrects decolonial tensions, especially at the start of the Philippine Commonwealth and immediately following World War II, and the efforts to wrest intellectual power from U.S. scientists practicing in the Philippines.

The center of this chapter is not a plant with heavily reported economic or medicinal value but instead an ornamental known commonly in Tagalog as *pitogo* or in English as Wade's *pitogo*. *Pitogo* can broadly refer to various *Cycas* species endemic to particular islands in the Philippines. Leaves of *pitogo* serve as palm branches for ceremonial Holy Week activities, and seeds go into the manufacturing of crafts, toys, and decorative ephemera (Agoo, Madulid, and Callado 530). I am interested in how the idea of *C. wadei* enamored early twentieth-century colonial scientists—the idea of its being a new species, uprooted from its local context and worthy of a unique description and a different name. Surely a rich history of *pitogo* existed in the Philippines prior to the start of the U.S. colonial period in 1898, and the present study does not discount the history of the species prior to 1902. Rather, it emphasizes the temporally positioned, measured, and conscientiously recorded character of colonial scientists' engagement with flora they purportedly discovered in the colony. This chapter, therefore, stresses time, empire, and the intellectual context behind a plant species, especially as humanists criticize the atemporal, universalizing logics of taxonomic botany (Ryan).

Tracking the Culion Cycad

Elmer D. Merrill first arrived to the Philippines in 1902, only months before the end of the Philippine-American War (1899–1902), which ushered in U.S. occupation of the archipelago. From 1906 until his departure in 1923, he practiced as a botanist for the Bureau of Science, first named the Bureau of Government Laboratories (founded in 1901), in the colonial capital of Manila. While at the bureau, he published extensively on Philippine plants and directed the institution during his final four years in the colony. During one of his earliest surveys on the islands in 1902, he and other U.S. scientists visited the province of Paragua, later renamed Palawan, to identify a location for a leper colony. On the northeastern provincial island of Culion, which had been selected as the site, Merrill collected samples of the cycad.

Colonial health officials identified leprosy as a pressing public health concern upon U.S. arrival to the Philippines and sought a location spacious enough for agriculture, hospitals, residences, and recreational facilities that could also prevent escape. Conversion of Culion into a leper colony began in 1902, and in 1904 the island was declared a formal reservation. Three years later, the Philippine Commission formalized forced apprehension and detention of all those suspected or diagnosed with leprosy (Escalante 95). Leaving the colony after treatment was unlikely, and permanent isolation was a marked feature of institution (Dado). The "colony within a colony" became one of many experimental efforts of the U.S. colonial administration in the Philippines that gained international attention. The cycad's discovery points to the multipronged deployment of scientific personnel to establish a firmer intellectual and sanitary hold over the archipelago. Botanical concerns ran aside medical ones, and colonial officials carried out extra-disciplinary work while establishing their own disciplinary-specific outfits in the colony.

After Merrill's spotting of the cycad, the plant appeared intermittently in botany publications as a passing reference (Merrill, *Dictionary of the Plant Names* 97), lacking a definitive identification that aligned with the unusual features presented by the Culion species. A more determined study of the plant did not reemerge until 1923, when requests to find more sample material from the island surfaced. Plant physiologist William Henry Brown, appointed director of the Bureau of Science upon Merrill's departure from the Philippines, requested that researchers stationed on the island find more samples of the cycad. Herbert W. Wade, who first arrived to the Philippines in 1916 as a bacteriologist and pathologist, was tasked with tracking the cycad following his restationing to Culion in 1922. In 1924, he relayed the pleasurable news that he had photographed and collected proper cycad specimens for Brown, suggesting he found the original cycad that Merrill observed in 1902 (Wade to Brown, 18 September 1924).

While Brown had received these new cycad samples at the bureau, Merrill had separately commissioned Albert W. C. T. Herre, an ichthyologist and lichenologist who had been appointed chief of fisheries at the bureau in 1920, to collect cycad material on his behalf. He received and reviewed Herre's samples in New York, where he had taken a directorship at the New York Botanical Garden (NYBG) in 1930, and pronounced his own enthusiasm regarding what he determined to be a new species. In August 1931, Merrill wrote Brown about the "undoubtedly undescribed species," which he dubbed *C. herrei* (Merrill to Brown, 10 August 1931).

Nomenclatural Patronage

The benefit of the modern moment assures us the species was, in fact, named *C. wadei*. The difference, however, merits pause. Historians have studied Latin naming conventions at length and how these conventions have signaled acts of status making and status giving. Aside from names drawn from morphological features of species, Latin plant names have tended to honor scientists, locations of species collection, collectors, and patrons. The history behind nomenclatural conventions likewise reminds us that names are embedded in the veneration of scholarly endeavor within a broader arena of imperial relations and international politics—an arena not immediately visible through a Latin name's longevity.[2]

Brown responded hastily to Merrill's letter with a two-page justification for naming the new species after Wade, who, Brown emphasized, "might feel I have been negligent and let someone else to describe it under another name" (Brown to Merrill, 26 September 1931). He also revealed that he would have already published a description of the interesting species but could not collect proper developmental material from the cycad specimens growing on bureau grounds. Conceding that he would send his collected material, photographs, and manuscript descriptions to Merrill, Brown closed the letter, "As far as I am concerned, it is immaterial whether you or I or we together describe the species. . . . Of course, I cannot object if you publish as the species was your find."

Then as now, publishing on a new species is a career-making accomplishment. Brown and Merrill's correspondence demonstrates an academic propriety common among early twentieth-century botanists. This polite ethos could obfuscate the actual professional competitions in the colonial Philippines. The archipelago presented a tremendous frontier for botanists seeking to systematize its plant life and to make a name for themselves, particularly as botany became an international field dominated by imperial interests at the turn of the century (Gutierrez, *Region of Imperial Strategy* 164). In his earliest years in the Philippines, Merrill remarked on the scientifically "neglected" landscape of the colony, which provided the "stimulus" to study the flora of the islands (*Botanical Work* 5). Over the course of the U.S. colonial period, colonial scientists, botanical enthusiasts, and independent collectors participated in a feverish search for undescribed species. Based on their exchange, Brown evidently had begun collecting material on the same cycad under

Merrill's study. The correspondence reveals that Brown would have pub-lished first had his specimens properly pollinated—notice he may not have given Merrill had Merrill not reached him first about *C. herrei*. Such an act was not without understood gain in ostensibly unchartered colonial terrain.

Local Desperation amid Global Crisis

Amid the competition, much of the success of Merrill's publication on the new cycad was due to his professional relationships with Filipino botanists and U.S. scientists stationed in the Philippines. Chief among them was Edu-ardo Quisumbing. Their friendship began in the early 1900s and continued throughout the remainder of Merrill's life.[3] Quisumbing trained at the Col-lege of Agriculture in the province of Laguna before completing a doctorate at the University of Chicago in 1923. After working briefly with Merrill at the University of California, Berkeley, he returned to the Philippines to conduct research on behalf of the bureau—and for many of its divisions following major institutional splits—through 1961. For decades, the two maintained regular correspondence, which has provided insight into pivotal historical moments in the Philippines such as World War II, the Battle of Manila, and the reconstruction of Manila in the 1940s and 1950s (Gutierrez, "Rehabili-tating Botany"). This insight is no less informative in their 1930s exchanges when Merrill looked to Quisumbing to send the needed cycad material when parcels from Brown were either delayed or incomplete (Merrill to Quisumb-ing, 1 June 1932).

The Great Depression surfaces most acutely in the letters between Mer-rill and Quisumbing and some of Merrill's other Philippines correspon-dence during his tenure at the NYBG in the early 1930s. At the outset of the Depression, the institution was financially bereft without adequate, updated equipment (Robbins 287). The decade-long worldwide economic downturn impacted scientific labor, especially that which relied on public moneys, and led to reduced salaries for government employees in the colonial Philippines (Merrill to Quisumbing, 1 June 1932). Global reverberations manifested in the scientific climate of the archipelago, motivating local researchers to seek support and employment in the U.S. metropole.

Besides Quisumbing, other civil service employees communicated to Merrill feelings of institutional unrest and financial precarity. Because of the downturn in Manila and elsewhere in the colony, several men appealed to

Merrill to work with him in New York, where they envisioned more research opportunities and fewer political squabbles. Ceferino D. Montejo, a research associate on the island of Leyte, asked about the quality of life for Filipinos in New York: "Is the racial feeling so keen as in the Pacific coast way down in San Francisco or Los Angeles, or Watsonville, where the riots were staged?" Curious if he could "get along all right" in New York with only enough fare to take him "across the Atlantic," Montejo inquired if Merrill could help him "get along with some thing to make a living to make body and soul meet together" (Montejo to Merrill, 20 October 1931). Leodegario E. Hachero, a botanical collector from Surigao, similarly reached out to Merrill for guidance. Hoping to continue his work in plant collection and preservation, Hachero offered to assist any of Merrill's flora work from the island of Mindanao (Hachero to Merrill, 1 January 1934).

Working on behalf of the Bureau of Science—either as contract labor or as a regular employee—had offered social and economic opportunity to locals in the Philippines. In exchange, colonial scientists like Merrill benefited from specimens and access to territory that would have been otherwise more difficult without field assistants, translators, and guides. The Philippine environment staggered U.S. scientists, and its contagions, tropical heat, and stewards presented roadblocks to intensive botanical study. As such, the safety and survival of U.S. colonial scientists necessitated collaboration with local personnel (Gutierrez, *Region of Imperial Strategy* 122). Yet, mutually beneficial collaboration had its limits: the Great Depression made clear the point at which U.S. colonial patrons could not offer financial support or employment to local scientific labor, no matter the extent to which such labors enhanced their own intellectual repute.

Merrill responded to both Montejo and Hachero with a bleak depiction of the economic and research environment in the United States and could not promise any Philippines-based collector or civil service employee gainful employment. He had been well aware, too, of the fraction of salary paid to Philippine-based personnel versus their equivalents in U.S. metropolitan institutions (Merrill to Clemens, 31 July 1927). To Montejo, he advised against traveling to New York under any circumstance unless he had the financial means to support himself, citing the NYBG's "retrenchment rather than expansion." Though during his two years in New York he "observed no anti-Filipino feeling," Merrill could not recommend their relocation (Merrill to Montejo, 30 November 1931).

"Anti-American Feeling" at the Emergence of the Commonwealth

During these years, institutional reorganization was underway at the Bureau of Science, suggesting why progress on the cycad's study had been delayed. The reorganization coincided with the approach of the Philippine Commonwealth, which began with the passage of the Tydings-McDuffie Act in 1934 and the declaration of Philippine independence through the Hare-Hawes-Cutting Act a year prior. The colony-wide impact of the Great Depression amplified Filipino and U.S. officials' anxieties about what independence could portend. "Filipinization," the policy of populating the government bureaucracy with local Filipino personnel instead of U.S. foreign counterparts advanced under U.S. governor-general Francis Burton Harrison (1914–20), furthered this uncertainty (Abinales 613), particularly since the last government unit to Filipinize was the Bureau of Science (W. Anderson 304).

The cycad letters reveal glimpses of how scientists reacted to the political changes afoot in the Philippines and of the surfacing racial antagonism between Filipino and U.S. researchers. The earliest U.S. scientists in the Philippines found Filipinization ill-timed and feared the erosion of scientific progress made in the colony (W. Anderson 304). Their protests, however, failed to halt the policy, and by the 1930s and the start of the Commonwealth, U.S. personnel held only the senior-most research positions while Filipinos populated the wide majority of scientific ranks (W. Anderson 305). On the state of Philippine political and institutional affairs at the time, Quisumbing dreaded the "drastic rearrangements" foreshadowed by the Hare-Hawes-Cutting Act and the bureau's possible reorganization (Quisumbing to Merrill, 23 January 1933). To Merrill, he denounced a government plan to transfer the bureau's herbarium well outside of Manila to the College of Agriculture in the province of Laguna. U.S. agriculturist Edwin Copeland, according to Quisumbing, had been at the forefront of the proposed transfer and had allegedly threatened authorities if the herbarium were not moved (Quisumbing to Merrill, 23 January 1933).

Quisumbing remitted to Merrill a confidential copy of a scathing seventeen-page memorandum intended to indict Copeland and to initiate his ouster from the government. He claimed Copeland had sought to fuse the College of Agriculture, the Bureau of Agriculture, and the Bureau of Science under his own leadership, which Quisumbing remarked was a "matter of record" throughout the decades of Copeland's station in the Philippines.

Citing "mental derangement" among other insults, Quisumbing lambasted the U.S. scientist for his public critiques of the bureau and snubbed his personal ambitions as those "fermenting, fermenting, but making very poor excuse for 'good beer.'" Copeland's institutional vision, he warned, was for the "aggrandizement of one man" and not for the sustained contributions to the wider scientific community the herbarium offered through its location at the Bureau of Science in Manila (Quisumbing to Vargas, 1934).

These squabbles peaked in 1934 with Brown's forced departure. While an obituary of Brown cites his early retirement from the bureau ("William Henry Brown" 532), a letter from Clarence J. Humphrey, a bureau U.S. mycologist, suggests otherwise and explains in part why the cycad material was slow to reach Merrill. According to Humphrey, the bureau's problems culminated in Brown's "forced resignation," and "the independence agitation . . . increased the Anti-American feeling, and a feeling of self-sufficiency on the part of the natives, which is strongly antagonistic to any Americans in government employ" (Humphrey to Merrill, 24 January 1934). He shared that he and other U.S. scientists speculated that Brown worked with Secretary Jorge B. Vargas to create "an Anti-American frame-up" and may have colluded with his "henchman" Copeland to stoke animosity among the U.S. and Filipino ranks. One of the gravest accusations running through the bureau halls, he confided, was that scientists were maintaining private collections even though all government employees were required to centralize collections with the bureau (Humphrey to Merrill, 24 January 1934).

Humphrey's disclosure sheds light on Quisumbing's allegations against Copeland, whom Quisumbing feared had been arranging to hoard scientific might and material away from the bureau. One might glean that Quisumbing was one of several native employees of the institution seeking to expose the ambitions of high-ranking U.S. colonial personnel who clashed with the bureau's purported ideals. He emphasized that Copeland had "made enemies" in the Philippines because of his "overbearing sense of superiority and omniscience." With the staunch opposition mounted against Copeland, Quisumbing insisted, "Dr. Copeland finally sees a ghost of which he is very fearful and this ghost is bothering his conscience and his soul. . . . Let [his ambitions] be shattered for the sake of peace and the success of science in the Philippines" (Quisumbing to Vargas, 1934). That Quisumbing had shared these complaints with Secretary Vargas, a suspected conspirator in the "anti-American" plot at the bureau, points to the political webs that encased the beginning of the Commonwealth. Such webs could, for instance, ennoble some U.S. personnel over others under the assumption that native cries for "self-sufficiency," in Humphrey's terms, could be instrumentalized to execute conspirators' whims. While the correspondence does not fully confirm the degree and extent of the anti-American orchestration, the possibility of independence left the few remaining U.S. researchers "watching their steps pretty carefully so as not to offend in any way the politics in power" (Humphrey to Merrill, 24 January 1934). The days of foreign colonial dominance at the bureau had been numbered.

Wrestling against strict U.S. administrative power of the Philippines had not only emerged during the Commonwealth deliberations. Factions of turn-of-the-century revolutionaries and politicians worked to negotiate or out-right dislodge the terms of U.S. governance in the Philippines. Humphrey's letter suggests that the revealed puppetry of U.S. scientists like Brown and Copeland may have intensified decolonial sentiment. Concealed in the white space behind a preserved cycad specimen, then, is the historical climate of discontent against the U.S. scientists deployed to the Philippines, alleged collaborators against one another or against the interest of local intellectuals like Quisumbing.

Soon after receiving Humphrey's letter and a similar one from Herre detailing the divisive events at the bureau, Merrill wrote to bureau researcher Richard C. McGregor, questioning the fate of the *Philippine Journal of Science* (founded in 1906), the longest-running science periodical established under the U.S. colonial administration. He stated he was not asking for "inside information" on Brown's sudden departure and instead wanted to determine where he would publish his complete manuscript on the cycad should the journal dissolve (Merrill to McGregor, 19 February 1934). Though a lacuna appears in his Philippines correspondence between his last letter to McGregor and his final letter written as director at the NYBG, Merrill sent his final manuscript and the original type specimens back to Manila in 1935 for review. The description of the cycad with its definitive and finalized Latin name appeared in an issue of the sixtieth volume of the *Philippine Journal of Science* a year later.

Reflections: Imperial Afterlives and Enduring White Space

I position this record of species collection, professional competition, racial animosity, decolonial efforts, and publication against the decontextualiz-

Fig. 2.2. Original image of herbarium sheet with *C. wadei* cones, ovules, and seeds.
These structures were photographed and published in the 1936 *Philippine Journal
of Science*. Series 1, Series 3 (Oversized), Elmer D. Merrill Papers. Archives of the
New York Botanical Garden, The Bronx, New York. 28 October 2019. Reproduction
permission courtesy of the Archives of the New York Botanical Garden.

ing quality of white space. Viewing dried *C. wadei* structures mounted on a white herbarium sheet erodes the history behind *C. wadei* in the first third of the twentieth century. Like the pictorial work of European naturalists, the mounting sheet in its whiteness starkly contrasts the specimen mounted upon it, removing a fuller sense of the past behind many specimens' discoveries and naming. To add to Bleichmar's analysis, white space is devoid not only of ecology and contextual history but also of the imperial afterlives that continue to underwrite a plant's study.

The existence of white space is contingent upon the excision of a plant from its original environment. This excision only becomes legible once marked by place and time, a common practice for most herbaria, which requires careful cataloging of collection dates and locations such that proper annotation of material is current yet privy to previous botanical collecting work. This annotative practice makes a species more accessible for studying, claiming, and (re)naming. As Quisumbing opined of the herbarium, "It is not merely a mass of dried, named plants. It is an aggregation of material made vitally alive by the reason of the commentaries, notes and annotations of the men who described the plants. These notes often in their own hand writing or that of equally able successors in the field of research and criticism" (Quisumbing to Vargas, 1934). His humanistic account of the herbarium stresses the labors memorialized by hand for generations of scholars. The vitality of such material depends on the historical sensitivity to the annotative acts of current taxonomists. While critical to and emblematic of a "science of the archive"—or a scientific discipline wherein its practitioners must be attuned to the past (Daston 160)—it is still a limited sense of the past. Theoretical bases for classification, Latin designation, previous nomenclatural assertions and descriptive mistakes, and a specimen's record of collection determine the boundaries of what past is worthy of communication.

Regrettably, Quisumbing spent the remainder of his career at the Bureau of Science rehabilitating the herbarium's collections (Gutierrez, "Rehabilitating Botany" 40–45). In 1934, Quisumbing had emphasized that the herbarium was "one of the greatest of the world and is known the world over. It could never under any circumstance be replaced if destroyed for the simple reason that the types of new species and the specimens of *unica* which it contains are not susceptible of duplication as any scientific man knows" (Quisumbing to Vargas, 1934). Yet, nearly a decade after publication on the Culion cycad, U.S. artillery razed the Bureau of Science during the Battle of Manila. Over 1.5 million volumes from national, scientific, university, and municipal libraries were estimated to have been lost.[4] The cycad's type specimen was also likely destroyed during combat. In a 1993 letter to the Royal Botanic Garden Sydney (RBGS), Domingo A. Madulid, former botany curator of the National Museum of the Philippines, wrote of the *C. wadei* type specimen: "We regret to inform you that we do not have these specimens in our collection. The type specimens of these specimens were probably included in the destruction of the [Philippine National Herbarium] during the Second World War" (Madulid to Briggs, 9 September 1993). His letter and colored photographs of the cycad take the place of a typical herbarium specimen sheet at the National Herbarium of New South Wales located in the RBGS.

The destruction of the Battle of Manila took with it many of the type specimens that were career making for dozens of U.S. colonial scientists. In the first half of the twentieth century, U.S. botanists were the staunchest advocates for the type concept in international botany. The establishment of a type ensured that a single specimen's morphology would be selected as the source of its published description, which could anchor other specimens in the same taxon. Merrill was one of the major proponents of the type principle and, under his leadership, co-instituted the type concept among his colleagues at the International Botanical Congress in 1930 (Gutierrez, *Region of Imperial Strategy* 143). Lamentably, U.S. military fire destroyed thousands of the specimens and numerous types that he worked to accrue while based in the Philippines. Indeed, even with what could be augured of Philippine independence during the Commonwealth, continued global imperial violence expunged the botanical work of Philippine and foreign personnel, thereby stressing the enduring nature of white space.

No matter how formalized the Culion cycad is in international botany, threat of its disappearance looms. *C. wadei* is currently a critically endangered species. With a steadily decreasing population, it only numbers five thousand mature specimens (Hill). Any destructive development or ecological disaster to its locality on Culion could mean the loss of the entire species, and fires set seasonally for cattle grazing and human settlement threaten the species (Madulid and Agoo 102). Other cycads, like *C. lacrimans* and *C. mindanensis*, grow in locations with rich nickel deposits and are threatened by aggressive domestic and internationally financed extractive activities (Agoo, Madulid, and Callado 536).

The province of Palawan is no stranger to this kind of environmental distress. Long-standing resource extraction, increased tourism, and corresponding environmental activism have marked its political ecology. Heightened mining activity in the province has sparked heated debates among business-oriented stakeholders, local politicians, and activists. The high-profile murder of journalist and wildlife veterinarian Gerry Ortega in Puerto Princesa in 2011 is but one startling indication of the province's ongoing environmental unrest. Studies that track the discovery, collection, and description of Philippine plants have the opportunity to highlight not only the vast endemic flora of the archipelago but also what the continued existence—or threatened nonexistence—of these species can mean. Working against the endurance of white space demands a recovery of the contexts in which species were discovered, collected, and described. These underline the workings of colonial intellectual pursuits and the afterlives of imperial war and extraction that leave debris in their midst. The very threats to the Philippine cycad species occur on multiple scales of human interaction, reminding us that the sustained intellectual interest in a species is beholden to its survival or looming disappearance.

Notes

Acknowledgments: A different version of this chapter appeared as "What's in a Latin Name? *Cycas wadei* and the Politics of Nomenclature" in the *Philippine Journal of Systematic Biology* in 2018. I thank the editorial team of the present volume and of the *Philippine Journal of Systematic Biology* for allowing me to publish this story of the *pitogo*. The Social Science Research Council's International Dissertation Research Fellowship, with funds provided by the Andrew W. Mellon Foundation, and the Fulbright–Hays Doctoral Dissertation Research Abroad program enabled the research and writing of this chapter. I dedicate this piece to Drs. Esperanza M. Agoo and Domingo A. Madulid, specialists of the Philippine Cycadaceae.

1. For exemplary single-species and genus studies, see Folch, "Stimulating Consumption"; Barnard, "The *Rafflesia*"; Carney, "African Rice" and *Black Rice*; De Jesus, *The Tobacco Monopoly*; Osseo–Asare, *Bitter Roots*; Appleby, "Ginseng and the Royal Society"; and Parsons, "The Natural History of Colonial Science."

2. For an account of nomenclatural standardizations in the North Atlantic in the latter half of the nineteenth century and in the first half of the twentieth century, see Mickulas, *Britton's Botanical Empire.*

3. Quisumbing and Merrill's notable professional relationship has been recorded by Quisumbing biographers. See Asis, "Quisumbing and Friend"; Barroga-Jamias, "Eduardo A. Quisumbing: Botanist Par Excellence and Father of Philippine Orchidology (1895–1986)"; and Price and Price, "Eduardo A. Quisumbing, Portrait of the Botanist as a Filipino."

4. According to estimates, three million volumes from public school libraries and two million from private institutions were also destroyed during World War II. See transcript of "Press Interview–Professor Gabriel A. Bernardo," 18 January 1946, Miscellanea, Box 7, Folder 1—Concerning work in the Philippine Islands, Harley Harris Bartlett Papers 1909–1960, Bentley Historical Library, University of Michigan, Ann Arbor.

Works Cited

Abinales, Patricio N. "American Rule and the Formation of Filipino 'Colonial Nationalism.'" *Southeast Asian Studies*, vol. 39, no. 4, 2002, 604–21.

Agoo, Esperanza M. G., Domingo A. Madulid, and John Rey Callado. "Novel Species of *Cycas* (Cycadaceae) from Mindanao Island, Philippines." *Cycad Biology and Conservation: The 9th International Conference on Cycad Biology*. New York Botanical Garden, 2018, 529–39.

Anderson, Elijah. "'The White Space.'" *Sociology of Race and Ethnicity*, vol. 1, no. 1, 2015, 10–21.

Anderson, Warwick. "Science in the Philippines." *Philippine Studies: Historical and Ethnographic Viewpoints*, vol. 55, no. 3, 2007, 287–318.

Appleby, John H. "Ginseng and the Royal Society." *Notes and Records of the Royal Society of London*, vol. 37, no. 2, 1983, 121–45.

Asis, C. V. "Quisumbing and Friend." *Natural and Applied Science Bulletin*, vol. 27, nos. 1–2, 1973, 1–73.

Barnard, Timothy P. "The *Rafflesia* in the Natural and Imperial Imagination of the East India Company in Southeast Asia." *The East India Company and the Natural World*, edited by V. Damodaran, A. Winterbottom, and A. Lester. Palgrave Macmillan, 2015, 147–66.

Barroga-Jamias, Serlie F. "Eduardo A. Quisumbing: Botanist Par Excellence and Father of Philippine Orchidology (1895–1986)." *National Scientists of the Philippines (1978–1998)*. Anvil Publishing, 2000, 164–74.

Bleichmar, Daniela. *Visible Empire: Botanical Expeditions and Visual Culture in the Hispanic Enlightenment*. U of Chicago P, 2012.

Brown, William Henry. Letter to Elmer D. Merrill. 26 September 1931. Series 2, Box 3, Folder 14. Elmer D. Merrill Personal Papers. Archives of the New York Botanical Garden, The Bronx, New York.

Carney, Judith. "African Rice in the Columbian Exchange." *Journal of African History*, vol. 42, no. 3, 2001, 377–96.

Carney, Judith. *Black Rice: The African Origins of Rice Cultivation in the Americas*. Cambridge, 2002.

Dado, Veronica A. "Spaces and Boundaries in Culion: Mobility amidst Segregation." *Hidden Lives, Concealed Narratives*, edited by Maria Serena Diokno. National Historical Commission, 2016, 113–39.

Daston, Lorraine. "The Sciences of the Archive." *Osiris*, vol. 27, no. 1, 2012, 156–87.

De Jesus, Edilberto C. *The Tobacco Monopoly in the Philippines: Bureaucratic Enterprise and Social Change*. Ateneo de Manila UP, 1998.

Escalante, Rene R. "American Public Health Policy on Leprosy, 1898–1941." *Hidden Lives, Concealed Narratives: A History of Leprosy in the Philippines*, edited by Maria Serena Diokno. National Historical Commission, 2016, 87–110.

Folch, Christina. "Stimulating Consumption: Yerba Mate Myths, Markets, and Meanings from Conquest to Present." *Comparative Studies in Society and History* vol. 52, no. 1, 2010, 6–36.

Gutierrez, Kathleen Cruz. "The Region of Imperial Strategy: Regino García, Sebastián Vidal, Mary Clemens, and the Consolidation of International Botany in the Philippines, 1858–1936." PhD diss., University of California, Berkeley, 2020.

Gutierrez, Kathleen Cruz. "Rehabilitating Botany in the Postwar Moment: National Promise and Encyclopedism of Eduardo Quisumbing's *Medicinal Plants of the Philippines* (1951)." *Asian Review of World Histories*, vol. 6, 2018, 33–67.

Hachero, Leodegario E. Letter to Elmer D. Merrill. 1 January 1934. Series 2, Box 3, Folder 14. Elmer D. Merrill Personal Papers. Archives of the New York Botanical Garden, The Bronx, New York.

Hill, Ken D. "*Cycas wadei.*" IUCN Red List of Threatened Species, 2010, http://dx.doi.org/10.2305/IUCN.UK.2010-3.RLTS.T42097A10631294.en. Accessed 25 April 2018.

Humphrey, C. J. Letter to Elmer D. Merrill. 24 January 1934. Series 2, Box 3, Folder 14. Elmer D. Merrill Personal Papers. Archives of the New York Botanical Garden, The Bronx, New York.

Madulid, Domingo A., and Esperanza M. G. Agoo. "Taxonomy and Conservation of Philippine Cycads." *Blumea*, vol. 54, 2009, 99–102.

Madulid, Domingo A. Letter to Barbara D. Briggs. 9 September 1993. Digital file. Esperanza Maribel Guiao Agoo Collection. Herbarium of De La Salle University–Manila, Manila.

Mascarenhas, Michael. "White Space and Dark Matter: Prying Open the Black Box of STS." *Science, Technology, & Human Values*, vol. 43, no. 2, 2018, 151–70.

Merrill, Elmer D. *Botanical Work in the Philippines*. Bureau of Public Printing, 1903.

Merrill, Elmer D. *A Dictionary of the Plant Names of the Philippine Islands*. Bureau of Printing, 1903.

Merrill, Elmer D. *Enumeration of Philippine Flowering Plants*, Volume I. Bureau of Printing, 1922.

Merrill, Elmer D. Letter to William H. Brown. 10 August 1931. Series 2, Box 3, Folder 14. Elmer D. Merrill Personal Papers. Archives of the New York Botanical Garden, The Bronx, New York.

Merrill, Elmer D. Letter to Mary S. Clemens. 31 July 1927. Clemens–E.D. Merrill 1925–1929, Box 5. University Herbarium, Bentley Historical Library.

Merrill, Elmer D. Letter to Richard C. McGregor. 19 February 1934. Series 2, Box 3, Folder 14. Elmer D. Merrill Personal Papers. Archives of the New York Botanical Garden, The Bronx, New York.

Merrill, Elmer D. Letter to Ceferino D. Montejo. 30 November 1931. Series 2, Box 3, Folder 14. Elmer D. Merrill Personal Papers. Archives of the New York Botanical Garden, The Bronx, New York.

Merrill, Elmer D. Letter to Eduardo Quisumbing. 1 June 1932. Series 2, Box 3, Folder 15. Elmer D. Merrill Personal Papers. Archives of the New York Botanical Garden, The Bronx, New York.

Merrill, Elmer D. "A New Philippine Species of Cycas." *Philippine Journal of Science*, vol. 60, no. 3, 233–39.

Merrill, Elmer D. "William Henry Brown." *Science*, vol. 90, no. 2345, 531–32.

Mickulas, Patrick. *Britton's Botanical Empire: The New York Botanical Garden and American Botany, 1888–1929*. New York Botanical Garden, 2007.

Montejo, Ceferino D. Letter to Elmer D. Merrill. 20 October 1931. Series 2, Box 3, Folder 14. Elmer D. Merrill Personal Papers. Archives of the New York Botanical Garden, The Bronx, New York.

Osseo–Asare, Abena D. *Bitter Roots: The Search for Healing Plants in Africa.* U of Chicago P, 2014.

Parsons, Christopher M. "The Natural History of Colonial Science: Joseph-François Lafitau's Discovery of Ginseng and Its Afterlives." *William and Mary Quarterly*, vol. 73, no. 1, 2016, 37–72.

"Press Interview–Professor Gabriel A. Bernardo." 18 January 1946. Miscellanea, Box 7, Folder 1—Concerning work in the Philippine Islands. Harley Harris Bartlett Papers 1909–1960. Bentley Historical Library, University of Michigan, Ann Arbor.

Price, Grace A., and Mike G. Price. "Eduardo A. Quisumbing, Portrait of the Botanist as a Filipino." *Kalikasan: Philippine Journal of Biology*, vol. 5, 2–18.

Quisumbing, Eduardo. Letter to Elmer D. Merrill. 23 January 1933. Series 2, Box 3, Folder 15. Elmer D. Merrill Personal Papers. Archives of the New York Botanical Garden, The Bronx, New York.

Quisumbing, Eduardo. Memorandum to Jorge B. Vargas. 1934. Series 2, Box 3, Folder 15. Elmer D. Merrill Personal Papers. Archives of the New York Botanical Garden, The Bronx, New York.

Robbins, William J. "Elmer Drew Merrill, 1876–1956." *National Academy of Sciences Biographical Memoirs.* National Academy of Sciences, 1958, 273–333.

Ryan, John C. "Cultural Botany: Toward a Model of Transdisciplinary, Embodied, and Poetic Research into Plants." *Nature and Culture*, vol. 6, no. 2, 2011, 128–30.

Wade, Herbert W. Letter to W. H. Brown. 18 September 1924. Series 3 (Oversized). Elmer D. Merrill Personal Papers. Archives of the New York Botanical Garden, The Bronx, New York.

3

Rust and Recovery

A Study of South Indian Goddess Films

Chitra Sankaran

The goddess genre of films is popular in India. The goddess, as she is represented in the Hindu imaginary, is made most accessible through the goddess films and, more recently, its offshoot, the goddess serial drama. The goddess film genre has stood the test of time. Many of the themes and plots of the goddess films, an identifiable subgenre under mythological films, are a hotchpotch of legends and stories sourced from Hindu texts that range over two or more millennia, that is, from the Vedic, Upanishadic, and Puranic texts and the epics, both classical (in Sanskrit) and regional (in regional languages). Separated by vast stretches of time, these texts understandably reflect vastly differing worldviews. I examine goddess films in order to excavate the unexpected parallels that emerge with Ann Laura Stoler's idea of imperial debris. I approach this by drawing on the similarities between the goddess as projected on the silver screen and the idea of rust as discussed by Jonathan Waldman. I also refer to Julia Kristeva's idea of the "abject" and discuss how both rust and the goddess in the films engage with the idea of the abject in ways that invoke Stoler's idea of colonial "ruination."

Since its inception in the 1950s, the goddess film has taken many avatars. It began as mythological, faithfully reproducing stories from the epics and Hindu *Puranas*. In the 1960s, it morphed into domestic drama, using the genre to comment and revile marital abuse of young brides, with the goddess taking the side of the subdominant domestic female, reinstating *stree-shakti* (female energy), and punishing the arrogant male and nonbelievers. In the 1970s, it co-opted features of the superhero genre, where Good and Evil clashed on the big screen and the goddess morphed into a superhero. Increasingly in the 1990s, technological advancements enabled this genre of films to foreground fantastic spectacles on the big screen. In the twenty-first century, when attention has turned to the place of the human in the ecological chain, the goddess films have once again adapted to become topical and relevant to these times. Hence, the goddess film genre is complex and evolving, constantly reinventing itself in order to stay current.

I examine two blockbuster goddess films, *Amman* (1995) and *Devi* (1999), and other films both older and more recent to study how the reinvention of certain traditional themes that connect the Hindu goddess with manifest nature has the potential to transform several entrenched ecological perceptions. I argue that the goddess films visually and graphically reinvent the goddess as a superhero and also paradoxically as a liminal figure who can exist on the borders of abjection, like rust. I also assert that these kinds of non-Western perspectives that combine representations from two ends of the mainstream spectrum (superhero and the abject), emerging from within specific, national, and cultural contexts (South India), can open up alter-visions for ecofeminism.

Spiritual feminism, alternately referred to as "spiritual ecofeminism" or "myth feminism," seeks to empower women spiritually. The goddess is often centered in this seeking. In *The Dictionary of Feminist Theory*, Maggie Humm describes this branch of feminism as emphasizing "the spiritual dimension as being as, or more, important than material rights to women's happiness" (274). Within spiritual ecofeminism, there has long been a move to turn toward the "wisdom of women," as Thomas Berry phrases it in *The Great Work: Our Way into the Future*. Others such as Susan Griffin in *Woman and Nature: The Roaring Inside Her* and Charlene Spretnak in "Ecofeminism: Our Roots and Flowering" emphasize the importance of a new spiritual vision, where matricentric perspectives replace patricentric ones. They believe that this will, among other things, open up a world of enchantment, magic, and imagination. Berry believes this is crucial since this shift will enable a more earth-centered perspective to emerge.

Aspects of Hinduism, the oldest living religion in the world, long ago initiated these ideas of the spiritual ecofeminists. Hinduism has three main schools of worship, *Shaivism*, *Vaishnavism*, and *Shaktism*. This third, often referred to as the *Shakta* school, is dedicated to the worship of the goddess as the supreme being. It envisages the goddess as, among other things, Mother Earth (*bhoodevi*) and the source of all cosmic energy, *shakti*. She is also manifest nature. Indeed, for Hindus in general and especially *Shaktas*, the goddess is a complex figure who incorporates within her traits that are generally polarized as masculine and feminine in mortal discourse. She is life giver and destroyer, primal matter or *prakriti*, and transcendent spirit or *Brahman*. In Sanskrit, *prakriti* literally means the natural condition or state of anything that is found in creation. *Pra* means "in the beginning," and *kriti* means "creation" or "composition." Hence, in Hindu thought, the natural world is not *prakriti* per se, that is, "the natural condition at the beginning," but a *manifestation* of it. The world emerges from *prakriti* as a projection, a modification, a transformation. All these conflicting and contradictory traits of the goddess—as both spirit and matter—are utilized in the goddess film genre.

Berry believes that the "macrocontext" for personal and communal self-understanding is developed by communities through religions with their creation stories and myths. Peter Berger also asserts that such beliefs with their myriad manifestations in society could be labeled its "nomos," from which meaning is derived and actively maintained. He regards religion as the "most powerful and comprehensive nomos, serving to place humans in a divinely inspired Universe and translate some notion of the sacredness of the natural world" (cited in Godfrey 97). The goddess films, as a far more accessible medium, unlike the Vedic texts, combine both Vedic and folk narratives about the goddess. Therefore, one could argue that the goddess film genre provides the "macrocontext" for a large proportion of the Hindu populace, reinforcing ancient Vedic as well as popular myths about the goddess.

The goddess films that came out in the 1960s, 1970s, and 1980s represent the goddess based on Hindu creation myths from the *Shakta* school. Here the goddess is both transcendent and immanent. Marilyn Strathern's observations in her book *After Nature* is relevant to our examination of the goddess film genre, where she discusses the theory of "social constructionism," the idea that human development is socially situated and knowledge is constructed through interaction with others (McKinley). The goddess films then become illustrative of this since knowledge of the goddess gets enriched, expanded, and augmented in the populace through the conversations about tradition and progress of (wo)man's place in nature and ecosystems, provoked by the goddess film genre. While examining this concept, Strathern remarks that "implicit in the theory/model is the assumption that change is a mark of activity or endeavor whereas continuity somehow is not" (2). She inverts this to explore how change and continuity are interdependent. This view is very pertinent to examining the goddess film genre, where the understanding of the Hindu goddess as cosmic energy and as *prakriti* or manifest nature is the "constant" against which is situated the "performance" of the goddess as the protagonist in the protean genre of the goddess films with its differing plot structures.

The goddess, though traditionally associated with *prakriti*—generally parsed as Nature or manifest reality—is also *maya*, or illusion, since within Hinduism, manifest reality is also considered as illusory, a projection of the transcendent *Brahman* or Cosmic Consciousness. In a way, therefore, the goddess on the silver screen as a "projection" is neatly illustrative of a more abstruse idea, and the irony of this speaks to the initiated Hindu audiences. More complexly, we also see how, even in her Vedic conception, the goddess traverses conventional boundaries. The Hindu goddess as an aspect of the transcendent *Brahman* but simultaneously yoked to *prakriti* emerges as a composite, contradictory figure. An attempt to describe this complexity invokes the yoking of opposites—such as evolution and extinction, death and rebirth, and, indeed, continuity and change. These would be in keeping with the Hindu cosmogony with its cyclical concept of time. This film genre itself, therefore, becomes a symbol of modernity engaging with tradition and deflecting it in interesting ways.

Also, the provocative word "after" in the phrase "after nature" that Strathern uses acquires diverse significations when approached in the light of the imaging of the goddess in these films. "After" could mean "post-nature" as in a world where there is no "nature" left; it could also rehearse a certain idea of temporality, where the hope of an *evolving* or adaptable nature has lapsed; alternately, it could signal an attempt to recapture an atavistic vision of nature in the hope that it will help us reorder our current relationship with it. This resonates with what Jonathan Waldman claims in *Rust: The Longest War*— that rust is not only the underside of cosmopolis but an agent of time. Rust sponsors stories of collapse and recovery, of evolution and extinction, and interrogates them. Rust would also offer material signs of colonial ruination, imbricating imperial rule with ecological ruin, and point to the persistence of imperial debris. Therefore, an engagement with rust enables the questioning of ways in which the goddess films merge Hindu cosmology with ideas about nature, incorporating a postcolonial-ecocritical vision. The goddess, like rust, signals the underside of cosmopolis or indeed "modernity." An exploration of these modes of perceptions would help re-cognize ecofeminist ideas about nature and offer alter-visions of nature.

Andrew Tudor describes a film genre as "a conception existing in the culture of any particular group or society; it is not a way in which critics classify films for methodological purposes but the much looser way in which an audience classifies its films" (118). Tudor's description is very suitable for identifying the "goddess film genre," which has the goddess as the protagonist and an avid, if somewhat prescribed, set of age- or class-specific followers, usually either the older female viewers across all class groups or rural viewers of both genders and across all age groups, though predominantly women. The audiences have no trouble identifying the distinct features of this genre. If we keep in mind Thomas Schatz's observation that "a genre film involves familiar . . . one-dimension characters acting out a predictable story pattern within a familiar setting" (6), we would be able to readily identify the goddess film genre with its stock characters of the devout, pure maiden or chaste wife, who has a special relationship with the goddess and is a favored devotee, the initially skeptical but well-meaning male, who, persuaded by the faith of the female devotee, is gradually brought into the "goddess's fold" to eventually pit his wits against the evildoer, who is the prime antagonist. Here both the male and female devotees are aided by the goddess.[1]

To reiterate an earlier point, rust as a concept can create critical alliances with the Hindu goddess. As Jonathan Waldman clarifies, rust is complex and pervasive and appears indestructible. So also is the Hindu goddess. She has countless dimensions that are not easily classifiable. Just as rust is vitality, materiality, and quintessence, so too is the goddess. Both rust and the goddess are cognized as pervasive yet invisible, always underestimated. With rust this leads to underpreparedness in anticipating and managing the damage caused by rust. In the goddess films, it is again a lack of cognizance of the pervasive and immediate presence of the goddess. In all goddess films, this attitude is central to the unfolding plot. There is frequently a divide along gender lines. While women (and "non-alpha" males) intuitively cognize the power of the goddess, the arrogant or cerebral male invariably underestimates her power and magnitude and is brought to heel. This cerebral male is aligned with progress, cosmopolis, reason, and technology. The goddess, however, establishes her presence as antithetical to these positions. She stands for tradition and intuition and is aligned with primordial nature. The rational male is eventually made to heed the goddess. Those who fail to do so meet a dire consequence. In the film *Amman*, for example, the evildoer mocks the goddess as mere stone. The goddess gives him ample opportunities to rectify his evil ways and ultimately manifests as the avenger and tears out his entrails.

The unfolding plot structure is worth noting as it invokes interesting allegiances. Rust calls up an abject aspect of Nature. Julia Kristeva defines "abjection" as that which marks a "primal order" that escapes signification in the

Lacanian Symbolic Order. In *Powers of Horror*, Kristeva refers to the moment in our psychosexual development when we established a border or separation between human and animal, between culture and that which preceded it. In relation to archaic memory, Kristeva refers to the primary desire to separate ourselves from the animal. She asserts that "by way of abjection, primitive societies have marked out a precise area of their culture in order to remove it from the threatening world of animals or animalism, which were imagined as representatives of sex and murder" (12–13). This concept is useful in examining the representation of the goddess in the films.

The Hindu goddess appears to precisely threaten this nature/culture divide, inhabiting a conceptual hinterland. An explanation of this phenomenon may exist in the ancient *Puranic* text on the goddess called *Devi Mahatmya*—a sixth-century compendium on Devi or goddess and acknowledged as a comprehensive source of all knowledge on the goddess—where the phenomenon that Thomas Hopkins has described as "the Brahminical synthesis" can be clearly distinguished. Thus, in this text, pre-Aryan goddesses are slowly but surely being incorporated into the canon of Aryan/Brahminical goddesses, all identified under one name—Devi. A result of this attempt at co-option and the merging of pre-Aryan elements is that the goddess emerges as both sacred and profane, associated with worship but also manifesting as "primal matter" beyond culture, a boundary figure who mocks the human/animal or nature/culture divide. This amalgam can be clearly traced and is often foregrounded in several goddess films where the goddess is unproblematically associated with the animal and the animalistic but is simultaneously also projected as the caring mother. In the film *Nageshwari* (*naga*, "snake"; *ishwari*, "goddess"), the snake—a reptile, feared; a figure of horror; an ancient enemy—is also worshiped by the devout as the snake goddess or *Nageshwari*. The snake as goddess nurtures the baby and is also the feared reptile that avenges her devotee's murder. In fact, in film after film in this genre, the goddess and the animal cannot be separated.

In *Amman*, in the final scene, the goddess merges into her *vahana* (vehicle), the *simha* (lion). The goddess, often known as *simhavahini* (one who rides a lion), morphs into a lion to tear the entrails of the evil demon who is terrorizing her devotees. She then emerges as the "monstrous feminine." This is interesting since in this conception, there is no divide between the "divine feminine" and the "monstrous feminine," nor is there a difference between the divine and the animalistic. Barbara Creed argues that concepts of the monstrous feminine within horror films are psychosocial effects mirroring male anxieties regarding female sexuality and fears of male castration. Creed argues that there are a variety of different appearances of the monstrous feminine, all of which reflect female sexuality: archaic mother, monstrous womb, vampire, monstrous mother, witch, and castrator. Though Creed's ideas are useful in analyzing the goddess films, unlike in Creed, where the "monstrous feminine" is othered, the goddess, even in her monstrous feminine form, which she assumes to annihilate evil, is never othered. She is agentic sexually since she is both *yogini* (one who performs yoga) and *kamini* (one who has *kama* or sexual desire; one who is desirable). She may morph into the monstrous, but *in* her, opposites are resolved and amalgamated.

The goddess is thus both subject and abject. As the archaic mother-incarnate and the divine-feminine, she is definitely the subject. But when she assumes the monstrous feminine form, she can manifest variously as the devouring womb or the animalistic. I would further provocatively argue that the goddess as subject/abject is akin to rust not just through superficial similarities but more inherently. We all know that rust and temporality are closely linked. In *Shakta* conception, goddess as "transcendent power" is beyond time, but as "manifest nature" she is bound by time. The goddess films faithfully reflect this paradox, where eternity and temporality are both invoked.

Moreover, most cultures associate rust with entropy. It is seen as the end result of a process of natural decay. Rust can function both as abject and as art. As Waldman explains, in Japanese aesthetics *sabi* is the beauty of natural aging and aged materials; what is new is not as lovely as what has weathered. From this perspective, rust becomes beautiful and rusty metal becomes an art object (34). The Hindu goddess can be equally complex. Like rust, she incorporates within her contrary traits that generally stand polarized in discourses about mortals. She is both nurturer and destroyer. As destroyer, the goddess stands for entropy. For, as manifest nature, she also brings about its evolutionary decay and death. She is both mother and monster, the embodiment of both refinement and savagery. Thus, she can be dainty and coarse. But she is also transcendent and local, for, in the films, the goddess as mother is often associated with one village only and her powers appear restricted to its borders. Devotees are protected by the goddess in *that* village, but when they leave its borders, they are open to attack by the archaic evil power. In many goddess films, this henotheism is centered. In short, as Waldman labels rust, the goddess, too, is a "high-maintenance lady" (14). The graphic illustrations of these contrary sides of the goddess abound in these films as in popular Hindu iconography.

The goddess as *prakriti* stands for nature in its most pristine form outside of history and the human context. Goddess as *prakriti* is an essential principle and foundational category, a ground for both being and society. However, as *prakriti*, she is also nature and, therefore, to use Soper's description of Nature, represents "an independent domain of intrinsic value, truth, or authenticity" outside of culture (140). Soper's view is designed to reify (and challenge) the nature-culture binary. But we note that the goddess traverses this, for, as nurturing mother, she is habitually ensconced in the middle of worshiping communities, the mother who lovingly and graciously looks after her children but has the freedom to do so as the monstrous, the animal, or the animalistic.

To demonstrate this, let us take a closer look at the narrative of the goddess film *Amman*. The film begins with a community of women performing a ritual worship to invoke the goddess in order to ward off smallpox. The filmic diegesis opens with the idea that the goddess, though an elemental, transcendent force, will also form strong links within the community to fight with the people and safeguard their interests. The goddess enters as a mysterious guest and is ensconced in the house of a naive, young devotee. The goddess tasks the young village maiden with spraying medicinal water around the village to prevent smallpox from entering it and gives her word to the young girl that she will not leave her cottage until the maiden's return. When the initially unsuspecting girl discovers by accident her lady guest's true identity, she decides that the only way to permanently retain the goddess in her village is for her to never return home. Hence, she commits suicide.

Again, in the film *Devi*, a snake goddess, a folk deity, descends to a village and gets romantically involved with a local man. She builds bonds with his family and becomes a much-loved family member. These plots are interesting at several levels. First, the transcendent goddess is irrevocably localized. She is perceived very much as residing in one particular village unavailable to people outside it. However, this perception is not outside of Dravidian traditions. David Shulman, in *Tamil Temple Myths*, identifies henotheism, or the localized worship of a deity (even if s/he is acknowledged as an aspect of a more centralized deity), as an essential element of South Indian temple worship (139). Second, the great power inherent in the transcendent goddess is now tied up irrevocably with her corporeality. The transcendent goddess then gets localized, acquires materiality and its associated traits, and becomes the specific village goddess. As mentioned earlier, the goddess is simultaneously conceived as both spirit and body and exhibits immanence and transcendence. Furthermore, as *prakriti* and hence the equivalent of manifest nature, and as the village goddess standing for culture, she links both.

As the arbiter of both nature and culture, the goddess is shown to constantly reify Hindu/Indian culture. For this purpose, very often, myth and even historical episodes are harnessed in the plots of the films. The iconic film *Adiparasakthi* has an episode that works alongside both ecofeminist and postcolonial trajectories. The film enacts a recorded incident from colonial days. Peter Rous was the collector of the town of Madurai from 1812 to 1828. This town has the biggest temple dedicated to the goddess Meenakshi. Peter Rous was an emancipated thinker for his times. He respected people of all faiths. As collector, he also oversaw the finances and accounts of Meenakshi temple. His residence stood on one side of the temple, while his office stood on the other. Peter did due diligence by always removing his footwear when crossing the temple as a mark of respect for the goddess. He is also reputed to have diligently safeguarded the temple and its wealth. One night, as tradition has it, when a storm was raging outside, Peter was fast asleep in his house. He was suddenly woken up by the sound of anklets. He saw a little girl imperiously beckoning him to follow her. He is recorded as having described her as wearing precious jewelry and silk garments. He followed her out into the downpour. Minutes later, his house was struck by lightning and collapsed. He was stunned by his near death and miraculous escape and turned to find the little girl, his savior, walking off at a distance. He began running after her but found that he could never quite catch up. She ran straight into the sanctum sanctorum of the Meenakshi temple and merged with the deity. Acknowledging his debt to the mother goddess, Peter Rous donated a pair of golden anklets studded with rubies to the temple, which is still part of the temple jewelry. For many devotees, in this story, myth and history merge very satisfactorily.

The episode is also vital because it centers on a quintessential debate that was pervasive in Victorian England. As Giorgia Shani observes, in colonial India of the nineteenth and early twentieth centuries, "religious identities were essentialized and racialized. The centrality of religious affiliation, along with caste, marked out, for the British, India's essential 'difference' from the rational, enlightened West" (20). Therefore, to mark out a historical moment when "a miracle of the goddess" was acknowledged both through faith and materially through a donation by a British officer, holding high office becomes a salient, postcolonial moment, which, to borrow Ann Laura Stoler's words, refocuses attention on "the more protracted imperial processes that saturate the subsoil of people's lives and persist, sometimes subjacently, over a lon-ger durée" (192). The highlighted moment where the (Hindu) goddess goes beyond her sect or race of believers to "save" a white Christian then becomes a moment that not only establishes the glory of the goddess but also insists on the "moral superiority" of the Indians as always, already evolved beyond the racialized discourse subtly and overtly adopted by imperial Britain and indeed by Christianity under the empire. Moments like these in the goddess films hence become "vital refigurations" of what Stoler terms "microecologies of matter and mind" (10), wherein the goddess's glory is celebrated and, simul-taneously, a political point is nailed into place. Furthermore, by recapturing such moments that hover between myth and history, the goddess's power, though ancient, is shown as all-pervasive, contemporary, and relevant.

In Shakta cults within Hinduism, the goddess is the most ancient power in the universe. She is *Ādisakti*, or primordial power. But as Robin Rinehart clarifies in *Contemporary Hinduism: Ritual Culture and Practice*, "The nar-rative of the *Devi Mahatmya* indicates the fluid, ever-changing nature of the goddess within Hinduism. In this *Purana*, she creates new forms for herself and reabsorbs them into her supreme form" (47), an idea that is constantly rehearsed in the goddess films.

Just as rust is associated with contrary ideas of both evolution and extinc-tion, so too is the goddess. In keeping with the motto of the city of Detroit, Michigan—*Resurget Cineribus*, "It will rise from the ashes"—the goddess as Sati repeatedly resurrects herself from her ashes. One of the most ancient mythological stories about the goddess (as Dakshāyini) is the one about her being the primordial sati, burning herself in protest at her father's (Daksha or the Himalayas) refusal to invite her consort, Shiva, to his *yagnja* (fire worship), with Shiva arriving in outrage to resurrect her. This act of sati is graphically reenacted in *Devi*. The snake goddess, while praying to her Shakti (primordial) aspect, who is the divine mother, immolates her material body by setting fire to herself and becoming a sati like the original Dakshāyini. The scene that follows shows the goddess resurrected from her ashes encompass-ing the entire earth in her monstrous serpent form. The goddess as snake col-lapses irreconcilable categories of transcendence and animality, giving new meaning to the idea of an agentic nature.

Rust, however, has also acquired strong associative connotations in most cultures. It constitutes the darker side of progress. It stands opposed to narra-tives of growth, evolution, and advancement tarnishing such "splendour." Rust is inherently organic and hence also stands opposed to technology. Interestingly, a similar discourse surrounds the goddess, especially in these films, for not only does she deride the male who is aligned to reason and progress, but the goddess also appears to actively celebrate the simple-minded and the credulous. Therefore, even as the agency of the goddess is being promoted, in a parallel but reverse movement, the credulous mortal woman as protagonist is usually reinscribed into conservative ideologies. Furthermore, through a loose alliance with the more banal scriptural texts,[2] it propounds reactionary and conservative ideologies. Hence, goddess films emphasize rituals believed to ensure prosperity or safety in a turbulent world. Predictably, given the inscription of such reactionary ideologies within its diegesis, women characters are constructed as safeguarding and transmitting traditional values that inevitably valorize the imbrication of women in traditional hierarchies of power. The goddess in these films propagates the ideal of the woman as the "domestic goddess." Invariably, like in traditional Western fairy tales, where the only mortal women with a modicum of agency (such as the stepmother, the [disobedient] daughters, and the witch) are vilified, here, too, women who are shown to, in any way, disregard patriarchal strictures about proper feminine conduct are portrayed negatively. Women with agency are vilified. There is no representation of the modern, educated, or professional woman in the goddess genre except in a negative light and usually as a contrast to the devout, simple, home-loving girl, who evolves into the long-suffering wife. However, one interesting consequence of this negative gender representation is that the goddess's authority itself remains ultimately unchallenged, and she reigns supreme. As such, in recent films, there has been an emphasis on the links between the goddess-mother and the earth-mother and how desecrating the latter will be tantamount to mocking the former, an idea that has always been central to Hindu belief systems though, in practice, flouted, as elsewhere in various cultures, the power imagined as residing in idealized concepts of motherhood differs vastly from that available to actual mothers. However, as an effect of the divine–earth-mother link, some positive environmental images have emerged from the goddess films. This puts a new twist on an old debate within ecofeminist thought.

Women's conventional association with the natural world in Western culture, which, as ecofeminists like Carolyn Merchant point out, is ubiquitous (3–26), has received approval from writers such as Aldo Leopold and has continued to be celebrated by ecofeminists like Sharon Doubiago. But this woman/nature association has been contested by other ecofeminists. Janet Biehl, Catriona Sandilands, and several others have been troubled by this essentializing of both woman and nature, which they perceive as being reductive of the diversity of women, collapsing various ecological predicaments into one. They see this as ultimately disempowering to women and not useful for ecological preservation. But the goddess, conceived of as traversing boundaries of nature and culture, adds a hitherto missing dimension to this debate. The goddess as powerful archaic mother is also pro- and proto-feminine. She is an herbalist, always outwitting technological prowess that is showcased by the male antagonists. She is supremely assured, autonomous, and disdainful of human discourses of power over nature, and she celebrates her primordial connection with nature. As such, her conception stands above and beyond that of the mortal feminine. This is no doubt problematic in ways mentioned by theorists above. But it is also empowering in ways that are not adequately addressed in Western debates.

The transcendence and transgression of binaries construct the goddess as an unresolvable puzzle. In effect, therefore, in the goddess figure, such binaries collapse. This is unique to the Hindu goddess phenomenon and is particularly identifiable in the goddess film genre. These abstract conceptual ideas about the Hindu goddess, buried for millennia in philosophical religious treatises accessed by Vedic scholars in Sanskrit, are made graphically clear through the films. With the goddess both as *manifest nature* in all its aspects, as animal, the animalistic, and plant—the holy basil, the neem tree, and so forth—all associated with the goddess, and as *abstract spirit*, beyond and above human knowledge and cognition, the current debates about women inscribed within nature as passive objects take on a far more interesting and complex twist, for the final irony is that in the goddess film, the goddess also often takes on the mortal feminine form and as such is unrecognizable as the goddess to both the devout and the skeptical. Inevitably, from the perspective of the goddess films, ecofeminist debates that are arraigned around neat binaries are superseded.

On the other hand, given that the only agency that women are allowed in the goddess films is through the construction of the goddess as *prakriti* or Nature with its flora and fauna, it can be argued that the goddess-as-nature sends a powerful message about the sanctity of the earth and the need to conserve it to viewers, many of whom are rural, illiterate, or semiliterate women with little access to literatures revolving around global warming or its counter-effects. This does not make them alienated from or indifferent to ideas of positive earth identification. In fact, many of them, as subsistence farmers or enfolded into ecologically nurturing occupations, readily identify with earth conservationist sentiments. In fact, it can be argued that given the popularity of the goddess films with this demographic, such connections enable a greater environmental awareness and convey the urgency of conserving our planet. Thus, I submit that these kinds of non-Western perspectives, emerging from within a specific, national, and cultural context, open up alter-visions for ecofeminism.

Notes

1. See Chitra Sankaran, "Materiality, Devotion and Compromise."

2. Such texts abound in Hinduism, since, not being a founded religion and with no central monitoring body, inevitably there are several texts, both ancient and modern, that profess to be sacred but can be extremely esoteric or frankly eccentric, to which a small cult could subscribe. Some of these texts (for instance, Gowli Panchangam, or gecko astrology, which makes a claim that depending on a gecko's movement one can predict the future) can also be very insistent on rituals that need to be performed in precise ways. For instance, as Sarah Caldwell of the Harvard Divinity School remarks: "Tantric religious traditions provide specific means for ritual worship of and yogic meditation upon the goddess, directing the worshipper to a state of complete identification and union with her" (http://www.infinityfoundation.com/mandala/i_es/i_es_caldw_goddess_frameset.htm).

Works Cited

Berger, Peter. *The Sacred Canopy: Elements of a Sociological Theory of Religion*. Random House, 1990.

Berry, Thomas. *The Great Work: Our Way into the Future*. Bell Tower, 1999.

Biehl, Janet. *Finding Our Way: Rethinking Ecofeminist Politics*. Black Rose Books, 1991.

Creed, Barbara. "Horror and the Monstrous-Feminine: An Imaginary Abjection." *Screen*, vol. 27, no.1, 1 January 1986, 44–71.

Doubiago, Sharon. "Mama Coyote Talks to the Boys." *Healing the Wounds: The Promise of Ecofeminism*, edited by Judith Plant. Green Print, 1989, 40–45.

Godfrey, Phoebe C. "Ecofeminist Cosmology in Practice: *Genesis Farm* and the Embodiment of Sustainable Solutions." *Capitalism, Nature, Socialism*, vol. 19, no. 2, 2008, 96–114.

Gopalakrishnan, K. S., director. *Adi Parasakthi*. Chitra Productions, 1971.

Griffin, Susan. *Woman and Nature: The Roaring Inside Her*. Harper and Row, 1978.

Hopkins, Thomas J. *The Hindu Religious Tradition*. Dickenson Publishing, 1971.

Humm, Maggie. *The Dictionary of Feminist Theory*. Ohio State UP, 1990.

Jagadeesan, K., director. *Melmaravathur Adhiparasakthi*. Movieland, 1985.

Kristeva, Julia. *Powers of Horror: An Essay on Abjection*. Trans. Leon S Roudiaz. Columbia UP, 1982.

Leopold, Aldo. *A Sand County Almanac and Sketches Here and There*. Oxford UP, 1968.

McKinley, J. "Critical Argument and Writer Identity: Social Constructivism as a Theoretical Framework for EFL Academic Writing." *Critical Inquiry in Language Studies*, vol. 12, no. 3, 2015, 184–207.

Merchant, Carolyn. *Earthcare: Women and the Environment*. Routledge, 1995.

Narayan, Ram, director. *Nageshwari*. Anand Cine Service, 2001.

Ramakrishna, Kodi, director. *Amman*. Super Good Films, 1995.

Ramakrishna, Kodi, director. *Devi*. Eagle Entertainment, 1999.

Rinehart, Robin. "Introduction: The Historical Background." *Contemporary Hinduism: Ritual Culture and Practice*, edited by Robin Rinehart. ABC Clio, 2004, 1–67.

Sandilands, Catriona. *The Good-Natured Feminist: Ecofeminism and the Quest for Democracy*. U of Minnesota P, 1999.

Sankaran, Chitra. "Materiality, Devotion and Compromise: A Study of Goddess Films of South India." *Material Religion*, vol. 11, no. 4, 2015, 443–64.

Schatz, Thomas. *Hollywood Genres: Formulas, Filmmaking, and the Studio System*. Random House, 1981.

Shani, Giorgia. "Empire, Liberalism and the Rule of Colonial Difference: Colonial Governmentality in South Asia." *Ritsumeikan Annual Review of International Studies*, vol. 5, 2006, 19–36.

Shulman, David Dean. *Tamil Temple Myths: Sacrifice and Divine Marriage in the South Indian Śaiva Tradition*. Princeton UP, 1980.

Soper, Kate. "Naturalized Woman and Feminized Nature." *The Green Studies Reader: From Romanticism to Ecocriticism*, edited by Laurence Coupe. Routledge, 1996, 139–43.

Spretnak, Charlene. "Ecofeminism: Our Roots and Flowering." *Reweaving the World: The Emergence of Ecofeminism*, edited by Irene Diamond and Gloria Orenstein. Sierra Club Books, 1990, 3–14.

Stoler, Ann Laura, editor. *Imperial Debris: On Ruins and Ruination*. Duke UP, 2013.

Strathern, Marilyn. *After Nature: English Kinship in the Late Twentieth Century*. Cambridge UP, 1992.

Tudor, Andrew. "Genre and Critical Methodology." *Movies & Methods*, edited by Bill Nichols. U of California P, 1976, 118–25.

Waldman, Jonathan. *Rust: The Longest War*. Simon and Schuster, 2016.

4

"If We Return We Will Learn"

*Empire, Poetry, and Biocultural Knowledge
in Papua New Guinea*

John Charles Ryan

In 1984, the Ok Tedi Mine opened in the Western Province of Papua New
Guinea (PNG). The mine would soon acquire an "international reputation
as an environmental disaster" with an average of eighty million tons of tailings discharged into rivers each year (Filer and Jenkins 29). As the first major
resource extraction project of the newly formed PNG government, Ok Tedi
precipitated the ecological ruin of the floodplain on which the Yonggom rely
(Kirsch, "Indigenous Movements" 305). Andok Yang, a Yonggom woman who
lives downstream from the mine, recalled that "the river became muddy and
the fish and prawns died. At the same time, the sandbanks that later covered
our gardens began to form" (qtd. in Kirsch, "Return to Ok Tedi" 659). Around
the time that Ok Tedi commenced, Vincent Warakai published "Dancing Yet
to the Dim Dim's Beat," a poem lamenting the neo-imperial state that PNG
had become less than a decade after independence. Seventy years of imperial
control by Australia (1905–75) had impacted the environment and destabi-
lized land-based traditions. Rather than an expression of sovereignty, agency,
and identity, drumming presents a haunting metaphor of an uncertain future:
"Yes, It is signalling, not the bliss, / But the impending crisis" (Warakai 169,
lines 35–36). The poem's final lines evoke the interlinked environmental and
social crises of postcolonialism in the Asia-Pacific region.

    The history of Australian colonialism in Oceania has many parallels with
the history of American imperialism in Asia and the Pacific, namely, the
appropriation of natural resources, the ruination of the environment, and the
dispossession of Indigenous communities. In both regions, imperial states

enforce resource exploitation paradigms that marginalize the sovereignty of non-Western nations and prolong the aftereffects of colonial rule through contemporary forms such as economic globalization (Young). The history of colonialism and imperialism is a history of entwined ecological and cultural degradation. In PNG since independence, the Bougainville conflict (1988–98) represents another biocultural catastrophe. The violent ten-year dispute over the secession of the Bougainville Province was fueled by community grievances emerging from the Panguna mega-mine (Wallis). Inundated with tailings from Panguna, coastal lowlands turned into toxic swamps, and the once-thriving fisheries of the Kawerong-Jaba river system deteriorated (Ross 400). Resource extraction continues to impact Bougainville's people and places. The Jaba glows eerily with the heavy metals dumped by Bougainville Copper Limited. Notwithstanding the risks, villagers pan the sand-choked river for gold to garner a living from a landscape that no longer supports subsistence agriculture (Loewenstein 95). With implications for human and more-than-human lives, Ok Tedi and Panguna represent the *imperial debris* of ninety-one years of Western colonialism in PNG. Ann Laura Stoler defines this term as "remnants that slip from immediate vision, detritus that is harder to grasp—intimate injuries that appear as only faint traces, or deep deformations and differentiations of social geography which go by other names" ("'The Rot Remains'" 18). Imperial remnants—those reinscribed by multinational mining conglomerates—"saturate the subsoil of people's lives and persist, sometimes subjacently, over a longer durée" (5).

This chapter extends Stoler's theorization of imperial debris to PNG poetry written during the colonial and postcolonial eras. I examine Stoler's assertion that "stories congeal around imperial debris, as do critiques" ("'The Rot Remains'" 19). The poetry of Apisai Enos (b. early 1950s) and Steven Edmund Winduo (b. 1964) interrogates the ruination of ancestral environments. The poets' use of vernacularisms and local lexicons reveals a hybridization of textuality and orature—stories, myths, legends, songs, and chants—that implicates ecological decline in the (post)colonial disintegration of biocultural formations. More than nostalgic reverie, their writing intervenes in imperial "processes of decimation, displacement, and reclamation" (Stoler, "'The Rot Remains'" 8). Enos's collections *High Water* (1971), *Warbat* (1971), and *Tabapot* (1975) interweave traditional motifs with an anti-colonial politics. In the post-independence milieu, Winduo's *Lomo'ha I Am, in Spirits' Voice I Call* (1991) and *Hembemba* (2000) poeticize the oral traditions of East Sepik as a means to critique biocultural disintegration. Composed in English, Tok Pisin, and

Nagum Boiken, the inflections of *Hembemba* counter Anglocentric imperialism by embracing Winduo's homeland as an embodiment of biocultural sovereignty. The performative-restorative strategies of their work help to recover
land-based traditions undermined by climate change, habitat degradation,
and species decline. The idea of *performative-restorative ecologies* highlights
the centrality of poetic expression—lyrical-textual performance—to political resistance and ecological recuperation. Moving beyond the depiction of
imperial ruination, contemporary PNG poetry invites the (re)imagining of
potentialities for nature-culture assemblage. Rather than being limited to
colonial critique, the poetry of Enos and Winduo preserves, innervates, and
imparts biocultural knowledge to audiences. The integration of written and
spoken modes, however, is not unique to these writers but reflects strategies
of colonial disruption enacted in early works of PNG literature.

"Fragile and Durable Substance": Empire, Environment, Poetry

At the end of the 1960s, PNG literature emerged in response to decades of
British, German, and Australian occupation. Writers with nationalistic ideals
evoked traditional cosmologies, cultural motifs, and mythological personae
as expressions of resistance to imperial intrusion (Sharrad). During these
years, traditional orature—combined with concerns about colonialism—
influenced the development of a Papuan literary style (Gorle 83). Politician
and academic Joseph Sukwianomb suggests that the growth of PNG literature in the late 1960s and early 1970s reflected "the build-up of tension, anxiety and restless voices of the local population against the violent and oppres-
sive cultural colonialism and imperialism" (qtd. in Gorle 84). In 1884, Britain
proclaimed the southeastern quarter of New Guinea a protectorate, while, in
the same year, Germany created a protectorate in the northeast and adjacent
island groups, initially managed by the New Guinea Company (Waiko 28, 41).
Four years later, Britain annexed British New Guinea. Under the Papua Act
of 1905, Australia assumed control of the British Protectorate, renaming the
territory Papua (57). At the beginning of World War I, Australia placed German New Guinea under military administration, and, from 1921, a League of
Nations mandate directed Australian governance of the territory for another
twenty years (84). PNG achieved full political autonomy in September 1975.

   During the late colonial and early postcolonial periods, literary expression contributed to the momentum toward autonomy through a return to land-based traditions. Narrating the protagonist Hoiri Sevese's process of coming to terms with colonial trauma, Vincent Eri's novel *The Crocodile* (1970) brought attention to the implications of imperialism for communities outside of Port Moresby. One year earlier, scholar-editor Ulli Beier released the pilot issue of *Kovave*, featuring poetry, prose, and folklore in translation to English. The magazine's name invokes an initiation ceremony among the Orokolo people of the Gulf Province. *Kovave* propelled a cohort of young writers to prominence as Papuan voices. Poetry collections by Kumalau Tawali and John Kasaipwalova further fomented literary nationalism in the years preceding independence. Parodying imperial apparatuses, these works set generational Papuan knowledge of land in contrast to the narrow purview of Anglo-European bureaucrats.

Since independence, PNG has become the neocolonial object of multinational conglomerates intent on exploiting its resources while minimizing social and ecological responsibilities. Positioned at the crossroads of Southeast Asia and the Pacific Islands, PNG is bioculturally complex and known for its "multi-dimensional megadiversity" (Filer 256). Bordering Indonesia to the west and facing Australia southward, PNG encompasses a central region—part of the largest tropical island on Earth—and numerous archipelagoes. What's more, the country contains the third most extensive closed-canopy rainforest in the world and harbors 6–8 percent of all known species on 0.5 percent of the global land area (Convention on Biological Diversity 7). Ethnically and linguistically heterogeneous, PNG is also home to an estimated 854 languages—about one-sixth of those thought to exist worldwide—sustained over generations through the performance of narratives involving cultural figures and natural forces (Winduo in Wood 86). Nevertheless, *Papua New Guinea's Fifth National Report to the Convention on Biological Diversity* observes that "the porosity of its national borders, huge demands for cash windfalls . . . from logging companies, expanding population, and growing demands for food and wildlife resources" continue to threaten to erode biodiversity (Convention on Biological Diversity 8). Biodiversity loss, in turn, is an erosion of cultural and linguistic diversity—and vice versa. Performative-restorative ecologies in PNG poetry counter this loss by providing a living record of interlinked biological, cultural, and linguistic diversity. In this way, the poetic narratives of Enos and Winduo preserve and disseminate traditional biocultural knowledge of plants, animals, the land, and human-nature relations.

Environmental deterioration has also beset neighboring South Pacific islands. In Micronesia, for instance, the forests of Pohnpei Island vanished almost completely between 1975 and 1995 due to commercial agriculture, and on Nauru Island phosphate mining largely expunged the island's biological communities (Manner, Mueller-Dombois, and Rapaport 106). As in the cases of Ok Tedi and Panguna, nature-culture imbrications in PNG have been degraded by commercial logging, mineral exploitation, hazardous waste, marine pollution, species overharvest, and global warming. Marked by the violent accrual of imperial debris, neoliberal development in PNG has privileged resource extraction and export. In the short term, industrial-scale activities prove remunerative for the government and foreign corporations but catastrophic for the land and local people (Gorle 82). Indigenous culture-environment assemblages, moreover, are ruptured by the "twin forces of colonialism and capitalism" (Filer 258), or what Stoler describes aptly as "imperial architectures" ("Imperial Debris" 141). Stoler characterizes "ruined ecologies as the profit of some and the ruination of others" ("'The Rot Remains'" 14). In a neocolonial context, the impetus toward development reinforces "the longevity of structures of dominance" ("Imperial Debris" 193). She elaborates further, "To speak of colonial ruination is to trace the fragile and durable substance of signs, the visible and visceral senses in which the effects of empire are reactivated and remain" ("'The Rot Remains'" 11). For Enos, Winduo, and other writer-folklorists, poetry enables the perception of imperial processes. More specifically, Winduo's work probes the consequences of epistemological violence and the erosion of cultural attachments to land as materializations of imperial debris (Winduo, "Unwriting Oceania" 605).

"Pregnant with Secrets": Orality, Bioculturalism, Nostalgia

The poetry of Enos and Winduo is neither romanticized nostalgia nor "mourning contingent and concomitant with what colonialisms destroy" (Stoler, "'The Rot Remains'" 16) but, instead, performs bioculturalism as a counterforce to the hegemonic apparatus. In PNG, Indigenous orality constitutes a vital element of poetic intervention that resists the alienation of the resource extraction paradigm. Characterizing Pacific Island societies as "essentially oral," Winduo calls attention to writers' hybridization of knowledge systems, including myths, metaphors, and motifs, "both introduced and traditional, as remedial measures" ("Unwriting Oceania" 601, 603). Winduo refers to this process as the *unwriting* of imperial discourses through multi-modal and polylingual narratives. *Unwriting* can be understood as a literary process of decolonization that counters the dominant imperial constructions of Indigenous culture by restoring attention to traditional oralities. Such unwriting, however, is oftentimes typecast by Western literary critics as revisionist, naive, and nostalgic (Winduo, "Unwriting Oceania" 607). In terms of memory and affect in pre-independence PNG poetry, for example, William McGaw identifies its two primary impulses as "*nostalgia* for traditional tribal values and traditional tribal ways and *anger* at the white culture which has subverted them" (83; emphasis added). For McGaw, reading the work of Southern Highlands writer Dus Mapun, PNG poetry written prior to 1975 constructs the past "in the context of a post-lapsarian present" toward the preservation of an "adulterated" heritage (84). Within this narrow dipole, Mapun's poem "My Land" accordingly becomes pastoral idealization and nostalgic reverie rather than anti-hegemonic catharsis and biocultural recuperation:

> The trees on this land will shade you by day
> And by night you will kindle your fire.
> The water on it will wash your feet.
> (in Jawodimbari and Mapun 17, lines 12–14)

A prevailing emphasis on nostalgia fails to acknowledge that the verbs *shade*, *kindle*, and *wash* instantiate biocultural sovereignty. Indeed, to interpret Mapun's poem as nostalgic yearning for a precolonial idyll is to negate its power as decolonial resistance or *unwriting* (Tuhiwai Smith).

In PNG and elsewhere in the Pacific, traditional forms of orality (re)-inscribe knowledge of culture and ecology—of the interdigitation of human and more-than-human lives. As a case in point, Enga men of the Eastern Highlands perform a song called *sangai nemongo titi pingi* or "bachelor purification praise poem" (Clarke 1). One poem, a praise song for the bog iris employed in purification rites, narrates the journey of the speaker's ancestors from the Ambum Valley to the Sau Valley to acquire the plant from another Enga group. The song-poem expresses "the network through which sacred and other objects passed from one Enga sub-region to another" (1). The plant-poem-performance assemblage countervails the commodification of these networks by the colonial state. The generative friction between the traditional and modern, moreover, is palpable in Herman Talingapua's poem

"Hidden Power" (1972) in its evocation of *leleki* baskets as culturally rever-
berative objects:

> Leleki baskets
> hang from the roof of the men's house
> pregnant with secrets. (Talingapua 8, lines 11–13)

Neither nostalgia nor mourning can sufficiently convey the material-semiotic
agency of the *leleki*—notwithstanding its elusive episteme—in contradistinc-
tion to the suit, case, and electronics invoked later in the poem. The narrative
encodes specifics of place (within view of Mount Kumbu in West New Britain Province), botany (palms, coconuts, and sago), and culture. Like the bog
iris, the baskets are linked to male initiation ceremonies; the speaker later
declaims he is "uninitiated."

Oral-textual hybridity is further evident in Allan Natachee's "Poems of
Contact," the first verse in English published by a Papua New Guinean. Structured with quatrains, the ten-part poem opens a longer polylingual work
entitled "Mekeo Poems and Legends" published in 1951. Mekeo is a Central
Province language group. With its anti-colonial subtext, the poem makes use
of "counter-mimicry," defined by Graham Huggan and Helen Tiffin as "an
ironic version, which is also an inversion" that parodies the imperial speaking
position (95). Natachee ventriloquizes the colonial impetus through references to Mekeo knowledge of land enunciated in song performances or *sing-
sing*. The section "Our Papuan Garden," for example, narrates the protocols
and proscriptions involved in subsistence forestry:

> Then comes the time of dealing with big tree fellings,
>   Which is the work of males only,
> Joining the noise of falling trees with our yellings.
> (Natachee, "Mekeo Poems" 151, lines 9–11)

While representing Mekeo spiritual ecology, the figure of the god of emp-
tiness appearing in later lines satirizes colonial authority in the manner of
Tawali's lampooning of the kiap. Also included within "Mekeo Poems and
Legends" is "Mekeo 'Sing-Sings' of Nature," a seven-part, chant-like sequence
in both English and Mekeo comprising sing-sings of birds, gardens, rivers,
and thunder (152–54). In this context, Natachee published in 1968 the short
chant-poem "Love Charm," summoning the seductive power of the yellow-
flowering *kapok* tree:

I shall come and enter your heart, woman!
Leaf of Kapok shall entice you!
Weeping leaf of Kapok shall entice you! (Natachee, *Aia* 27)

Natachee's writing reflects the intersection of textual and oral narrativities during the pre-independence era. The agency of Kapok—its power to entice—suggests an interspecies intimacy that countervails imperial narratives of resource exploitation premised on the estrangement of human beings from the more-than-human world.

In a manner that similarly discloses nature-culture imbrications, politician Albert Maori Kiki's autobiography *Ten Thousand Years in a Lifetime* (1968) includes detailed references to traditional uses of fauna, flora, and fungi among the Parevavo of the Gulf of Papua. He recalls that women would combine a bitter grass known as *ero'o* with the juice of the plant *havai* to produce a botanical contraceptive (Kiki 14). Villagers processed the poisonous vine *ii* to kill fish and collected the luminescent *hiri* fungus to make natural bush lamps (19). Kiki concludes the first chapter, "Growing Up in Papua," with an incantation his mother instructed him to say while planting his first banana tree. The short verse invokes Maruka Akore, the ancestral deity of the clan and "the greatest protector we have, in war and in peace" (7). The mythological figure came to life when a woman named Namora became pregnant after swallowing a large fish. Sucking on a piece of sacred bark, Kiki sang:

As I am planting this banana,
go into the earth before it,
give it power. (Kiki 20)

Honoring Maruka Akore ensures the growth of the banana. Read in conjunction with the poetry of Natachee, Talingapua, and others, Kiki's narrative points to the integral role of orality in PNG literature. The oral-textual nexus recuperates nature-culture assemblages rendered vulnerable by imperial compulsions. Notably in the case of "Mekeo Poems and Legends" and other examples, prosody reflects the structure of orality through stanzaic repetitions and other formal features. Vernacularisms comprise not only colonially referent terms but also local nomenclatures for species (*ero'o*), objects (*leleki*), and ancestral personae (Namora) (see, for example, Sharrad). These poems show us how biological diversity is implicated in cultural and linguistic heterogeneity. Moreover, the temporal structure of the works absorbs elements of sung narratives and, accordingly, counters the imposition of hegemonic colonialist time as a fixed, linear progression rather than a cyclical, recursive phenomenon. Aiming to replace localized time-reckoning with a universalized paradigm, imperial administrators regarded PNG as a "*terre sine tempore*—a timeless land" lacking the sense of orderliness generated by minutes, hours, weeks, months, years, and other temporal constructions (Nanni 60). As a countercurrent to the colonization of time, the poetry of Kiki, Natachee, and other Papua New Guineans recuperates the land-based temporal cadences encoded in traditional songs.

"Soft Like Iba Blossom": Enos's Performative Ecologies

The narratives of Albert Maori Kiki and Allan Natachee reveal how the oral-textual interface inspired writers of the colonial era. Their calling upon bio-cultural epistemologies and motifs provided a strategy for conferring voice to themselves as emerging writers in relation to social and biological communities outside the purview of the urban elite. Postcolonial scholar Helen Gilbert contends that "orality should not be relegated to the realm of the archaized pre-literate . . . rather, orality is a practice and a knowledge, a strategic device potentially present in recuperating indigenous voices, potentially effective in de-scribing empire" (110). Alongside the "nationalistic—often overtly anticolonial—emphasis" (Gorle 86) of these early works is a distinctive amalgamation of spoken/performed and written/inscriptional modes. Born in East New Britain, Apisai Enos was active in the 1970s as a poet, editor, and folklorist (Powell 188). In the transitional years preceding independence, Enos advocated a "Pidgin literary corpus" (Keown 154) through his publications *High Water* (1971), *Warbat* (1971), and *Tabapot* (1975). With the author Russell Soaba, he edited *How* (1978), an anthology of folklore. In the 1980s, he also wrote and recorded children's poetry based on Pacific motifs (Ellerman 171). Influenced by studies in theater and drama, his poetry investigates "precontact aesthetic systems" and "lived experience outside of colonialism" (322).

Enos's essay "Niugini Literature" promotes the development of a Niuginian English and of written literatures in Tok Pisin and Motu, the language of the Indigenous owners of the land where, in 1873, Captain John Moresby established the capital city. PNG orature comprises lullabies, love songs, praise poems, playful chants, children's rhymes, supernatural incantations, ghost stories, animal fables, and "aetiological tales" (Enos, "Niugini Literature" 46). Traditional literature "relates experience to the immediate environment" and engages "non-sequential perception" (47). He characterizes transitional literature as "a political weapon, a natural response to colonialism," and a "polemic exercise to rebel against alienation" (47). Enos's idea of estrangement signifies the separation between people and the more-than-human world resulting from the commodification of land under colonial paradigms. The hybridization of spoken and written literatures renders Enos's poetry a counterforce to imperial discourses of ecological "decimation, displacement, and reclamation" (Stoler, "'The Rot Remains'" 8). Literary scholar Regis Tove Stella understands Enos's poem "New Guinea" as an imagining of a past "constructed out of what is conceived as a European-created, chaotic present" despoiled by colonization (33). For Stella, Enos's poem operates "in a recuperative sense" that recovers "indigenous identity" (33).

As Stella observes, "New Guinea" celebrates the entwined biological and cultural heritages of PNG. The narrative thematizes oral motifs but also structurally enacts orality. The songlike composition uses anaphora—repetition at the beginning of lines—to generate a performative effect and a catalogic density of allusions. More than nostalgic reverie, the poem invokes the traditional agents that hegemonic discourses relegate to primitivism:

> land of *haus tambaran, dukduk* and *eravo*
> land of *kovave* masks and *gope* boards
> land of *hiri, kula* ring and fire dance. (Enos, *High Water* 10, lines 26–28)

A concentration of biocultural references marks the poem. The Tok Pisin term *haus tambaran* denotes the ancestral houses of worship in East Sepik where initiated men conduct ceremonies such as the yam cult (Jell and Jell-Bahlsen). *Gope boards* embody protective spirits. The sacred shields are constructed from a light wood known as *ibua* used also in canoe making (Frankel). Through the non-Anglophonic resonances of objects and places, the speaker revels in the topophilic and incantational senses. *Kundu* is an hourglass-shaped drum covered in reptile skin, whereas *garamut* is a drum fashioned from a log slit. "New Guinea" is descriptive of orality but also becomes a performative poem-object in itself within a wider textual ecology that implicates narrative language in human and more-than-human lives. As decolonial expression, Enos's narrative celebrates the performative traditions—of singing and dancing—linked to biocultural objects. The aurality, tactility, and sensation of "New Guinea" counter the protracted (neo)colonialization of "the visible and visceral senses in which the effects of empire

are reactivated and remain" (Stoler, "'The Rot Remains'" 11). This exultant reclamation of intergenerational sensory experience is central to performative-
restorative ecologies.

Enos addresses other poems in *High Water* to more-than-human beings.
As a culturally resuscitative practice, naming figures prominently in "Ingal,"
directed to an "elusive spirit" with "delicate hair soft like *iba* blossom" (Enos,
High Water 7, lines 13, 23). The irregular indentation, alternating line lengths,
and absence of punctuation conjure the ontological elusiveness of Ingal. Ingal
appears to its communicant in revelatory dreams as either the incarnation of
deceased man or a bush entity who discloses the magical uses of wild plants
(Wagner 141–44). Plant juices applied to one's face attract Ingal. Another technique involves the killing of a light-colored snake known as *bo*, which is then
placed inside an areca palm. Once the snake has decomposed, the Ingal seeker
consumes the *maut*, or fermented juices. Other strategies involve *worowos*,
a termite nest, and *bubu*, a flower put under one's pillow to entice the spirit.
Although the poem does not explicate these traditions, "Ingal" is indexical of
ancestral engagements with land mediated by supernatural forces. "Escape in
the Wind" is also composed to a mythological being, Posana, "stretched on
the tapa cloth / deep in the forest beside the river" (Enos, *High Water* 5, lines
24–25). Minimally punctuated and irregularly lineated, the poem embodies
the metaphysical terrain to which it refers. Enos's narrative hybridization of
spiritual energies and environmental knowledge influenced Winduo's debut
poetry collection, *Lomo'ha I Am, in Spirits' Voice I Call* (Wood 89). Although
writing before and after independence, respectively, Enos and Winduo share
a common concern with the imperial debris that occludes "microecologies of
matter and mind" (Stoler, "'The Rot Remains'" 10).

"Each Mark Carved on Trees": Winduo's Restorative Ecologies

Winduo comes from the village of Ulighembi in the Kubalia area of East Sepik
Province in the northwest region of the mainland (Winduo, *Hembemba* 124).
He writes from a hybridic position in English, Tok Pisin, and Nagum Boiken,
his native language (Winduo, "Transition" 174). His short stories incorporate
traditional themes. "Twin Dilemma," for instance, recounts the life of the
bachelor Jolomo and the death of his twin sister, Suaraukha. Based on *fakhi*,
or Nagum Boiken tales, the narrative alludes to a gray-feathered *kowi* in a
kapok where "each tree's height told of how old the village was" (5). The nar-

rative invokes toponyms—the Paminjin River is one—and integrates Nagum Boiken vernacularisms such as "numbo wia raukhua nien" describing a hardworking woman from the mountains (5).

As a young writer, Winduo found inspiration in the work of Nora Vagi Brash, Arthur Jawodimbari, John Kasaipwalova, and other voices for independence (Wood 89; Winduo, "Transition" 173). Although compelled by the "fiery nationalism" of Kasaipwalova's poem "The Reluctant Flame" (Winduo, "Transition" 171), he prefers to "leave the issue of politics to the imagination of the reader" (Wood 90). Winduo edited *Savannah Flames*, a journal of literature, language, and culture, frequently using his own resources because, as he explains, "no-one is prepared to put money into publishing literary works" in PNG today (qtd. in Modjeska 50). Although Winduo problematizes the "narrowing of reading culture" in the last few decades (51), he promotes Pacific literature as a writer-scholar and centralizes performative-restorative ecologies in his work. During ceremonial exchanges and special feasts, Nagum Boiken people compose and recite poetry (Wood 92). A recurring figure in these performances is Lomo'ha, the cultural hero who visited the spirit world (88).

Among Ulighembi clans, the figure of Lomo'ha offers a parable of exile, of leaving—and returning to—one's homeland (Winduo, *Lomo'ha* 40). Winduo elaborates that "while out collecting okari nuts in his part of the jungle Lomo'ha accidentally unplugged the lid that sealed the passage into the spirits' world, or the *waliwuiya*" (40). Following the reemergence of the hero, the shocked villagers used ginger and medicinal bark to expel the spirit residues from him. The narrative associates Lomo'ha and the otherworldly with okari, a tree providing an almond-flavored nut grown, eaten, and processed into butter. Punctuated by stanzas in Nagum Boiken—including the declarative "*Nuwo Lomo'ha ne*," or "I am Lomo'ha"—the collection's opening poem is told in the voice of the being remembering *waliwuiya* (1, l. 9). Freed from the realm of the dead but no longer at ease in the world of the living, Lomo'ha embraces the land. Rather than an unpopulated wilderness or neo-imperialized commodity, the forest is a cultural, spiritual, and semiotic terrain, one that heals: "I learned about each mark carved on trees / By unknown hands which spoke to me" (1, lines 15–16). Evocative of Enos's "Ingal," Winduo's incantational poem narrativizes biocultural interconnections embodied in a mythological persona but is also a performative-restorative object in itself.

In affective terms, the speaker of "Epilogue to Lomo'ha" identifies with the exile of the spirit being. Written while Winduo was a graduate student in New Zealand, the narrative evokes the isolation faced by Indigenous poet-scholars in the Pacific, many of whom occupy a liminal position between the local and the transnational, the vernacular and the imperial, the traditional and the hypermodern. At the poem's conclusion, however, a bird-of-paradise presents a material-semiotic intervention into postcolonial malaise. The narrator recounts a dream of a long-lost brother:

> I walk up to him
> With a beautiful bird of paradise
> In my hand and say I have returned. (Winduo, *Lomo'ha* 39, lines 16–18)

Prized for its colorful plumage and recognized for its elaborate courtship rituals, the bird-of-paradise is culturally salient but highly threatened. The blue bird-of-paradise, for instance, is found only in the montane rainforests of PNG, where it is hunted by local people for its feathers. Yet Winduo's subtext is one of conservation in which the living bird in hand—not reduced to its plumage—signifies human-non-human recovery from imperial trauma. A restorative ecology preserves the value of the bird-of-paradise within Nagum Boiken tradition while sustaining the species over the longue durée. Accordingly, the poem imbricates natural and cultural orders in which each is inseparable from the other. For Winduo, imperial debris registers in the "aftermath of rearrangement of the indigenous psyche to one of disillusionment, trauma, and paranoia" ("Transition" 169). Notwithstanding his political reticence, he advocates the critique of "the values of colonialism" and urges Papua New Guineans to "erase the stigma born of the colonised experience" (171).

The recuperative process described by Winduo involves the recovery of dialogical relations to the more-than-human. Just as Lomo'ha ameliorated its dispossession by regaining the ability to read the earth after returning from *waliwuiya*, so too must postcolonial PNG continue to uphold the longstanding connections between environment and narrative. This performative-restorative nexus orients his second collection, *Hembemba*, a Nagum Boiken term for "river of the forest" (Wood 85). Part IV includes poems in Nagum Boiken and Tok Pisin alongside their English translations. "Canoe Making in Megiar," or "Sapim Kanu Long Megiar" in Tok Pisin, calls attention to the intergenerational communication of traditional marine knowledge:

> The story of the sea and tides
> Leaves the mouth of the old man
> He begins from the source of the story. (Winduo, *Hembemba* 106, lines 7–9)

Also from the collection, "Kowi" echoes Winduo's early story "Twin Dilemma" by reinvoking the sacred bird that was banished from Nagum Boiken society for disclosing the intimate secrets of a couple (Winduo, *Hembemba* 122). The poem opens:

> I have known the songs of Kowi
> Without words to say to me
> What of the world did the Kowi see. (Winduo, *Hembemba* 70)

Winduo foregrounds the need for his people to learn to listen to the more-than-human world once more—"To our mute neighbour" (70, l. 23)—and recover the capacity of Nagum Boiken ancestors to exist in discourse with natural beings and supernatural entities. For Winduo, poetry reinvigorates biocultural heritage in the aftermath of empire "gouged deep in sensibilities of the present" (Stoler, "'The Rot Remains'" 2).

"Our Traditions Are Still Alive":
Performative-Restorative Ecologies as Resistance

Hybridizations of orality and textuality—what I have described as performative-restorative ecologies—signify the importance of poetic expression as ecopolitical resistance and biocultural recovery in PNG. Winduo's polylingual poem "Pasin/Ways" voices optimism that traditions will endure and that the spiritual landscape will prevail:

> If we return we will learn
> Our traditions are still alive
> Ways to look after our land are there. (Winduo, "Pasin/Ways" 69–70,
>   lines 3–5)

As narrated in the tale of Lomo'ha, returning involves the recuperation of identity as a function of ancestral ecologies. It is no coincidence, then, that Stoler begins her theorization of imperial debris with Saint Lucian writer Derek Walcott's "Ruins of a Great House," characterizing the poem as "a harsh clarion call and a provocative challenge to name the toxic corrosions and violent accruals of colonial aftermaths, the durable forms in which they bear on the material environment and on people's minds" ("'The Rot Remains'" 2). I have argued, however, that the writing of Enos, Winduo, and other Papua New Guineans is much more than a catalog of "toxic corrosions." In their rendering of poems as vibrant, performative, and polylingual objects in themselves, these writers preserve, energize, and transmit biocultural knowledge to audiences. At the performative-restorative nexus, their poetry enables the imagining of potentialities for nature-culture assemblage beyond the protracted "rot" of empire that Stoler compels us to consider.

Works Cited

Beier, Ulli, editor. *Kovave: A Journal of New Guinea Literature*, vol. 1, no. 1, 1969, 1–63.

Clarke, William. *Man, Land, and Poetry: Geography in Poetic Expression*. U of Papua New Guinea, 1975.

Convention on Biological Diversity. *Papua New Guinea's Fifth National Report to the Convention on Biological Diversity*. Government of Papua New Guinea, 2017.

Ellerman, Evelyn. "Literary Institution in Papua New Guinea." PhD diss., U of Alberta, 1994.

Enos, Apisai. *High Water*. Papua Pocket Poets, 1971.

Enos, Apisai. "Niugini Literature: A View from the Editor." *Kovave*, vol. 4, no. 1, 1972, 46–49.

Eri, Vincent. *The Crocodile*. Jacaranda Press, 1970.

Filer, Colin. "Interdisciplinary Perspectives on Historical Ecology and Environmental Policy in Papua New Guinea." *Environmental Conservation*, vol. 38, no. 2, 2011, 256–69.

Filer, Colin, and Phillipa Jenkins. "Negotiating Community Support for Closure or Continuation of the Ok Tedi Mine in Papua New Guinea." *Large-Scale Mines and Local-Level Politics: Between New Caledonia and Papua New Guinea*, edited by Colin Filer and Pierre-Yves Le Meur. Australian National UP, 2017, 229–59.

Frankel, David. "Carving a Gope Board." *Artefact*, vol. 33, 2010, 49–55.

Gilbert, Helen. "De-Scribing Orality: Performance and the Recuperation of Voice." *De-Scribing Empire: Post-Colonialism and Textuality*, edited by Chris Tiffin and Alan Lawson, Routledge, 1994, 98–111.

Gorle, Gilian. "The Theme of Social Change in the Literature of Papua New Guinea, 1969–1979." *Pacific Studies*, vol. 18, no. 2, 1995, 79–113.

Huggan, Graham, and Helen Tiffin. *Postcolonial Ecocriticism: Literature, Animals, Environment*. Routledge, 2010.

Jawodimbari, Arthur, and Dus Mapun. *Wicked Eye*. Papua Pocket Poets, 1973.

Jell, George, and Sabine Jell-Bahlsen. "From 'Haus Tambaran' to Church: Continuity and Change in Contemporary Papua New Guinean Architecture." *Visual Anthropology*, vol. 18, no. 5, 2005, 407–37.

Keown, Michelle. *Pacific Islands Writing: The Postcolonial Literatures of Aotearoa/New Zealand and Oceania*. Oxford UP, 2007.

Kiki, Albert Maori. *Kiki: Ten Thousand Years in a Lifetime*. F. W. Cheshire, 1968.

Kirsch, Stuart. "Indigenous Movements and the Risks of Counterglobalization: Tracking the Campaign against Papua New Guinea's Ok Tedi Mine." *American Ethnologist*, vol. 34, no. 2, 2007, 303–21.

Kirsch, Stuart. "Return to Ok Tedi." *Meanjin*, vol. 55, no. 4, 1996, 657–66.

Loewenstein, Antony. *Profits of Doom: How Vulture Capitalism Is Swallowing the World*. Melbourne UP, 2013.

Manner, Harley, Dieter Mueller-Dombois, and Moshe Rapaport. "Terrestrial Ecosystems." *The Pacific Islands: Environment and Society*, edited by Moshe Rapaport. U of Hawaiʻi P, 2013, 95–108.

McGaw, William. "The Sense of the Past in Pre-Independence Papua New Guinean Poetry." *The Writer's Sense of the Past: Essays on Southeast Asian and Australasian Literature*, edited by Kirpal Singh. Singapore UP, 1987, 83–93.

Modjeska, Drusilla. "PNG Writing, Writing PNG." *Meanjin*, vol. 62, no. 3, 2003, 46–54.

Nanni, Giordano. *The Colonisation of Time: Ritual, Routine and Resistance in the British Empire*. Manchester UP, 2012.

Natachee, Allan. *Aia: Mekeo Songs*. Papua Pocket Poets, 1968.

Natachee, Allan. "Mekeo Poems and Legends." *Oceania*, vol. 22, no. 2, 1951, 148–61.

Powell, Ganga. "Biographical Index of Authors." *Through Melanesian Eyes: An Anthology of Papua New Guinean Writing*, edited by Ganga Powell. Macmillan Company of Australia, 1987, 188–91.

Ross, Corey. *Ecology and Power in the Age of Empire: Europe and the Transformation of the Tropical World*. Oxford UP, 2017.

Sharrad, Paul. "'Ghem Pona Wai?': Vernacular Imaginations in Contemporary Papua New Guinea Fiction." *Cross/Cultures*, vol. 181, 2015, 121–44.

Soaba, Russell, and Apisai Enos, editors. *How*. Institute of Papua New Guinea Studies, 1978.

Stella, Regis Tove. *Imagining the Other: The Representation of the Papua New Guinean Subject*. U of Hawaiʻi P, 2007.

Stoler, Ann Laura. "Imperial Debris: Reflections on Ruins and Ruination." *Cultural Anthropology*, vol. 23, no. 2, 2008, 191–219.

Stoler, Ann Laura. "'The Rot Remains': From Ruins to Ruination." *Imperial Debris: On Ruins and Ruination*, edited by Ann Laura Stoler. Duke UP, 2013, 1–35.

Talingapua, Herman. "Hidden Power." *Modern Poetry from Papua New Guinea*, edited by Nigel Krauth and Elton Brash. Papua Pocket Poets, 1972, 8.

Tuhiwai Smith, Linda. *Decolonizing Methodologies: Research and Indigenous People*. Zed Books, 2012.

Wagner, Roy. *Asiwinarong: Ethos, Image, and Social Power among the Usen Barok of New Ireland*. Princeton UP, 1986.

Waiko, John Dademo. *A Short History of Papua New Guinea*. Oxford UP, 1993.

Wallis, Joanne. "Ten Years of Peace: Assessing Bougainville's Progress and Prospects." *The Round Table*, vol. 101, no. 1, 2012, 29–40.

Warakai, Vincent. "Dancing Yet to the Dim Dim's Beat." *Through Melanesian Eyes: An Anthology of Papua New Guinean Writing*, edited by Ganga Powell. Macmillan Company of Australia, 1987, 167–69.

Winduo, Steven Edmund. *Hembemba: Rivers of the Forest*. Institute of Pacific Studies, 2000.

Winduo, Steven Edmund. *Lomo'ha I Am, in Spirits' Voice I Call*. South Pacific Creative Arts Society, 1991.

Winduo, Steven Edmund. "Pasin/Ways." *Huihui: Navigating Art and Literature in the Pacific*, edited by Jeffrey Carroll et al. U of Hawaiʻi P, 2015, 69–70.

Winduo, Steven Edmund. "Transition and Transformation: Steven Winduo Examines the

Challenges of Being a Writer in PNG and How He Has Met Them." *Meanjin*, vol. 62, no. 3, 2003, 169–77.

Winduo, Steven Edmund. "Twin Dilemma." *Ondobondo*, vol. 8, 1987, 5–6.

Winduo, Steven Edmund. *The Unpainted Mask*. UPNG Press, 2010.

Winduo, Steven Edmund. "Unwriting Oceania: The Repositioning of the Pacific Writer Scholars within a Folk Narrative Space." *New Literary History*, vol. 31, no. 3, 2000, 599–613.

Wood, Briar. "An Interview with Steven Winduo." *Journal of Postcolonial Writing*, vol. 42, no. 1, 2006, 84–93.

Young, Robert J. C. "Postcolonial Remains." *New Literary History*, vol. 43, 2012, 19–42.

PART II

Militarized Environments

"Nuclear Family"
Craig Santos Perez

"The militarization of light has been widely acknowledged as a historical rupture that brought into being a continuous Nuclear Age, but less understood is the way in which our bodies are written by these wars of light."

    —ELIZABETH DELOUGHREY, "RADIATION ECOLOGIES
      AND THE WARS OF LIGHT" (2009)

~

7
In the beginning, _____ and _____ stood
on the bridge of heaven and stirred the sea
with a jeweled spear until the first island was born.
    Then one day, men who claimed to be gods
said: "Let there be atomic light," and there was
a blinding flash, a mushroom cloud, and radiating fire.
"This will end all wars," they said. "This will
bring peace to the divided world."

6
In the beginning, _____ and _____
ascended from the First World of darkness
until they reached the glittering waters

of this Fourth World, where the yellow snake,
Leetso, dwelled underground.

    Then one day, men who claimed to be gods
said: "Let there be uranium," and they dug
a thousand unventilated mines. They unleashed
Leetso and said: "This will enrich us all."

5

In the beginning, _____ spoke the islands
into being and created four gods to protect
each direction. The first people emerged
from a wound in the body of _____.

    Then one day, men who claimed to be gods
said: "Let there be thermonuclear light," and there were
countless detonations. And they said: "Bravo!
This is for the good of mankind."

4

In the beginning, _____ transformed the eyes
of _____ into the sun and moon, and his back
into an island. Then her body transformed
into stone and birthed my people.

    Then one day, men who claimed to be gods
said: "Let there be bone seeker," and trade winds
rained strontium-90 upon us, and irradiated ships
were washed in our waters. And they said:
"This is for national security."

3

In the beginning, _____ created earth from mud.
Then his younger brother, _____, carried
a woven basket full of the first people to the Great Basin.

    Then one day, men who claimed to be gods
said: "Let there be plowshare," and the desert
cratered, and white dust snowed upon the four corners.
And they said: "This is for peaceful construction."

2

In the beginning, there was no contamination.
Then the men who claimed to be gods said:
"Let there be fallout," and our sacred homes
and bodies became proving grounds, waste dumps,
and tailings. "Let there be fallout," and there was
a chain reaction of leukemia and lymphoma,
miscarriages and birth defects, lung and liver cancer,
breast and uterus cancer, thyroid and bone cancer.
      And we learned that there is no half-life of grief
when a loved one dies from radiation disease.
There is no half-life of sorrow when our children
inherit this toxic legacy, this generational
and genetic aftermath, this fission of worlds.

1

In the beginning, there was peace.
Let there be peace across our atomic cartographies.
Let there be peace for Hiroshima and Nagasaki.
Let there be peace for the Marshall Islands.
Let there be peace for the Navajo and Shoshone Nations.
Let there be peace for Mororua, Fangataufa, In Ekker,
Kiritimati, Maralinga, and Amchitka. Let there be peace
for Malan, Montebello Islands, Malden Island, Pokhran,
and Ras Koh Hills. Let there be peace for Chagai District,
Semipalatinsk, Novaya Zemlya, Three Mile Island,
Chernobyl, Punggye-ri, and Fukushima. Let there be
peace for the downwinders, from Guam to Utah to
every radiation ecology and every irradiated species.
      Let there be the safe disposal of waste
and the cleaning of abandoned mines. Let there be
the disarmament of the violent nucleus within nations.
Let there be a proliferation of peace and justice
for our entire nuclear family.

5

Environmental Violence and the Vietnam War in lê thi diem thúy's *The Gangster We Are All Looking For*

Emily Cheng

This chapter examines lê thi diem thúy's 2003 novel, *The Gangster We Are All Looking For*, through an environmental lens that considers environmental tropes in relation to the larger context of U.S. imperial intervention in the Vietnam War and the contradictions of Vietnamese resettlement as refugees and immigrants in the United States. The novel is loosely a coming-of-age story told from the perspective of an unnamed female protagonist. As a young child, the narrator flees South Vietnam with her father by boat and settles in San Diego. They are joined a couple of years later by her mother, whom they were forced to leave behind in Vietnam. Speaking to the loss of homeland and refugee resettlement in Southern California, the girl's narrative of her childhood is grounded in the legacies of the trauma of war and refugee resettlement and racialized poverty in the United States. In the context of the complexities and contradictions of this experience, we see a gap in the young narrator's ability to articulate a rational explanation of the events of their lives and to understand the social and political dimensions of her experience.

The narrative of the text is "elliptical" in that the narrator does not clearly tell us what is happening in the external world but focuses on her inner life and child's understanding of the world ("The Gangster We Are All"). Isabelle Thuy Pelaud characterizes this as lê's writing practice to "tell-without-revealing," in which the "narrative is told from the perspective of a child who does not understand what is going on around her. From this perspective, the narrator is not accountable for what she sees" (102, 101). Lacking a linear plot, the novel is made up of many interrelated stories and remembrances.

Crossing space and time, the narrative shifts fluidly between Vietnam and the United States and various moments in the past, present, and future.

However, by considering figures and objects from a more-than-human natural world that pervade the novel, we can see how the human narrator's connection with this realm helps to develop the narrative. The child often makes sense of what is happening or explains her perspective through animals or plants. For instance, she is fascinated by a preserved butterfly that she believes is trapped in glass and must be liberated, imagines that glass animal figurines are living friends, and tells of the ways water and trees appear vividly in her childhood. While some of these instances may seem like a young child's active imagination or confusion over the world around her, she draws attention to material objects from her environment and their relationship to the human realm. Her narration of animals and plants in fact helps to make sense of the complex world of refugee settlement and racialized poverty and to grapple with the losses and violence of displacement and war.

At a larger level, attending to the connection between the human and more-than-human world also productively puts environmental humanities and material ecocriticism in conversation with critical refugee studies. In the context of Vietnamese American studies, this focus on the narratives illuminated through the material world adds to the telling of marginalized stories of the Vietnam War and its aftermath. As Viet Thanh Nguyen writes, "So much is told about Viet Nam, and so little is understood. . . . If screen memories from movies like *Apocalypse Now* or *The Deer Hunter* are what Americans remember, they are what I and many other Vietnamese Americans want to forget: peasants massacred on a boat, prisoners playing Russian roulette with the Viet Cong" ("Speak of the Dead" 13). In the context of dominant memories highlighting the meaning of the war in U.S. narratives of democracy that foreground veterans and in refugee success stories that confirm U.S. intervention as rescue, an environmental lens helps articulate other narratives.[1]

The girl's relationship with plants and animals tells dimensions of her story beyond what she explicitly states. Iovino and Opperman have articulated material ecocriticism as "the study of the way material forms—bodies, things, elements, toxic substances, chemicals, organic and inorganic matter, landscapes, and biological entities—intra-act with each other and with the human dimension, producing configurations of meanings and discourses that we can interpret as stories" (7). The nonhuman material forms in the novel are not just foils or even metaphors but agentic objects with stories to tell, and they are entangled with the narrator's experience in ways that illuminate the narrative. Material ecocriticism offers a framework through which to "[examine] matter both *in* texts and *as* a text, trying to shed light on the way bodily natures and discursive forces *express* their interaction whether in representations or in their concrete reality" (2). Examining how dimensions of the narrative gain substance through material objects speaks to Yên Lê Espiritu's statement of the need in Vietnamese American studies for "more attention to strategic and self-imposed silence than to the power-laden process of silencing, to the ways that subjugated histories are told 'quietly' or told without words" (*Body Counts* 20).

While the child does not explicitly articulate the nuances of the family's experiences, her relationship to the material world helps to illuminate the long-lasting effects of U.S. imperial violence in Vietnam. Ann Laura Stoler asks us to consider how "imperial formations persist in their material debris, in ruined landscapes and through the social ruination of people's lives" (10). The narrator's close relationship to the material of her environment brings to the fore the structuring of the ongoing violence and trauma in the refugee characters' lives by imperial formations. Through this connection between the narrator and her environment, lê portrays the persistence of the violence of racialized poverty, resettlement, and trauma in the United States that is connected to their displacement from Vietnam in the aftermath of U.S. intervention.

Water as a Connector across Space and Time

Appearing as metaphor, a symbol for the reader and the characters, and a physical entity in fluid, gaseous, or solid state, water permeates the text. From the outset, it frames the shifting meaning of the boundaries of the nation and citizenship and illuminates the imperial formations manifest in U.S. intervention in Vietnam and in the resettlement of Vietnamese American refugees. lê's epigraph explains that "in Vietnamese, the word for *water* and the word for *a nation, a country*, and *a homeland* are one and the same [nu 'ó'c]." Water evokes the complex meanings of Vietnam and the United States as home countries and the connection between the two through the liquid form of the water that characterized refugee flight by boat and the ocean connecting the two spaces. Water also conveys the intertwined geopolitics that mediate the contradictions of home and nation for the characters, as they are displaced from Vietnam and struggle to make a home in the United States, in the face of the complexities of U.S. involvement in their country of origin.

For instance, the narrator connects the two spaces through water in the form of the shoreline where the ocean meets land. The family was separated during their departure from Vietnam, as the boat carrying the narrator and her father was forced to leave her mother among others stranded on the shore. In her early days in San Diego, the young girl imagines her mother to still be at the beach and longs to go there to reunite with her. In response to her request, her father responds: "No. Not possible. There's no reason for us to go there. But Ma's there, I said. No she's not, Ba said . . . you told me she was at the beach" (13). When he responds, "not the beach here. The beach in Vietnam," she thinks to herself, "what was the difference?" (13) Her child's understanding of geography does not recognize that the respective beaches are parts of distinct land masses 8,000 miles apart. However, taking her perspective on the beach seriously, we can see how water draws our attention to the significance of her equation of these two sites across the Pacific Ocean.

If water evokes home and the beach is the meeting point of land and water that represents the physical and political demarcation of the homeland, by viewing the beach in Vietnam and California as literally the same, the narrator destabilizes the boundaries of the nation-state. The connection between Vietnam and the United States highlighted by a material ecocritical perspective is in line with the geographical framework of critical refugee studies, which, in Viet Nguyen's words, "challenge[s] the very viability of the nation-state" ("Refugee Memories" 30). As Espiritu notes, "This field begins with the premise that the refugee, who inhabits a condition of statelessness, radically calls into question the established principles of the nation-state and the idealized goal of inclusion and recognition within it" (*Body Counts* 10). The beach may appear to be where the narrator orients away from the home to the ocean beyond, yet the fluid movement of the ocean connects the two spaces of home for the family. The meeting of water and beach not so much evokes the family's division across autonomous nation-states but invites consideration of the political, material, and affective connections across these spaces.

In particular, water interacts with narratives of other material forms to convey the transnational and transtemporal reach of war. The narrator recounts what she has been told about the war in Vietnam:

> Ma says war is a bird with a broken wing flying over the countryside, trailing blood and burying crops in sorrow. If something grows in spite of this, it is both a curse and a miracle. When I was born, she cried to know that it was

war I was breathing in, and she could never shake it out of me. . . . War has
no beginning and no end. It crosses oceans like a splintered boat filled with
people singing a sad song. (87)

The bird as a metaphor conveys the sadness of war; however, it also operates
on a material register to convey the physical devastation of crops, forests,
and fauna, including humans, in the Vietnam War. At the human level, war
infuses the narrator's life from the moment of birth, and the figurative language of the boat carrying singing people gives voice to the importance of
escape by water in the Vietnamese refugee experience. Through the fluidity of
the water linking land masses across the Pacific Ocean, the novel makes clear
that war and refugee flight are not discrete moments of trauma that can be
left behind in the past. As war and its effects travel across time and space by
crossing water, it is an entity without a singular origin or endpoint.

Thinking of the voices of those left behind on the shore of Vietnam,
including her mother, the narrator tells us that "years later, even after our
family was reunited, my father would remember those voices as a seawall
between Vietnam and America or as a kind of floating net, each voice linked
to the next by a knot of grief" (105). The voices of the Vietnamese refugees
are solidified as walls and nets that cross the ocean, making their expression
of loss and sadness audible in the United States.

Water's intra-action with the seawall, a barrier that seeks to protect
human-built environments by physically disrupting wave action upon the
shore and the natural deposition and erosion of sand, gives form to the personal trauma of the war that persists across oceans and the human structures
that create and complicate this process. As a built barrier that seeks to protect the environments valued by humans, the seawall of voices gives a solid
form to the personal trauma of the war that persists across oceans. Yet while
in its protective capacity the seawall may represent a protection from grief,
this human-made barrier is always being stressed by the forces of the wave
action upon the shore and the natural deposition and erosion of sand it seeks
to ward off and will not last forever. In this sense, the seawall also conveys the
tensions and conflicts within the frameworks of the refugee and nation-states
that also persist in the nets of violence and trauma across the ocean.

The connection across space and time through water emphasizes the
family's ongoing experience of loss and violence. As the ocean physically and
metaphorically connects Vietnam and the United States, it also connects the
multiple losses that come with claiming American citizenship and entering

into the narrative of U.S. democracy. The focus on water highlights the contradictions of the U.S. role in the violence of the war that leads to the family's displacement and of the social violence of their resettlement in the United States, the site of refuge. The narrator's perspective offers an alternative to the temporal and spatial dimensions of dominant teleological narratives of Vietnamese Americans and the Vietnam War, in which violence and any blemishes in U.S. democracy were circumscribed by the years of the U.S. intervention in Vietnam.

In this conventional logic, Vietnamese American refugee narratives of assimilation and upward mobility have been central to the recuperation of the Vietnam War from a debacle for U.S. democracy, an unpopular and failed war, back into the narrative of U.S. exceptionalism, with its framing of U.S. wars abroad as performance of democracy rather than imperial intervention. The refugee is figured in a teleology from an abstracted Third World, impoverished condition to the improvement of living in the United States, with assimilation and model minority status as Vietnamese Americans as vindication of the rightness of the U.S. war and rescue. In the recasting of national memory of the war, Espiritu writes that Vietnamese refugees "have ironically become constituted as the featured evidence of the appropriateness of U.S. actions in Vietnam: that the war, no matter the cost, was ultimately necessary, just and successful" ("We-Win-Even-When-We-Lose" 329). The exemplary good refugee, a figure that flattens the heterogeneity of U.S.-born Vietnamese Americans, immigrants, exiles, and transnational migrants, is framed in a narrative of the "desperate-turned-successful" who aspires to and attains the American Dream as a model minority (Espiritu, "Toward" 410).

The narrator tells us of her family's journey that defies assumptions of rescue by Americans and the unidirectional narrative of the "good refugee." Water emphasizes their lack of directional intent: "Linda Vista, with its rows of yellow houses, is where we eventually washed to shore. . . . Ma was standing on a beach in Vietnam while Ba and I were in California with four men who had escaped with us on the same boat. Ba and I were connected to the four uncles, not by blood but by water" (3). Water symbolically brings these characters to the United States, although in their literal journey, they leave Vietnam by boat and arrive in the United States by airplane after being in a refugee camp. The language that they "washed to shore" indicates a process governed by outside forces, where the human occupants of the boat are not in control, and conveys their limited agency within the greater structures of war and global geopolitics. These flows of the ocean represent forces so powerful as to be able to transform the characters' social identities, as new kinship configurations and social identities as refugees are made in the experience of escaping by water.

While the ruination of the war follows the characters across the oceans, we can continue to see the quotidian violence in the lives of the narrator and her family in the United States through examination of the natural world. Rob Nixon theorizes the long scope of slow violence, which "occurs gradually and out of sight, a violence of delayed destruction that is dispersed across time and space, an attritional violence that is typically not viewed as violence at all" (2). Drawing on this concept, we can see how attending to not only the spectacular violence of wartime but also the everyday damage of refugee resettlement and racialized poverty can highlight the continued devastation the family faces in the United States.

Water also tells of the ongoing losses and the lack of control the family has in the United States. Unable to find a stable home in San Diego, the family is displaced multiple times. Water, in the symbolic form of a tarp, speaks to both the family's longing for home and lack of control in the face of racialized housing inequities and the forces of gentrification. When living among "Vietnamese, Cambodian, and Laotian refugees from the Vietnam War" in former Navy housing bungalows, the narrator says that "living next to Anh's family reminds [Ma] of Vietnam because the blue tarp suspended above Anh's backyard is the bright blue of the South China Sea" (88, 89). When this Southeast Asian enclave is razed to make way for development of a higher rent complex, the tarp is also lost. This incident registers the family's thwarted agency in making a home in the United States that is also linked to an affective and symbolic connection to Vietnam as home through the tarp. Having to trespass into the house to recover their possessions the night after being evicted, the mother laments their loss through water's representation of home in the form of the tarp: "Ma starts to cry. 'What about the sea?' she asks. . . . I want to know . . . who is doing this to us? . . . Why are we always leaving like this?" (97). Watching the demolition of their old house, the family looks for signs of the connection to the natural world that had made it home, such as "the scent of lemongrass" or "our blue sea" (99).

Overlooking this destruction, the narrator concludes that "there is not a trace of blood anywhere except here, in my throat, where I am telling you all this" (99). Her focus on water in the form of the tarp thus brings voice to the violence of their continued displacement from temporary homes in the United States that are framed by the shadow of their dislocation from

Vietnam. That there is not a trace a blood visible to the outside highlights for us the marginalization of her story and the pain of telling it. Adding to the explicit human narration of the novel, water draws our attention to the material, metaphoric, and affective registers of the violence of displacement and gentrification that the family continues to experience in the United States.

The Stories Told by Palm Trees

The palm tree is another material form from the other-than-human natural world that is intertwined with the narrative of refugee resettlement in the novel. While water connects Vietnam and the United States in the novel, the palm tree is especially significant in examining the characters' lives in the United States. It functions as a living being that intra-acts with the characters to tell stories of the contradictions of the family's lives as they live in a present inseparable from the past.

The stories the palm reveals are multifaceted. For instance, the chapter title, "palm," captures at least two meanings of the word, the tree itself and the palm of a human hand, that infuse the chapter. The palm of the hand is one way the narrator makes sense of her environment and how her environment impacts her body. For instance, in her exploration of a boy's body, she puts her "lips against his palm" and notices that "his palm felt warm" (63). She describes her changeable experience of feeling her own "palms in the dark," as the lines she finds sometimes feel like the "roots of the trees my mother says are growing inside of me" (64). If she cannot "feel a single line on my hand . . . that's when I imagine that my palms are all sand, desert" (64).

While the chapter mentions many palm trees present in the neighborhood, the central instance is the tree that appears on the courtyard of the family's apartment building. The apartment complex's courtyard was originally occupied by a swimming pool and served as a gathering spot for the Vietnamese American residents. Families spent evenings sitting on the terrace overlooking the pool, as "adults talked among themselves while the kids played" (51). This includes a group of boys who regularly jump off the second-floor railing, despite warnings by the adults. Angered by the boys' actions and the damage to the entry gate that the narrator's mother has caused with the family car, the landlord "silently cursed his tenants" and has workers cover the swimming pool with cement and place a palm tree on top (41).

This tree is an object that represents the landlord's control and the ten-

ants' relative lack of power. From the narrator's story, the tree is the culmi-
nation of a process of loss through the swimming pool. She tells us that it
looked "like a strange sand-colored skin that had grown over the swimming
pool, the cement took the pool's shape, even its curved edges. It hid from us
nothing but the water" (53). The palm caps the process of closing off the pool,
when the "workmen . . . carried in a big wooden planter, and whatever was
in the planter was covered with a black plastic bag. They placed the planter
in the center of the courtyard, right in the middle of where the water used to
be. When they cut away the plastic, what we saw was a squat baby palm tree"
(53). The baby palm tree in this barren space is a representation of violence
and loss of the water, with its resonance of home, for the family. We are told
that after the workmen leave the palm, "that night, my parents had an argument" ostensibly about "why the landlord had done it" (53, 54). In this fight
borne of the frustration over loss of autonomy, the parents react to the landlord's actions but through the changed landscape:

> "It doesn't matter," my father said. He turned toward the wall. My mother
> said, "It does matter. It's ugly. What is there to look at now?" My father didn't
> answer. My mother said, "I open the door and what is there to see?" "Well,
> what do you want to see?" my father asked. "Not a desert," my mother said.
> Then no one said anything. What was there to say? (54)

If a desert is characterized by "sparse vegetation and a limited population of
people and animals," in this case, the process of the diminishment of life has
a human agent in the landlord ("What Is a Desert"). The covering of the pool
and the placement of the tree become the way the parents talk about their
frustrations without voicing them directly. Here we see how paying attention
to the tree tells a story that the human characters do not articulate explicitly.
In its particular manifestation in the courtyard, the tree represents a narrative of not being able to put down roots. It is trapped in its planter box and
placed on impenetrable cement. The tree's circumstances thus tell a story of
the displacement and tenuous access to a new home that the child experiences. While her own telling of the story tells us about the fights and snippets
of observations about the other tenants and the landlord, the palm tree draws
our attention to the landlord's power over their circumstances.

The tree is a living manifestation of the landlord's control over the space
through ownership and of the tenants' lack of control. Due to their morphology of having a small root ball, palm trees are "fungible; nurseries raise them

in standardized containers. Like orchids, palms can be precisely monetized" (Farmer 412). Able to appear on demand as a commercialized product, the palm also speaks to the capitalist dimensions of ownership as central to the American Dream, of which the California Dream is a heightened version. If the economic achievement of Vietnamese refugees is a core tenet of the mainstream success story, the novel's portrayal of the economic struggle and the inability of the family to claim ownership over their home offers an alternative story. Its narrative is manifest through trees and plants, particularly if we consider the meanings associated with them in the dominant ideologies of capitalist success.

The palm in California cannot be thought of without considering its iconography in the imaginary of the state. As Don Mitchell writes, "Quite literally, we *see* California *as*—as palm trees, golden hills, extensive orchards, suburban sprawl, apartments scaling hillsides in San Francisco, towering redwoods, the valleys of Yosemite and Imperial" (8; original emphasis). The centrality of the palm to the construct of Southern California in particular was created historically through the work of developers, city boosters, and so forth that elevated the palm to be a "metasymbol for the desirable city itself" (Farmer 361). Coming to represent the California good life, palms were used to adorn yards and swimming pools in the Southland (390). In this context, the palm replacing the swimming pool seems to emphasize the inaccessibility of the California Dream, with its promise of comfortable living in one's own home, as it emphasizes the landlord's ownership of the property.

The family's distance from home ownership indicates both their inability to make a home in this space where they arrived under duress and their alienation from the American Dream. The geography of residential neighborhoods manifests the "gaps in material, social, cultural, and academic capital between the refugees and their American neighbors," as Xiaojing Zhou writes (301). Adjacent to the old Navy housing where the Southeast Asian refugees live is the new Navy housing where the narrator "see[s] the Navy people watering their lawns, their children riding pink tricycles up and down the cul-de-sac" (lê 89). This quintessential image of the suburban idyll contrasts the lives of those displaced through U.S. military intervention abroad and the Americans who serve on the side of U.S. military might.

Not only does the palm tree express meaning in relation to human action, but the properties of the tree itself also offer a way to rethink the temporality of the refugee narrative. The palm tree is a monocot that does not grow new secondary vascular cells in its trunk after it reaches adulthood, in contrast to the conventional notion of trees characterized by secondary vascular growth, whereby new cells form outer layers of living tissue as the interior layers cease to provide nutrient transport functions. In the latter, the age of the tree is correlated with its girth; however, with a palm, the trunk does not grow wider with age. Looking at a palm does not accurately reveal its age. Further, palms undergo what can be a prolonged juvenile establishment phase during which the stem grows to its full adult girth underground before emerging aboveground.[2] When we see a small palm, it may already have been alive for a period of time on the order of decades. The morphology of the tree conveys ways to think about time outside of rationalist linearity and underscores the ways in which temporal boundaries are blurred in the novel.

That the vascular bundles in the palm's stem continue to function for the life of the tree presents another dimension to the nonlinear temporal thinking that resonates with the anti-teleological narrative of Vietnamese Americans in the text. Botanist P. Barry Tomlinson and plant biologist Brett Huggett have suggested that "the extended stem cell longevity of palms therefore raises interesting questions as to how this cell longevity is possible and if palms differ from other trees in fundamental features of cell metabolism. One could even claim in this context that palms are the longest-lived trees" (1891). As the metabolically active differentiated cells of a palm trunk can live for centuries, the cells of the palm's trunk are all alive, in a colloquial sense. Whatever the palm experiences in its lifetime has been experienced by its presently living cells in its trunk. This living connection between past and present parallels the slippages across temporalities and the ongoing effects of trauma and displacement narrated in the human realm of Vietnamese refugees in the novel. Going back to the example of the palm that the workers place in the family's apartment complex, the tree is both a symbol of devastation to the characters and itself a living witness to the long duration of the family's struggle that connects the violence of wartime to the present.

The father's work as a gardener brings together the multiple registers of the meaning of the tree as a symbol and an object that can convey meaning to the human realm. Leaving his job as a welder for an air conditioner manufacturer, the father fulfills his aspiration of self-employment as a gardener. To prepare, he sends the narrator to the "library to check out books about plants and trees for him. . . . There were many varieties of palm trees. Among them, the Alexandra, the Australian feather, the betel-nut, the book, the broom, the coconut, the date, the dwarf, the fern, the fishtail, the wine, and the walking stick" (106). If palms are symbolic of California, the father and daughter's study of palms performs their education in claiming California for themselves as the father prepares for this work of labor with the land and the autonomy of having his own business.

The trees and plants to which the father tends tell their own stories that in fact can serve as a proxy for direct communication between humans. His relationship with the plants to which he tends maps an alternative geography based in labor and care for the natural world rather than possession. The father does invisible labor in his clients' yards, where he "trimmed hedges, swept walkways, raked up fallen leaves and hauled away broken tree branches. My father and the people he worked for rarely saw each other. He would come to their homes after they'd left for work in the morning and was sure to leave before they returned in the evening" (106). The father is able to do his work without speaking to his clients. The plants in the garden speak for him, signifying that he has been there and has done his work. If this gets done, there is no need for them to interact or recognize the other as occupying the same space. Doing so would bring to the fore the inequalities of the social space of the suburban home around race and nation, between the marginalized lives of the refugees and the employers living the American Dream in single-family suburban homes.

When the garden indicates to the clients that the father has done his job, the two worlds do not need to intersect. However, the trees and plants can also communicate the father's distress. He becomes violent as the narrative progresses, physically lashing out with what may be PTSD symptoms. One day, "he starts digging a trench around the base of a palm tree in the garden of one of the people he works for. He digs until his hands bleed. When he remembers that no one has asked him to do this, he packs up his equipment, pulls the lawn mower into the truck bed and drives away. Let them call. Let them curse into the answering machine. He will never go back to that house again" (115). Though the clients do not witness the act and do not know for certain what caused it, the tree's state signals that there has been an act of violence done to it. Even if the father does not interact with the clients directly, they will be forced to witness the evidence of his trauma that is usually hidden in their privileged sphere of the suburban landscape. By refusing to take their calls, the father refuses accountability and prevents the clients from seeking restitution or gaining closure to this incident, thus disrupting the power relationship between the two sets of actors.

By way of conclusion, I turn to the role of plants in conveying the marginalized and silenced narratives of the family. Whereas the father's work in the garden is done behind the scenes, and the plants are what is visible, in the case of the family's own garden, the plants are not visible to outsiders. As the narrator describes a "hot and dusty" Southeast Asian ethnic enclave her family lives in within San Diego, "Some people think it's dirty but they don't know much about us. They haven't seen our gardens full of lemongrass, mint, cilantro, and basil. Driving by with their windows rolled up, they've only seen the pigeons pecking at day-old rice and the skinny shade of skinny trees. Have they seen the berries that we pick, that turn our lips and fingertips red?" (90).

The plants in the lush herb garden convey their vitality through their growth and their physical rootedness in the soil. The agency of the plants acts upon the human realm; that the family's consumption of the berries stains their skin highlights this interconnection of human and plant agency. It is this connection that the outsiders miss as they fail to notice the agency of either the plants or the residents of this Southeast Asian enclave. Their visual and olfactory beauty does not register in the sensory perceptions of strangers who neither see nor smell as they pass by the house in their sealed up cars. This separation keeps the outsiders from recognizing human connections across difference and between humans and the more-than-human natural world. They instead make assumptions about the dirtiness of racialized, refugee poverty based on seeing pigeons, an animal whose association with dirtiness is itself a recent story, and trees that appear impoverished.

This alienation speaks to the displacement and exclusion from social citizenship to which the narrator gives voice through these plants and animals. Using this approach of considering objects from nature in relation to the human characters in the novel, we can see how both create meaning that enhances the narrative of the Vietnamese American refugee community. Given the ways we can think of the ecology of the novel as made up of disparate material objects, whether alive or not, this approach shows how interdisciplinary thinking about the environment can add to Vietnamese American studies. Paying attention to the environment and nature adds to consideration of the material and structural circumstances that ground Vietnamese American narratives and thereby works against the retelling of these stories through teleological ideologies that emphasize the depoliticized personal narratives of individual suffering or perseverance.

Notes

1. See Mimi Thi Nguyen, *The Gift of Freedom: War, Debt, and Other Refugee Passages* (Duke UP, 2012).

2. For a description of the juvenile phase of the sabal palm, which has an average juvenile phase of sixty years, see David George Haskell, *The Songs of Trees: Stories from Nature's Great Connectors* (Penguin, 2017), 69–70.

Works Cited

Espiritu, Yến Lê. *Body Counts: The Vietnam War and Militarized Refugees*. U of California P, 2014.

Espiritu, Yến Lê. "Toward a Critical Refugee Study: The Vietnamese Refugee Subject in US Scholarship." *Journal of Vietnamese Studies*, vol. 1, no. 1–2, February/August 2006, 410–33.

Espiritu, Yến Lê. "The 'We-Win-Even-When-We-Lose' Syndrome: U.S. Press Coverage of the Twenty-Fifth Anniversary of the 'Fall of Saigon.'" *American Quarterly*, vol. 58, no. 2, June 2006, 329–52.

Farmer, Jared. *Trees in Paradise: A California History*. W. W. Norton, 2013.

"The Gangster We Are All Looking For." *Publishers Weekly*, www.publishersweekly.com/978-0-375-40018-6

Iovino, Serenella, and Serpil Opperman. "Introduction: Stories Come to Matter." *Material Ecocriticism*, edited by Serenella Iovino and Serpil Opperman. Indiana UP, 2014, 1–17.

lê, thi diem thúy. *The Gangster We Are All Looking For*. Anchor Books, 2003.

Mitchell, Don. *The Lie of the Land: Migrant Workers and the California Landscape*. U of Minnesota P, 1996.

Nguyen, Viet Thanh. "Refugee Memories and Asian American Critique." *positions: east asia cultures critique*, vol. 20, no. 3, Summer 2012, 911–42.

Nguyen, Viet Thanh. "Speak of the Dead, Speak of Viet Nam: The Ethics and Aesthetics of Minority Discourse." *New Centennial Review*, vol. 6, no. 2, Fall 2006, 7–37.

Nixon, Rob. *Slow Violence and the Environmentalism of the Poor*. Harvard UP, 2011.

Pelaud, Isabelle Thuy. "War, Gender, and Race in lê thi diem thúy's *The Gangster We Are All Looking For*." *The Vietnam War: Topics in Contemporary North American Literature*, edited by Brenda Boyle. Bloomsbury Academic, 2015, 95–114.

Stoler, Ann Laura. "'The Rot Remains': From Ruins to Ruination." *Imperial Debris: On Ruins and Ruination*, edited by Ann Laura Stoler. Duke UP, 2013, 1–35.

Tomlinson, P. Barry, and Brett A. Huggett. "Cell Longevity and Sustained Primary Growth in Palm Stems." *American Journal of Botany*, vol. 99, no. 12, December 2012, 1891–1902.

"What Is a Desert?" USGS, https://pubs.usgs.gov/gip/deserts/what/

Zhou, Xiaojing. *Cities of Others: Reimagining Urban Spaces in Asian American Literature*. U of Washington P, 2015.

6

Toxic Waters

Vietnamese Ecologies in the Afterlives of Empire

Heidi Amin-Hong

On April 6, 2016, Vietnamese diver Chu Van Dai discovered dead fish surrounding a waste discharge pipe from Taiwanese company Formosa Ha Tinh Steel's plant in central Vietnam.[1] Noticing "a bitter taste in his mouth" and sudden exhaustion, Dai and his fellow divers ended work early, suspecting toxic chemicals in the water (Trang). Soon after, locals saw millions of dead fish washed up on the shores of the central coast of Vietnam. Formosa officials denied culpability for the fish deaths, instead stating publicly that Vietnam must "choose between catching fish and shrimp and building a modern steel industry" (Reuters Staff). Posing environmental destruction as an unfortunate but necessary consequence of infrastructural development, the Taiwanese corporation established global capitalism, industrialization, and disregard for nature as an inevitable future. The logic of global capitalism aligns nature in the form of "fish and shrimp" to a backward, unproductive past that is antithetical to modern advancement. To achieve the dream of a developed urban society, the Vietnamese state has also adopted these logics of rapid industrialization and reinforced a historical amnesia that rejects environmentalist critiques of war and development.

Though Formosa and the Vietnamese state frame ecological disaster as a side effect of modernization, I contextualize the ruination of Vietnamese waterscapes within a longer colonial history of U.S. militarism and East Asian sub-imperialism in Southeast Asia. I contend that the ruination of Southeast Asian waters and marine life is constitutive of the rise of new "subimperial" powers, formed from an assemblage of multinational corporations, global capitalism, and centralized state power (Chen 17). My goal is not to delineate a causal relationship between the Vietnam War and current ecological emergencies but to dwell in overlapping histories of ecocide—spaces where imperial violence ripples or echoes across the natural environment—and their material and psychic effects on the present. Furthermore, while ruination is often read simply as a symptom of spectacular violence, I trace the generative potential of ruin for both institutions of power and the human and more-than-human beings living with/in contaminated spaces. Drawing attention to the effects of empire's material residue on human and nonhuman lives, Vietnamese artist Tien Van Mieu and writer Bao Ninh both articulate multispecies intimacies and alliances among Vietnamese populations, nonhuman animals, and natural elements unfolding in spaces of ruin.[2] Through a reading of their cultural texts, this chapter examines a Vietnamese environmental aesthetics of ruin emerging alongside forms of imperial dominance, focusing specifically on representations of water and toxicity in the aftermath of war and industrialization.

The Imperial Logics of Ruination

Taiwan's rise as an "economic miracle" and a sub-imperial power is deeply connected to its ties to American neocolonial power in the Pacific as well as the exploitation of Taiwanese labor and natural resources through "export processing zones" designed to accelerate export-oriented industries. During the Cold War, Taiwan received significant military and economic aid from the United States, which solidified its status as an economic power with rapid industrialization and economic expansion (Chen 17).[3] Founded in 1954 through a strategic U.S. loan, Formosa Plastics Corporation was one of the early Taiwanese companies to benefit from U.S. aid during this period, eventually expanding into a multinational corporation with subsidiaries in the United States and Southeast Asia. After environmental regulations in Taiwan became stricter in the 1990s, corporations such as Formosa moved their operations to China and Southeast Asia in search of cheaper labor and materials costs.[4] In the Formosa case, Vietnamese territories were made available to toxic dumping through the state's partitioning of "special economic zones" that granted tax incentives and exceptions to foreign investors. In the context of shrinking resources and polluted environments, the exploitation of natural resources in Vietnam and other regions drives new imperial formations that depend on collaboration with local governments and Indigenous dispossession to bolster profitable development in sub-imperial centers.

Large-scale environmental devastation on Vietnamese lands and waters was also a crucial objective and consequence of the American war in Vietnam from 1955 to 1973.[5] While 1954 marked the signing of the Sino-American Mutual Defense Treaty, which provided startup funding for Taiwanese companies such as Formosa, it also signaled a shift of increased U.S. military involvement in Vietnam. The war's ongoing environmental legacies, including systemic destruction of flora and fauna, toxic dumping of Agent Orange into rivers and oceans, and infrastructural warfare, set up the logics of development for Vietnam's participation in a neoliberal economy. As this excerpt from a 1968 article in *Chemical Engineering News* demonstrates, the U.S. military justified environmental ruination in Vietnam with the logics of capitalist profit and opportunity, viewing defoliation as an opportunity to create new economies and industries:

> The Army scientist [C. E. Minarik] told the meeting that defoliation greatly improves visibility. This exposes enemy movements and hideouts, reducing the chances of ambush, and virtually eliminating sniper fire on both troops and civilians. The civilian by-products include increased accessibility of mangrove wood for production of charcoal, release of land for agricultural uses, improved commerce in isolated village areas, release of Viet Cong-captured rice for food, and improvements in communication lines. (qtd. in Zierler 68)

Minarik's portrayal of chemical warfare as a "civic or developmental project" argues that nature must be destroyed to pave the path to civilization, technology, and networked communication. The militarized U.S. state envisions a Vietnamese landscape that is "cleared" of forests in favor of industrialized production, characterized by the extraction of natural resources such as mangrove wood for charcoal and "land for agricultural uses." Improving commerce would open up new markets for U.S. exports and make Vietnamese land available to house factory production. Ecocide and the creation of waste were not side effects of warfare but deliberate strategies to convert Vietnamese land, forests, and water into profitable economies that would eventually strengthen U.S. economic control of Southeast Asia. These logics of profit-driven ecocide, as well as the devastation of existing Vietnamese economies during the war, would set the stage for the continued exploitation of Vietnamese lands and waters in the global economy.

Created in response to these two distinct but overlapping histories, the artistic and literary works of Tien and Ninh outline an aesthetics of ruination tethered to water that challenges the sub-imperial logics of transnational infrastructural development and resource extraction. Produced in the aftermath of the Formosa disaster, Tien's *The Dead Sea* series visually assembles the toxic ruins of extractive capitalism with the lasting impact of ecological destruction on Vietnamese bodies and psyches. Ninh's novel *The Sorrow of War* confronts the traumatic legacy of the Vietnam War for Vietnamese soldiers, whose memories of war are narrated through observations of the natural environment. Written in a historical moment that predates current structures of East Asian capitalism and extraction, *The Sorrow of War* elucidates the enduring logics and overlapping violences of imperial ruination on Vietnamese waterscapes. While multinational corporations in Asia visualize Southeast Asian territories as "special economic zones" emblematic of technological efficiency and rapid modernization, Tien and Ninh map a relationship to water that is attuned to the entanglements of human and nonhuman bodies and histories with the dispersed material waste of militarism and global capitalism.

Toxic Waters: Visualizing Oceanic Debris

In the Vietnamese environmental imagination, water is a life-sustaining force that is synonymous to a personal sense of home and a political feeling of national belonging. As lê thi diem thúy professes in the epitaph to *The Gangster We Are All Looking For*, "In Vietnamese, the word for water and the word for a nation, a country, and a homeland are one and the same: nước" (lê 1). As Huynh Sanh Thong points out, nước's multiple meanings also encompass "the juice from fruits," "body fluid," the "outward gloss" of a diamond, and "the complexion of skin" (Tran, Truong, and Luu vi). Thus, nước denotes a material connection between the human body that is composed of 60 percent water, the flora and fauna that nourish human life and depend on water to survive, and the bodies of oceans that shape and exceed national boundaries. Water gives life and enables the human body to enter into political identification, but it also underscores human interdependence with fish, coral reefs, and other lively and contaminated matters that are entangled in its currents.

Water is also a militarized, territorialized space, a conduit for transnational flows of capital, and a connective tissue for communities enmeshed in neo-imperial networks. Historically, the coastline of Vietnam bordering the South China Sea has been a space of contention between Vietnam and militarized U.S. and Chinese powers.[6] Since the Vietnam War, the United States has maintained the militarization of Southeast Asian waters through strategic occupation of the Pacific.[7] The federally funded Center for Naval Analysis has published widely on the stakes of maintaining "unhindered access to the waters of the South China Sea," citing "economic dynamism" and international trade alongside "America's ability to project military power" as key strategic stakes in Southeast Asia in 2013 (McDevitt, Taylor Fravel, and Stern 3). The coupling of military power and free trade reveals the co-constitutive relationship between militarization and neoliberal capital, which Pacific currents embody and enable. In the post–Cold War moment, China has adopted similar logics of militarization and economic dominance, increasingly clashing with Vietnam and the Philippines over claims to Southeast Asian waters. China has engineered islands in the Spratly Islands by artificially moving sediment onto reefs in order to house military facilities and an airstrip, reinforcing Chinese territorial claims in the region (Watkins). The militarization of ocean waters bordering Vietnam poses threats to Vietnamese sovereignty and fragile marine ecosystems, which will bear damage from sediments laced with heavy metals and chemicals from construction sites.

Thinking about water as an ambivalent and contradictory force enables more nuanced understandings of alliances and frictions that emerge in maritime spaces. U.S. imperialist projects in the Pacific Ocean have forced intimacies among communities in Southeast Asia, the Pacific Islands, and North America, which have all been unevenly exposed to militarized toxins. In his congressional testimony before the subcommittee on Asia, the Pacific, and the global environment, Eni F. H. Faleomavaega, a representative from American Samoa, draws an explicit connection between Agent Orange poisoning in Vietnam and U.S. nuclear testing in the Pacific, which has displaced Pacific Islanders from the Marshall Islands and exposed the Marshallese to radiation poisoning (Committee on Foreign Affairs). In his comparison, Faleomavaega views the Pacific Ocean as a fluid space that connects the toxic debris of war in Vietnam, the South Pacific, and the U.S. mainland where radioactive materials have spread. The material debris of toxic warfare, surfacing in bodies of water and flesh, become part of a shared ongoing condition of U.S. empire.

Water not only facilitates transit and connection across geographical boundaries but also serves as a conduit of memory and a witness to history, breaking down temporal boundaries that dismiss Vietnam's colonial past as no longer relevant in its pursuit of foreign investment capital and economic growth. Carrying sedimented waste from militarized Chinese-made islands, industrial runoff from Formosa's steel plant, and byproducts of Agent Orange incinerated in the Pacific, ocean currents collapse militarized and imperial histories into toxic matter that lingers in marine life. These layered histories and chemical dispersals evidence what Stoler calls "the uneven temporal sedimentations in which imperial formations leave their marks" (2). While the Vietnamese state maintains what artist Tiffany Chung describes as a "politically driven historical amnesia" that ignores the lasting psychic impact of war on Vietnamese people and diasporic refugees, the sea serves as a haunted reminder of these collective histories (Chung). For Vietnamese and other Southeast Asian refugees fleeing the aftermath of war, water symbolizes both a lost homeland and a site of death and decay in the perilous journey across the Pacific. For former North Vietnamese soldiers, whose traumatic memories do not fit into the state-enforced narrative of the war as an unequivocal victory against empire, water recalls the human and environmental consequences of these continuous struggles for self-determination. This chapter harnesses an eco-materialist analytic to turn toward these toxic waters in Vietnam to consider the uneven distributions of imperial debris in the afterlives of empire.

The Visceral Ecologies of *The Sorrow of War*

Based on the author's own experiences as a North Vietnamese soldier and one of the few survivors of his battalion, Ninh's novel *The Sorrow of War* merges militarized violence against human and animal bodies with environmental haunting in its visceral descriptions. Told in a nonlinear narrative that weaves scenes from the war with the protagonist Kien's reflections in the aftermath, the novel portrays water as essential in shaping memories of war and making the detritus of empire visible. In the opening scene, Kien travels to the water-soaked jungles of Vietnam's central highlands to recover the remains of missing-in-action soldiers. Here, Ninh uses the sounds of rain to depict natural elements as witnesses that amplify the haunting presence of ruined bodies and trapped souls:

> The old tarpaulin covering the truck is torn, full of holes, letting the water drip, drip, drip through onto the plastic sheets covering the remains of soldiers laid out in rows below Kien's hammock. . . . The stream moans, a desperate complaint mixing with distant faint jungle sounds, like an echo from

another world. The eerie sounds come from somewhere in a remote past, arriving softly like featherweight leaves falling on the grass of times long, long ago. (Ninh 4)

Dripping onto the tarp covering the soldier's remains and moaning "a desperate complaint," water is personified as grieving for those lives lost. At the same time, the stream serves as a material conduit for the lost soldiers to express their grief, as their bodies and histories decompose and dissolve into the natural environment. While the "plastic sheets" attempt to shelter bodies from the rain, the stream's "moans" of pain mixed with "faint jungle sounds" echo, recalling human and nonhuman histories that refuse separation. Disrupting a linear human-centered temporality, Ninh deploys the sonic here to describe an elongated history that incorporates minor natural events such as "leaves falling on the grass" in times that predate human existence. While those "eerie sounds" could be considered as nature's lament for those times of peace, they also echo the impossibility of return to a precolonial past, divorced from history.

In his attention to minor events, Ninh uses the sonic to juxtapose the spectacular violence of war against the everyday conditions of communities living with/in postwar ruins. In another scene, Ninh invokes the drip of water again in a reflection about the protagonist Kien's neighbors:

On summer evenings when there were power blackouts and it was too hot inside, everyone came to sit out in front, near the only water tap servicing the whole three-story building. The tap trickled, as drop by drop every story was told. Nothing remained secret. (Ninh 62–63)

Here, the water tap is the infrastructure that unifies the neighbors' stories, as they gather by a shared resource and gossip about each other. Though Kien as the narrator attempts to convince the reader that "nothing remained secret" and that the story of their daily lives was "not a war story," Ninh emphasizes that these daily experiences of melancholy, poverty, and loss are deeply tied to the war and its unacknowledged memories. Echoing the rain falling on broken bodies and environments of the battlefield, the sound of the water's trickle serves as a metaphor of the everyday lives that have been overlooked in historical accounts. As Ninh writes, "The most attractive, persistent echo of the past is the whisper of ordinary life, not the thunder of war, even though the sounds of ordinary life were washed away totally during the long storms of war" (63). Thus, these "whispers" of the everyday, characterized by the dripping of tap water, the snipping of a barber's scissors, and the neighbors' gossip, congeal into a powerful affective force that persistently recalls the effects of militarized ruination. In contrast to the thunder of war taking place in the "Pacific theater," the whispers of the mundane afterlives of war may be temporarily drowned out, yet they always reemerge as a collective amalgamation of voices and sounds.[8]

In his attention to the visceral waste(making) of militarized operations, Ninh also utilizes smell to evoke the enduring nature of rot as the material sign of war and its multispecies entanglements. He describes the shocking aftermath of a battle that Kien recalls:

> After the Americans withdrew, the rainy season came, flooding the jungle floor, turning the battlefield into a marsh whose surface water turned rust-colored from the blood. Bloated human corpses, floating alongside the bodies of incinerated jungle animals, mixed with branches and trunks cut down by artillery, all drifting in a stinking marsh. When the flood receded everything dried in the heat of the sun into thick mud and stinking rotting meat. (Ninh 5–6)

While Ninh describes the spectacle of violence on the battlefield, here he focuses more on the waste of its aftermath. The "flooding" of the jungle battlefield pushes the atrocities of war to the surface, where human corpses float next to "incinerated jungle animals" and broken tree branches. The flood is an agential force that exposes the connectivity of violence against human bodies and the environmental harm done to nonhuman animals and trees. Water not only renders war's debris visible but also erases the material distinctions between human, animal, and forest, as these distinct forms decompose into indistinguishable matter—"thick mud and stinking rotting meat." Here, Ninh uses rot to describe an active assemblage of human, animal, water, and soil that bears the weight of militarized empires. Rot, as an active substance with a history containing multiple lifeforms, is already haunted by the layered violences against human and nonhuman life. Although rot itself is not always visible, its vibrant, unruly qualities—stench, texture, and the ability to spread—bring into relief the underbelly of empire and industrial progress. For Ninh, the stench of rot uniquely functions to refuse the impulse to bury the past, as smell—intricately tied to memory—cannot be easily exorcised. Stench lingers and has a life of its own that is borne from the intimacies of human and nonhuman matter, unfolding in the ruins of U.S. imperialism.

Through these visceral descriptions of ecological elements, Ninh invokes haunting as a political strategy against state censorship that erases the traumatic, lingering effects of war and colonization. As Ninh's narrative contradicts the official historical record of a victorious war, his writing has been deemed politically controversial for drawing attention to human and environmental costs that have been forcibly forgotten. Vietnam's national ban on *The Sorrow of War* was not lifted until 2006, fifteen years after its original publication (Inani). Thus, Ninh alludes to the "eerie" echo of the jungle and stream as material signs of haunting, a process by which the past comes to bear on the present in ways that can no longer be ignored. Avery Gordon has described haunting as a particular way of drawing attention to the "dense site where history and subjectivity make social life" (8). While Gordon views the ghost as a "social figure" that recalls what is missing or deliberately forgotten in dominant social narratives, I suggest that ecological entanglements with ghosts also operate to highlight the enmeshment of human and nonhuman histories in these social formations. These intimacies emerging from spaces of destruction have the potential to challenge existing political structures that suppress forms of dissent. Manifesting in both sonic and olfactory registers, haunting in Ninh's narrative is the deliberately suppressed past echoing in and reshaping the material environment of the present. The accumulation of jungle sounds and dripping water also signifies haunting as a process of sedimentation, as the debris from past instances of violence builds up in scenes that are otherwise ordinary.

The Dead Sea: Aesthetics, Politics, and Ecological Entanglement

Ninh's visceral narrative reverberates against artist Tien Van Mieu's *The Dead Sea* series, which uses assemblage art to chronicle a contaminated sea laden with biological and chemical waste after the Formosa marine disaster. Like Ninh, Tien emphasizes the materiality of water in relation to other beings as he crafts an aesthetics that is attentive to the interconnected violence of imperialism and extractive capitalism. A prominent Vietnamese artist and activist, Tien attended the Hanoi Industrial College of Fine Arts and established himself in Hanoi and Saigon as a performance and assemblage artist before turning to experimental painting. His early performances of *The Art Space* in 1997 at the Temple of Literature, Vietnam's national university and monument to Confucian teachings, subtly critique the Vietnamese state's monopoly on cultural meaning and deference to Chinese culture. After the controversial performance, Tien moved to Ho Chi Minh City and produced several conceptual projects that address industrial waste, development, state surveillance, and communal art. Unlike the work of other underground artists in Vietnam, his projects have been documented and strategically made available to a global audience through his website and social media. Compared to Tien's earlier work, the *Dead Sea* series is a more overtly political project that critiques both the Taiwanese production of waste and Vietnamese state negligence. Suspended in dirty waters, Tien's haunting hybrid figures represent the material harm done to Vietnamese bodies and fish populations; yet, the image of bloodied figures drifting together also invokes the ghosts of war and displacement. While Tien's paintings do not explicitly reference war or empire, I pair his evocative images of ecological violence alongside Ninh's visceral descriptions to critically highlight the continuities of war and global capitalism. Focusing on their aesthetic parallels, I argue that both Ninh and Tien employ an aesthetics of "rot" to complicate boundaries between human and nonhuman life and to refuse political and historical amnesia. Akin to Ninh's novel, Tien's paintings are a form of political protest that recalls historical forms of imperial violence—such as centuries of Chinese imperialism and the American war in Vietnam—in a critical moment of resistance against Taiwanese sub-imperial capital and Vietnamese state repression.

In the first piece from *The Dead Sea*, Tien depicts a ghostly, skeletal figure with arms raised as it is submerged in blood. The figure's hollow face, open mouth, and outstretched hands convey both an abject position of surrender and a cry for help. Behind him, the white corpse of a fish floats in a pool of blood that spreads across the canvas. Though formally simplistic with bold lines and flattened shapes that could be read as crude, the painting deliberately adopts the aesthetics of anti-Formosa protestors who held up handmade signs at organized demonstrations depicting polluted waters and dead fish. Often unsophisticated and ideologically driven, protest art is created in response to a state of emergency and assembled quickly with available materials, slogans, and provocative images. With its thick outlines and contrasting colors, this piece clearly articulates a political imperative to challenge the conditions of suffering for Vietnamese divers and marine life. Inscribed on the straw hat dangling from the figure's arm, the words "I love Vietnam" read like a slogan proclaiming patriotic allegiance, alluding to the affective ties of nationhood. The drowning figure memorializes the divers that were poisoned

Fig. 6.1. Image of *The Dead Sea II*, a multimedia painting created with acrylic and other materials on canvas. Artwork by Nguyễn Văn Tiến, 2017. Reproduction permission courtesy of Nguyễn Văn Tiến.

at sea, neglected by the state and Formosa as they become entwined with the corpse of the fish. Although Tien's work never explicitly criticizes the Vietnamese government, its evocative content alludes to the conditions of neglect and oppression and gestures to the fate of environmental organizers and journalists who were recently incarcerated for their activism. Even as Tien's work proclaims patriotism, the crooked slogan on the hat points out the diver's precarious relationship to a nation that sacrifices its working class and rural populations for industrial development and profit.

The Dead Sea also senses the parallels between the loss of human life and the destruction of marine life in its critique of the nation-state's complicity in global capitalism. Featuring human bodies merging underwater with the ghostly shapes of fish, Tien's paintings expose the interconnected damage done to Vietnamese bodies and bodies of water, rendered as tainted with blood and rust. Through his use of vivid red brushstrokes that highlight the iridescent fish and the bleeding body dissolving into each other, Tien draws a direct relation between the suffering of Vietnamese people and the poisoning of the fish. While the human figure is foregrounded and evokes sympathy, the fish with its smooth white torso is more defined and dimensional as it looms behind the figure; it appears to be bleeding into the water. Pooling from the fish's form, the red water stains almost half the canvas, signaling a destructive force that cannot be contained within national boundaries. The red water abruptly merges into a large gash near the human figure's torso, emphasizing an open wound that resembles a mouth with a tongue or the gaping lips of dying fish. Although red alludes to blood, Tien's aesthetic choice also gestures to the phenomenon of algal bloom known as "red tide," which Formosa offi-cials and the Vietnamese government have cited as the "natural" cause for the mass deaths of both farmed and wild fish. While Formosa in collusion with the Vietnamese state has dismissed waste from the steel mill as nontoxic, Tien poses a political intervention that redirects the viewer to the "slow vio-lence" of contaminated waters and its effects on humans and fish (Nixon).

Contrasted with the smooth lines and flattened forms of *The Dead Sea 1*, Tien's *Fisherman and the Dead Sea* is multilayered and chaotic. While the first painting is one-dimensional, *Fisherman and the Dead Sea* is an assem-blage of watercolor abstractions, semantic symbols, and everyday objects. In the foreground, a fisherman with a straw hat looms in an almost blacked-out shadow in front of protest signs, a restricted symbol, and drawings of fish. These objects come into focus against a backdrop of a turbulent sea, framed by a large white- and rust-colored border. Tien mixes pigments and water on the surface of the canvas to create a diluted texture that is dependent on the process of water traveling across the surface and evaporating. This experi-mental choice highlights water's material qualities and movement as it shifts and pools on the canvas, becoming more viscous as different pigments are added. Fluid and unruly, water on Tien's canvas demonstrates a liveliness of its own that operates outside of the artist's control. Its fluidity symbolizes an agential force that becomes entangled with man-made waste but cannot be completely contained. The metal strainer attached to the top of the canvas faces down toward the "dirty" water, its mesh potentially referencing the fish-ing nets that Vietnamese fishermen used. In contrast to the chaotic sea, the metal strainer is a man-made object that resembles steel and represents the transnational steel industry's impact on everyday life. Tien traces the strainer

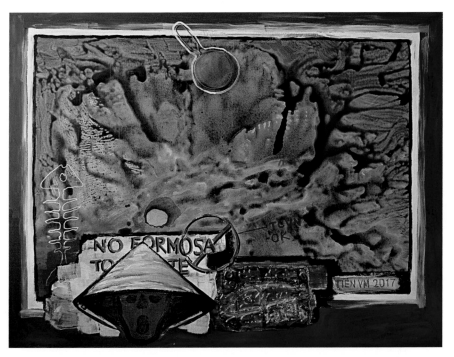

Fig. 6.2. Image of the painting *Fisherman and the Dead Sea*, created with acrylic and other materials on canvas. Artwork by Nguyễn Văn Tiến, 2017. Reproduction permission courtesy of Nguyễn Văn Tiến.

with the same white outline that he uses to render the bones of the fish float-ing on the left side and the frame containing the ocean. The repetition of the rough white outline memorializes a polluted ocean, dead fish, and the loss of livelihoods symbolized by the metal strainer.

Applying red on top of wet blue paint, Tien mixes the colors in the cen-ter of the canvas to create a brownish texture that spreads with the flow of the water to cover most of the canvas. The bold and cacophonic textures in the visualized water replicate the porous and uneven surfaces of rust, which forms when iron corrodes after exposure to water and oxygen. Rust, the deterioration and transformation of inorganic matter, combines with and becomes indistinguishable from the rot of fish carcasses and human bodies. Tien's layering of rust and rot attests to the entanglement of nature and indus-trialization, as the distinctions between organic and inorganic matter break down. Rust disrupts the promise of the industrial economic zone as a sleek model of modernity and progress built on constant extraction and regeneration; instead, its grit, undesirability, and corrosion signal alternative understandings of industrial capitalism as a destructive force. At the same time, rust is a material marker of a different temporality that operates alongside the temporalities of fast capitalism. As the heavy metals of Formosa's factory waste take on new forms in the water, they become submerged and temporarily hidden from view. By drawing attention to the rust that forms under the surface, Tien forces the viewer to acknowledge the underbelly of capitalist progress, which is marked by processes of slow ruination and deterioration. Dwelling in the messiness of rust, Tien also reveals corrosion and decomposition as transformative processes that fundamentally alter the relationship between man-made materials and the environment. The rust spreading out from the center of the canvas coalesces to form a circular shape that appears like the eye of a fish, with a ghostly body that dissolves into the bold renderings of protest signs in the foreground. His use of rust as an aesthetic directly condemns the Taiwanese steel industry as the perpetrator of environmental harm but also opens up possibilities for collective resistance and resilience shown in the protest slogans and signs gathering in front of the frame.

Tien offers an aesthetics of ecological relationality that is in dialogue with contemporary Vietnamese environmental protests, which are often represented in his artwork. The stark lines framing the fisherman and the protest signs in the foreground separate them clearly from the chaotic sea behind them, creating an assemblage effect where the objects in the foreground appear pasted. The partially obscured protest sign is overlaid on top of a fish skeleton and jagged brushstrokes that suggest a plethora of signs held up by protesters. The rough sketch of a fish outline labeled with the English word "fish" resembles a child's drawing, referencing the children who became involved in making their own signs and marching with their parents. Alluding to the activist signs that use drawings and photos of fish coupled with English and Mandarin slogans to mobilize a transnational base to protect the sea, Tien uses English to signal a transnational and trans-species connection among protestors and fish affected by Formosa. The use of multiple textures, frames, and everyday objects in Tien's assemblage art represents the complex political forces and multiple actors involved in staging ecological destruction. The overlapping abstractions of fish, protest slogans, quality control acronyms, and ghostly human figures signal an emerging multispecies alliance among fishermen and marine life who exist within states of ruin, as well as other Vietnamese people coming into political consciousness through their roles as witnesses of ecocide.

In the long colonial history of Southeast Asia, tracing imperial debris offers tools to identify continuities and ruptures from the past, reflecting the structures of empire as simultaneously enduring and shifting. Contextualizing the Formosa marine disaster within longer legacies of U.S. imperialism and East Asian sub-imperialism in Vietnam, I suggest that these two seemingly disparate moments of war and contamination are connected by material legacies and multispecies histories. Following debris turns our attention to not only disasters on a massive scale but also how they fit into prolonged states of violence and dispossession. What Stoler calls the "psychic and material spaces" of debris elucidate the dialectical relationship between the material effects of toxic waste, global warming, and extractive capitalism and the affective dimensions of loss, kinship, and resilience (2).

Ninh's *The Sorrow of War* and Tien's artistic responses to the Formosa marine disaster both articulate an aesthetics of ruin that exposes the material effects of militarism and industrialization on human and nonhuman bodies. While Ninh harnesses the visceral sensations of sound and smell to explore multispecies entanglements in the aftermath of the Vietnam War, Tien uses texture and assemblage art to stage a political reorientation of the human and environmental stakes of industrialization and sub-imperial development. Attending to minor ecological histories and the everyday conditions of those living with war's material and psychic legacies, Ninh reveals that these seemingly insignificant engagements have the greatest potential to amplify the legacies of empire. Ninh's and Tien's attention to the materiality of rot and water's lively properties reveals empire's waste(making) as deliberate and generative.

As war and empire attempt to drown both human and nonhuman life, the ocean and the tide render their detritus visible and vibrant. Turning to toxic entanglements in the sea allows us to see the Pacific Ocean not as a space of conquest or extraction but as a home to the ghosts of war and of those who have been erased from national memory but resurface in vengeance. As toxic waste sediments into waterscapes and the bodies of humans and fish, the material composition of its surrounding environment is transformed. When the currents wash up marine debris and decay onto the shore, ruin resurfaces where it is not expected, coheres after it has been suppressed by the logics of capitalist development. Submerged underwater and pushed onto shore, rotting fish carcasses become a material sign of the rot of colonial capitalism;

they enable Vietnamese activists to align ecological violence with imperial and state violence against Vietnamese people. In their attention to human entanglements with nonhuman life, artists and activists provide an alternative perspective that views the ocean as a space of sustenance rather than a dumping ground.

Notes

Acknowledgments: This chapter is indebted to the powerful work of Nguyễn Văn Tiến, who graciously granted permission to reprint his artwork on the Formosa disaster here. I would also like to thank my coeditors, Jeffrey Santa Ana, Rina Garcia Chua, and Xiaojing Zhou, for their invaluable feedback on this chapter. All flaws are my own.

1. Formosa Ha Tinh Steel Corporation is a subsidiary of the Taiwanese conglomerate Formosa Plastics Group, which began as Formosa Plastics Corporation.

2. Known to the art world as Tien Van Mieu, Tien also goes by Nguyễn Văn Tiến.

3. Taiwan has a complex history of colonization, being subordinated by Holland in the Ming Dynasty and Japan in the early twentieth century. See Chen, chap. 1.

4. Taiwan and specifically Formosa Plastics have a history of environmental violations and toxic dumping in Cambodia and Malaysia and in the United States.

5. The United States spilled 72 million liters of Agent Orange throughout Vietnam during the war, with the bulk of the chemicals applied between 1966 and 1969. See Haond et al.

6. Vietnam established an exclusive economic zone along its coast in 1977, delineating 200 nautical miles from the baseline as under Vietnamese jurisdiction. While the creation of special economic zones in coastal regions and port cities encourages foreign direct investment, exclusive economic zones establish exclusive fishing rights to protect Vietnam's maritime resources.

7. The U.S. military has established and maintained military bases on Guam, Okinawa, and Hawai'i, cementing a structure of land acquisition and Indigenous dispossession that Juliet Nebolon has termed "settler militarism."

8. For more on the political construction of the Pacific Theater during World War II as a space for competing imperial powers, see Camacho and Shigetmatsu.

Works Cited

Camacho, Keith, and Setsu Shigetmatsu. *Militarized Currents: Toward a Decolonized Future in Asia and the Pacific.* U of Minnesota P, 2010.

Chen, Kuan-Hsing. *Asia as Method: Toward Deimperialization.* Duke UP, 2010.

Chung, Tiffany. "Interview." *Japan Foundation Asia Center.* 16 Feb. 2017, https://jfac.jp/en/culture/features/asiahundreds-tiffany-chung/4/. Accessed 1 Feb. 2019.

Committee on Foreign Affairs, U.S. House of Representatives. "Agent Orange: What Efforts Are Being Made to Address the Continued Impact of Dioxin in Vietnam?" 4 June 2009. https://www.govinfo.gov/content/pkg/CHRG-111hhrg50112/html/CHRG-111hhrg50112.htm

Frame, Mariko Lin. "The Neoliberalization of (African) Nature as the Current Phase of Ecological Imperialism." *Capitalism Nature Socialism*, vol. 27, no. 1, Jan. 2016, 1–19.

Gordon, Avery. *Ghostly Matters: Haunting and the Sociological Imagination.* U of Minnesota P, 1997.

Ha, Viet, and Brooks Boliek. "Algae and Toxins, Not Steel Mill Waste, Blamed for Vietnamese Fish Kill." *Radio Free Asia*, 27 Apr. 2016, https://www.rfa.org/english/news/vietnam/algae-and-toxins-04272016160930.html. Accessed 15 Feb. 2019.

Haond, Sophie Arnaud, et al. "Genetic Recolonization of Mangrove: Genetic Diversity Still Increasing in the Mekong Delta 30 years after Agent Orange." *Marine Ecology Progress Series*, vol. 390, 2009, 129–35.

Inani, Rohit. "The Long Silence of Bao Ninh." *Diacritics*, 14 Dec. 2018, http://diacritics.org/2018/12/the-long-silence-of-bao-ninh/. Accessed 1 Feb. 2019.

lê, thi diem thúy. *The Gangster We Are All Looking for.* Knopf, 2003.

McDevitt, Michael A., M. Taylor Fravel, and Lewis M. Stern. "The Long Littoral Project: South China Sea. A Maritime Perspective on Indo-Pacific Security." Center for Naval Analysis, March 2013, https://www.cna.org/research/long-littoral. Accessed 10 Apr. 2018.

Nebolon, Juliet. "'Life Given Straight from the Heart': Settler Militarism, Biopolitics, and Public Health in Hawai'i during World War II." *American Quarterly*, vol. 69, no. 1, 2017, 23–45.

Ninh, Bảo. *The Sorrow of War: A Novel of North Vietnam.* Translated by Frank Palmos. Pantheon Books, 1995.

Reuters Staff. "Vietnam Media Ties Massive Fish Kill to Formosa Plastics Unit." *Reuters*, 27 Apr. 2016, https://www.reuters.com/article/vietnam-formosa-plastics-environment/vietnam-media-ties-massive-fish-kill-to-formosa-plastics-steel-unit-idUSL-3N17U2KH. Accessed 30 Mar. 2018.

Stoler, Ann Laura. *Imperial Debris: On Ruins and Ruination.* Duke UP, 2013.

Tien, Van Mieu. *The Dead Sea.* 2017. http://tienvanmieu.com/en/gallery/

Tran, Barbara, Monique T. D. Truong, and Khoi Truong Luu, editors. *Watermark: Vietnamese American Poetry and Prose.* Asian American Writers' Workshop, 1998.

Trang, Doan. "Timeline: The Formosa Environmental Disaster." *The Vietnamese*, 8 Nov. 2017, https://www.thevietnamese.org/2017/11/timeline-the-formosa-environmental-disaster/. Accessed 30 Mar. 2018.

Watkins, Derek. "What China Has Been Building in the South China Sea." *New York Times*, 31 July 2015. https://www.nytimes.com/interactive/2015/07/30/world/asia/what-china-has-been-building-in-the-south-china-sea.html

Zierler, David. *The Invention of Ecocide: Agent Orange, Vietnam, and the Scientists Who Changed the Way We Think About the Environment.* U of Georgia P, 2011.

7

Haunted by Empires

Micronesian Ecopoetry against Colonial Ruination

Zhou Xiaojing

On the Runit Island of the Enewetak Atoll, west of the Marshall Islands, half-way between Australia and Hawaii, lies the Runit Dome, aka "The Tomb" by local Marshallese. It is an 18-inch thick dome of concrete at sea level, encapsulating an estimated 85,000 cubic meters of radioactive waste, including plutonium-239, with a half-life of 24,000 years (Willacy). These highly contaminated materials were debris left by 43 U.S. nuclear weapon detonations on the Enewetak Atoll between 1946 and 1958. According to Mark Willacy of the Australian Broadcasting Corporation, "Four of Enewetak's 40 islands were completely vaporised by the tests, with one thermonuclear blast leaving a two-kilometre-wide crater where an island had been just moments before." As the photograph in figure 7.1 illustrates, a U.S. atomic detonation left a crater, where an islet used to be. In figure 7.2, the photograph of the dome shows how close it is to the sea.

Entombed in a crater left behind by one of the nuclear blasts, the waste gathered by about four thousand U.S. servicemen over a three- to four-year period (1977–1980/81) continues to poison the soil, water, and lives of the area (Wernick). With the sea level rising due to climate change, the contamination is on the verge of spreading far beyond the Enewetak Atoll. A report commissioned by the U.S. Department of Energy in 2013 reveals that the radioactive materials were leeching out, threatening the already tenuous existence of Enewetak locals (Willacy). Water is "penetrating the underside of the dome," whose pit was not lined with concrete as it should have been because of cost considerations, and typhoons with increased ferocity threaten to breach the dome (Wernick). The result would be catastrophic contamination of "the whole Pacific," says Alson Kelen, a Marshall Islands climate change activist (qtd. in Willacy). For Kelen, the Runit Dome is "the connection between the nuclear age and the climate change age." Kelen's remarks foreground the magnitude of ongoing damage of imperial militarism in the Marshall Islands and beyond. For the children of Enewetak, the dome is "a poison" in their island. Christina Aningi, the head teacher of Enewetak's only school, says, "This is like a graveyard for us, waiting for it to happen" (qtd. in Willacy). Poisoned by nuclear pollution since 1946, the Marshallese contaminated bodies, like their mutilated islands, bear witness to the persistent violence of U.S. imperial militarism.

The Runit Dome and the ghostly presence of the vaporized islets embody what Ann Laura Stoler calls colonial and imperial "ruination"—"an active, ongoing process that allocates imperial debris differently," with detrimental impact on racially marked locations ("'The Rot Remains'" 7). Stoler's emphasis on "ruination" by "imperial debris" as "an active, ongoing process" calls critical attention to "what people are 'left with': to what remains, to the aftershocks of empire, to the material and social afterlife of structures, sensibilities, and things" ("Imperial Debris" 194). Even though the United States stopped nuclear testing in the Pacific Islands more than half a century ago, the impact of 67 detonations in the Marshall Islands continues to damage the Marshallese and the ecosystems of the atolls and other Micronesian countries such as Guåhan (Guam).[1] Situated approximately 1,200 miles directly west of the Marshall Islands, Guam and its inhabitants have been affected by the fallout and decontamination runoffs. According to the *Blue Ribbon Panel Committee Action Report on Radioactive Contamination in Guam between 1946–1958*, authored by Charles L. S. Briscoe, U.S. Navy ships "present during the nuclear testing were decontaminated in Guam harbors" and the acidic detergents and the runoff from testing operations went directly into the "local fishing and reef environments" (2). The destructive long half-life of isotopes hidden in the environments and people's bodies is part of the ongoing socioecological ruination of colonialism, causing "different types of genetic damage to biological organisms, the longer the debris being suspended in the environment of Guam, the more damage the island would sustain" (2). Yet, "reports from the Navy indicated that they had full knowledge and did not warn or help the local population," whom they were supposed to protect (3). Such disregard of the well-being of Guam and its local population is inseparable from the island's colonized status. As Craig Santos Perez, a Chamorro poet from Guam, notes, "Guam is currently on the United Nations' lists of non-self-governing territories and has been one of the longest, continuously colonized places in the world" ("A Testimony" 155).

Fig. 7.1. The dome on Runit Island with a crater left behind by another nuclear test. Photograph by Greg Nelson, 2017, in "A Poison in Our Island" by Mark Willacy. Reproduction permission courtesy of Mark Willacy.

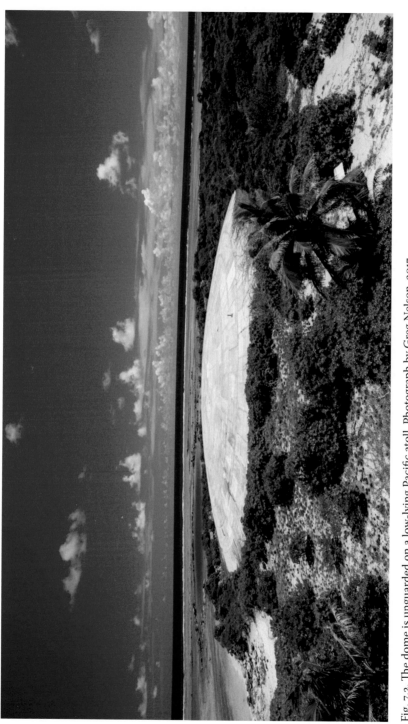

Fig. 7.2. The dome is unguarded on a low-lying Pacific atoll. Photograph by Greg Nelson, 2017, in "A Poison in Our Island" by Mark Willacy. Reproduction permission courtesy of Mark Willacy.

Colonized by Spain, Japan, and the United States, Guåhan and its Indigenous population have suffered more than three centuries of colonial conquests and subsequent socio-ecological devastation. The assault on the island's environment is exacerbated by the U.S. military buildup on the island. According to historian Robert Rogers, when the United States took over Guam from Spain in 1989 as part of its $20-million offer to Spain for the cession of the Philippines and Guam, it established a "[c]olonial military government" as did Spain (107, 101). President William McKinley issued Executive Order 108-A on December 23, 1898, placing Guam "under the control of the Department of Navy." Appointed by Secretary of the Navy John Davis Long, Captain Richard Phillips Leary became "the first U.S. naval governor of Guam" (108). When the U.S. reclaimed Guam from Japan in 1944, it "reestablish[ed] the navy's authority on Guam" through a proclamation by Admiral Chester W. Nimitz in the style "of the Spanish kings, and of Captain Richard Leary back in 1899 and of General [Tomitaro] Horii in 1941" (181–82). Nimitz asserted "All powers of government and jurisdiction in Guam and adjacent waters, and over the inhabitants thereof, and final administrative responsibility . . . as Admiral, United States Navy, commanding the forces of occupation and as Military Governor" (182). Aiming to expand its bases on the island of Guam, the U.S. military acquired "huge tracts of land, particularly around the harbors and at the sites of the planned airfields" by simply confiscating "whatever land was needed" and overlooking Indigenous people's ownership and delaying "eminent domain procedures" (182).

The expanded U.S. military operations in Guåhan led to the spread of toxic erosion in the ecosystems of the island. In her article "Rethinking 'Collateral Damage' in the Vietnam War: The *Other* Others in the Circuits of U.S. Empire," Yến Lê Espiritu notes that by 1956 the 20,000-acre U.S. Andersen Air Force Base on the island of Guåhan had become Strategic Air Command's chief base in the Pacific, which played "a 'legendary' role in the Vietnam War, launching devastating bombing missions over North and South Vietnam for close to a decade" (136). Guåhan was also a site for the storage of defoliants, including Agent Orange, Agent Purple, and Agent Blue, used in the Vietnam War. The Andersen Air Force Base in Guam remains a source of toxic contamination, its waste disposal sites leaching chemicals into the soil and aquifer. Moreover, recent U.S. military buildup in Guam, as depicted in Perez's poems, has resulted in further degradation of both the marine and the terrestrial ecosystems of the region, as well as Chamorros' lives, cultures, and environments.

Like the Marshall Islands, Guam is a converging site of multiple vectors of "the more protracted imperial processes that saturate the subsoil of people's lives and persist, sometimes subjacently, over a longer durée" (Stoler, "'The Rot Remains'" 5). The interconnections among these two Micronesian countries, and between the island countries and their colonizers, reveal "the relationship between colonial pasts and colonial presents, the residues that abide and are revitalized" (5). Drawing on Stoler's concept of imperial debris, I explore the ways in which two Micronesian poets, Kathy Jetñil-Kijiner and Craig Santos Perez, foreground "how empire's ruins contour and carve through the psychic and material space in which people live and what compounded layers of imperial debris do to them" (2).

I argue, moreover, that the ecopoetry of Jetñil-Kijiner and Perez exposes more than prolonged social and environmental destruction by imperial conquest. In confronting the ongoing, structural colonial ruination, Jetñil-Kijiner's and Perez's respective ecopoems enact the politics of mourning irrecoverable loss as protest against ecological, environmental injustice and as a refusal of the violent erasure and dispossession of Micronesian ancestral lands, histories, cultures, and knowledge. In fact, mourning in their poems entails a decolonial process of recuperating Indigenous identities and ways of knowing. This process disrupts colonial subjugation and "unknowing" through an anti-anthropocentric ecopoetics from Indigenous perspectives, performing what critic Nelson Maldonado-Torres calls "epistemic decolonization," which reclaims Indigenous cultures and knowledge (3).[2] The thematic concerns and poetic strategies of the two poets reveal complex entanglements of past and present empires beyond what Espiritu has rightly identified as "a constellation of U.S. former and current colonial territories in the Asia-Pacific region" and "the collateral damage produced by the Vietnam War" (134). They situate U.S. colonialism in the Pacific Island countries in longer colonial histories and in a larger constellation of colonial territories.

Kathy Jetñil-Kijiner: Trans-Corporeal Ecopoetics of Mourning and Recuperation

Evoking the poisoned, damaged, and defiled land of the Marshall Islands, Jetñil-Kijiner portrays the Indigenous women's body as a site bearing witness to colonial, imperial violence and a site for articulating Indigenous protest and resistance. Her poems enact what David Eng and David Kazanjian have termed "the politics of mourning." In their introduction to *Loss: The Politics of Mourning*, Eng and Kazanjian argue that the "politics of mourning might be described as that creative process mediating a hopeful or hopeless relationship between loss and history" (2). Mourning as a refusal to forget, a refusal of closure, is a continual engagement with the ongoing colonial and imperial ruination in the Marshall Islands. At the same time, mourning in Jetñil-Kijiner's poems is a complex process of exposure, critique, protest, and emotional, psychological recuperation of the damaged land, body, family, and culture.

The prose poem "Monster," which Jetñil-Kijiner wrote after her visit to the Runit Dome, is a salient example of how she enacts the politics of mourning through innovative incorporation of an Indigenous folktale to capture the lingering violence of imperialism that haunts the Marshallese physically and psychologically. She reinterprets the Marshallese folktales about the *mejenkwaad*—a female wandering demon, the undead spirit of a woman who died in childbirth or who has eaten her own baby—to tell a different story. By reimagining and rearticulating this demon in her poem, Jetñil-Kijiner links the baby-eating woman monster to mothers who had abnormal births resulting from radiation contamination by the U.S. nuclear weapon tests. She re-represents the *mejenkwaad* from the perspectives of Marshallese women who were nuclear survivors, and whose testimonies were collected by anthropologist Glenn Alcalay in an unpublished field report, "The Sociocultural Impact of Nuclear Weapons Tests in the Marshall Islands." Jetñil-Kijiner read this report while doing research for her poem "Monster." She incorporates various testimonies from Alcalay's report and Bella Compoj's testimony at the UN in her poem, using one statement in particular as the refrain to emphasize the horror of nuclear contamination that Marshallese women have experienced: *"Nerik gave birth to something resembling the eggs of a sea turtle and Flora gave birth to something like intestines."*[3] These nightmare births "Show the world what happens. When the sun explodes inside you" ("Monster").

As the poem develops, the ruination of U.S. imperial violence hidden in Marshallese women's bodies becomes evident as the source of monstrosity:

these women who bore unholy things—created from exploding spit and ugly things.

And how these women buried their nightmares. Beneath a coconut tree. Pretended it never happened. Sinister. Hideous. Monster. More jellyfish than child. ("Monster")

Jetñil-Kijiner connects the Marshallese mothers and their nightmares to the dreaded *mejenkwaad*, thus simultaneously re-representing the female monster and calling into question the monstrosity associated with women and gendered suffering as a naturalized female attribute:

> Were the women who gave birth to nightmares considered monsters? Were they driven mad by these unholy things that came from their bodies? Were they sick with the feeling of horror that perhaps there was something

> wrong. With them. ("Monster")

She then recuperates both the woman monster and the Marshallese women as grieving mothers, who turned "monster from agony" and out of love for the newborn struggling for breath in pain swallows her nightmare baby to "bring the child peace" by bringing it into its "first home" inside her body ("Monster"). In so doing, she enacts the politics of mourning that "offers a capaciousness of meaning in relation to losses encompassing the individual and the collective, the spiritual and the material, the psychic and the social, the aesthetic and the political" (Eng and Kazanjian 3). Through mourning unrecoverable losses in her prose poem "Monster," Jetñil-Kijiner raises the question: "How many stories of nuclear war are hidden in our bodies?" ("Monster").

Engaging with history and imbued with Indigenous culture, many of Jetñil-Kijiner's poems are characteristic of what might be called "trans-corporeality" that is shaped by Marshallese cultural perspectives, which highlight the impact of colonialism and U.S. nuclear tests. Stacy Alaimo, in her book *Bodily Natures: Science, Environment, and the Material Self*, theorizes the epistemological, ethical, and political aspects of "trans-corporeality," which highlights "the interconnections, interchanges, and transits between human bodies and nonhuman natures" (2). With an emphasis on the "movement across bodies, trans-corporeality . . . acknowledges the often unpredictable and unwanted actions of human bodies, nonhuman creatures, ecological systems, chemical agents, and other actors" (2). Emphasis on "the material interconnection of human corporeality with the more-than-human world" and recognition of "material agency," Alaimo adds, can necessitate "more capacious epistemologies" that allow "us to forge ethical and political positions that can contend with numerous late twentieth- and early twenty-first-century realities in which 'human' and 'environment' can by no means be considered as separate" (2). This concept of the trans-corporeality helps deepen our understanding of nuclear contamination and subsequence genetic mutations in Marshallese women's bodies and the ethical, political implications of Indigenous people's storied land and body.

Trans-corporeality in Jetñil-Kijiner's poems, however, has similar, yet broader, meanings and implications, including kinship between humans and nonhumans. It can be traced to Micronesian legends, and their epistemological, ethnical, and political implications allow Jetñil-Kijiner to confront and counter colonial production of knowledge and subject. She reinvents and revitalizes Marshallese folktales as resistance to Eurocentric colonial knowledge and as protest against environmental racism, through mourning multi-layered loss—the loss of lives, habitats, islands, and Indigenous languages and cultures. In Marshallese legends, human bodies interface and intertwine with nonhuman bodies in the creation of the Micronesian world, cultures, foodways, and medicine. The trans-corporeality in these legends counters settler colonialists' possessive relationship with "nature." In Micronesian legends, trans-corporeality is ubiquitous, showing an ecological ethics, episteme, and affect underlying Micronesians' kinship, identities, cultures, and ways of relating to the more-than-human world. For example, in "The Beginning of This World" as told by Kuwjleen Jelibōr Jam, a woman gives birth to a ripe coconut and names her child "Ḷakaṃ." She "treasured it highly" and plants it after three days of careful consideration. From this coconut came coconut trees, which provided people with food and materials for making baskets, fires, sennit and, eventually, canoes, houses, and medicine. Later, around the flourishing Ḷakaṃ many other kinds of vegetation appeared, including breadfruit and pandanus, among other plants and fruit trees (Tobin 11–16). Trans-corporeality also characterizes the tale about the origin of the banana plant on Arṇo Atoll, where the first banana plant grew from the spot where a magician was buried on Ḷōñar Island (81–82). Underlying these stories about the beginnings of the islands and lives are inseparable interconnections and interdependence of all things and all lives. This ecological web underscores the extent of wreckage on the Marshall Islands by U.S. nuclear weapon tests.

The fact that the Republic of the Marshall Islands became the nuclear testing ground of the United States reveals the "tenacious qualities of colonial effects"—their "protracted temporalities" in the formation of imperialism (Stoler, *Duress* 7). After centuries of successive colonial rule by Spain, Germany, and Japan, the Marshall Islands became part of the "Trust Territory of the Pacific Islands," pursuant to UN Security Council Resolution 21 in

1947, and the United States was designated as the Administering Authority, entrusted "to protect the land, resources, and health of Micronesia's inhabitants" (Georgescu 4). But, rendered a virtual colony of the United States, the Marshall Islands became its "proving ground" for atomic weapon tests. "From 1946 to 1958, the US detonated sixty-seven atomic and thermonuclear bombs in the Marshall Islands," whose total explosive yield "was equivalent to more than seven thousand Hiroshima bombs" (Johnston 140, 144). In 1956, the United States Atomic Energy Commission regarded the Marshall Islands as "by far the most contaminated place in the world" (Cooke 168).

The history of the Marshall Islands and the contamination of the Marshallese land, water, and bodies demonstrate the ways in which colonial ruination continues in our times through tangible and invisible forms. As a colonized and racialized Other, the Marshallese victims of the U.S. nuclear weapon tests continue to be deprived of their basic human rights. They became subjects of laboratory studies without being informed of the effects of contamination on their bodies and the environment. According to a Marshallese nuclear survivor, Lijon Eknilang, some Marshallese were used as the "control group," who were sent to the contaminated Rongelap Atoll to test the effect of radiation (qtd. in Johnston 141). The fallout poisoned the entire food chain of the islands and damaged the Marshallese's health for generations. Eknilang explained, "Some of our food crops, such as arrowroot, completely disappeared. Makmok, or tapioca plants, stopped bearing fruit. What we did eat gave us blisters on our lips and in our mouths and we suffered terrible stomach problems and nausea. Some of the fish we caught caused the same problems" (141). While Marshallese suffer from a variety of cancers, Marshallese women "suffer silently and differently" from "many reproductive cancers and abnormal births." Because conventional Marshallese cultural beliefs suggest that "reproductive abnormalities are a sign that women have been unfaithful to their husbands," Eknilang notes, "many of my friends keep quiet about the strange births they had. In privacy, they give birth, not to children . . . but to things we could only describe as 'octopuses,' 'apples,' 'turtles,' and other things" (142–43). Even when children were born normal, some died of leukemia before reaching their teens.

Jetñil-Kijiner's poems protest against Micronesians' raced and gendered physical, psychological damage by U.S. nuclear tests and reclaim Marshallese women's bodies, subjectivities, and important roles in Micronesian society by retelling Indigenous stories and mourning irrecoverable losses. The poems in the opening section of her collection *Iep Jāltok: Poems from a Marshallese Daughter* recuperate the earthbound, seafaring, life-giving, and creative female figure of Micronesian legends. This recuperation, however, entails confronting the impact of colonialism on the Indigenous culture, as depicted in the prose poem "Liwātuonmour." Birthed "by fire and sea," Liwātuonmour and her sister Lidepdepju were stones who gave birth to the clans and the chiefly lineage, the Irooj. These two sacred stone sisters were also mothers of Indigenous Marshallese cultures. Through poetic language and images in sections 6 and 7 of her prose poem, which reimagines and retells this legend, Jetñil-Kijiner captures the vitality and magic of matter and its intertwining relationship with Marshallese people, society, and culture. Her employment of the prose poem form and numbers for the narrative sequence enact Marshallese storytelling that enhances the content of the poem and its decolonial agency: "**6**. Mothers who shaped the sounds of midday and dusk. **7**. They found the words inside their blood inside their pulse inside the stars and the waves" (*Iep Jāltok* 8). Jetñil-Kijiner situates her retelling of the legend in a colonial context that includes a European missionary, Dr. Rife, to whom the two sisters "were nothing more. Than rocks. Nothing more. Than stone" (8). She emphasizes in her essay "Luerkoklik" that Rife throws Liwātuonmour into the ocean in an attempt to "stamp out 'pagan' practices."

The missionary's arrogant anthropocentric view and action lead to the "revenge" of the bereaved sister stone, which demonstrates the agency of apparently inert material. The outraged lonely Lidepdepju "is destroying us all" and "our fleet of canoes" (*Iep Jāltok* 8). The trans-corporeality of this Marshallese origin story illustrates Micronesians' ecological view that recognizes and respects the agency of matter. The articulated kinship between humans and stones counters colonialist possessive domination over nature, which is reduced to profitable resources. As Jetñil-Kijiner says, the legend tells the "beginning of our clans. How we came from stone, from earth." It also reminds us that "Land has power to destroy us. It has eyes. It remembers" ("Luerkoklik"). Countering the missionary's anthropocentric view and action, she performs a ritual of reverent offering to the remaining sister stone in her poem, "Lidepdepju." The speaker takes the reader to the Aur Island, where Lidepdepju can be seen in the form of a pile of rocks, "to pay tribute, to ask" for her guidance and strength (*Iep Jāltok* 9).

But the strength of the female figure entangled with the sea, the earth, and the Marshallese people and culture is severely undermined by the socio-ecological devastation resulting from the lingering impact of colonialism and

U.S. nuclear weapon tests. Jetñil-Kijiner evokes past European missionaries' attempts to eliminate Indigenous beliefs and practices on the Marshall Islands in her critique of the U.S. military's coercion of the Marshallese, in the name of God, to allow nuclear tests on their islands. In her poem "History Project," she quotes a U.S. military officer's words—*"for the good of mankind"* and *"God will thank you"*—in addressing a crowd of Marshallese, who were persuaded to "hand over our islands / let them blast / radioactive energy / into our sleepy coconut trees / . . . / our busy fishes that spark like new sun / into our coral reefs" (*Iep Jāltok* 21). These lines expose how settler colonial projects are "predicated on the very systems that propagate and maintain the dispossession of indigenous peoples for the common good of the world," as Indigenous studies scholar Jodi Byrd has noted (xix).

In her other poems, Jetñil-Kijiner further relates prolonged U.S. nuclear destruction in the Marshall Islands to U.S. imperial expansion to the Pacific. In "Fishbone Hair," which is about her six-year-old niece Bianca, who died of leukemia at age eight, Jetñil-Kijiner links her memory of Bianca to the Marshallese fishermen who were exposed to nuclear fallout more than fifty years before to highlight the protracted violence of nuclear colonialism in Marshallese peoples' everyday life.[4] She situates the Marshallese's bodily damage in the U.S. colonial conquest and dispossession of Indigenous peoples by alluding to the westward expansion of the U.S. empire in the name of "manifest destiny," as she depicts Bianca's body corroded by cancer resulting from nuclear contamination: "white cells had staked their flag / they conquered the territory of her tiny body / they saw it as their destiny / they said it was manifested" (*Iep Jāltok* 25).[5] In another poem, "On the Couch with Būbū Neien," Jetñil-Kijiner indicates that the invisible attritional violence of nuclear tests entails the dying of native language and cultural traditions along with the dying of people, lagoons, corals, and plants of the islands:

My grandmother has tongue cancer.

Words
are ripped
from the belly of
her throat
before they can be born.
Before they can flutter
in this space

between us—
an unturned layer of earth I
can no longer cultivate. (*Iep Jāltok* 42)

By using "an unturned layer of earth" that the speaker "can no longer cultivate"
as a metaphor for the "space"—the gap between her and her grandmother—
Jetñil-Kijiner calls the reader's attention to the degradation of ethnobiodiversity, the rupture in the Marshallese's native tongues, legends, and plant-based
traditional foodways and medicine.[6] Colonial settlement and U.S. nuclear
weapon tests have led to the loss of islands, habitats, plant species, migrations of people, "rapid urbanization, and over a century of the expansion of
coconut plantations onto almost all available land" on the Marshall Islands
(Thaman 41). The intertwined physical, cultural, and socio-ecological damage to the Marshallese reveals an ecology of empire that alters the colonized
landscapes and their webs of lives, communities, and ecosystems.

Haunted by the ruination of U.S. "imperial debris," Jetñil-Kijiner's trans-
corporeal ecopoems are at once haunting and healing through the mourning of irremediable losses. By interweaving Marshallese women's testimonies
with Marshallese folktales, Jetñil-Kijiner recuperates damaged bodies, landscapes, and cultures and exposes disavowed, hidden colonial ruination that
continues like the radioactive remains buried under the Runit "Tomb."

Craig Santos Perez's Ecopoetry as a Living Archive of Imperial Ruination and Indigenous Resistance

Engaging with past and present colonialism in Guåhan, Craig Santos Perez
enacts a complex process of critique, protest, mourning, and recuperation in
the open, capacious space of his multilingual, multi-genre ecopoetry. While
this process exposes the intertwining of continuous ecological degradation in
the island, resulting from colonial conquests by Spain, Japan, and the United
States, it demonstrates Chamorros' persistent resistance to colonial subjugation through grassroots activism in reclaiming Indigenous people's cultures,
ways of knowing, and ways of being, which are intertwined with Chamorros'
ancestral land and waters.

Perez's ecopoetry, then, enacts a decolonial process of "epistemic de-
linking" (Mignolo 450) and "epistemic reconstruction" (Quijano 176), one
that the Togan and Fijian anthropologist Epeli Hau'ofa calls for in his writings.

In "Our Sea of Islands," Hau'ofa points out, "People in some of our islands are in danger of being confined to mental reservations, if not already to physical ones." He proposes a reconceptualization of colonized Asia-Pacific countries by turning to "the myths, legends, and oral traditions, and the cosmologies of the peoples of Oceania" (152). In addition, he emphasizes the importance of Indigenous constructions of history and production of knowledge by bringing "into the center stage grassroots resistance and other unnoticed but important events for our peoples. . . . The new knowledge and insights we could gain from this reversal of historical roles could open up new and exciting vistas" (Hau'ofa, "Epilogue" 458). Resistance as such that includes both Indigenous grassroots movements and writings is characteristic of what the Argentine scholar and anthropologist Walther Mignolo defines as "epistemic de-linking," a "decolonial shift," such as "the radical political and epistemological shifts enacted by Amilcar Cabral, Aimé Césaire, Frantz Fanon, Rigoberta Menchú, Gloria Anzaldúa, among others" (452). These perspectives call critical attention to the cultural, epistemological dimensions of protracted colonial ruination, which Perez, like Jetñil-Kijiner, confronts while enacting Indigenous interventions in their respective poems.

Critics on Perez's poetry have pointed out what could be called an "epistemic reconstruction." In his provocative essay "Guahan (Guam), Literary Emergence, and the American Pacific in *Homebase* and *from Unincorporated Territory*," Hsuan Hsu contends that Perez's work features a "literature emergence" that reflects "counterdiscourses . . . emerged from Guam and the Chamorro diaspora." These counter-discourses include grassroots activism in reintroducing the Chamorro language "to all public schools" and restoring "traditional Chamorro practices" (287). Cathy Schlund-Vials addresses similar issues in her essay "'Finding' Guam: Distant Epistemologies and Cartographic Pedagogies" by highlighting the way Perez's poems at once expose and counter the systemically "*disremembered*" U.S. imperialism, "unmasking the absented registers of American empire" (46). As its book title, *from unincorporated territory*, indicates, Schlund-Vials contends, Perez's poems "underscore a longstanding relationship between indigenous subject, refugee body, and colonized territory that is part and parcel of past/present U.S. foreign policy, particularly with regard to westerly militarized campaigns across the North American continent and into the Pacific" (52). In his reading of Perez's poems, Paul Lai also situates Guam's legal status in "the imperial topography of the United States," which highlights "Native American reservation spaces within the boundaries of the contiguous states, offshore territories in the Caribbean and Pacific oceans (including Guantanamo Bay, Cuba) and the two outlying states of Alaska and Hawai'i" (3). These readings of Perez's poetry highlight the emergence of Indigenous decolonial activism against territorial expansion of the U.S. empire.

Moreover, Perez contends that critical analysis of imperialism and settler colonialism "should extend" the concept of territoriality. He states:

> Territoriality signifies a behavioral, social, cultural, historical, political, and economic phenomenon. Territoriality demarcates migration and settlement, inclusion and exclusion, power and poverty, access and trespass, incarceration and liberation, memory and forgetting. . . . Humans, animals, plants, and environments all struggle over territoriality. ("Transterritorial Currents" 620)

Enmeshed in a web of such entanglements, Perez's ecopoetry is a site of the intersections of what he calls "transterritorial currents." Building on existing scholarship, my reading of Perez's ecopoetics seeks to spotlight the ways in which Perez exposes complex ecological, cultural, ideological, and historical entanglements of imperialism and Chamorros' epistemic delinking and reconstruction, through an innovative ecopoetics of mourning. By breaking away from the lyric "I" as the organizing principle of his poems, Perez opens up the poetic form to allow multiple voices, heterogeneous texts, and different locations and historical periods to enter to form multilayered juxtapositions and counter-discourses. His poems are like a living archive, which documents not only past and present colonial destruction in Guam but also Chamorros' resistance and intervention.

The poem "*from* **achiote**," included in Perez's first collection, *from unincorporated territory* [*hacha*], is a salient example of intertwined social, cultural, and material transformations following the Spanish, Japanese, and American conquests of Guam. This poem begins with an illustration of the achiote plant named "Bixa orellana" from *Flora de Filipinas* (1880–1883?) by Francisco Manuel Blanco, a member of the Augustinian order of friars, whose assignments included the Philippines, and whose book of comprehensive flora of the Philippines was categorized according to the system of Linnaeus. Countering the uniform, hierarchical taxonomy of colonial production of knowledge about "nature," Perez lists varied common names of achiote, including those used by Indigenous peoples in Peru and Brazil. He achieves historical span and complex perspectives through intertextual juxtapositions, while interlacing the achiote plant through various spaces and temporalities.

The way the plant features in different places and at different moments in history marks the impact of colonialism across continents. In the Americas, achiote was integral to Mayan culture, foodways, and medicine (*[hacha]* 17). In present-day United States, however, achiote becomes an exotic spice "in the ethnic foods aisle of some grocery store," its intimate relationship with Indigenous Americans being lost with the decline of Mayan society following the Spanish conquest. Perez tactfully juxtaposes the description of achiote's remedy for *"skin problems, burns, venereal disease, and hypertension"* with the Spanish colonizers' presence in Guam and their imposition of Catholicism with its "catechism lessons," "flagellation physics *disciplina* a cilice" on Chamorros. Children who did not say their prayers at Sunday school would have "bruises" on their bodies (19).

As the poem develops with his interlacing of Spanish colonialism with the achiote's functions in Chamorros' everyday life, Perez reveals that the violence brought by Spanish colonialists led to Chamorro resistance and brutal suppression by the Spanish military. He juxtaposes the picture and caption of Chief Mata'pang's killing of Padre San Vitores, who baptized the chief's newborn daughter without permission, with the following statement: "*after the death of san vitores, the native population collapsed from 200,000 to 5,000 in two generations as a result of spanish military conquest" (*[hacha]* 21). The impact of colonial conquest continues in Guam, as can be seen in the landscape marked by the presence of past and present empires in the island. Perez shows that in Tumon Bay of Guam, tourists can "stay at the *Hilton, Westin, Grand Plaza, / Marriott, Hyatt,* and *Holiday Inn,*" which are located off "*San Vitores Road*" that "runs parallel to *Marine Drive* / which was renamed *Marine Corps Drive.*" And on the site where Magellan's ship landed, "the shrine of father sanvitores lies / between *Guam Reef Hotel* and *Sails Restaurant—*" (23). These landmarks are signs of the colonial "rot" that continues with further dispossession of Chamorros by transnational capitalism and the U.S. military. Their names and dominant presence mark what they have erased.

Perez's employment of the achiote as a "connective tissue" serves to highlight the contour of empire's ruin that "carve[s] through the psychic and material space in which people live and what compounded layers of imperial debris do to them," to quote Stoler again ("'The Rot Remains'" 2). The following lines illustrate layers of colonial ruin in the material, cultural, and psychic spaces of Chamorros:

My grandmother used achiote to make hineksa agaga
   so young when the japanese army invaded and
renamed hagåtña "akashi"
     the "red city" "bright red stone"

       ~

. . . .
"mata'pang" used to mean "proud and brave"
    used to mean "alert eyes"
he led the rebellion against the spanish
    before he was captured and killed

now it means "silly" or "rude" or
     "misbehaved" or "uncivil" (*[hacha]* 24)

Placed directly below these lines is a drawing of the achiote plant, with its flower and seed dissected and named "Bixa orellana" identified as from *Flora de Filipinas* (1880–1883?) by Francisco Manuel Blanco (*[hacha]* 24). The dissected, fragmented, isolated parts of the plant (fig. 7.3) reduced to a passive object to be mastered and controlled embody the production of colonial knowledge that resonates with the colonizers' violation of Indigenous Mayan and Chamorro identities, cultures, and societies.

Moreover, the ending lines of this poem about Chamorros' use of the achiote plant *"as an antivenom for snake bites. / to heal wounds"* anticipate the ecological devastation on the island by the invasion of the brown tree snake brought by the U.S. military during and after World War II (*[hacha]* 24). Perez documents the environmental transformation, ecological degradation, and species extinction in Guam following the U.S. military shipment of *"equipment and salvaged war material to permanent bases and scrap metal processors on Guam"* (*[hacha]* 89). In a decade after the first brown tree snake was reported to be found in Apra Harbor in 1953, *"the snakes had colonized half the island,"* and by 1968, they had spread to the northernmost Ritidian Point of Guam, leading to the extinction of native birds and the dying of local forests.[7]

Perez foregrounds the connection between ecological devastation and U.S. military buildup in the following lines, which indicate that the ruination by colonial empires continues to corrode the colonized island country:

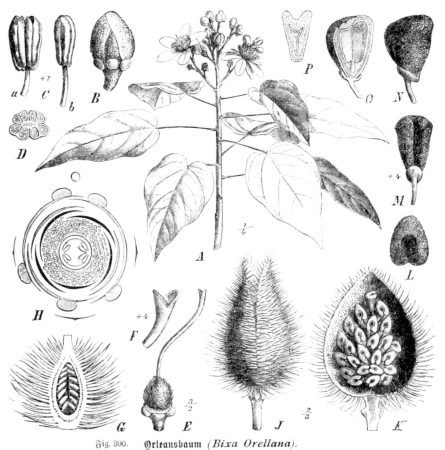

Fig. 390. **Orleansbaum** (*Bixa Orellana*).

A Blühender Zweig. *B* Blütenknospe. *C, D* Staubblätter. *E* Stempel. *F* Narbe. *G* Fruchtknoten im Querschnitt. *H* Schematischer Grundriß. *J* Frucht. *K* Dieselbe, eine Klappe entfernt. *L—N* Same *O, P* Derselbe im Längs= und Querschnitt.

Fig. 7.3. *Bixa orellana*, from E. Gilg and K. Schumann, "Das Pflanzenreich. Hausschatz des Wissens" (The plant kingdom: Treasure of knowledge), ca. 1900. (Published online by Kurt Stüber, www.biolib.de; available at Wikimedia Commons, https://commons.wikimedia.org/w/index.php?curid=651669)

The snake population grew exponentially, reaching a density of 13,000 per square mile. At the same time, declining bird populations were noticed. [*8,000 Marines and their dependents will be transferred to Guam from Okinawa by 2014 through a joint effort of the United States and Japan.] ([hacha] 93)

The expansion of the U.S. military in Guam parallels the explosion of the brown tree snake population on the island. The subsequent ecological consequences have also eroded the Chamorros' everyday experience and threatened the lives of infants, who are most vulnerable to the snakebite. Perez interlaces those facts to reveal the entanglements of the human and more-than-human lives affected by the violence of colonization: "*At present, Guam has lost all its breeding populations of seabirds, 10 of 13 endemic species of forest birds, 2 of 3 native mammals, and 6 of 10 native species of lizards. Also, there have been over 100 infant deaths reported in the last 50 years*" ([hacha] 95). An ecology of empire embedded in these intertwined destructions, altered habitats, and degraded environments becomes more overt and multifarious in Perez's later collections.

In his second collection, *from unincorporated territory [saina]*, Perez weaves a more complex web of intricate ecological, cultural, and sociopolitical entanglements of colonial conquests and Indigenous resistance. The book's title captures both the colonization of Guam and the Chamorros' decolonial activism. In juxtaposition to "*unincorporated territory*," which foregrounds the subjugation of Chamorros and the erasure of their Indigenous traditions, Perez counterpoises the name of a sakman, an outrigger canoe—"saina," meaning "parents elders spirits ancestors" in Chamorro (*[saina]* 15). He begins his second collection with an evocation of Chamorro ancestors—"taotaomo'na"—and asserts their indomitable spirit as embodied in the rebuilt sakman—saina (13). Perez documents the violent suppression of Chamorro culture by the Spanish as a way to contain the Indigenous people's mobility: "following the Chamorro-spanish [sic] wars [1671–98] the Spanish colonists began destroying the sakman and forbade chamorros to sail the ocean" (14). But a 33-foot sakman was rebuilt in 2007 by members of the Chamorro organization of "traditions about seafaring islands" under the guidance of master navigator and canoe builder Manny Sikau from Polowat in the federated states of Micronesia. It was the largest sakman built on Guam in centuries, which embodies the recovery of Chamorro Indigenous cultural traditions (15).

The recuperation of Chamorro Indigenous culture, however, coexists with the continuing socio-ecological ruination by colonial conquest and the expansion of the U.S. empire. Perez employs intertextual juxtapositions to demonstrate these intertwined processes of domination and resistance, destruction and recuperation. He incorporates excerpts from "A Testimony before the United Nations" which Perez presented on behalf of the Guåhan Indigenous Collective before the United Nations Special Political and Decolonization Committee (Fourth Committee) on the question of continued colonization of Guåhan (Guam), on 7 October 2008.

He interweaves ten excerpts from this testimony throughout the book, beginning on page 17 and ending on page 127. These extended intertextual juxtapositions illustrate the extent of colonial ruination, including environmental contamination, exacerbated by the expansion of the U.S. military bases in Guam, against which Perez counterpoises Chamorros' protest and critique. He uses strikethrough to cross out the excerpts from the testimony to indicate the marginalization of Chamorros' perspectives, which are mostly ignored in the decision-making about Guam. Paradoxically, the strikethrough calls the reader's attention to the testimonial statements. Excerpt 4 reveals that the contamination of Chamorros' social, cultural, physical, and environmental health by the U.S. military operations continues in Guam:

> 4. ~~our environmental, social, physical and cultural health, since world war two, military dumping and nuclear testing has contaminated the pacific with peb's and radiation. in addition, peb's and other military toxic waste have choked the breath out of the largest barrier reef system of guam, poisoning fish and fishing grounds, as recently as just of this year, the uss houston, a u.s. navy nuclear submarine home ported on guam, leaked trace amounts of radioactivity into our waters~~. (*[saina]* 60)

Perez highlights through intertextual juxtapositions the connection between imperial military occupation and the creation of toxic waste dumps in Guam. The U.S. Navy owned and operated the Ordot Dump before and after World War II. During its occupation in Guam, the Japanese army used the dump for its disposals.[8] In addition, Perez links the ecological, physical devastation to psychological damage of the Chamorros in Guam, who are endangered by more than toxic contamination. Excerpt 9 from the testimony reveals that Chamorros suffer disproportionately "~~high rates of incarceration, family violence, substance abuse, teenage suicides, and school drop outs~~" because "~~our mental health is woven to our physical health~~" (*[saina]* 114). Perez's use of strikethrough paradoxically illustrates and counters the erasure of Chamorros and their suffering from colonialism and military imperialism.

By lamenting Chamorros' continuing loss of homeland and situating it in complex historical contexts, Perez's composite poems offer provocative ways for investigating "the political, economic, and cultural dimensions of *how* loss is apprehended" and for exploring what new possibilities reside in "what remains," as Eng and Kazanjian have argued for the politics of mourning. By "animating the remains of loss as an infinite number of new" possibilities, Eng and Kazanjian suggest that mourning is a way of investigating how loss is interpreted as it "opens up the present and orients it toward unknown futures" (5–6). In confronting the afterlife of past colonialism and the present expansion of U.S. empire in Guam, Perez counters Chamorro peoples' dispossessions and displacements in the same poem that mourns the loss of Chamorros' ancestral home. He shows that Chamorros have reinvented their home/house/refuge and reclaimed their Indigenous identity and cultures through activism and reimagining, reinventing their connections to their ancestral home. Against the *"permanent loss,"* against the *"cage"* of second-class U.S. citizenship, and against *"removal from"* ancestral land, Perez ends the poem with a celebration of the building of a canoe house by Traditions Affirming our Seafaring Ancestry. Named "Guma' Latte Marianas," the canoe house evokes Guam's magnificent Indigenous latte, stone structures that "formed the foundations of homes, schools, canoe shelters, food sheds, and communal spaces" dating back to AD 900, most of which were destroyed by the Spanish (*[guma']* 18). The canoe house embodies a new sense of home, affirming Indigenous culture through a new way of belonging, of being Chamorro, like the *"aerial and sub-aerial roots"* of the banyan tree, connecting to Marianas' ancestors and home *"from multiple points of migration and return"* (40). So, too, do Perez's poems affirm the Chamorros' connection to Indigenous culture and ancestors, *"because every poem is a navigational chant . . . because [our] bones are twenty percent water hunggan hunggan hunggan magahet"* (40). As Eng and Kazanjian contend, "Avowals of and attachments to loss can produce a world of remains as a world of new representations and alternative meanings" (5).

Perez's poems as navigational chants are also songs of mourning irrecoverable and impending losses resulting from colonialist conquests in Guam. They sing the names of numerous Chamorros in the U.S. Army and U.S. Navy killed in Iraq, Afghanistan, and Kuwait, along with the name of an ancestral latte village, Pågat, where Chamorros still travel to "collect medicinal herbs;

to learn about Chamorro culture and history"; and "to seek guidance from the ancestral spirits that dwell there." However, Pågat, "also home to the Mariana eight-spot butterfly, an endangered native species" is under imminent threat by the U.S. military's plan to build a "live firing range complex" in the area where Pågat is (*[guma']* 59–60). In enacting the politics of mourning by interweaving different periods of colonial histories, Perez brings the past to bear witness upon the present, thus allowing the past to remain "steadfastly alive to the political work of the present" (Eng and Kazanjian 5).

In both Jetñil-Kijiner's and Perez's respective ecopoems haunted by empires, the political work of the present is rendered even more urgent by a multifaceted investigation of loss and ruination through mourning. By allowing their poems to be haunted by what Stoler calls "the hardened, tenacious qualities of colonial effects," Jetñil-Kijiner and Perez mourn the ongoing loss and what remains of multifarious colonial ruination in their poems. Their mourning produces a politics that engages with the past and orients toward the future. The politics of their ecopoetics offers "a capaciousness of meaning in relation to losses," which entails both "the capacity to 'hold out'" and "'to endure,' as a countermand to 'duress' and its damaging and disabling qualities," as Stoler says of the concept of "duress" in understanding imperial durability in our times ("Critical Incisions" 7). Their poems demonstrate that to endure the losses entails reclaiming through the agency of imagination. Jetñil-Kijiner's poem "Of Islands and Elders" and Perez's poem "*ginen* aerial roots" illustrate how to endure, how to hold out despite the ongoing ruination:

> And how do we mourn elders
> who were islands
> lush with knowledge and story?
> . . . .
> But look–
> right there
>
> There exists
> still
> some
> green
>
> Even after

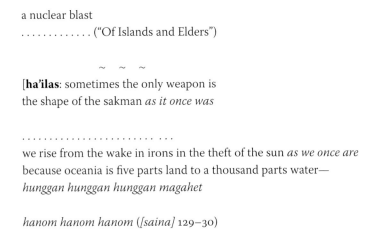

a nuclear blast

. . . . ("Of Islands and Elders")

~   ~   ~

[**ha'ilas**: sometimes the only weapon is
the shape of the sakman *as it once was*

. . . .

we rise from the wake in irons in the theft of the sun *as we once are*
because oceania is five parts land to a thousand parts water—
hunggan hunggan hunggan magahet

hanom hanom hanom (*[saina]* 129–30)

In countering the durability of colonial ruination, the ecopoetry of Jetñil-Kijiner and Perez enacts the ways in which Indigenous spirit, cultures, and struggles endure beyond imperial ruination.

As such, the respective ecopoems by Jetñil-Kijiner and Perez perform the entanglements of "monsters" and "ghosts," demonstrating what Anna Tsing and her coeditors might call "arts of living on a damaged planet." Yet, their monsters are more than the embodiment of "the wonders and terrors of symbiotic entanglement in the Anthropocene" (Swanson et al. M2). They reveal the intertwined ecological, cultural, and social transformations shaped by past colonial conquests and new imperial operations, as well as by Indigenous resistance and reinvention. The "ghosts" in their poems haunt not only landscapes altered by nuclear tests, species extinction, but also diseased, monstrous bodies produced by imperial debris. In fact, these landscapes and bodies themselves are at once haunted and haunting, like the poems by Jetñil-Kijiner and Perez. The "ghosts" in their poems, moreover, entail Micronesian ancestral spirits and Indigenous cultures that refuse to be forgotten. Their unsettling presence disrupts historical amnesia of disavowed, obscured enduring ruination of particular places on the damaged planet Earth, places marked by the difference of race and the long durée of imperial colonization and Indigenous resistance.

Notes

Acknowledgments: I am indebted to my coeditors—Jeffrey Santa Ana, Heidi Amin-Hong, and Rina Garcia Chua—and the anonymous reviewers for the University of Michigan Press for their insightful, constructive suggestions, which helped make this chapter stronger. All the oversights in it are mine. I am also grateful to the following individuals and presses for their permissions to use the materials as identified: Photographs of the Runit Dome by Greg Nelson in Mark Willacy's article, reprinted by permission of Mark Willacy. Excerpts of poems by Craig Santos Perez from his books—*from unincorporated territory [hacha]* (2017); *from unincorporated territory [saina]* (2010); and *from unincorporated territory [guma']*—reprinted by permission of Omnidawn Publishing. All rights reserved. Excerpts of poems by Kathy Jetñil-Kijiner from her collection *Iep Jaltok: Poems from a Marshallese Daughter.* © 2017 Kathy Jetñil-Kijiner. Reprinted by permission of the University of Arizona Press.

1. The name "Guam" was officially changed to "Guåhan" by a bill passed by the Guam Legislature in 2010. See Craig Santos Perez, *from unincorporated territory [guman']*, 84. I use "Guam" and "Guåhan" interchangeably, as does Perez in his writings, which acknowledges Chamorros' different perspectives on the name of the island.

2. I draw from the theorization of "colonial unknowing" by Manu Vimalassery, Juliana Hu Pegues, and Alyosha Goldstein, as an integral part of settler colonial elimination of indigeneity and Indigenous people's claims to place.

3. See Kathy Jetñil-Kijiner's statement about the source of this quote in note 3 of "New Year, New Monsters, New Poems," 15 Jan. 2018, https://www.kathyjetnilkijiner.com/new-year-new-monsters-and-new-poems/

4. For more information about nuclear colonialism beyond the Marshall Islands, see Huang Hsu, "Representing Environmental Risk in the Landscapes of US Militarization."

5. In discussing "Fishbone Hair," a poem about the death of her niece, Bianca Lanki, Kathy Jetñil-Kijiner says that Bianca passed away from leukemia at age eight, though she is six in the poem as she struggles with treatment. See https://www.kathyjetnilkijiner.com/fishbone-hair-full-poemvideo/

6. See R. R. Thaman, "An Introduction to the Ethnobiodiversity and Plants of the Marshall Islands"; and Irene J. Taafaki, Maria Kabua Fowler, and Randolph R. Thaman, editors, *Traditional Medicine of the Marshall Islands: The Women, the Plants, the Treatments.*

7. See Elizabeth Wandrag and Haldre Rogers, "Guam's Forests Are Being Slowly Killed Off—By a Snake."

8. For reports on toxic contamination on Guam, see The Old Blue Water Navy Site US Military Contamination of Guam, particularly Part 7, "Mapping Toxic Waste Sites" by Dr. Luis Szyfrey, http://www.oldbluewater.com/guamcontamination1.htm. Dr. Szyfrey's report includes a map that shows more than 100 dumpsites with toxic chemicals on a 30-by-8-mile island; see http://www.oldbluewater.com/guam/guamsites.jpg. I am grateful to Craig Santos Perez for calling my attention to this map.

Works Cited

Alaimo, Stacy. *Bodily Natures: Science, Environment, and the Material Self.* Indiana UP, 2010.

Briscoe, Charles L. S. *Blue Ribbon Panel Committee Action Report on Radioactive Contamination in Guam between 1946–1958.* 12 Nov. 2002, 1–97, https://www.worldcat.org/title/blue-ribbon-panel-committee-action-report-on-radioactive-contamination-in-guam-between-1946-1958/oclc/608426696?referer=di&ht=edition

Byrd, Jodi. *The Transit of Empire: Indigenous Critiques of Colonialism.* U of Minnesota P, 2011.

Cooke, Stephanie. *Mortal Hands: A Cautionary History of the Nuclear Age.* Black, 2009.

DeLoughrey, Elizabeth. "The Myth of Isolates: Ecosystem Ecologies in the Nuclear Pacific." *Cultural Geographies*, vol. 20, 2013, 167–84.

DeLoughrey, Elizabeth, Jill Didur, and Anthony Carrigan, editors. *Global Ecologies and the Environmental Humanities Postcolonial Approaches.* Routledge, 2015.

Eng, David L., and David Kazanjian. "Mourning Remains." *Loss: The Politics of Mourning*, edited by Eng and Kazanjian. U of California P, 2003, 1–26.

Espiritu, Yến Lê. "Rethinking 'Collateral Damage' in the Vietnam War: The *Other* Others in the Circuits of U.S. Empire." *Asian American Literary Review*, vol. 6, no. 2, Fall 2015, 133–39.

Flores, Alfred Peredo. "'No Walk in the Park': US Empire and the Racialization of Civilian Military Labor in Guam, 1944–1962." *American Quarterly*, vol. 67, no. 3, September 2015, 813–35.

Georgescu, Calin. *Report of the Special Rapporteur on the Implications for Human Rights of the Environmentally Sound Management and Disposal of Hazardous Substances and Wastes.* Human Rights Council, United Nations General Assembly, 3 Sept. 2012, www.converge.org.nz/pma/A-HRC-21-48-Add1.pdf. Accessed 15 May 2017.

Haberman, Clyde. "Agent Orange's Long Legacy, for Vietnam and Veterans." *New York Times*, 11 May 2014, http://www.nytimes.com/2014/05/12/us/agent-oranges-long-legacy-for-vietnam-and-veterans.html. Accessed Mar. 18, 2016.

Hauʻofa, Epeli. "Epilogue: Pasts to Remember." *Remembrance of Pacific Past: An Invitation to Remake History.* U of Hawaiʻi P, 2000, 453–71.

Hauʻofa, Epeli. "Our Sea of Islands." *Contemporary Pacific*, vol. 6, no. 1, Spring 1994, 148–61.

Hsu, Hsuan L. "Guahan (Guam), Literary Emergence, and the American Pacific in *Homebase* and *from Unincorporated Territory*." *American Literary History*, vol. 24, no. 2, Summer 2012, 281–307.

Hsu, Hsuan L. "Representing Environmental Risk in the Landscapes of US Militarization." Virtual Exhibitions, Rachel Carson Center for Environment and Society/LMU Munich, 2014 No. 1, http://www.environmentandsociety.org/exhibitions/risk-and-militarization

Jetñil-Kijiner, Kathy. *Iep Jāltok: Poems from a Marshallese Daughter.* U of Arizona P, 2017.

Jetñil-Kijiner, Kathy. "Luerkoklik and the Role of the Land in the Climate Movement." *Ke Kaupu Hehi Ale*, 26 June 2015, https://hehiale.wordpress.com/2015/06/26/luerkoklik-and-the-role-of-the-land-in-the-climate-movement/

Jetñil-Kijiner, Kathy. "Monster." *KathyJetñil-Kijiner.com*, 25 Jan. 2018, https://www.kathyjetnilkijiner.com/new-year-new-monsters-and-new-poems/

Jetñil-Kijiner, Kathy. "New Year, New Monsters, New Poems," 15 Jan. 2018, https://www.kathyjetnilkijiner.com/new-year-new-monsters-and-new-poems/

Jetñil-Kijiner, Kathy. "Of Islands and Elders." *KathyJetñil-Kijiner.com*, 2 Mar. 2018, https://www.kathyjetnilkijiner.com/dome-poem-part-ii-of-islands-and-elders/

Johnston, Barbara Rose. "Nuclear Disaster: The Marshall Islands Experience and Lessons for a Post-Fukushima World." *Global Ecologies and the Environmental Humanities*

Postcolonial Approaches, edited by Elizabeth DeLoughrey, Jill Didur, and Anthony Carrigan. Routledge, 2015, 140–61.

Lai, Paul. "Discontiguous States of America: The Paradox of Unincorporation in Craig Santos Perez's Politics of Chamorro Guam." *Journal of Transnational American Studies*, vol. 3, no. 2, 2011, 1–28.

Maldonado-Torres, Nelson. "Thinking through the Decolonial Turn: Post-continental Interventions in Theory, Philosophy, and Critique—An Introduction." *Transmodernity: Journal of Peripheral Cultural Production of the Luso-Hispanic World*, vol. 1, no. 2, Fall 2011, 1–15.

Mignolo, Walter. "Delinking: The Rhetoric of Modernity, the Logic of Coloniality and the Grammar of De-Coloniality." *Cultural Studies*, vol. 21, no. 2–3, 2007, 449–514.

Perez, Craig Santos. *from unincorporated territory [guma']*. Omnidawn Publishing, 2014.

Perez, Craig Santos. *from unincorporated territory [hacha]*. Omnidawn Publishing, 2017.

Perez, Craig Santos. *from unincorporated territory [saina]*. Omnidawn Publishing, 2010.

Perez, Craig Santos. "A Testimony before the United Nations." On behalf of the Guåhan Indigenous Collective. *Diálogo*, vol. 19, no. 1, Spring 2016, 153–56.

Perez, Craig Santos. "Transterritorial Currents and the Imperial Terripelago." *American Quarterly*, vol. 67, no. 3, Sept. 2015, 619–24.

Quijano, Aníbal. "Coloniality and Modernity/Rationality." Translated by Sonia Therborn. *Cultural Studies*, vol. 21, no. 2–3, 2007, 168–78.

Rogers, Robert F. *Destiny's Landfall: A History of Guam*. U of Hawai'i P, 1995.

Schlund-Vials, Cathy. "'Finding' Guam: Distant Epistemologies and Cartographic Pedagogies." *Asian American Literature: Discourses and Pedagogies*, vol. 5, 2014, 45–60.

Stoler, Ann Laura. "Critical Incisions: On Concept Work and Colonial Recursions." *Duress: Imperial Durabilities in Our Times*, edited by Stoler. Duke UP, 2016, 1–36.

Stoler, Ann Laura. "Imperial Debris: Reflections on Ruins and Ruination." *Cultural Anthropology*, vol. 23, no. 2, 2008, 191–219.

Stoler, Ann Laura. "'The Rot Remains': From Ruins to Ruination." *Imperial Debris: On Ruins and Ruination*, edited by Stoler. Duke UP, 2013, 1–35.

Swanson, Heather Anne, Anna Tsing, Nils Bubandt, and Elaine Gan. "Bodies Tumbled Into Bodies." *Arts of Living on a Damaged Planet*, edited by Anna Lowenhaupt Tsing, Heather Anne Swanson, Elaine Gan, and Nils Bubandt. U of Minnesota P, 2017, M1–M12.

Taafaki, Irene J., Maria Kabua Fowler, and Randolph R. Thaman. *Traditional Medicine of the Marshall Islands: The Women, the Plants, the Treatments*. IPS Publications, U of the South Pacific, 2006.

Thaman, R. R. "An Introduction to the Ethnobiodiversity and Plants of the Marshall Islands." *Traditional Medicine of the Marshall Islands: The Women, the Plants, the Treatments*, edited by Irene J. Taafaki, Maria Kabua Fowler, and Randolph R. Thaman. IPS Publications, U of the South Pacific, 2006, 41–56.

Tobin. Jack A. *Stories from the Marshall Islands*. U of Hawai'i P, 2002.

Vimalassery, Manu, Juliana Hu Pegues, and Alyosha Goldstein. "On Colonial Unknowing," *Theory & Event*, vol. 19, no. 4, 2016, https://muse.jhu.edu/article/633283

Wandrag, Elizabeth, and Haldre Rogers. "Guam's Forests Are Being Slowly Killed

Off—By a Snake." *The Conversation*, 31 Aug. 2017, https://theconversation.com/
     guams-forests-are-being-slowly-killed-off-by-a-snake-83224

Weiss, Jasmine Stole. "GovGuam Lawsuit against Navy over Ordot Dump to Move Forward."
     Pacific Daily News, 1 Oct. 2018, https://www.guampdn.com/story/news/2018/10/01/
     govguam-lawsuit-against-navy-over-ordot-dump-move-forward/1484612002/

Wernick, Adam. "Seawater Is Infiltrating a Nuclear Waste Dump on a Remote Pacific Atoll."
     PIR: Public Radio International, 19 Feb. 2018, https://www.pri.org/stories/2018-02-19/
     seawater-infiltrating-nuclear-waste-dump-remote-pacific-atoll

Willacy, Mark. "A Poison in Our Island." *ABC* (Australia), 16 Nov. 2017, updated 8 Feb.
     2018,   https://www.abc.net.au/news/2017-11-27/the-dome-runit-island-nuclear-test
     -leaking-due-to-climate-change/9161442

PART III

Decolonizing the Transpacific

Settler Colonialism and Indigenous Resistance

"Praise Song for Oceania"
Craig Santos Perez

for World Oceans Day, June 8

"Belonging to Oceania becomes a matter of political and cultural commitment: Oceania means not only having a sense of history and cultivating a set of attitudes and beliefs, it means cultivating a sense of belonging to the earth and ocean as a bioregional horizon of care."

—ROB WILSON, "OCEANIA AS PERIL AND PROMISE:
TOWARDS THEORIZING A WORLDED VISION OF
TRANS-PACIFIC ECOPOETICS" (2012)

~

praise
your capacity
for birth your fluid
currents and trenchant
darkness praise
your contracting waves
and dilating horizons
praise our briny
beginning, the source
of every breath praise

your endless bio-
diversity praise

your capacity
for renewal your rise
into clouds and descent
into rain praise your underground
aquifers your rivers and lakes
ice sheets and glaciers praise
your watersheds and
hydrologic cycles praise

your capacity
to endure the violation
of those who name you
who claim dominion
over you who map you
empty ocean to pillage
who divide you into
latitudes and longitudes
who scar your middle
passages who carve
shipping lanes who exploit
your economy praise

your capacity
to survive our trawling
boats breaching
your open body
and taking from your
collapsing depths praise

your capacity
to dilute our sewage
and radioactive waste
our pollutants and plastics
our heavy metals
and greenhouse gases praise

your capacity
to bury our shipwrecks
our soldiers and terrorists
slaves and refugees to bury
our lost cities every last breath
to bury the ashes of our
loved ones praise

your capacity
to remember praise
your library of drowned
stories praise your museum
of lost treasures your archive
of desire your repository
of deep secrets praise
your uncontainable mystery
praise your tidalectic theory
praise our migrant routes
and submarine roots praise

your capacity to penetrate
your rising tides and
relentless storms
and towering tsunamis
and feverish floods praise

your capacity
to smother whales
and schools of fish
to wash them ashore
to save them from our cruelty
to show us what we're
no longer allowed to take
to starve us like your corals
are being starved and bleached
like your liquid lungs
choked of oxygen praise

your capacity to forgive please
forgive our territorial hands
and acidic breath please
forgive our nuclear arms
and naval bodies please
forgive our concrete dams
and cabling veins please
forgive our deafening sonar
and lustful tourisms please
forgive our invasive drilling
and deep sea mining please
forgive our extractions
and trespasses praise

your capacity for mercy please
let our grandfathers and fathers
catch just one more fish please
make it stop raining soon please
make it rain soon please
spare our fragile farms
and fruit trees please
spare our low-lying islands
and atolls please
spare our coastal villages
and cities please
let us cross safely to a land
without war praise

your capacity for hope
praise your rainbow
warrior and peace
boat your Hokuleʻa
and sea shepherd praise
your arctic sunrise and freedom
flotillas praise your nuclear free
and independent pacific movement
praise your marine stewardship
councils and sustainable

fisheries praise your radical
seafarers and native navigators
praise your sacred water walkers
praise your activist kayaks
and canoes praise your ocean
conservancies and surfrider foundations
praise your aquanauts and hydrolabs
praise your Ocean Cleanup
and Google Oceans
praise your whale hunting
and shark finning bans
praise your sanctuaries
and no take zones praise
your pharmacopeia of new
antibiotics praise your wave
and tidal energy praise your
#oceanoptimism and Ocean
Elders praise your blue
humanities praise

your capacity for echo
location our words for you
that translate into creation
stories and song maps
tasi and kai and tai and moana nui
and vasa and tahi and lik and wai tui
and daob and wansolwara

praise your capacity
for communion praise
our common heritage praise
our pathway and promise
to each other praise our
endless saga praise our most
powerful metaphor praise
your vision of belonging
praise your blue planet
one world ocean praise

our trans-oceanic
past present and future
flowing through
our blood

8

Risk and Resistance at Pōhakuloa

Rebecca H. Hogue

At the base of Mauna Kea on the Big Island of Hawaiʻi, the Pōhakuloa Training Area has hosted American military training exercises since World War
II. Located on a large flatland spanning over 108,000 acres of ceded lands
seized by the U.S. government after the 1898 annexation of the kingdom of
Hawaiʻi, the training facility currently operates on a 65-year lease at the cost
of one dollar. In anticipation of the current lease ending in 2029, two Kanaka
Maoli residents (Clarence Kūkauakahi Ching and Mary Maxine Kahaulelio)
filed a lawsuit with the Hawaii State Court in 2014 challenging that the U.S.
military was not adhering to the terms of environmental and cultural protection set out in its lease with the Hawaiʻi Department of Land and Natural
Resources and that therefore the department was not properly enforcing the
lease. Among several objections, they argued that Kānaka Maoli or Kānaka
ʻŌiwi as Indigenous peoples should have access, currently denied, to cultural
landmarks on the base under the terms of the Department of Land and Natural Resources and feared the destruction of cultural landmarks due to weapons testing. The suit was also concerned with the failure to properly dispose
of weapons and ammunition used on the land—a key point of contention as
many of those weapons contain depleted uranium. The presence of depleted
uranium, of which traces have been found in the public water system on the
island, inflicts environmental harm as well as corporeal risk to citizens in
the surrounding areas. Yet, reports released by the state government denied
the severity of these effects, privileging attention to perceived global security
risks instead of the immediate material as well as long-standing sociological
ramifications caused by the military presence at the Pōhakuloa Training Area.

The intertwining issues of land sovereignty and toxicity brought to light
by the suit highlight the discursive discord between Kānaka Maoli activists,
environmentalists, and the settler state governments of both Hawaiʻi and

the United States. These activists' arguments of slow and ongoing violence are further iterated in a 2014 short documentary: *Pōhakuloa: Now That You Know, Do You Care?* A 2007 poem by Kanaka Maoli poet Sage Uʻilani Take-hiro entitled "Progress at Pōhakuloa" also confronts how the military's presence at Pōhakuloa is a key site for interrogating the intersections of settler colonialism and Kānaka Maoli sovereignty in Hawaiʻi. The documentary and the poem invoke sacred genealogies to refute military rhetorical stratagems—which are, I would argue, another form of "training" that the U.S. military conducts at Pōhakuloa—as well as to complicate notions of risk societies as both material and metaphysical.

Since its inception as a military base, the Pōhakuloa Training Area has remained fueled by a perpetual perception of risk in the American imagination. In this chapter, I expand upon Anthony Giddens's and Ulrich Beck's articulations of "risk," which, according to Giddens, refers to "hazards that are assessed in relation to future possibilities," whereas Beck explains risk as "a systemic way of dealing with hazards and insecurities induced and introduced by modernization itself" (Giddens 22; Beck 21). Important to each of these definitions are an emphasis on the future and an imbrication with modernity, as Gidden's explanation of risk argues that "risk presumes a society that actively tries to break away from its past—the prime characteristic, indeed, of modern industrial civilization" (22). In the context of Hawaiʻi, however, risk is unevenly distributed and perceived depending on epistemological relationships with the future: for the U.S. military, training for speculative threats while presently detonating weapons with partially known future consequences; and for Kānaka Maoli, understanding risk as an *ongoing* process of living with the both known and yet to be determined effects of settler colonialism, militarization, and environmental degradation.

The American military rapidly expanded its already pervasive military presence in the Hawaiian Islands, along with the rest of the Pacific, when the United States entered World War II after the attack on Honolulu's Pearl Harbor. At the time of Pōhakuloa's first use as a military installation, the islands were operating as a U.S. territory, with statehood to come another 16 years later in 1959. Yet, Americans have always used risk as a rhetorical strategy for justifying their illegal and militaristic occupation of the Hawaiian archipelago. As early as 1840, a newspaper printed in Hawaiʻi advocated for an American military base to be built there to protect American whalers. With the Americans' annexing of both Alaska and Midway in 1867, the United States expanded its purview beyond the North American continent, and in

1887, it gained exclusive rights to Pearl Harbor as a coaling and repair station. When the United States illegally overthrew the Hawaiian Kingdom in 1893, and subsequently annexed the islands in 1898, the U.S. military rapidly began building its bases throughout Hawai'i, first at Fort Shafter (1907) and then at Pearl Harbor (1908), followed by another surge in building during World War II. Many of those bases, like Pōhakuloa, remain in operation as an essential part of what the U.S. Department of Defense has called "the Pacific Century" (Gibson and Cheatwood).

Currently, the Pōhakuloa Training Area (or PTA) serves, according to the U.S. Army website, as a "firing range [that] allow[s] units to conduct small-arms and crew-served weapons familiarization training," with most recent trainings prepping for combat operations in Iraq and Afghanistan. Furthermore, the U.S. Army's website acknowledges the very subject that I will address here—the base's relationship with the environment and Kānaka Maoli. According to the U.S. Army, the Pōhakuloa Training Area is "a vanguard of environmental and cultural protection." In the 1965 lease, the United States agreed to clean up ammunition in anticipation of public use: "In recognition of public use of the demised premises, the government [of the United States] shall make every reasonable effort to stockpile supplies and equipment in an orderly fashion and away from established roads and trails and to remove or deactivate all live or blank ammunition upon completion of a training exercise or prior to entry by the said public, whichever is sooner" (3). Furthermore, the lease includes language pertaining to protecting environmental features in order to "prevent unnecessary damage to or destruction of vegetation, wildlife and forest cover [and] help preserve the natural beauty of the premises, avoid pollution or contamination of all ground and surface waters and remove or bury all trash, garbage and other waste materials" (5). Cultural artifacts and structures also fell under these categories of relative protection, as the lease states that "the Government shall not deliberately appropriate, damage, remove, excavate, disfigure, deface or destroy any object of antiquity, prehistoric ruin or monument" (5).

After decades of denying that any depleted uranium existed on the property, the U.S. Army finally disclosed to the public in 2005 that the weapons used in the 1960s on the base had contained depleted uranium—this information had previously been classified. In 2013, the Hawai'i State Department of Health published a report entitled "The Facts about Depleted Uranium in Hawai'i" amid the growing concern that depleted uranium had entered the water supply on the Big Island of Hawai'i. This echoed an earlier 2010

report by Cabrera Services, a radiological science, engineering, and remedi-
ation company, which claimed that "no significantly increased risks for the
human receptors considered in this document exist at PTA. As a result, no
adverse human health impacts are likely to occur as a result of exposure to
the uranium present in the soil at PTA." Nevertheless, in 2014, Kamakako'i,
the online platform for the Office of Hawaiian Affairs, produced the short
documentary *Pōhakuloa: Now That You Know, Do You Care?* to highlight
the inconsistencies in the U.S. Army's reporting of both the presence and the
effects of depleted uranium and to call for Hawaiian sovereignty of Pōhakuloa. The documentary explores the cultural significance of the location of
Pōhakuloa and how the military's presence and its decades of weapons testing and training exercises are both desecrations of sacred lands and environmental disasters.

The rhetorical strategy of *Pōhakuloa: Now That You Know, Do You Care?*
begins with its title: that knowledge must engender action and empathy. Positioned as a presentation of previously unknown, if not covered up, information, the documentarians challenge the viewers in the form of a question to
care about the issue at hand. "Now" knowing this information, what will the
viewer do to address this issue? The documentary joins both Kānaka Maoli
activists and settler environmentalist discourses on why the public should be
concerned about the threat of not only the destruction of and displacement
from sacred Kānaka Maoli cultural sites but also the potential health effects
of depleted uranium for the community at large. In the opening moments of
the documentary, the voiceover of the narrator is heard over images of the
sunrise from a mountain view: "Since the beginning, Hawaiians have existed
as part of the living universe. For generations, families lived in harmony with
nature. This harmony is being destroyed, on what some would consider the
most sacred place on the island" (Carrillo). The documentary begins with its
argument that there is a violent distinction between the current actions of the
U.S. military and the cultural importance of the site.

In the opening sequence, activist Kalani Flores argues for remembering
Pōhakuloa's sacred status. "If people can just remember that these things are
still sacred, that Mauna a Wākea is still sacred, Pōhakuloa still sacred," he says,
"that if we all start to remember that, then there will be a shift in consciousness of humanity. Then these things won't be allowed to continue to occur."
Through this opening passage, Flores articulates the violence of forgetting as a
structural effect of settler colonialism and U.S. militarism; he advocates that if

people know of a place's sacred status, then these violences will not continue in the same way. As the Pōhakuloa Training Area sits at the base of Mauna Kea, its location holds great significance in Kānaka Maoli epistemologies as a wahi pana, a sacred place, as the site of the birthplace of the Hawaiian people according to multiple important mo'olelo (histories or stories). According to Flores, "We're right in the energetic piko (umbilical cord) in the center of the island." In the opening scene, Flores walks out to an ahu (altar) at Pōhakuloa and performs ceremony in the direction of Mauna Kea. In the voiceover, he explains the importance of this location, "the sacredness of the earth that we stand on—so from Wākea (sky father) to Papahānaumoku (earth mother) it's acknowledging all that ke akua the creator bestowed upon us."

For Kānaka Maoli, āina, most simply translated as "land" but etymologically translated as "that which feeds," functions not only as a provider of sustenance but also as a genealogical ancestor. As explained by geographer Katrina-Ann R. Kapā'anaokalāokeola Nākoa Oliveira in *Ancestral Places: Understanding Kanaka Geographies*, the Indigenous epistemologies of Kānaka Maoli and their conceptions of space and place are fundamentally different from those imposed by Western occupiers. Works such as Oliveira's and others attempt to disrupt colonial legacies of the built environment by using Kānaka Maoli understandings of ecology to draw attention to environmental concerns ignored by settler colonialists, such as the risks posed by depleted uranium. While the United States uses risk to justify security and militarization, Kānaka Maoli activists are using the language of risk to draw attention to the latent evironmental hazards. Nevertheless, such Kānaka Maoli rhetorics have continued to be obfuscated by militaristic discourse of national defense, and as I argue here, the documentary and the poem function as resistance to these violent paradigms.

Mauna Kea has recently (2015 and 2019–20) been the subject of controversy due to the debate over the prospective construction of the Thirty Meter Telescope upon its peak. In representations by contemporary media, the debate over the construction has been largely characterized as one of "myth" versus "science"—as Kānaka Maoli kia'i (protectors) defend the genealogy of Mauna Kea as piko and do not consent to it as an acceptable site for a telescope or any other construction. Historically and contemporarily, there are multiple important appearances of Mauna Kea's sacred status. In "Mapping Abundance on Mauna a Wākea as a Practice of Ea," Candace Fujikane documents the significance of Mauna Kea by explaining its genealogical origins:

The mauna is the piko or summit where the earth meets the sky. The mauna is also the elder sibling of both the kalo plant and the Kānaka, the people, all fathered by Wākea. Through this moʻokūʻauhau, this genealogy, Mauna a Wākea is the piko as the umbilicus, the cord that binds the people to their ancestors and all of their pulapula, the seedling descendants, all those who came before and all those who will come after. Mauna a Wākea thus embodies a profound sense of familial connectedness to the past, present, and future. (25)

Mauna Kea also figures in the *Kumulipo*, a more than 2,100-line ʻŌlelo Hawaiʻi creation chant, which explains not only the genealogy of Kānaka Maoli and its aliʻi (royalty) but also every aspect of Hawaiʻi life and ecology. More specifically, a *mele hanau*, or birth song, entitled "He kanaenae no ka hanau ana o Kauikeaouli," written in honor of the birth of King Kamehameha III, Kauikeaouli, in 1814, and published in a Hawaiian language newspaper called *Nupepa Kuokoa* (1866) explains the significance of Mauna Kea:

Moe Wākea moe ia Papa,	Wākea [slept] with Papa,
Hanau ka la na Wākea,	The sun was born to Wākea,
He keiki kapu na Wākea,	A sacred [child] of Wākea,
[. . .]	[. . .]
Hanau ka mauna	The mountain was born,
he makahiapo kapu na Kea.	the sacred first-born of Kea.
	(Maly 9)[1]

Furthermore, according to Candace Fujikane, this mele hanau was chanted by kiaʻi mauna (protectors of Mauna Kea) on 24 June 2015, thus extending its political pertinence into the contemporary movements. These two texts, the *Kumulipo* and "He kanaenae no ka hanau ana o Kauikeaouli," are among the most frequently cited as explaining the connection of the sacredness of the mountain to the Kānaka Maoli definition of land, ʻāina, as a genealogical ancestor.

In the *Kumulipo*, Wākea and Papa (short for Papahānaumoku), mentioned above, have two children. The first, named Hāloa, is born stillborn, and *kalo* (taro) grows in its place. The second child, also named Hāloa, considers the kalo kaikuaʻana (the older sibling to whom the younger one owes great respect), and, as Noenoe Silva explains, "This story of Hāloa is often invoked to symbolize the Kanaka belief in familial relationship to land and opposition to ownership over land" (101–2). 'Āina (land), "that which feeds," within Hawaiian cosmology is part of a larger, balanced agricultural system from the top of the mountain to the ocean, called ahupua'a. The notion of land as a familial, life-giving entity presents epistemological conflicts, as Silva explains, with non-Hawaiians, as the debate over Mauna Kea shows, as Hawaiian epistemologies are written off as "myth" or "religion." In this case, each group's understanding and determination of land use appear to be incommensurable. The state's dismissal of Hawaiian epistemologies in favor of continued military exercises at the Pōhakuloa Training Area demonstrates a clear privileging of Western epistemologies over Indigenous ones, one that draws its position from the long history of settler colonialism throughout Hawai'i. Conversely, the movement for the protection of Mauna Kea has been called by Kanaka Maoli political scientist Noelani Goodyear-Ka'ōpua as an opportunity for "futures-creation." As she explains, "In this movement Kānaka Maoli and settler allies work together to unmake relations of settler colonialism and imperialism, protecting Indigenous relationships between human and nonhumans through direct action and compassionate engagement with settler-state law enforcement" (185).

In *Pōhakuloa: Now That You Know, Do You Care?*, depleted uranium's environmental toxicity demonstrates the desecration of 'āina through both weapons testing on the base and the fenced-off enclosure of removing Kānaka Maoli from their ancestors. Both the known presence and the ambiguous risk of depleted uranium are causes for alarm among Kānaka Maoli and settler environmental activists alike. As Jim Albertini, founder of Malu 'Āina Center for Non-Violent Education and Action, describes in *Pōhakuloa: Now That You Know, Do You Care?*, depleted uranium is "creating a military toxic stew that we don't know the full implications of." He continues, "We can't do to the land or to the water or to the plants or the animals without doing to ourselves." Shared risk of toxicity between the 'āina and Kānaka Maoli becomes another connection between them. The imbrication of delayed temporality and harm is also key to the documentarian's argument; the health effects of depleted uranium may take a long time to fully ascertain, and land recovery once, or if, the military leaves will also take decades. The documentary also offers a counterexample of another military testing ground in Hawai'i—the island of Kaho'olawe, which was commandeered through martial law by the military and shelled for decades after World War II—to demonstrate the power of the military to take what it wants as well as its murky justifications for doing so. In the documentary, Kalani Flores states: "The Navy would say in the press conference that Kahoʻolawe is a strategic military, you know, bombing site, bombing practice area. It is significant to the national defense of the United States and we need it. But as we see they didn't really need it. Eventually the island was returned." Indeed, after decades of Kānaka Maoli activism resisting military testing at Kahoʻolawe, the island was eventually transferred back to the state of Hawaiʻi in 1993.

Though returned, Kahoʻolawe was environmentally devastated, littered with unexploded ordnances and metal debris after "underwater torpedoes; air-dropped, general purpose bombs; three, 500-ton TNT charges; target airfields; and other weapons were set off there" (Cerizo). After 25 years of cleanup and restoration, 10 of which were overseen by the military in a $400 million ordnance removal process, the island is still only about 75 percent cleared: "'There's probably never going to be an absolute clean-up of the island,' said Mike Nahoopii of the Kahoʻolawe Island Reserve Commission. 'Once you start using a piece of property for military bombing, you're never going to remove every single bomb'" (Deniz). The temporal injustice of environmental harm from military testing is aptly summarized by a title from *Hawaii News Now*: "The Bombing of Kahoʻolawe Went on for Decades: The Clean-up Will Last Generations." This again amplifies the urgency of the "now" in the documentary's title: *Pōhakuloa: Now That You Know, Do You Care?* Military-induced environmental-cultural destruction at Kahoʻolawe, and the slow but possible recovery from it, is a mirror to the merging of environmentalism, sacredness, and sovereignty that the documentary uses to resist military presence at Pōhakuloa, as stated in the voiceover by the narrator:

> It's up to us to ask the questions for all who live in Hawaiʻi. What are we doing to our land, our air, and our groundwater? If no one answers, there could be consequences for generations to come. If we don't push for action, who is held accountable for the health of our families, our children, and for the troops who put themselves in harm's way? If we are silent, who speaks for our culture and the preservation of our beliefs? Remember the lessons of Kahoʻolawe. If not for the voices of a brave few, where would we be today?

The Pōhakuloa Training Area, the documentary reminds its audience, is five times the size of the island of Kahoʻolawe, increasing the potential environmental harm of continued testing there exponentially. The documentary always remains clear that this is an issue of settler colonial interlopers, the U.S. government and military, destroying land and culture and bodies through its "testing." The documentary suggests that more than one type of training has been occurring at Pōhakuloa—not only the training of soldiers for war but also the training of Hawaiians into passivity, complacency, and ignorance regarding the 'āina, their genealogy, and sovereignty: "The worst thing we can do is nothing. The biggest obstacles to an acceptable outcome are apathy and inaction," the documentary's narrator concludes. The final lines of the documentary come from Skippy Ioane, a Kanaka Maoli activist: "You can say 'you don't know,' but this [*sic*] what this supposed to do—make you know. And if you know, do you care? Now that you know. And if you don't care, how come? What happened to you, you know, your cultural dignity? You're supposed to be mad!"

Like the documentary, Kanaka Maoli poet Sage Uʻilani Takehiro's "Progress at Pōhakuloa" seeks to undo settler colonial erasure of Indigenous histories and genealogical connection with the land for Kānaka Maoli individuals. It, too, invokes histories of Kānaka progeneration as a way to convey the importance of both physically and discursively reclaiming sacred places such as Pōhakuloa. In the poem, the poet juxtaposes, through a dialogue, a contemporary "Hawaiian Warrior" employed at the Pōhakuloa Training Area as a guard with the poem's speaker, who is honoring a sacred place in "the dirt under this American Military Training Camp" (5). The figure of the soldier, within the poem, embodies the subaltern positionality as both subjugated and utilitarian within the parameters of the colonial and military project. His role in the poem's narrative suggests the effects of mental colonization through an embracing of hegemonic narratives.[2] In the second stanza, the poem's speaker, conversely, begins the Warrior's *re*connection to the land by connecting his work at the base with their own work of honoring the land: "Love this dirt with me Hawaiian Warrior, as you do every day of / your career, guarding the entrance to the American Military Training / Camp" (6–8).

The speaker then removes the land from belonging to the "American Military" and returns it to the Warrior as a genealogical relationship, imploring the Hawaiian Warrior to "love this dirt that gave birth to your Grandfather" with "Both our feet firmly planted in Papahānaumoku" (8, 11). These lines recall not only the birth history of the Warrior's own genealogy but also the narratives of genealogy for his ancestors alongside the ancestry of the islands themselves. Papahānaumoku, etymolgically, "native-born—birth—island," figures as the "earth mother" and reminds the Warrior and the reader of the genealogical and also *living* connection to land. To be "planted" in this place insists and reminds him of the genealogical ancestor, Hāloa, the taro that grows in this place, and ʻāina, that which feeds. The relationship between human and earth is a nurturing and sustaining one—one that grows when planted. The relationship is not that of planted on, but "planted *in*" (my emphasis), insisting on the ways in which the human is always already imbricated with the land.

The speaker turns to ʻŌlelo Hawaiʻi and Hawaiian Creole English in her address of the Warrior in the third stanza. "E Hawaiian Warrior, I not pau yet," she states. "E" functions as an address but also as an imperative. "No can survive if we go back to da ancient days," the soldier states in Hawaiian Creole English or Pidgin. This adoption of the idea of indigeneity as past, as "da ancient days," reinscribes racist Western narratives of the native as primitive, recalls notions of the vanishing native, but most significantly, as distinct from and incompatible with modernity. The vision of progress held by the character of the Hawaiian Warrior is clearly that of a Western notion of progress—of Indigenous land dispossession, industrialization, and militarization. The speaker's "E" reclaims the Warrior's attention away from the colonial-imposed forgetting he has of his own genealogical connections—Indigenous relationships to the land that refute categorical distinctions between "ancient days" and the present used to justify the dispossession of their land.

In the confrontation of the Hawaiian Warrior, the speaker knows that warrior needs to understand his own disembodiment and displacement from the land, ʻāina. She therefore speaks of the Warrior's lack of knowledge and investment in Indigenous epistemologies as a physical blindness: "if I were to pluck out your ʻŌiwi eyes they would bleed, pulsate and die." To describe his eyes here is deliberate—to remind the Warrior of his indigeneity but also to force him to return to his body as a site of genealogy. She also suggests that even if he can't "see" it or doesn't know it, he remains "ʻŌiwi." "ʻŌiwi," as defined by Mary Kawena Pukui and Samuel H. Elbert, literally translates to "native, native son" and also has a secondary definition of "physique, appearance; to appear" (280). Etymologically, ʻŌiwi connotes "of the bones," suggesting not only that his indigeneity is in his bones but also that he is made of it, too. By turning, or returning, his eyes and body to the earth, the Warrior can have renewed intimacy with his past and future: "plopped on this / dirt, your dried eyeball juice will ejaculate in your wahine and those / ʻŌiwi eyes will generate in your children. They will come and give / love to this dirt they come from. How do you wish them to / see it?" (13–18). Immersed with the earth, he can make new kin, continue his genealogical connections, and see the earth anew. He will also create the possibility that his children will "see" the "dirt they come from" with "love," just as it loves them back.

The speaker invokes the long genealogies with the place where they stand, reminding the soldier of not only his past, as a child of Papahānaumoku and a symbol of the reproduction and continued presence of the Hawaiian people. The speaker specifically encourages his affective reconnection to Papahānaumoku as a means of reconnecting emotionally to the land:

> She watches you work long hours every day at Pōhakuloa. She sees the
> way you look at her, like you are in love. She wants you to say it out
> loud so everyone can hear you say, "I am proud to be Hawaiian." She
> is not ancient. She stands before you. She will stand after you. She
> stands in beauty, despite the unexploded ordnances scattered like
> pimples on her nose.
>
> She loves us, as we are her children. Care for her so that she can care
> for you. Love her. Love her out loud. Aloha. She forgives you
> Hawaiian Warrior. She forgives me. (29–37)

The speaker takes away the settler control of time, linearity, and progress and instead reminds the Hawaiian Warrior of what truly holds power now—"She stands before you"—and what truly endures—"She will stand after you . . . despite the unexploded ordnances scattered like / pimples on her nose." He regains power and self-determination by emotionally connecting to a past that is also his future: "Love her. Love her out loud. Aloha." The mana, the power, the "progress" at Pōhakuloa, then, is not the military as a source of so-called advancement but the progression, the progeneration, and the perpetuation of Kānaka Maoli intimacies and ways of knowing.

In August 2019, the Hawaiʻi Supreme Court ruled on the suit brought by Ching and Kahaulelio, voting 5–0 that the state of Hawaiʻi had not properly managed the ceded lands at Pōhakuloa. Establishing that the state had failed to execute their terms of the lease and oversee the military's use of the land, the decision now requires the state to "develop and execute a plan to conduct regular, periodic monitoring and inspection [and] take an active role in preserving trust property and may not passively allow [trust lands] to fall into ruin" (Burnett). The decision is a landmark victory in holding the U.S. military and the government of Hawaiʻi accountable for, respectively, their destructive tactics on ceded land and subsequent inaction to protect and preserve the land. The documentary, the poem, and the persistence of social movements in Hawai'i denote important shifts in awareness and knowledge dissemination about not only the actions of settler colonial militaries and governments but also the re-insistence of Indigenous epistemologies in the public sphere. Settler colonialism in Hawai'i aims to undermine Indigenous connection to the land by violently displacing them physically, mentally, and emotionally from the 'āina, their kin and genealogical ancestor. *Pōhakuloa: Now That You Know, Do You Care?* and "Progress at Pōhakuloa" educate settlers and insist upon the continued and ongoing presence of Kānaka Maoli ways of knowing and their continued significance for self-determination as well as ecological sustainability through relationality and care.

Note

1. Translated by Maly and Maly (2005). Replacement translations were added by the author. "He kanaenae no ka hanau ana o Kauikeaouli" is well-known to have incorporated kaona, what Brandy Nālani McDougall calls "the intellectual practice of hiding and finding meaning that encompasses the allegorical, the symbolic, the allusive, and the figurative," and therefore can have multiple interpretations, meanings, and translations (6).

2. The poem, by including the character of the "Hawaiian Warrior," also invokes the large recruitment of Indigenous peoples into the armed forces from the American states and territories in the Pacific: Hawai'i, Guam, American Samoa, and the Northern Mariana Islands.

Works Cited

Beck, Ulrich. *Risk Society: Towards a New Modernity*. Sage, 1992.
Burnett, John. "High Court Rules State Breached Trust Duties at Pōhakuloa Training Area." *Hawaii Tribune-Herald*, 23 Aug. 2019, https://www.hawaiitribune-herald.com/2019/08/23/hawaii-news/high-court-rules-state-breached-trust-duties-at-pohakuloa-training-area/
Cabrera Services. "Final Pōhakuloa Training Area Firing Range Baseline Human Health Risk Assessment for Residual Depleted Uranium." *U.S. Army*, June 2010, https://home.army.mil/pohakuloa/application/files/9515/5961/2205/PTA_BHHRA_Report_Rev_2.pdf
Carrillo, Ruben. *Pōhakuloa: Now That You Know, Do You Care?* April 11, 2013. https://vimeo.com/63867248
Cerizo, Kehaulani. "25 Years Hence, Recovery Work Continues on the Island of Kahoolawe: Anniversary of Sign-over Ceremony Is a Time for Reflection and Vision." *Maui News*, 5 May 2019, https://www.mauinews.com/news/local-news/2019/05/25-years-hence-recovery-work-continues-on-the-island-of-kahoolawe/. Accessed 29 Sept. 2019.
Deniz, Lacy. "The Bombing of Kaho'olawe Went on for Decades. The Clean-up Will Last Generations." *Hawaii News Now*, 27 Feb. 2018, updated 15 Aug. 2019, https://www.hawaiinewsnow.com/story/37604472/the-bombing-of-kahoolawe-went-on-for-decades-clean-up-will-take-generations/. Accessed 29 Sept. 2019.

Department of Defense. "Depleted Uranium on Hawaii's Army Ranges." *U.S. Army*, http:// www.garrison.hawaii.army.mil/du/faq.htm. Accessed 15 Oct. 2016.

Fujikane, Candace. "Mapping Abundance on Mauna a Wākea as a Practice of Ea." *Hūlili: Multidisciplinary Research on Hawaiian Well-Being*, vol. 11, no. 1, 23–54.

Gibson, Daniel, and Jon Cheatwood. "The Army, Engagement, and America's Pacific Century." *Military Review*, January–February 2016, https://www.armyupress.army.mil/ Portals/7/military-review/Archives/English/MilitaryReview_20160228_art013.pdf. Accessed 25 Sept. 2019.

Giddens, Anthony. *Runaway World: How Globalization Is Reshaping Our Lives.* Taylor & Francis, 2003.

Goodyear-Kaʻōpua, Noelani. "Protectors of the Future, Not Protestors of the Past: Indigenous Pacific Activism and Mauna A Wakea." *South Atlantic Quarterly*, vol. 116, no. 1, 2017, 184–94.

Maly, Kepa, and Onaona Maly. *"Mauna Kea–Ka Piko Kaulana O Ka ʻĀina" (Mauna Kea—The Famous Summit of the Land): A Collection of Native Traditions, Historical Accounts, and Oral History Interviews for: Mauna Kea, the Lands of Kaʻo.* Kumu Pono Associates, 2005.

McDougall, Brandy Nālani. *Finding Meaning: Kaona and Contemporary Hawaiian Literature.* U of Arizona P, 2016.

Oliveira, Katrina-Ann R. Kapāʻanaokalāokeola Nākoa. *Ancestral Places: Understanding Kanaka Geographies.* Oregon State UP, 2014.

Pukui, Mary Kawena, and Samuel H. Elbert. "ʻŌiwi." *Hawaiian Dictionary*, edited by Mary Kawena Pukui and Samuel H. Elbert. Revised and Enlarged Edition, U of Hawaiʻi P, 1986.

Silva, Noenoe. *Aloha Betrayed: Native Hawaiian Resistance to American Colonialism.* Duke UP, 2004.

State of Hawaii, Board of Land and Natural Resources. *State General Lease No. S-3849; U.S. Lease, Contract No. DA-94-626-ENG-80.* State of Hawaiʻi, Department of Land and Natural Resources, 24 Aug. 1964, http://www.nhlchi.org/images/GL3849--Original-Document-1964-08-17.pdf. Accessed 25 Sept. 2019.

Takehiro, Sage Uʻilani. *Honua.* Kahuaomanoa Press, 2007.

Wood, Houston. *Displacing Natives: The Rhetorical Production of Hawaiʻi.* Rowman and Littlefield, 1999.

9

"Disentrancing" the Rot of Colonialism in Philippine and Canadian Ecopoetry

Rina Garcia Chua

In November 2015, the known Catholic nation of the Philippines witnessed a rare (but often occurring) show of solidarity among its sectarian and non-sectarian religious communities: bishops, priests, pastors, and the faithful all gathered outside the Mindanao Mines and Geosciences Bureau's office and held up banners that cried "Stop Militarization and Plunder in Minda—NOW!" in response to the violent displacement of the Lumad peoples from their ancestral land for mineral mining that still prevails.[1] The island of Mindanao, where the Lumad peoples have ancestrally lived, has rich deposits of copper and nickel. This widespread displacement and destruction of the environment have been a cause largely ignored by previous government administrations, despite being undertaken by many powerful support groups—mostly nongovernment organizations.[2] The specific act of ignoring the rights of the Lumad is also in direct violation of the law, for in 1\997, the Republic Act No. 8371 (otherwise known as the Indigenous Peoples Rights Act of 1997) was signed into Congress. It even requires the state itself to protect the Filipino Indigenous communities' right to their ancestral land without discrimination or distinction and with respect to their "customs, traditions, values, beliefs, interests, and institutions" (Const., Rep. Act 8371, Chap. 1, Sec. II).

This incident can be viewed as parallel to what happened to Canada's Indigenous peoples 150 years ago. The British North America Act of 1867, or the Indian Act, ensured that the welfare of the "Indians" and their lands was under federal responsibility. The reserves were subsumed under the Canadian Ministry of Indian and Northern Affairs, including the well-being of the Indigenous peoples living within these reserves. Furthermore, an "Indian agent" (another white settler) was assigned to a particular reserve, from whom the Indigenous peoples needed to ask permission to sell crops they had grown or harvested themselves or to wear their traditional dress off reserves. Even worse, the law was seemingly manipulated and abused to allow for extensive mining, forestry, farming, and settlement by the non-Indigenous inside the reserve lands. When Indigenous peoples began to fight for the recognition of their rights to land ownership and against the abuse of power and corruption within the Indian Act, "the Act was amended to make it an offence for an Aboriginal person to retain a lawyer for the purpose of advancing a claim" (Hutchings). In relation, Renisa Mawani asserts that the Indian Act at the provincial level was enforced not to finally serve as recognition of Indigenous rights but rather to alleviate the colonial anxiousness in maintaining "distinct boundaries around Indian-ness" (51). Now, the Indian Act takes on different roles for the many First Nations communities in Canada—some sign their own treaties with their provincial government, while some have signed onto the First Nations Land Management Act of 1999.[3] Others remain governed by the Indian Act, as they appreciate some of its benefits (e.g., tax exemptions in some reserves) while denouncing its problematic historical context.

I argue, then, that the parallelism is distinct: both the Philippines' Indigenous Peoples Rights Act of 1997 and Canada's Indian Act of 1867 were laws that appeared as giant strides toward the diverse concepts of reconciliation for both countries; however, they appeared and are appearing as yet another manifestation of the systemic imperial tendencies of previously colonized spaces.[4] The parallelism here, however, invites thoughtful and embodied consideration of comparative indigeneity that exists in different lands. Though the injustices of the Indigenous peoples in the Philippines and Canada may appear similar, the interlocking systems of oppressions that occur within each community are complex and differentiated. Awareness of these realities is the reason why I refer to these oppressions as "intersections" throughout the chapter.

These intersections between the two acts in two different countries somehow emphasize this pervasive "rot" that has continued to permeate much of the previously colonized spaces in different parts of the world. Ann Laura Stoler, in her introduction to *Imperial Debris: On Ruins and Ruinations*, uses a phrase from Derek Walcott's poem "Ruins of a Great House" to distinguish a symbol of "ruination" that appears in colonial zones of vulnerability: "the rot that remains." What is rot in postcolonial countries? To determine the rot is "to delineate the specific ways in which peoples and places are laid to waste, where debris falls, and whose lives it accumulates" (Stoler 29). Integral to identifying ruination within postcolonial systems is also to make visible these forms of rot that different colonial legacies have affected. Furthermore, in pinpointing where the rot remains, there may be an answer to one of the questions Stoler raises: "How do imperial formations persist in their material debris, in ruined landscapes and through the social ruination of people's lives?" (10).

The ruination is pervasive in the two sociohistorical situations in the Philippines and Canada, and it is enacted through the act of "ignoring" the plight of Indigenous peoples or racialized minorities. Though motions for reconciliation have been initiated, most predominantly in Canada by its government and in the Philippines by certain religious groups, activist clusters, and nongovernment organizations, the act of ignoring Indigenous rights to ancestral lands still prevails. This act of ignoring has extended also to turning away from the overt acts of violence toward the Indigenous—whether through the enforcement of paramilitary forces, subversive racism, or even environmental starvation, often in capitalist and neoliberal ventures. The striking parallelisms between the two nation-states make me wonder: Will reconciliation with the Indigenous communities ever be achieved if the governments in power persistently ignore their ancestral, lawful, and human rights? I also argue in this chapter that the constant violations of Indigenous rights by the ruling hegemony in both countries have allowed the citizenry's majority to be ambivalent to the plight of these communities; this ambivalence, in turn, has enabled these violations to continue. With this, I operationalize two ecopoems—"Guilt" by Achilles B. Mina of the Philippines and "The Man Who Logged the West Ridge" by Tom Wayman of Canada[5]—to illustrate that the Filipinx[6] postcolonial subject and the Canadian white settler citizens have been kept in a "trance" by the appropriation brought about by preconceptions of how reconciliation should be and that this kind of trance most of us are in is *still* a debris of imperial power that is rotting within many of us as a cultural paradigm. This rot must be recognized and acknowledged before we can "disentrance" ourselves from ruining Aboriginal communities and their relationship with multiple environments—environments that most of us occupy.

The Philippine Postcolonial Subject

At this point, I must devote space for my genealogical disclosure: I am classified in the Filipinx society as mestiza—my mother is half-Spanish and my father is half-Chinese. I am what Angela Reyes (211) reminds us is one who contains bodily and linguistic doubleness; I signify "the privilege associated with collaborating and containing workings of power." It is perhaps significant to note, uncomfortably, that my Chinese grandfather married into my grandmother's family, and she is the youngest daughter of a prolific politician and educator. My individual history, at times, make me feel that I interpellate five hundred years of colonial and neocolonial rule that has been historicized as vile and violent and has discombobulated many present local systems; perhaps I do.

Despite being a second-generation Filipinx citizen[7] in my family, I am still what I would call a "postcolonial subject"—a body that does not erase the debris of colonialism that is genealogically a part of me. The privileges of this very genealogy—no matter how far removed I am from its previous elitism—separate my materiality from Indigenous Filipino citizens like the Lumad peoples who do not share the same opportunities that I do. My identity is one that is an "iconization of mixedness and excessiveness" (Reyes 212); it is a distinction of Philippine elite types—a regurgitation of the colonial hierarchy that allowed Spanish colonizers to dominate and subjugate the native Filipinos, or as they called them during colonial times, the *indio*.

Further, the privileges of my mixedness have allowed me certain advantages that many Filipinxs do not have access to, which is a chance to find multiple opportunities within the Western gaze. The postcolonial struggle of the Philippines as an independent nation is oftentimes marred by existing colonial systems that are incessant under different manifestations of imperial exigencies. As a postcolonial subject, the Filipinx is, then, at the crosshairs of the struggle for identity and independence and the imperial Western hegemony that still permeates much of the national systems. Oftentimes, this struggle is apparent in a Filipinx's rejection of traditional values and religion (mostly Catholic) and the yearning for modernization (i.e., Western ideals) or in the deep-seated unwavering faith in Catholicism and loyalty to traditional values. There is also the apparent vitriol against those who have succumbed to "modernization" (eventually as modernized Filipinx are said to be a national betrayal).

Also, it is important to espouse that

scholars have tied modernity to many things, most notably emergent capitalist structures, as well as industrialization, surveillance, and military power (Giddens 1990). If Europe's "laboratories of modernity were its colonies, not

the metropole" (Stoler and Cooper 1997), then modernity is also inseparable
from colonialism (Quijano 2007). (Reyes 216–17)

To become modern and to embody what is demanded of or afforded by this
"mixedness" means to reject those that are deemed impediments to modernization. The Third World situation of the Philippines means that it still
strives for economic gains so that it hopefully becomes, one day, a developed
country where all of its citizens purportedly enjoy their rights and privileges
like any Westerner is able to do in their own chosen and occupied spaces.
However, the governments in power have allowed the exploit of the country's
rich natural resources to those who can afford to invest in them (e.g., China,
the United States, and even Canada)—natural resources that are usually
within the lands of the Indigenous communities. For the sake of economic
gain and modernization, resources have to be and have been utilized despite
the laws that are in place to ensure the right to land of the Indigenous. What
has happened is that modernization is favored over the Indigenous rights,
and, in turn, modernization and promises of socioeconomic prosperity for
many Filipinxs have allowed violent Indigenous land grabbing to fly below
the consciousness of many citizens. As a postcolonial subject, one that is still
within the grips of the imperial exigencies of the empire, the Filipinx is both
complicit to and powerless against the hegemonies that enforce the violations
of Indigenous rights.

I find that this kind of persistent imperial rot is present in Achilles B.
Mina's ecopoem "Guilt"—a poem of irony that encapsulates how a postcolonial subject in the Philippines reacts to, at times, the blatant atrocities against
Indigenous communities. Here, the persona is confronted with a burning on
a mountain as he is traveling on a bus. He wonders who could be burning
wood up in the mountains when he knows that the tribes that used to reside
in them have long fled their ancestral homes:

> The tribe has long left the detritus floor, the understory,
> Their story lost in their haste, their labored retreat
> From the falling trees, from the fallen ghosts of the keep. (lines 7–9)

The act of forgetting the tribe's stories and losing these narratives as they have
left their lands is an instance of the rot in the ecopoem. It is not uncommon to
lose the Indigenous ways of living and their respective cultures once they are
driven away from their spaces; thus, when the persona likens them to "fallen

ghosts," it is an indication that the rot's effects have defeated these cultures— they have been defaced from their lands by "losing" a battle that they have never even been an active part of. Furthermore, in removing the Indigenous from their lands, they have been rendered invisible again. Therefore, is there a chance for self-reflexive reconciliation for the postcolonial subject in the ecopoem? Mina continues:

> I, too, would have run from the trees
> Had I seen the birds fall.
> But the bus had its nose toward the light
> And I had my brow toward sleep
> At last lost from last remembrances. (lines 14–18)

I go back once more to the ecopoem's title, which seems to be in direct contrast to the last few lines—the persona would have, say, been more concerned about the plight of the Indigenous ("I, too, would have run from the trees") but has succumbed to sleep (or has chosen to sleep instead?) to lose "last remembrances." It may appear that there is no "guilt" at all there and that the postcolonial subject narrative does not even move beyond the point of historicizing the embattled mountain. Yet, "Guilt" may suggest more. Is the persona ignoring *rather than* remembering? Also, in being guilty, is the persona refusing to continuously ignore what he has ignored before and, in doing so, disentrancing one's self from the violence of the national hegemony? This may be an interesting take on what is initially a passive ecopoetry of witnessing; in considering the concept of "disentrancing," this may show how potent ecopoetry is as a space for self-reflexive reconciliation—of remembering and understanding complicity and unpacking the repercussion of this acquiescence.

The Canadian White Settler Subject

Ariel Hernandez (93) warns against the "banner of nationhood" that citizens of a country are oftentimes subjected to. It is when there is an imagined national identity standing in the ideologies of the cacique democracy[8] that violence is used as a weapon of erasure and cohesion. Whatever does not fit the national "mold" is subjected to erasure, and whoever is not serving the cohesive structure of hierarchical relations that are enforced by the hegemonies is eradicated. It is disheartening to further note that "an outburst of violence is frequently the predictive outcome of nation-building" (Hernandez 94). The violence talked about here is not only the material violence that is apparent in some areas in the Philippines—where politicians actively eliminate by violence their opposing camps (such as the appalling Maguindanao Massacre[9])—but also the *symbolic violence*, where the desire to protect the imagined national identity and to erase whatever does not fit the cohesive structure is embedded in the cognition and actions of Filipinx citizens. This symbolic violence is at times so embedded into societal consciousness that, when it occurs, it is not immediately acknowledged and visible. Thus, what the Filipino Indigenous communities symbolize for the postcolonial Filipinx citizen does not often fit the hierarchical relations of a stable system that is essentialized by the Philippine national hegemony. These hierarchical relations range from socioeconomic satisfaction, to Western acceptance, to the ever-elusive desire to be a part of the First World.

Though a different kind of complexity, a thread of symbolic violence (oftentimes enacted as material violence) also predominantly runs through the enculturation of Canadian national identity. The complexity in this kind of violence against Canada's First Nations communities that still exists until now has been tied to the discourse of settler colonialism—the permanent occupation of territory at the expense of forcibly removing Indigenous peoples from their lands to build and protect a distinct Canadian national identity.

It is imperative to stress that colonialism and white settler colonialism are different, yet these terms inform one another. The former is a historical discussion, and the latter is a necessary *historicized* discourse that exists right here, right now, and not in the past (Bonds and Inwood 716). The prominence and obvious persistence of settler communities in Canada have pushed the historicized discourse even further to see it as one that endures because of the desire to eliminate Indigenous populations—once again, to serve the distinct national identity of a Canadian who is hardworking, polite, productive, and (hopefully) ethnically white. In other words, the social reproduction of whiteness has to ensure that the citizen is as respectable as the "white working-class" citizen. Further, it is the national image of the white working-class Canadian that is enforced here, and more oftentimes this involves symbolic violence against what the Indigenous communities interpellate to the white settlers—they are seen as alcoholics, lazy, criminals, and many other negative connotations.[10] In short, the Indigenous are seen as vulnerable bodies to which the national identity is built *against*; they are the reference point to which Canadian national identity is contrasted as something it must *not* be.

The material production of this hegemonic ideal of the Canadian national identity circumscribes the kind of violence that is enforced on the Indigenous. It is a violence that aims to erase their cultures and families and to sever their sacred relationship with the land. Anne Bonds and Joshua Inwood (716) attest that extermination of Indigenous communities "necessitates" the building of new settlements for the country's socioeconomic gain: the eradication of Indigenous populations, the seizure and privatization of their lands, and the exploitation of marginalized populations in a system of capitalism are established by and reinforced through racism. Now, the violence against Indigenous communities is oftentimes complicated by neoliberal tendencies and conservative discourses that appeal to national values treasured by the citizens' hegemonic majority. Why are the Indigenous peoples' rights to their lands continually sacrificed for the sake of building a strong economy and the necessary national identity of a hardworking white Canadian citizen?

Perhaps the best example in this case is the Keystone Pipeline XL issue, which affects both Canada and the United States. Indigenous peoples in North America have vigorously protested against the pipeline, as its negotiations have failed to meet a suitable treaty with the affected communities, since its construction on ancestral lands will significantly affect those who live there economically, physically, emotionally, and spiritually. Yet, the push for the construction of the pipeline by the Alberta government (led by former premier Rachel Notley and aggressively pursued by succeeding premier Jason Kenney) has seen contentious disagreements among the provinces of Alberta and British Columbia and has affected states in the United States such as Texas.[11] What is lost among these national discourses, at most, are the voices of the affected Indigenous communities who claim that they have not been rightly consulted and that a consensus among the chiefs have not been rightly reached before the government assumed that it has "consent" to pursue the pipeline's construction. Recently, the Royal Canadian Mounted Police started clearing the blockage set up by some clans of the Wet'suwet'en First Nations at Mile Marker 7, the community's traditional lands. The blockage is in protest of a part of the pipeline that is to be built near the Morice River Bridge,[12] within the Unist'ot'en camp. Some negotiations have been underway, and the involved parties have reached compromises. Yet, the question remains about who has spoken for the Indigenous peoples and whether their voices were ever truly considered in the building of this contentious pipeline.

Kari Marie Norgaard (99) has said that "the word ignore is a verb. Ignoring something—especially ignoring a problem that is both important and disturbing—can actually take quite a bit of work." I agree, for the act of ignoring as citizens in postcolonial countries can be translated to "willful neglect" of what is a bigger societal and environmental issue against the Indigenous. I wonder if, in continuing to ignore the violently obvious, we are building another empire of (neoliberal) colonial rule in our own countries against our own fellow and most vulnerable citizens. I suggest that this act of ignoring is also a rot of the empire's crimes—that the colonial hold is so strong in postcolonial and white settler subjects that we are in a "trance" to persist in keeping the invisible invisible.

Tom Wayman's poem "The Man Who Logged the West Ridge" reveals the persistent rot of white settler colonialism and its deleterious effects on the communities that are left to deal with its debris. This poem tells the story of Canada's mythological abundance: how a place's natural resources are obliterated by one man to the point of complete domination, as shown in what he shouts at a pickup truck driving below the ridge:

> I don't have to talk to you.
> I am leaving a few trees. I don't have to do that.
> Bug me, and I'll level this place completely. (lines 20–22)

These lines show a more direct manifestation of the rot that permeates white settler narratives, and it is the belief that nature and people can be dominated through force, coercion, and threats. In addition, it is a challenge to the ecosystem—the man in the poem believes he "owns" the land to the point of privileged exploitation. As the ecopoem demonstrates, the rot seeps through the domination not only of ancestral lands but even of public environmental spaces. The ecopoem's persona stresses that the ridge is part of the valley and is still an empty reminder of what was once there for the rest who still live within the valley. Eventually, the ridge is emptied and the logging corporation packs up and leaves, but somehow the rot remains among the people who live there:

> - its shadow continues to slip down its creekbeds
> every afternoon
> darkening the land as far as the river
> while the other side still receives the sun.

> That shadow, once of a forest,
> now is born from an absence, from money,
> from eight weeks' work. (lines 48–54)

The effects of the rot are catastrophic—they are not only environmental but also socioeconomical. The man has already abandoned the deforested ridge, but the people who live around the area are still haunted by its absence. Perhaps it also shows the domination enforced by entranced white settler subjects? This understanding is where self-reflexive reconciliation may occur, for to grapple with the absence of what once was there may be a point of disentrancing from the larger myth of Canadian abundance as established by the imperial monolith: to contemplate the lost may be a path toward the kind of resistance required to move beyond the rot.

An Attempt at Disentrancing

The challenge of merging historicized racial and environmental discourse between the two countries is to unmap the relationship of identity and space. Sherene Razack asks questions regarding this particular kind of unmapping:

> What is being imagined or projected on to specific spaces and bodies, and what is being enacted there? Who do white citizens know themselves to be and how much does an identity of dominance rely upon keeping racial Others firmly *in place*? How are people kept in their place? And, finally, how does place becomes race? (5)

These queries may not be apparent in the concept of disentrancing, yet in order to problematize the relations of race and environment in two different sociopolitical and economic contexts, it is still useful to address these questions to consider how the act of ignoring pressing Indigenous issues is perpetuated by both the postcolonial subject and the white settler citizens.

How do we disentrance ourselves then from the larger narrative that the imperial has established in our histories and personal systems? It is back to Stoler and Rob Nixon where I have seen the possible signs of disentrancing. Stoler mentions that there is an opportunity to approach language in literary works as "a harsh clarion call and a provocative challenge to name the toxic corrosions and violent accruals of colonial aftermath" (2), while Nixon notes that "the neoliberal era . . . has also intensified resistance, whether through isolated site-specific struggles or through activism that has reached across national boundaries in an effort to build translocal alliances" (4). I believe the manifestation of this rot is in the hierarchical relations that accentuate the liminal space; it is where the cohesive national identity is enforced by the hegemonic system in order to "vanquish" that which does not fit that imagery (Razack 14). It brings about the citizen's willful neglect, and this act of ignoring may be more potent in ensuring that imperial machinations endure. This concept may also be related to what Nixon has termed "slow violence," which is "violence that occurs gradually and out of sight, a violence of delayed destruction that is dispersed across time and space, an attritional violence that is typically not viewed as violence at all" (2). In ignoring our potential role in the situation of the Indigenous communities in both countries, despite being far removed from the direct atrocities of colonialism, we may be reinforcing the slow violence of rot to percolate in our respective societies.

At this point, I believe that the environmental humanities provide the space for discussing and highlighting what has been ignored for so long as the "harsh clarion call" for postcolonial and white settler subjects. Moreover, it may be a point of resistance against the rot—a venue to execute self-reflexive reconciliation as a subject of the citizenry—and a step to rebuilding genuine sustainable, productive relationships and ecosystems with or for the Indigenous communities.

The recognition of being a postcolonial subject and/or white settler *and* the acknowledgment that one has been complicit in the ongoing ancestral and environmental struggles of the Indigenous peoples is a hard pill to swallow. Pushing against the government's and society's paradigm of neoliberal colonialism (and capitalism) is another mountainous hurdle, especially in a Third World country like the Philippines that has shadow paramilitary and/or vigilante groups in the offing (and a past president who had publicly boasted of carrying out drug-related murders himself) as enforced by the persistent cacique democracy. For me, it is clear that no aspirations of reconciliation can be genuine unless the reconciliation is self-reflexive; however, to be vocal about this admittance may be another struggle in itself.

John Collins (182) says that these realizations may "under certain circumstances, become deployed in social action in such a way that they stand mimetically within or closer to actions in ways that continue to comment on what has supposedly already passed." This statement means that deployment in social action (occupying an informed stance, e.g., that may lead to different forms of activism) is the likely logical step when one is disentranced from complicity, but the next step is to do it in terms that are safe, secure, and effective. Ecopoetry (and environmental literature in general) may then be able to provide a tentative and pliable space for that discussion to abound and for multiple narratives from all sides of the liminal space to be considered. Mina's "Guilt" has operationalized irony in remembrance as a form of admitting what one has ignored, while Wayman's "The Man Who Logged the West Ridge" illustrates the consequences of limitless white settler dominion and how it affects the entire nation's environmental and societal ecosystems. These two ecopoems also show that this realization of rot is not an easy feat— one may have to undergo the painful process of disentrancing first before the larger goals of reconciliation (especially on a national level) may ever be considered.

Borrowing from Norgaard, "disentrancing" is also a verb, one that involves a constant internal negotiation with the self as a postcolonial subject or white settler—to fully accept the capability to have been either a part of or a passive witness to the violence against the Indigenous communities' lives and ecosystems.

At the same time, it is also to accept that we may be able to translate (*not* appropriate or abrogate) these for those who are invisible. Nixon offers a possibility for us subjects to do more than just disentrance: he states that those who "stand above the immediate environmental struggles of the poor yet remain bonded through memory (and through their own vertiginous anxieties) to the straitened circumstances from which they or their families emerged" can be "go-betweens" or at least "highly motivated translators" for the plights of the Indigenous, of the invisible (26). Then again, this may be a tricky situation to navigate—for translating can easily spill over to appropriation, which may further exacerbate the complexities of these issues.

What is clear though is that these negotiations and actions, whether they work in a practical setting or not, are the first step to the foundations of transnational ecocritical conversations and perhaps may offer a more conceivable analysis of postcolonial ecocriticism. What is inevitable here is the need for someone like me, a mestiza, to subvert the agency back to myself from the national hegemony—and, ultimately, to those who I need to fight for until I can fight alongside and/or behind them. This rot has to end if we want our Indigenous communities, and ultimately *our* nations, to survive the future.

Notes

1. Unfortunately, the displacement of the Lumad still continues in the southern Philippines. This ongoing act of violence has prompted the United Nations Human Rights Office of the High Commissioner to publish a statement warning the Philippines of the irreversible impact of its continued militarization in Mindanao for the Indigenous communities there. The United Nations reminded the Philippines to "observe its obligations to the Lumad communities" ("Philippines Warned").

2. An example is former Department of Natural Resources secretary Gina Lopez's No to Mining in Palawan movement, which has drawn much-needed support from schools and universities all over the country. This is part of her larger foundation, the ABS-CBN Lingkod Kapamilya Foundation, which promotes ecotourism in embattled areas in the country so that the environment and livelihood of the inhabitants can be sustained.

3. The treatises themselves are interpreted in multiple ways. For most Indigenous peoples, the treatises are sacred and binding and allow them to assert their rights over lands that they have owned and cultivated for hundreds of years before colonization. Meanwhile, at the time when the treatises were established by King George III in the Royal Proclamation of 1763, they were used to recognize Indigenous rights; however, the treatises now are predominantly seen as self-serving deals that enable non-Aboriginals to utilize natural resources often found on sacred First Nations land. More can be gleaned from https://www.thecanadianencyclopedia.ca/en/article/aboriginal-treaties (accessed 5 Mar. 2019).

4. I will use the term "previously colonized spaces" to describe integral parts of the Philippines and Canada in order to keep the term distinguished from a postcolonial space—a space that, I believe, is consciously and/or unconsciously decolonizing itself from the imperial tendencies of the hegemony. It is obvious that I am arguing that both countries are still struggling to *become* postcolonial in their sociohistorical and material conditions and that further unpacking of the colonial influence in many machinations of both countries must still be desired.

5. I have underlined similar themes of postcolonial and white settler subject narratives in two anthologies: the anthology of Philippine ecopoetry that I have edited, *Sustaining the Archipelago*, and the anthology of Canadian nature poems entitled *Open Wide a Wilderness*, edited by Nancy Holmes. "Guilt" is from *Sustaining the Archipelago*, while "The Man Who Logged the West Ridge" is from *Open Wide a Wilderness*.

6. I use the term "Filipinx" with care here, recognizing that it is a diasporic label that many ethnic and/or mixed Filipinos use from outside the "nation" as a way to assert against colonial and gendered vowels from the Spanish language. It is a term that many Filipinos *within* the heartland disavow, for they feel that it is another way that diasporic Filipinxs appropriate and capitalize their struggles—which are admittedly different from those of us who are living away from the archipelago. Many Filipino scholars also remind the diaspora that "Filipino" in itself is already gender neutral in its usage; this is information that I still grapple with. In this chapter, I will use "Filipinx" to refer to Filipinos *as a whole* (including those living away from the Philippines, unless they have a hybrid designation such as Filipino American or Filipino Canadian) and refer to those who are living within the country as "Filipinos," unless I personally know that the person prefers one label over the other.

7. In citizenship, there are "subjects" or individuals "who have consented to a sov-

ereign's rule and who, by according to that consent, have certain rights and obligations" (Ahluwalia 66). A natural-born citizen of a country, say, the Philippines or Canada, does not give that "consent" but is immediately the "subject" of a larger power; whereas if one does give "consent" to be naturalized, that one obviously understands (to some extent) the agreements that comes along with the citizenship. Questions that can be asked here are the following: have I, as a postcolonial subject, grasped the "consent" I have intentionally or unintentionally given to the governmental monolith by largely "ignoring" the atrocities against the Lumad peoples? At the end of the day, I am still a "subject" of my country, and "what is perhaps easily forgotten is that the very subjects of empire have endured different forms of colonialism and that it is these different forms of power which need to be recovered" (69). I emphasize here an imperative commitment to reconcile within one's self that there has been active complicity in the exploitation and erasure of Indigenous rights by "ignoring" the existence and enforcement of these rights—or what appears to be an apathetic stance toward Indigenous issues.

8. Benedict Anderson in "Cacique Democracy in the Philippines: Origin and Dreams" describes the feudal political system in the Philippines as a "cacique democracy"—a system that sees local leaders as wielding warlord-like powers in order to assure the strength of their political campaigns.

9. The Maguindanao Massacre was one of the deadliest events for journalists in the history of the Philippines. On 23 November 2009, mass graves that were halfway buried (by a backhoe) were found in Ampatuan in Maguindanao province. Fifty-eight people (journalists, family members, and plain citizens alike) were on their way to file candidacy for Esmael Mangudadatu, the vice mayor of Buluan town, in a grand convoy. As they were on their way, they were kidnapped and killed in massive shootouts. Mangudadatu was filing candidacy to challenge the longtime ruler of Ampatuan in the province. Though some members of the Ampatuan political party were jailed and tried for a case, they were eventually released for "lack of evidence." Until now, no one has been tried and convicted for the massacre.

10. The myth associated with rampant alcoholism in First Nations communities in Canada stems from the Prohibition era, when the Crown established stipulations in the Indian Act to prohibit Aboriginals from trading for or purchasing alcohol from outside the reserves (most traded furs and other items for alcohol with traders—mostly Americans—before the enforcement of the Indian Act). It is said that the "ban" stems from the belief of white settlers that if the Aboriginal has access to alcohol, they will not diligently work on their "farmland." However, the persistence of alcoholism in First Nations communities stems from the deep-seated trauma of the violence enforced by the white settlers. Those who "survive" the atrocities in residential schools use alcohol to cope, especially since access to mental health resources for First Nations communities still continues to be challenging. More can be read at https://www.ictinc.ca/blog/first-nations-prohibition-of-alcohol (accessed 6 Mar. 2019).

11. According to the TC Energy website, the Keystone Pipeline and the company's relations with the government of Alberta have been terminated effective 9 June 2021. Read the official statement here: https://www.tcenergy.com/announcements/2021-06-09-tc-energy-confirms-termination-of-keystone-xl-pipeline-project/ (accessed 9 Sept. 2021).

12. Some of information about the Keystone Pipeline protests can be found in this informative timeline by the NRDC: https://www.nrdc.org/stories/what-keystone-pipeline (accessed 28 April 2022).

Works Cited

Ahluwalia, Pal. "When Does a Settler Become a Native? Citizenship and Identity in a Setter Society." *Pretexts: Literary and Cultural Studies*, vol. 10, no. 1, 2001, 64–73.

Anderson, Benedict. "Cacique Democracy in the Philippines: Origins and Dreams." *New Left Review*, vol. 1, no. 169, May 1988.

Bonds, Anne, and Joshua Inwood. "Beyond White Privilege." *Progress in Human Geography*, vol. 40, no. 6, 2016, 715–33, https://www.doi.org/10.1177/0309132515613166

Collins, John. "Ruins, Redemption, and Brazil's Imperial Exception" *Imperial Debris: On Ruins and Ruination*, edited by Ann Laura Stoler. Duke UP, 2013, 162–93.

Esmaquel, Paterno II. "Cardinal Tagle to Military: Leave the Lumad in Peace." *Philippine Rappler*, 11 Nov. 2015, https://www.rappler.com/nation/cardinal-tagle-military-lumad-mindanao

Hernandez, Ariel. *Nation-Building and Identity Conflicts: Facilitating the Mediation Process in Southern Philippines*. Springer Fachmedien Wiesbaden, 2014.

Hutchings, Claire. "Canada's First Nations: A Legacy of Institutional Racism." *Tolerance*, 19 Oct. 2015, http://knelsonhota.weebly.com/uploads/6/0/4/2/60421151/canada's_first_nations__the_legacy_of_institutional_racism.pdf

Mawani, Renisa. "In Between and Out of Place: Mixed-Race Identity, Liquor, and the Law in British Columbia, 1850–1913." *Race, Space, and the Law: Unmapping a White Settler Society*, edited by Sherene H. Razack. Between the Lines, 2002, 47–70.

Mina, Achilles B. "Guilt." *Sustaining the Archipelago: An Anthology of Philippine Ecopoetry*, edited by Rina Garcia Chua, UST Publishing, 2017, 45.

Nixon, Rob. *Slow Violence and the Environmentalism of the Poor*. Harvard UP, 2011.

Norgaard, Kari Marie. *Living in Denial: Climate Change, Emotions, and Everyday Life*. The MIT Press, 2011.

Office of the High Commissioner, United Nations Human Rights. "Philippines Warned over 'Massive' Impact of Military Operations on Mindanao Indigenous Peoples." Press Release, 27 Dec. 2017, https://www.ohchr.org/en/press-releases/2017/12/philippines-warned-over-massive-impact-military-operations-mindanao

Philippine Constitution. Republic Act No. 8371, Chapter 1. *Official Gazette*, 29 Oct. 1997, https://www.officialgazette.gov.ph/1997/10/29/republic-act-no-8371/

Razack, Sherene. *Race, Space, and the Law: Unmapping a White Settler Society*. W. Ross MacDonald School Resource Services Library, 2017.

Reyes, Angela. "Inventing Postcolonial Elites: Race, Language, Mix, Excess." *Journal of Linguistic Anthropology*, vol. 27, no. 2, 2017, 210–31. https://doi.org/10.1111/jola.12156

Stoler, Ann Laura. *Imperial Debris: On Ruins and Ruination*. Duke UP, 2013.

Wayman, Tom. "The Man Who Logged the West Ridge." *Open Wide a Wilderness*, edited by Nancy Holmes. Wilfrid Laurier UP, 2009, 325–26.

10

Representing Postcolonial Water Environments in Contemporary Taiwanese Literature

Ti-Han Chang

In contemporary literary studies, Taiwan, a politically marginalized island in the Pacific Ocean, is mostly known for its literary contribution to the contextualization of postcolonial history in the Asia-Pacific region. Taiwan underwent complex historical phases of colonization under the rule of the Japanese Empire (1895–1945) and the Kuomintang (hereafter KMT) military regime (1949–87).[1] In recent years, Taiwanese literature addressing domestic environmental problems has also been on the rise. It is the crossing of these two domains—the postcolonial and the environmental—that perhaps best characterizes the new dynamic of contemporary Taiwanese literature. This chapter investigates the representation of postcolonial water environments in the literary works of Syaman Rapongan 夏曼藍波安[2] (1957–), an Indigenous Tao writer and activist, and Fang Hui-chen 房慧真 (1976–), an independent journalist who specializes in environmental and social issues. I argue that this increased attention to environmental issues sheds new light on the postcolonial history of the Asia-Pacific region. Moreover, I suggest that the new environmental dimension of Taiwanese literature, which emerged in the late 1980s and early 1990s, may be able to provide an alternative perspective for other similar postcolonial states in the region (e.g., South Korea, Malaysia, and the Philippines), allowing them to revisit their colonial experience and potentially contributing also to the development of an original postcolonial environmental discourse stemming from the regional particularity of the Asia Pacific.

Given Taiwan's specific geographical features (i.e., an island surrounded by oceans featuring high mountains and abundant streams and waterfalls), themes that revolve around oceanic or water imaginary have become established as a major literary convention in the last few decades. Quite a few contemporary authors, such as Liao Hung-chi 廖鴻基 and Lu Ze-zhi 呂則之, apply this convention in their literary creations. Yet, not all of them make explicit attempts to articulate issues relating to postcolonialism and environmentalism. I have thus chosen to conduct a comparative study of Syaman and Fang, for both authors are considered writer-activists, politically dedicated to fighting social inequality and environmental injustice. Syaman's semi-autobiographical literary essays and Fang's essay collection underline the urgency of approaching the problem of heavily polluted water ecologies through a postcolonial lens. Scrutinizing their literary representations, I argue that the legacies of colonial developments in Taiwan during the Japanese imperial rule and KMT (neo)colonial occupation, as well as of the U.S. neoliberal domination over the Third World economy in the Asia Pacific, continue to produce negative impacts not only on the water environment themselves but also on the Indigenous Tao people and the Taiwanese population as a whole.

Colonial Ruination: Contextualizing Taiwan's Water Environmental History

The present chapter advances a postcolonial ecocritique of Taiwan's "colonial ruination." "Colonial ruination," as Ann Laura Stoler presents the concept, is what people are *left with* and continue to endure in their everyday life in the colonial aftermath (9). As such, it is "an ongoing corrosive process that weighs on the future" and, within that process, a political project that "lays waste to certain people, relationship and things . . . in specific places" (9). For example, the substantial changes of the geographical, cultural, and economic features of Taiwan caused by Japanese exploitation of the agricultural industries (mainly water-intensive crops, such as rice and sugar) continue to affect negatively the lives of Indigenous and postcolonial peoples in Taiwan. As Leo T. S. Ching notes, following the arrival of Sakuma Samata (the fifth Japanese governor-general) in Taiwan in 1910, a series of actions such as land expropriation and forced relocation of Taiwanese aboriginals were immediately put in practice. "The goals of the Japanese," Ching explains, "were to confine the aborigines and incorporate them into standard administrative units, to restrict their hunting activity, to encourage rice cultivation and finally, to exploit the abundant forest, timber and the camphor resources" (134–35).

These negative environmental changes and cultural dynamics are also underlined in Williams and Chang's *Taiwan's Environmental Struggle*. The two authors draw particular attention to the Japanese government's exploitation of Taiwan's water resources and the environmental repercussions thereof.[3]

From this historical perspective, the colonial ruination that remains part of Taiwanese life is inseparable from the exploitation that occurred under the Japanese colonial occupation and the KMT military rule. As mentioned earlier, given Taiwan's specific geographical features, exploitation is often linked to water environments. In his essay collection *Jia li shuibian name jin* 家離水邊那麼近 (So much water so close to home) (hereafter *Jia*), the renowned Taiwanese ecological writer Wu Ming-yi 吳明益 foregrounds this issue through the example of the Mugua River 木瓜溪. As Wu recounts, during the Japanese occupation of Taiwan, the colonizers constructed several hydroelectric power plants, exploiting both the water resources of the Mugua River and the human labor of the local Indigenous population (*Jia* 76–77). The exploitation did not cease after the termination of Japanese rule. On the contrary, the Taipower company[4] further expanded the construction of dams and hydroelectric power plants in order to meet the development needs of the west coast as well as of the heavy industries promoted by the KMT government (76–77).[5] Wu refers to Yang Guai-san's 楊貴三 article, which explains how hydroelectricity generation upstream and quarrying and irrigation downstream have, over the past one hundred years, led to the drying up of the abundant flow of the Mugua River, resulting in a great loss of aquatic biodiversity (82).

Colonial ruination, as Stoler further elaborates, is *not* simply the direct result of a colonial or imperial project. Ruination can also be the legacy of its underlying mechanisms—via the transfer of the colonial capitalist system to the neoliberal/neocolonial exploitation of the Third World—which continue to operate in contemporary postcolonial states (Stoler 18). Colonial ruination can therefore be found in an ongoing impetus for the postcolonial state to engage in such political projects as the importation of hazardous industries from the First World or the designation of land for industrial farming, chemical waste disposal, and nuclear waste storage. Degraded water environments in Taiwan generally result from these sorts of political projects, which occurred above all during the period of U.S. financial investment in the development of Taiwan's neoliberal economy. This fits perfectly with Stoler's conceptualization of colonial ruination. During the Cold War period, the U.S. geopolitical strategy and military agenda to counterbalance the growing influence of Communism in the Asia-Pacific region secured a political alliance with the Republic of China (Taiwan). Since the establishment of the U.S. Military Assistance and Advisory Group in 1951, Taiwan had "benefited and enjoyed" U.S. nonmilitary economic aid as part of its political agreement. Between 1951 and 1965, the United States offered $1.5 billion in nonmilitary aid to Taiwan (approximately $100 million per year), and this large sum of economic aid constituted about 40 percent of capital formation in Taiwan (Wang 325–28). According to Peter Chen-main Wang's research, most of this aid was spent on communication, electricity, and transportation, which helped to advance agricultural and industrial development (325–28). These economic investments were generally perceived as great benefits to Taiwan, given that they created the conditions for Taiwan to rise as an industrial power and thus enjoy the "economic miracle" of the 1960s and 1970s.

Nonetheless, from an environmental point of view, the disastrous impacts on natural environments and public health linked to this artificially generated growth, bankrolled by the United States, are now considered a case of irrevocable "colonial ruination" affecting the Taiwanese population in general. Wu Ming-yi has pointed out that the "generous" financial investment from the United States was also intended for Taiwan to quickly make the transition from an agriculturally based Third World economy to an industrially based developing economy ("Shengtai" 234). From 1966 onward, Taiwan was transformed into a labor-intensive and export-oriented economy. Wu notes that textile and electronic appliance manufacturing businesses—both of which are highly toxic industries—were the foundation of Taiwan's industrial economy, supporting its export-focused model (234–35). He further cites Jane Ive's *The Export of Hazard* and argues that America had strategically planned to move these polluting industries to its Third World allies, where environmental regulations were either non-existent or much more relaxed (Wu, "Shengtai" 235). Taiwan, as one of America's Third World allies, was determined to accept the export of hazardous industries. Although Wu does not provide a specific example, his argument is well supported by the case study presented by Williams and Chang. As these scholars show, Radio Corporation of America (RCA) pioneered its investment in Taiwan in the late 1960s and moved its production line of black-and-white televisions from Memphis to Taoyuan (Williams and Chang 44–45). The company used organic solvents to clean and degrease mechanic components. Since there were no enforced environmental rules, RCA simply discarded the used solvents into sewers and toilets or threw them out onto the grass without any treatment, causing significant degradations to neighboring water environments and also posing threats to people's health (45). Williams and Chang conclude that two of the solvents used are believed to be carcinogens and that "for more than two decades, workers and residents in the neighbourhood had been drinking and using the water, and claimed higher than normal rates of cancer" (45).

We therefore understand that colonial ruination can be found not just in what is physically left over but also in an ongoing impetus in the postcolonial state to engage in certain political projects, as demonstrated above. In the following analysis, I will show that the works of Syaman and Fang articulate issues that are essentially linked to these sorts of political projects. Furthermore, while Stoler's concept of "colonial ruination" is useful for providing a postcolonial ecocritique of Taiwan's water environments, this chapter seeks also to link this concept to Syaman Rapongan's proposed notion of "nomad body," an unstable and liminal subjectivity brought about through violent changes to an individual's external surroundings that force the individual to confront and articulate heterogenous values (modern/colonial and traditional/Indigenous) arising from different spatialities and temporalities. I will further show how this "nomad body" is represented not only by Syaman and his fellow Tao people but also, albeit in a very different context, by the marginalized urbanites as depicted in Fang's writing. These two theories not only provide an appropriate framework for the study of both literary works but also allow for a better understanding of the postcolonial exploitation of water environment and its negative effects on the local inhabitants, in both rural and urban Taiwan.

The "Nomad Body" as Colonial Ruination: Syaman Rapongan's *Hanghaijia de lian*

This section looks into the human ecology that is directly linked to the production of colonial ruination. To this end, the concept of "nomad body," drawn from Syaman's semi-autobiographical work, represents a significant form of colonial ruination, particularly as it occurs at the interface between colonial exploitation and the degradation of water environments. I also suggest, however, that the concept of the nomad body does not apply exclusively to Syaman's work and that it should not be limited to understanding the formation of Syaman's aboriginal subjectivity in a liminal space, as suggested in Lee Yu-lin's 李育霖 reading of Syaman's writing. Instead, this concept may be broadly applied to the study of other texts that portray the liminal subjectivity of various populations (e.g., migrant workers, social outcasts, and urban Indigenous people), who occupy or reside nearby degraded Taiwanese water habitats.[6]

A nomad body is constituted by a liminal subjectivity that arises from an individual's specific bodily experiences in relation to violent changes in their external surroundings. These experiences prevent the individual from consolidating subjectivity in a homogeneous manner and also prevent the individual from occupying a specific point of reference in the process of subject identification. On the contrary, the individual is condemned to occupy an ambivalent state as regards his or her subjectivity. As Syaman's daughter once said to him:

> Father, for us (the modern), you have torn your body to earn little money. Yet, your spirit follows the values of our grandparents (the tradition). Most of the tribesmen of your generation have already given up on maintaining this way of life. I can see that you are so tired and so exhausted![7] (*Hanghaijia* 9)

Dwelling on his daughter's words, Syaman replies, "My nomad body vacillates between these two different rhythms of life, unable to settle with the heterogeneity of these incompatible values" (9). As Syaman describes, his body is torn between two different temporalities and two different sets of values. It is torn between the modern and the traditional and between the desire to earn money to support his family in a modernized world and the longing to continue the traditional aquacultural work that is accompanied by so much hardship.

In *Hanghaijia de lian* 航海家的臉 (The face of a navigator) (hereafter *Hanghaijia*), Syaman and the Tao people he describes well illustrate these features of the nomad body. Being a Tao writer, Syaman attempts to connect with a fading culture on the brink of disappearance. He portrays a tribal society that is gradually being replaced by the knowledge and economic production of modernity (Lee 182). This tribal society is overwhelmed by technology, and to a certain extent, it is also environmentally degraded by wastes and pollutions (182). The subjects, the Tao people and Syaman himself, therefore undergo *a constant search for their possible existence* (i.e., a desire for life or an urge to survive) *in a liminal space* (182–83). This liminal space is determined by the crisis that the subject experiences, be it *a cultural crisis* staged in a confrontation between the Tao tribal values and the value of modernity or *an ecological crisis* that threatens the integral existence of the Tao people and their natural surroundings. Experiencing these crises thus obliges the subject to *become a nomad*, oscillating between the incompatible conditions and modes of his or her survival. In *Hanghaijia*, Syaman presents the sorrows of his wife and his own frustration vis-à-vis both a dying culture and their urge to survive as a family:

> My wife, she understands the pain of not having flying fish at home, and yet she adores eating fish.[8] . . . A vague idea of preserving our traditions and priding ourselves with these traditions has been clouded by the infinite amount of everyday worries that occupy her mind. . . . Both her heart and her mind were torn between the choices of our traditional tribal economy and the capitalist economy of modern society. She cries out with anger, "ah . . . for the body that comes after us, for our gold (i.e., child),[9] stop being so stubborn. . . . I need a life with a pay." . . . Apparently, everything that is passed down by our ancestors can no longer keep up with a reality underlined by payments and salaries. I stand under the waterfall nearby a taro field, trying to cool down my frustration with the water. Next day at dawn, I carry my axe to the mountain to cut down some wood [for building the fishing boat]. . . . While I sit on the pile of wood that I cut down, I murmur to myself, hoping that a salary is not the only answer to our happiness. (79–80)

This scene presents a liminal space determined by a cultural crisis that the subject experiences and that turns both Syaman and his wife into nomad bodies oscillating between the incompatible conditions of their family's survival and the pursuit of a traditional tribal lifestyle. As Syaman points out, they are subjected to the violent change imposed on a tribal system that must rapidly adapt itself to modern capitalist society. While the wife's body desires the taste of flying fish and her mind wants to feel the pride for having those fish on the drying rack, her desires are denied, first of all, by the conditions set up within the capitalist economy, and second, by the imperial debris of postcolonial Taiwanese society's fractured relationship to water. The "torn heart and mind" of Syaman's wife characterizes the nomad body. Here, this nomad body can be seen as the individual inhabiting these incompatible temporalities simultaneously, thus producing a heterogenous subjectivity.

It is also important to understand how the aboriginal subjectivity is transformed into a liminal one. According to Lee Yu-lin, Syaman's memoir writing about his tribal life and culture does not serve naively to advocate the preservation of the Tao's aboriginal culture, nor does it function as an ethical call for environmental protection; instead, it is *a process of involvement, a full engagement* of the political, social, cultural, and ecological dimensions of postcolonial life (183). In that sense, Syaman's actual experiences in the tribe and his writing about them become a medium that helps us to think about alternatives of coexisting with these struggles, thus offering new possibilities in this liminal space and new potentialities for the nomad body in postcolonial Taiwanese society (183). One can see that the subjectivity that arises in Syaman's works does *not* follow a process of subject identification, which is often enclosed within an individual, nor does it seek a homogenous logos (183–84). On the contrary, this subjectivity can only be found in a *pre-personal* context, and it is an *opening out* toward the natural environment (especially an opening out toward the water ecologies that occupy the center of the Tao's holistic conception of nature), as well as toward different aspects of society, such as the affirmation of ethnicities, social interactions, or individual relations to the state apparatuses (184). The *pre-personal* context, in the Tao's worldview, can be interpreted as that form of perception we share with nonhuman beings and is accessible either through dreams or when one is immersed in a natural environmental or working with and in nature (e.g., axing wood to make canoes, catching fish, sleeping on the beach, etc.).[10] In many traditional oral tales documented by Syaman, the protagonists have the ability to communicate with nonhuman beings (flying fish, cetaceans, crabs, or rocks), but this agency relies also on passing through one's "ancestors," understood not as specific individuals but rather in the collective sense of all those who came before oneself. When Syaman talks of "*everything that is passed down by our ancestors,*" he invokes a pre-personal symbolic realm contextualized by the Tao tribal culture and their ways of living with the surrounding oceans. The subject (Syaman) has to undergo a process of struggle and reconsider their relations with society—in a confrontation with the economic pressures arising from modern capitalist values. In the meanwhile, he must also *open* himself *out* toward his natural environment—as he stands under a waterfall or sits on a pile of wood. This *opening out* toward the environment does not represent a desire to evade liminality by choosing one or the other branch of the dilemma he faces. Again, it is an attempt to fully engage himself in the *pre-personal* context, while accepting to live with these struggles.

The nomad body therefore oscillates between the modern and the traditional, the nation and the tribe, technology and nature, the colonial and the postcolonial. And, in fact, these confrontations would not have arisen if there had not been a neoliberal exploitation of Orchid Island, as Syaman underlines in *Hanghaijia*. Colonial ruination is not necessarily a direct consequence of a specific colonial project, for it can also be the result of a general capitalist legacy, which exploits the colonized region or Third World country. In *Hanghaijia*, Syaman emphasizes the exploitation of the marine systems that was carried out on Orchid Island in the 1980s. This decade is well-known as an era in which Taiwan's economic growth surged, and its economy was subsequently included as one of the "Four Asian Tigers." This "economic miracle," as Syaman notes, came at the price of the "total destruction of [Orchid Island's] marine ecosystem," bearing in mind that it was seen very much as peripheral in the eyes of the Taiwanese government (*Hanghaijia* 164–65). During this period, Taiwanese businessmen had exploited Tao divers as cheap marine laborers in order to meet the growing demand of the fishing industry and aquarium tourism. When their catch supplies could not meet market demand, raft teams of Taiwanese fishermen were dispatched to spray a "sodium cyanide mixture"[11] to poison tropical fish or to use underwater dynamite to kill them (164). These devastating methods led to a significant amount of dieback on some coral reefs (i.e., coral bleaching), and the clear ocean gradually turned muddy white, which put further strain on Orchid Island's marine biodiversity (165). Syaman's description compels us to see the direct link between the legacy of colonialism and socio-ecological degradation. Taiwan's economic success, it turns out, cannot be dissociated from the environmental price paid by other people on the periphery. This is most visible on the damaged coastline and the destroyed marine biodiversity of Orchid Island. However, the cheap Tao laborers mentioned above also exemplify colonial ruination, given that the surplus value generated by their work is appropriated by the beneficiaries of this same economic system. We can further compare the cheap Tao laborers to Syaman and fellow tribesmen. Between having a better quality of life supported by higher incomes and a life that depends on maintaining the traditional tribal economy and fishing culture, these Tao laborers have also involuntarily become nomad bodies.

Degraded Water Environments, Social Outcasts, and Colonial Ruination—Fang Hui-chen's *Heliu*

Starting her career as a journalist in her late thirties, Fang Hui-chen quickly moved from being a news agent of a local tabloid in Taiwan to becoming a senior reporter for what is currently Taiwan's largest online independent media outlet, *Baodaozhe* 報導者 (The reporter). Unlike academically trained reporters, Fang, in her writings, often shows her conscientiousness and attentiveness to issues that relate to individual suffering, environmental exploitation, and social or cultural inequality. I now turn to Fang's essay collection *Heliu* 河流 (River) (2013) to show how her ecofeminist approach and her sophisticated skill of image-text composition directly bring together the issues of environmental and social injustice in Taiwan. Although Fang never describes herself as an ecofeminist, her literary writing draws a parallel between the patriarchal commodification and exploitation of the female body and the human domination of nature. This approach echoes the thinking of some ecofeminists, "which [attempts to unmask] and tries to dismantle the abstract framework of the supremacy, oppression, commodification" (Ranjith and Pius 18).[12]

Similar in style to George Orwell's *Down and Out in Paris and London* (1993), in which the author recounted his own life experiences on the margins of society, Fang's *Heliu* sharply captures the lives of "unwanted" people in the busy urban areas of Taiwan. Like Syaman, Fang interweaves her portrayals of the outcasts with depictions of degraded water habitats. She carefully presents the homeless people, the economic migrants from Southern Taiwan, the city-squatting aboriginals, the Hongkongnese or Taiwanese prostitutes, and the Tanka people,[13] who reside at the riverside of the Tamsui River 淡水河 and the Keelung River 基隆河 in Taipei. To a great extent, Fang's description of their lives and her choice to focus on the highly urbanized Taipei city can be read as a reaction to the colonial legacies manifest in the form of both the neocolonial capitalist economy and degraded water environments.

In one of the essays, "Fudao senlin" 浮島森林 (Floating forest island), Fang portrays the female sex workers and the environments in the Wan Hua 萬華 district. As she tells us, Wan Hua, situated along the Tamsui River, specializes in the sale of Chinese herbal medicine, while also being the most notorious area in Taipei for men to seek sexual pleasure. A double connotation is evoked here: Wan Hua not only provides cures for one's physical health; it also offers remedies for the sexual desire of urban loners. And these cures are available only via exploitation of the environment and of female bodies. In a sense, Fang's emphasis on the marginalized female prostitutes reaffirms the ecofeminist view on the links between the exploitation and commodification of both nature and women's bodies. The chapter begins by recounting various individual life stories of the prostitutes in Wan Hua. A mentally handicapped aboriginal girl voluntarily takes up prostitution in order to provide a living for her aged father (Fang 45). The wife of a middle-age couple serves a "customer" while her handicapped husband guards the door with their only child (46). A divorced Hongkongnese woman in her late fifties comes to Taiwan to be a migrant sex worker because she could not bear to bring shame to her family (46–47). The portrayal of these marginalized prostitutes outlines the (in)visible social and economic inequalities in the urban life of Taipei; moreover, the author also interweaves these portrayals with the theme of degraded water environments. Toward the end of this chapter, Fang writes:

> Most of the traditional herbal medicines that are sold in the shops on the "Green Grass Lane" [in Wan Hua] come from the floating island that is not far from the [Tamsui] river side. . . . On the island, people grow their vegetables, cultivate their herbal plants. . . . The nutrients of the soil come from the discarded waste water. However, the herbal plants that grow out of this island are the most famous "life-saving" cures. . . . The prostitutes in Wan Hua are the same. They float, they sway, unable to find a place to settle. . . . They are exiled to the margin of the world . . . yet blossom the most resilient flowers from the dirtiest and the most polluted soil. (47–48)

The "nomad bodies" (i.e., the marginalized prostitutes) described by Fang also try to navigate a liminal space determined by the crisis of social displacement. Nevertheless, the way Fang's writing relates to the production of colonial ruination is very different from that of Syaman. In *Hanghaijia*, both the Tao people and Syaman himself are subjected to direct exploitation in a neocolonial economic system, as well as to the loss of marine biodiversity. Fang's writing, on the other hand, presents rather a metaphorical comparison between the marginalized female sex workers and the degraded urban water environments, thus articulating an ecofeminist critique of the commodification of nature via female bodies.

Furthermore, the two elements found in Fang's writing, the degraded water environments and the marginalized population, work together to produce an unconventional aesthetic representation that calls for a reimagining of our relationship with the polluted environment. Looking at the formal features of her book, one immediately sees Fang's attempts to bring these two elements to the fore through both image and textual arrangement. Photographs are inserted between the texts, producing a cinematographic effect. For instance, a shot of an empty street with several manhole covers outside a window is spread across three pages and inserted between two chapters. The awkward visual effect, presenting half of the photo on the first two pages and the other half on the following page, renders a continuity of the image and of the stories told. The photograph also seems to suggest that, under these manhole covers, the currents of the filthy watercourse and of the lives of the marginalized urbanites run together through the path of the essays. By means of this specific image-text arrangement, Fang's writing displays a fluidity that resembles the flow of water, calling to mind how a filmmaker might roll the camera to shoot the actual life of the people she portrays.

Another technique that Fang experiments with to produce cinematographic effect involves placing text over an image. In figure 1, for example, a text box is placed directly on an image of a footpath in Taipei, giving the effect of a cinematic voice-over. While the image outlines the fast movement of cars, scooters, bike riders, and pedestrians in the hustle and bustle of the city, the written text turns the reader's attention to the slow pace of the marginalized urban Indigenous population who reside at the bank of the Danhan River 大漢溪, a polluted stream at the periphery of urban Taipei. Fang further notes that, unable to afford the expensive cost of living in the city on their minimum wages, these people were in perpetual conflict with the city government for the land they "illegally" occupied over the last thirty years. In the photo, however, both the marginalized Indigenous people and the river are nowhere to be found. What dominates the image is the overground rail track, moving the metropolitan urbanites forward at great speed. This contrast can be interpreted as Fang's specific style of making the invisible (i.e., the urban Indigenous people and the polluted Dahan River) visible.

In fact, despite that the book is called "River," very few pictures are actually images of river. They are scenes of urban life—the empty street, the spiral-shaped stairs, the shop signs spilling out onto the streets. In an unusual manner, these images together offer an ensemble effect that resembles the continuity of water flow. In short, Fang's deliberate design produces an unconventional aesthetic representation that is both powerful and striking and that allows readers to acknowledge the concealed polluted watercourses and the marginalized population often imperceptible in daily life.

Fang also employs a specific symbolic reference in her writing—sewage or concealed water channels—to represent the link between the invisible people and the hidden pollution of the waterways. Sewage can be easily read as a signifier for the marginalized outcasts and the hidden pollution, representing the buried legacy of colonial ruination. Fang presents the particular

傳統，無零工可打時，河邊空地還可種菜，水裡可抓魚，挨著城市邊

緣，自給自足。

挨著城市的邊角角，自給自足。三十幾年來，經歷無數次公權力的拆除，爾

大漢溪畔的三鶯部落，卻不是遺世獨立，不被打擾，

後住民仍一點一滴重建家園，

城市以光速行進，跟不上的人，便被拋到橋下。

前進的巨輪不斷在頭上翻過，無所謂的，拋到橋下，種菜，抓魚。

升起炊煙，在大橋下，取得了一種庇蔭。

Fig. 10.1. Scanned image of *a skywalk footpath in Taipei with text* on page 82 and 83 of Fang, Hui-chen 房慧真 *Heliu* 河流 (River), Yinke wenxue, 2013. Reproduction permission courtesy of the author, Fang Hui-chen 房慧真.

case of urban development at Shezi sandbank 社子沙洲, showing that the logic of an obscure city project reflects a neocolonial exploitation of marginalized economic minorities. Located at the confluence of two rivers, Shezi sandbank was originally formed by the earth that was washed down from the Tamsui 淡水 and Keelung 基隆 Rivers. However, as a result of its geographical features and lowland location on the periphery of Taipei city, it was designated as a site for the processing of all the sewage emitted from Taipei's city center. But it is not only the unclean wastewater that is washed down to Shezi. Being a lowland area, Shezi is also liable to flooding and eventually became an area where low-income populations reside. Shezi's economic activities gradually stagnated, and no further urban planning was considered necessary to transform or improve the quality of life there. Shezi then turned into a place that gathers most of the "unwanted people"—sex laborers for the city loners, gangsters of the underworld, and economic migrants coming from Southern Taiwan who cannot afford the expensive housing costs of the city center (Fang 52). Commenting on an obscure development proposal for turning Shezi into a red-light district, Fang writes, "As always, rubbish and scraps of leftovers as well as the used dirt in construction sites are all washed down to the island with wastewater emitted in the city" (52). Even though the proposed project has never been realized, one can see a general lack of government enthusiasm or effort to consider alternative ways to improve the environment and well-being of Shezi's inhabitants.[14] In a sense, when Fang mentions the "rubbish and scraps of leftovers" washed down to Shezi, she is referring not only to the actual waste that is dumped on the island, for the rubbish and scraps carry also metaphorical meanings relating to those marginalized workers or prostitutes deserted on the urban periphery.

A final thing that needs to be highlighted about Fang's writing is the structure of her collected essays. In several individual essays of her book, Fang starts with a detailed depiction of certain marginalized characters but ends with unusually ghastly scenes that demonstrate the awful degradation of the water environments. In doing so, she raises a variety of environmental issues related to the water habitats she describes, including direct water pollution, environmental degradation resulting from dam construction, and the problem of excessive general waste. Referring once more to the example of Shezi sandbank, Fang points out that the wastes and used earth from construction sites piled up on the island are mostly the result of the government's failed urban planning. The mouth of the Keelung River is always filled with floating pollutants. According to Fang, the main reason for this is the dam built upstream, which means that clean water is intercepted for city use; and then from the midstream onward, the water quality deteriorates rapidly (55). In the downstream sections, wastewater emissions from factories and households are "poured" into the river en masse (55). Since the ownership of certain parts of Shezi sandbank is unclearly defined, private companies often casually dump the used earth from construction sites without obtaining legal permission (54). These observations of Fang demonstrate that it is usually the marginalized urban outcasts who suffer the most from water pollution. The pollution of the watercourses in cities and its effects on human inhabitants can be read as a form of ruination that remains obliquely linked to the colonial legacy of Taiwanese society (i.e., the neocolonial capitalist system). In view of the above, we can see that the specific structural arrangement of Fang's text calls for ethical and political reflection on the part of the reader regarding the degraded water environments of urban areas. From the exhibition of invisible watercourses through particular text-image arrangements to the emphasis on social inequality in her portrayals of degraded urban water environments, Fang's writing not only presents the social outcasts and the polluted waters as forms of colonial ruination but also, more importantly, calls on the readers to reimagine how we might live with these colonial ruinations in the context of contemporary capitalist society.

Through its application to the literary works of Syaman and Fang, the concept of "colonial ruination" proposed by Ann Laura Stoler takes on a concrete form. The colonial ruinations depicted in these texts, be they destroyed coastline, damaged marine biodiversity, or polluted city watercourses, are in one way or another connected to the colonial legacies manifested most visibly in the capitalist economic system. These (in)visible colonial ruinations are not only what people are left with and have to endure, for they have also turned the people into part of the colonial ruins. As seen in Syaman's and Fang's works, the exploited Tao laborers, the discriminated sex workers, and the marginalized urban aboriginals are rendered "nomad bodies" by socio-ecological degradations, and their subjectivity thus lingers on in a liminal space. Through these authors' literary representations, I have mapped out the exploited human and natural ecology that arises in the continuation of Taiwan's colonial past to its neocolonial present.

This chapter not only demonstrates that a new ecocritical literary approach for revisiting the (post)colonial history of Taiwan is on the rise but also shows that this ecological perspective can offer a more comprehensive understanding of how the colonial mechanism and its legacies are correlated with regional specificities, in this instance the marine and river environments of Taiwan. The specific attention to water environments gives a new ecocritical lens that incorporates some specific features of the Asia-Pacific region and thus avoids seeing "nature" as a homogenous category. Apart from Syaman and Fang, more and more contemporary Taiwanese writers, such as Wu Ming-yi or Wang Jia-xiang 王家祥, have adopted this new approach. And some of them have also obtained international recognition for the writing they have produced.[15]

To conclude, as mentioned at the beginning of the chapter, I consider that Taiwanese literature's greatest contribution to the contemporary literary world is its contextualization of the colonial and postcolonial experiences in the Asia-Pacific region. This can be understood at two different levels. First, by incorporating an ecological perspective that highlights the *water environments* so often present in postcolonial Taiwanese literature, this new approach can further shape other works of ecoliterature produced in the region, especially in those countries that have shared similar colonial experiences. For example, Taiwan and Korea both endured long-term Japanese imperial occupation until the end of World War II partially as a result of their valuable natural resources, and they also underwent American neocolonial and economic control in the Cold War period largely for geopolitical reasons. Although there are studies of Korean water policy reforms that examine river basin development and its negative environmental impacts during the Japanese imperial occupation,[16] little discussion of water environments has taken place in the literary domain. In this regard, the examined Taiwanese ecoliterature might be able to lend itself as a model. Second, the theoretical concept of the "nomad body," which emerges from Taiwan's Indigenous ecowriting, can also form part of a strategy of decolonial reading and so could potentially be applied to other Indigenous ecocriticism from other Pacific archipelagos. Researching this new literary paradigm would thus appear to have significant potential with regard to the development of an alternative ecocritical theory stemming from the regional particularity of the Asia-Pacific countries.

Notes

1. Regarding the Kuomintang military regime, in 1949, the Republican government of the Kuomintang 國民黨 (Nationalist Party), led by Generalissimo Chiang Kai-shek 蔣介石, retreated to Taiwan after losing the battle against the Communist Party in Mainland China. After the immediate takeover of Taiwan, the Kuomintang authoritarian one-party state ruled under the "Order of Martial Law" (*Jieyanling* 戒嚴令) for nearly forty years. This period, also known as White Terror (*Baise kongbu* 白色恐怖), left a strong mark on contemporary history, and it stands as one of the longest martial law periods in the world.

2. The name Syaman Rapongan 夏曼．藍波安 in Tao language actually means "the father of Rapongan." In Tao culture, when one becomes the father of a firstborn child, he will no longer be known for his given name but only be referred to as "Syaman (the father) of . . ." The grandfather of the firstborn will also be referred to as "Syapan (the grandfather) of . . ." As neither Syaman nor Rapongan stands for the author's family name, in the chapter, I choose to reference the author as Syaman, but readers should note that in other publications the same author might be referred to as Rapongan.

3. Williams and Chang's research points out the Japanese exploitation of Taiwan's natural resources, including agricultural goods, forestry, and water habitats initiated by the Japanese and further expanded under the KMT regime. The exploitation continues to burden the future of the Taiwanese. They further state that the Japanese government's interests in forest and water resource exploitation in the inner mountain area of the island—building dams to satisfy electricity or irrigation needs and constructing freshwater lakes (e.g., Sun Moon Lake) for recreational purposes—led to serious environmental repercussions that have recently provoked political controversy in Taiwan. See Williams and Chang 15–16.

4. Taipower company, also known as Taiwan power company, is a government-run electric company in Taiwan. During the KMT military regime, heavy industries were the key focus of the government's general economic plan from the 1950s to the 1960s, which explains the huge demand for electricity.

5. It is important to note that the development of heavy industries in Taiwan had many negative impacts on the environment, as were experienced also by many other developing countries during the postwar era. It should be highlighted that these heavy industries were largely financed by the U.S. government because the Americans had a geopolitical interest in the Asia-Pacific region, especially in countries like Taiwan, South Korea, and the Philippines. This point will be further elaborated in the following paragraphs.

6. This point will be more fully discussed when we move on to the literary analysis of Fang's writing.

7. The original text is written in Chinese. The passage quoted here has been translated into English by the author. This applies to all other quotes from Syaman Rapongan's and Fang Hui-chen's works, unless specified otherwise.

8. Catching flying fish is one of the traditional tribal economic activities of Tao people. In Tao culture, to become a *real* man, it is essential for a Tao man to show that he has the ability to bring home fish. As Syaman denotes, a drying rack full of flying fish in one's backyard demonstrates the presence of a *real* man in the household. Before sailing out for the fish hunt, the man also needs to prove that he has the skills to build his own ship from scratch, with fine woods he selects and cuts down. Syaman Rapongan, *Hanghaijia de lian*, 78–79.

9. In the Tao language, both the terms "the body that comes after us" and "our gold" mean one's child or children.

10. In Syaman Rapongan's work *Tiankong de yanjing* 天空的眼睛 (Eyes in the skies) (2012), an example of Syaman himself being invited by a cetacean to go on a journey under the water is presented in the preface. The cetacean, whose name is Bawon 巴甕 (meaning "sea waves"), came to Syaman in his dream. Syaman was surprised that Bawon knows his childhood name, but the cetacean told him that he learned it from Syaman's great-grandfather. Other similar examples of a protagonist sharing the world with nonhuman beings are also evoked in *Kavavatanen No Ta-u Jimasik* 八代灣的神話 (The mythology of Badai Bay) (2011).

11. Cyanide fishing is a method of collecting live fish mainly for use in aquariums. It involves spraying the sodium cyanide mixture into the desired fish's habitat, thereby paralyzing the fish.

12. Reshma Ranjith and T. K. Pius further point out that, in ecofeminism, the theoretical challenge is often presented via an exposure of the colonization of nature and marginalized humans, as well as of the commodification of women and nature. See Ranjith and Pius 18.

13. Tanka people are known as *Danjia* 蜑家 in Chinese. They are boat people originally from the southern coast of China, sometimes referred to as "sea gypsies."

14. A satirical web post from the Collective of Sex Workers and Supporters lampooned the irresponsible proposal from one of the former Taipei mayor candidates, who claimed he would transform Shezi into the Las Vegas of Taiwan if he were elected. See Miss GoGo 嬋's web post, "Shezi Dao Bian Lasi Weijiasi Songzhuxi Baodao Weilao" 社子島變拉斯維

加斯 宋主席寶刀未老 (Shzei Island becomes Las Vegas, Chairman Song is not yet over the hill).

15. For example, Wu Ming-yi's *The Stolen Bicycle* (2017), which addresses the (post) colonial history of Taiwan through an environmental perspective, was long-listed for the 2018 Man Booker Prize. His cli-fi (climate fiction) *The Man with the Compound Eyes* (2014) (originally published in Chinese in 2011), which imagines the occurrence of environmental apocalypse in Taiwan provoked by the Great Pacific Trash Vortex, also won the French literary prize Prix du Livre Insulaire in 2014.

16. See Choi et al. 9.

Works Cited

Ching, Leo T. S. *Becoming "Japanese": Colonial Taiwan and the Politics of Identity Formation*. U of California P, 2001, 134–35.

Choi, Ik-chang, et al. "Water Policy Reforms in South Korea: A Historical Review and Ongoing Challenges for Sustainable Water Governance and Management." *Water*, vol. 9, no. 9, 2017, 1–20. *MDPI AG*, https://doi.org/10.3390/w9090717

Fang, Hui-chen 房慧真. *Heliu* 河流 [River]. Yinke wenxue, 2013.

Ives, Jane H., editor. *The Export of Hazard: Transnational Corporations and Environmental Control Issues*. Routledge and Kegan Paul, 1985.

Lee, Yu-lin 李育霖. "Youmu de shenti: Syaman Rapongan de xuni shentaixue" 游牧的身體: 夏曼藍波安的虛擬生態學 [Nomad body: Syaman Rapongan's virtual ecology]. *Nizao xin diqiu* 擬造新地球 [The fabulation of a new earth]. Guoli Taiwan daxue chuban zhongxin, 2015, 182–246.

Miss GoGo 嬋. "Shezi Dao Bian Lasi Weijiasi Songzhuxi Baodao Weilao" 社子島變拉斯維加斯 宋主席寶刀未老 [Shezi Island becomes Las Vegas, Chairman Song is not yet over the hill]. *Ririchun guanhuai huzhu xiehui* 日日春關懷互助協會 [Collective of sex workers and supporters], 25 Oct. 2006, http://coswas.org/archives/533. Accessed 1 June 2019.

Ranjith, Reshma, and T. K. Pius. "Ecofeminism, Patriarchy, Capitalism and Postcolonialism in the Indian Scenario: A Short Study." *IOSR Journal of Humanities and Social Science*, vol. 22, no. 9, 2017, 18–24. *IOSR Journals*, https://doi.org/10.9790/0837

Stoler, Ann Laura. *Imperial Debris: On Ruins and Ruination*. Duke UP, 2013.

Syaman, Rapongan 夏曼藍波安. *Hanghaijia de lian* 航海家的臉 [The face of a navigator]. Ink chubanshe, 2016.

Syaman, Rapongan 夏曼藍波安. *Kavavatanen No Ta-u Jimasik* 八代灣的神話 [The mythology of Badai Bay]. Lianjing chubanshe, 2011.

Syaman, Rapongan 夏曼藍波安. *Tiankong de yanjing* 天空的眼睛 [Eyes in the skies]. Lianjing chubanshe, 2012.

Wang, Peter Chen-main. "A Bastion Created, a Regime Reformed, and Economy Reengineered, 1949–1970." *Taiwan: A New History*, edited by Murray A. Rubinstein. Routledge, 2015, 320–38.

Williams, Jack F., and Ch'ang-yi David Chang. *Taiwan's Environmental Struggle: Towards a Green Silicon Island*. Routledge, 2008.

Wu, Ming-yi 吳明益. *Jia li shuibian name jin* 家離水邊那麼近 [So much water so close to home]. Eryu wenhua, 2007.

Wu, Ming-yi 吳明益. *The Man with the Compound Eyes.* Translated by Darryl Sterk. Vintage, 2014.

Wu, Ming-yi 吳明益. "Shengtai zhimin yu zaizhixing shehui" 生態殖民與宰制型社會 [Ecological colonialism and the domination of society]. *Taiwan ziran shuxie de tansuo 1980–2002 － yi shuxie jiefang ziran* 臺灣自然書寫的探索 1980–2002 － 以書寫解放自然 [Exploration modern nature writing of Taiwan 1980–2002—Liberating nature by writing], vol. 1. Xiari chuban, 2012, 209–66.

Wu, Ming-yi 吳明益. *The Stolen Bicycle.* Translated by Darryl Sterk. Text Publishing, 2018.

PART IV

Climate Justice and Ecological Futurities

"Age of Plastic"
Craig Santos Perez

"Plastic is wholly swallowed up in the fact of being used: ultimately, objects
will be invented for the sole pleasure of using them. The hierarchy of
substances is abolished: a single one replaces them all: the whole world *can*
be plasticized, and even life itself."

—ROLAND BARTHES, *MYTHOLOGIES* (1957)

~

The doctor presses the plastic probe
onto my wife's pregnant belly.
Plastic leaches estrogenic and toxic chemicals.
Ultrasound waves pulse between fluid,
tissue, and bone until the embryo echoes.
Plastic makes this possible. At home,
she labors in an inflatable plastic tub.

Plastic disrupts hormonal and endocrine systems.
After delivery, she stores her placenta
in a plastic freezer bag. *Plastic is the perfect
creation because it never dies.* Our daughter
sucks on a plastic pacifier. *Whales,
plankton, shrimp, and birds confuse plastic
for food.* The plastic breast pump whirrs—

breast milk drips into a plastic bottle.
Plastic keeps food, water, and medicine fresh.
Yet how empty plastic must feel
to be birthed, used, and disposed
by its degradable creators. *In the oceans,*
there exists one ton of plastic for every three tons
of fish. How free plastic must feel

to finally arrive at the Pacific gyre—
a paradise far from us. *Will plastic*
make life impossible? Our daughter
falls asleep in a plastic crib,
and I wish that she was composed
of plastic, so that she, too,
will survive our wasteful hands.

11

Climate Justice in the Transpacific Novel

Amy Lee

In the novel *Tropic of Orange*, Karen Tei Yamashita writes that climate change "had less perhaps to do with weather and more to do with disaster" (36). Set in Los Angeles, where one rarely experiences extreme weather events, *Tropic of Orange* regards the catastrophe of social and racial unrest for which the city is infamous as an epiphenomenon of climate change. An "aberrant orange"—the product of either global warming or "the industriousness of the African bees"—laced with cocaine sets in motion a plot punctuated by the transnational circulation of commodities, border crossings, and the fantastical reorientation of the Earth's geography, culminating in a spectacular traffic accident, and consequent traffic jam, on an LA freeway (11). The sensational image of an LA freeway engulfed in the flames of burning cars is a grand display of the costs of global capitalism and the extractive industries that form its foundations. Climate change manifests as a product of human behavior and as an urban ecology of imperial ruins.

Since the publication of *Tropic of Orange* in 1997, an evolving cast of hurricanes and wildfires has imprinted the specter of climate change most acutely as unfettered nature in the American consciousness. If the effects of global climate change have been largely imagined as offshore occurrences, for instance, in the figure of the drowning island, then the fallout from our overconsumption and overreliance on energy may have finally returned home with a vengeance. During this time, a growing body of American literature known as climate fiction (cli-fi) has emerged to portray a dystopian and postapocalyptic America rendered unlivable by environmental devastation.[1] In the post-racial worlds of these fictions, writers foresee the destructive impact of unchecked carbon emissions on a future world from which no one is safe. Yet, this literature neglects the ways in which communities of color have already been living with climate change, with "the historical *continuity* of dispossession and disaster caused by empire" (DeLoughrey 2). In contrast, Asian American novelists such as Chang-rae Lee, Karen Tei Yamashita, and Ruth Ozeki offer transnational and transpacific perspectives that illuminate how U.S. and Asian relations are imbricated in the militarism, global capitalism, and interimperial competition that lead to environmental ruin.

As a counterpoint to cli-fi renditions of the apocalyptic end of the world, this chapter considers literary texts that help us imagine ways of living through climate change. I focus my analysis on Chang-rae Lee's 2014 dystopian novel, *On Such a Full Sea* (hereafter *OSFS*), which depicts a precarious, unsustainable, and deeply stratified world seemingly wrecked by the unbridled drive for growth. Like Yamashita's novel, *OSFS* is set in a city of ruins (formerly Baltimore) and its surrounding areas. The novel tracks the adventures of Fan, the young female protagonist, as she travels through the stratified society in search of her missing fiancé. Although climate change is never named as the cause of urban and ecological ruin in the novel, the symptoms of climate change abound—resource scarcity, the spread of mysterious illnesses, mass displacement, and floods. What I find remarkable about Lee's novel is not his engagement with the effects of climate change but rather his dwelling on the question of transition and how to forge a climate consciousness in times of disaster. Lee grapples with the problem of creating a subject that is both a victim of climate change and responsible for its effects. In place of the liberal bourgeois individual, who is the subject who can participate in climate justice politics? The novel offers not a radical re-envisioning of possible worlds but rather a "just" transition to a livable—if damaged—world where we may have to relinquish our investments in individualism and consider how humans act upon the world as geophysical forces.

For communities of color, and writers of color, climate change discourse has never been restricted to discussions on carbon emissions, the weather, or even disaster; rather, climate change "is a symptom of a deeper crisis: resource intensive industrial production of the dominant dig, burn, dump economy" ("Just Transition"). Indeed, as Curtis Marez has argued, "Ecological disasters are historic and ongoing features of colonialism, capitalist resource extraction, and racialized and gendered labor exploitation" (xi). Just as racial capitalism is a root cause of "unjust environments," racism has concentrated the catastrophic effects of the fossil fuel economy in impoverished and racialized communities (Sze 7). Cli-fi, though an expanding and evolving literary field, has largely ignored the uneven distribution of climate risks and effects. Yet it is possible to harness the capacious resources of literature to articulate our responses to climate change, which is not restricted to one genre of writing.

It might be more useful at this juncture, given the dearth of literary fiction that explicitly engages with climate change, to advocate instead for a climate-conscious reading practice. If climate change marks a "world-changing rupture in a social and ecological system," cultural production would in no way be exempt from these dramatic shifts (DeLoughrey 7). Our energy sources, argues Patricia Yaeger, are "force field[s] for culture"; they fuel our cultural imaginary (308). A climate-conscious reading practice uncovers the ways in which our fictions—of "surplus," freedom, humanity—subsist on the forms of energy available to us (Szeman 324). It asks us to consider how our fictions evolve to meet the challenge of living in compromised worlds where the future is anything but guaranteed. In Lee's novel, global capitalism, as a stand-in for climate, wreaks havoc on the biosphere and urban environment. To read the novel on the register of climate change is useful to the extent that it alerts us to the irreversible shifts that have marked the Anthropocene and with them, undoubtably, the fundamental question of what it means to be human.[2]

While declarations of the end—of the world, of history, of capitalism, of empire, of theory—proliferate, it is becoming more and more clear that none of these systems and concepts ever end. For communities that have endured the ruinous effects of ecological calamities and capitalist accumulation and have already experienced the displacement and disappearance of their communities and livelihoods, the end of the world is not a compelling narrative. What many in the Global North fear is already a sealed fate for many in the Global South, as well as Black, Indigenous, and people of color communities everywhere. Yet, these provocations of end times are productive as indicators of the persistence of transition rather than ends. The survival of our communities facing the threat of disappearance depends on our ability to imagine and work toward a just transition. Because the climate crisis is an extension of environmental racism, both rooted in extractive, exploitative, and polluting industries, a just transition foregrounds the ways in which communities of color bear the brunt of the hazardous effects of industrial practices.[3] These industries enact a form of violence that Rob Nixon has called "slow violence": "a violence of delayed destruction that is dispersed across time and space, an attritional violence that is typically not viewed as violence at all" (2). Thus, industrial sites that disproportionally pollute poor neighborhoods are also responsible for increasing asthma rates; these "unhealthy" communities have a harder time weathering the effects of climate change such as intensifying heat waves and wildfires.

Contrary to the doom-and-gloom narratives of cli-fi, climate justice activists advocate for the necessity of a just transition, the "vision-led, unifying and place-based set of principles, processes and practices that build economic and political power to shift from an extractive economy to a regenerative one." A just transition requires a major cultural shift "to decolonize our imaginations, remember our way forward and divorce ourselves from the comforts of empire . . . where we live in just relationships with each other and with the earth" ("Just Transition"). Where cli-fi envisions a dystopic world that continues to get worse, such that the world may very well end before capitalism does, climate justice activists dream of the end of exploitation.

While the threat of climate change has often been envisioned in the trope of the island (DeLoughrey 6), the rapid industrialization and urbanization that attend imperial development and man's ultimate control over nature have also generated iconic images of the city "choking on growth."[4] In these images, we often see a panoramic view of the urban skyline occluded by smog or plumes of gas spewing out of smokestacks on the horizon. Lee's novel demonstrates how the remnants of the global American carbon economy have sedimented in cities such as Baltimore and Shenzhen. The specter of Asia, as symbolized by the rise of China and the threat of nuclear warfare,[5] figures prominently in American visions of environmental disaster. From the carbon economy that underwrites rapid industrialization to the occupation and development of native lands to labor exploitation and the domination of commodity markets, Asia's imperial reach would seem to mirror that of the United States. Yet, a narrow focus on Asian culpability in climate change, for instance, the responsibility of Chinese development for increasing global carbon emissions, eclipses the role of the United States, which depends on Chinese factories and labor to produce American goods.[6] That is, unchecked capitalist growth and political power in the Asia Pacific function, on the one hand, as an analogy for helping us understand the contributions of American imperialism and industrialization to climate change and, on the other hand, as a scapegoat obscuring American culpability. To the extent that the blame game (i.e., whoever is at greater fault for carbon emissions should do more to mitigate climate risks) has been ineffective in moving the conversation forward, scholars and activists have been enjoining us to look past national and identitarian differences to see ourselves in the same boat.

Lee collapses the distance between the United States and China and diminishes the economic competition between these two rivalries by casting the futures of these superpowers in mutual interdependence. The spectacular rise of China on the world stage may pose a threat to U.S. hegemony, but the threat of China has been neutralized in the novel and—vis-à-vis B-Mor—is quite literally embedded into the very fabric of American society. As Lee explains in an interview with *The New Yorker*, the idea for his novel transpired during one of his many train rides through a dilapidated section of Baltimore: "Maybe it was my frustration, my feeling of powerlessness, but I was suddenly struck by a very strange idea about re-populating this and other abandoned urban areas like it all in one stroke, boom, say with a homogenous colony of foreigners" ("The Chorus of 'We'"). What resulted is a speculative piece in which American society is stratified into three regions: the Charters, a wealthy community that owns the means of capital; B-Mor, an immigrant enclave and factory town made up of displaced Chinese migrants brought in to revitalize a decaying city much like the Baltimore that Lee saw on his train rides; and the Counties, lawless shantytowns left to languish as a wasteland with no hopes of development or progress. Lee's America is, in fact, a striking analogue to the division of the world into first, second, and third worlds. Either the world has supplanted America, or America has remade the world in its own image. To be sure, the notion that immigrants would resuscitate dying American cities is not purely speculative; this was really what happened to blighted cities all over the country.[7] In a sense, we may have already arrived at the world Lee augurs.

Originally planning to write a novel set in the factory towns of Shenzhen, the southern Chinese metropolis that became China's first special economic zone to open the country up to foreign investment, Lee transplanted Shenzhen to America instead. The new residents of B-Mor were forced to leave Xixu City in China, modeled on Shenzhen, after their city "was made uninhabitable by the surrounding farms and factories and power plants and mining operations, the water fouled beyond all methods of treatment" (*OSFS* 19). Xixu City had essentially become dead land.[8] Meanwhile, post-industrial Baltimore had been abandoned, its houses "basically shells" (20) and city blocks "utter[ly] dessicat[ed]" (21). "By dint of their collective will and the discipline of their leaders," the immigrants "transformed the desperate nothingness about them" (79). In this scenario, we are reminded that American prosperity is contingent on Chinese labor; at the same time, American precarity is linked to Chinese immigration. If B-Mor constitutes the future of a ruined China, then China projects hope for a ruined America. The idea that the ruination of one society could salvage the ruination of the other is a prime example of what might be called climate denial, a willful oblivion about the future based on a conservative and nostalgic desire to repeatedly recreate the bygone past: "What activity offers more immediate, honest gratification than shining up a seemingly ruined surface back to the distinctive grain of its essence?" (21). Yet, on some level, the collective "we" that is the narrator admits to the mutual harm that is part of this pursuit: "You can't help but crave some ruin in what you love" (112). The introduction of Chinese labor to restore a crumbling Baltimore ruined the city in another way by displacing B-Mor's historical inhabitants.

The novel begins with an answer to one of the most vexatious questions asked of immigrants, and in particular Asian Americans, "Where are you from?" The choral narrator responds: "It is known where we come from. . . . Except for a lucky few, everyone is from someplace, but that someplace, it turns out, is gone" (1). Forced to migrate because their hometown has been blighted by industrial pollution, these environmental refugees join a long line of migrants and trafficked persons for whom displacement is a permanent condition. Little remains of an Indigenous population, which interestingly includes "descendants of nineteenth-century African slaves and twentieth-century laborers from Central America and even bands of twenty-first-century urban-nostalgics" (21). Even if successive waves of migrants were to claim indigeneity, the places they claim will eventually die off as they themselves also disappear. Unmoored from the land, the experience of migration bespeaks a life of carcerality rather than mobility. For residents in the Counties, like those in Xixu city, "the loss of the land and resources beneath them" has displacing effects, but unlike the Xixu residents, Counties' people are "stranded in a place stripped of the very characteristics that made it inhabitable" (Nixon 19). The migrants from Xixu city "were brought in en masse for a strict purpose"—to perform the productive labor necessary to serve the needs of the Charters; their labor, which is "perpetually regenerative," essentially reproduces the very society from which they are displaced (*OSFS* 22). Even in the cocoon of privilege and wealth, a precarious future awaits Charters residents, so if they should fall, "there's no middle realm" likely expelling them to the Counties (62). Relatively isolated from each other, the Charters, B-Mor, and Counties are knowable to the "we" narrator only through the looking glass of Fan, the central protagonist.

In *OSFS*, which is structured as a picaresque novel, Fan sets out in the beginning on a quest to find her missing fiancé, Reg. Fan ventures through the three worlds and, for not quite discernible reasons, is able to adapt to every one of these environments. In B-Mor, she is a model worker and expert diver. In the Counties, she ingratiates herself to Quig and Loreen (her rescuers and keepers) by streamlining the bidding process and raising the bids offered for Quig's services. A family of entertainers, the Nickelmans, want to recruit Fan to perform in their show business while they plot to kill off Quig and Loreen. In the Charters, she is the object of much admiration and gratitude for the care and comfort she proffers both the girls kept as pets at Miss Cathy's house and her brother's children. She is the model minority par excellence with a real gift for the art of survival.[9] Whether Fan sets out to seek knowledge or freedom, her travels through the three worlds of the novel underscore one fundamental truth, which is that her survival depends on the instrumentality of her labor. As long as her body can be used or bartered for labor—productive, reproductive, emotional, and aesthetic—her livelihood is guaranteed.

Despite the clear distinctions drawn between the Charters, B-Mor, and the Counties, Fan's experiences reveal the ways in which these three worlds actually mirror each other. The narrator ponders in the first few pages of the novel "whether being an 'individual' makes a difference anymore" (3), a particularly pertinent question given the dubious efficacy of intention and agency in creating change. The "enigma of [Fan's] longing," the narrator tells us, "was of no longing" (304). Fan's adventures "down those unmarked and twisted roads . . . subjected to the warped designs of sundry citizenries" (304) constitute what Ann Kaplan has described as "border events" (xiv). Border events, such as Hurricane Sandy, have the effect of transforming our consciousness on climate change through, for example, "exposing our complete reliance on electricity," leaving us with an "immobilizing anticipatory anxiety about the future" (xix). Those moments in the novel when Fan realizes she is being used, when she appears to have little power, are also moments when "she [is] floated out, alone," to take control of her own life (*OSFS* 304). In a world besieged by climate change, humans simultaneously have too much power and too little power; though this consciousness is immobilizing, the urgency of the climate crisis compels us to seize upon the present moment.

In all three worlds, individualism is taken to such extremes that it poses a fundamental threat to society. Charters treat their selves as "exquisite microcosms, testing and honing and curating every texture and thread of their lives" (296–97). To become "Connoisseurs of Me," Charters cannibalize the labor of B-Mor in order to feed their carbon fantasies. The Charters is, after all, a community of fantasy makers: "real estate speculators, brokers of insurance, writers/creators of evening programs" (62). In a parodic mode, *OSFS* depicts a Charters' matron, Miss Cathy, keeping a group of young girls as pets for comfort, another collective that is available for cannibalism.[10] B-Mor, which by definition is a labor collective that organizes people in a "constant and interchangeable array" (53), also has its "lone agents" (265). These agents "are suddenly apart from us, as well as from one another. . . . They are playing solo. Perhaps because of this, they appear all the more anchored, all the more unitary" (265). Finally, the Counties is a dog-eat-dog world where being an individual risks cannibalization as a commodity to be bartered. In *OSFS*, individuals are parasites, terrorists (i.e., lone agents), and/or prey. Without idealizing the "individual," *OSFS* intimates that the individual has become the latest casualty of the "tragedy of the commons."

According to Jane Fiskio, two narrative threads dominate global climate change discourse: the "lifeboat" and the "collective." As opposed to the lifeboat narrative, which sees human beings as self-interested and exclusive even as they try to create sustainable communities, in the collective narrative, "what people need to face catastrophe is a sense of purpose and community" (Fiskio 22). In *OSFS*, B-Mor prioritizes the identity of the collective over that of the individual, but while Lee emphasizes the "psychic warmth of the hive" that envelops Fan, no specific belief system regulates B-Mor (*OSFS* 53). They "are ruled by one another as to what is optimal" and "abide by directorate regulations," practicing only "an undying habit of pragmatic attention and action" (171). The "sense of purpose and community" that Fiskio outlines is imperceptible in B-Mor's version of the collective. Others, the narrator warns, may even say that B-Mor is "amoral" (171). What good is having beliefs in a dystopian society? Or to put the question differently, might surrendering belief systems be one way of surviving the Anthropocene? Their pragmatism, after all, "endows [them] . . . with a certain equable stance that does not tip [them] either too far forward or back" (171). In the Charters, the anime-like girls kept by Miss Cathy may not be able to live without each other but are more akin to collectibles than a collective. Their purpose is to swaddle Miss Cathy: "For it was ultimately not a particular girl or girls who were most important but their totality, the way they could web and cocoon her" (285). *OSFS* queries whether these collectives could be mobilized for change or if they would simply fall apart. The "we" narrator reaches a daunting realization that "as conceived, as constituted, we may in fact be of a design unsustainable" (121). Yet the novel belies the view that sustainability, or sustainable living, would be the climate justice we are looking for. In the Counties, Fan encounters the Nickelmans, a cultish family of vegetarians, who strive to be completely independent by practicing a sustainable living that only uses the resources available to them on their compound. The problem is that they still have to feed their carnivorous dogs, and so, in what could be a scene from a horror movie, they try to capture Quig and Loreen as potential pet fodder. We can ascribe the lifeboat narrative here to sustainable practices that attempt to separate the microcosm from the larger ecosystem.

Without the means to initiate change, either through individual agency or collective action, the community pins their aspirations on Fan: "We needed Fan, in both idea and person" (121). That the community would be motivated by Fan's departure and the freedom it signifies—"We feel as free as Fan" (226)—is a bit curious given how unremarkable a character she is. Jiayang Fan writes in her review of *OSFS*: "As the ostensible heroine, Fan feels oddly puppet-like, a plot-advancing symbol rather than a complex character in her own right." Fan is not "the champion" or "the heroine who wields the great sword" or "the bearer of wisdom and light." Rather, "she is one of the ranks, this perfectly ordinary, exquisitely tiny person in whom we will reside, via both living and dreaming" (*OSFS* 230). It is precisely her ordinariness that evinces identification and transfigures her into "a kind of canvas that we all want to write on" (qtd. in Page 94). Lee elaborates on how the inspiration for the character of Fan was based on Moby Dick:

> The whale itself has no consciousness. The consciousness and presence that it is given come from those around it. . . . There's something about her that is absent of human consciousness in the ways we normally get consciousness in a maximal way in fiction. (qtd. in Page 94)

All the ways in which the "we" narrator lionizes Fan for possessing "wisdom," "clarity" (4), the "conviction of imagination" (7), "focus," "unwavering belief" (259), "freedom" (397), and "genius" (182)—all of which are unreliably narrated and may very well be the narrator's own desires and projections—almost read like an elegy of the subject itself.

The reviews on *OSFS* puzzle greatly over the characterization of Fan: is she a protagonist imbued with desires, intentions, and action, or is she a creature subject to the whims of the narrator and other characters? Christopher Fan argues that situating Fan within the "animacy hierarchy," as opposed to the human/animal divide, is more useful for understanding her

(677). He characterizes Fan as a form of "posthistorical animacy," his term for the "minoritized or waning protagonicity" associated with the status of the liberal bourgeois subject at the end of history (679). Rachel Lee claims that *OSFS* tests the limits of novelistic subjectivity by limning Fan as someone who exercises action "most mechanistically" in moments "resembling revolution" while in moments that resemble "complicity," "she displays . . . maximal intentionality. She is all intention and no action." She asks how we can recognize "direction without intention" and "intention without direction" as forms of historical agency (525). However Fan's subjectivity (or lack thereof) is comprehended, one concurrence we could be certain of is the death of the liberal bourgeois subject.

One of the central conundrums of climate activism is the astounding ways in which growing knowledge of climate change appears only to be matched, and even surpassed, by inaction. The more urgent the climate crisis, the more certain the solutions, the greater the impasse to the will to act. Anthropocene fictions underscore the discursive dimensions of the climate crisis, highlighting the "crisis of imagination" that stems from the difficulty of identifying the pertinent actors and causes of climate change (Mehnert 37). Nothing short of "a recalibration of theoretical knowledge" would seem to adequately address our analytical inability to get a firm grasp on climate change as it shapes our relation to the world (Johns-Putra 9). For instance, Timothy Clark argues that the Anthropocene induces a change in the "tectonic plates of human self-conceptions" (81) that involves a "kind of new, totalizing self-reflexivity as a species," one that perceives "being a person" as an "environmental problem" (86).

Given the mystery of Fan's intentions and how she exercises her agency, how might we consider her political subjectivity? I would argue that Lee's characterization of Fan typifies the subject of climate change discourse. According to Amitav Ghosh, it is precisely the modern novel's emphasis on the development of a liberal bourgeois subject, on the "rationalization" and "regularity" of modern life—which renders catastrophic climate events an impossible plot twist—that makes it impossible for serious fiction to engage with climate change. Our faith in the regularity of bourgeois life materializes as a kind of climate denial, a faith that Ghosh designates as the "Great Derangement." Dipesh Chakrabarty similarly argues that our inability to engage with climate change has to do with the ways in which our very conceptions of freedom, which can be traced back to Enlightenment ideals, are underpinned by the carbon economy ("Climate of History"). *OSFS* attests to the consequences of the carbon economy and the sense of living under siege; it engenders an affective space, or ecology, through Fan that mediates our movement through this world. The ambiguity of Fan's subjectivity underscores a climate consciousness that imputes responsibility for climate change to humans and at the same time renders them powerless in the face of it. That is, we might consider Fan not as a human subject per se but as a geophysical force, which is "the capacity to move things" but is "a form of collective existence that has no ontological dimension" (Chakrabarty, "Postcolonial Studies" 13). We may think of ourselves as individuals or as members of collectivities, but according to Chakrabarty, there is "no corresponding 'humanity' that in its oneness can act as a political agent" (14). Fan is part of a geophysical force known as humanity, but she cannot conceive of herself as such a force or as someone who can shape that force politically.

In the portrait of Fan that Miss Cathy's girls made, parts of the girls were drawn in so that "you could also think to see Five's fullish lips, or the most solid set of Three's cheek, or some distinctive notation of each of the girls" (*OSFS* 295). If Fan is not a typical protagonist, she might be more aptly viewed as an ecology.[11] Recall the narrator saying that they "reside" in her (230). She is weather, a climate, that moves through and enshrouds space:[12] "there is an altered thrum in the air" (337). Causing repeated disturbances, none cataclysmic, she incites others to adapt to her. She would often hold her breath underwater for much longer than she needed to, "summoning a different kind of force that would transform not her but the composition of the realm, make it so the water would not harm her" (7). Of her many gifts, she is also able to "acclimate to any temperature" (323). She allegorizes a climate resilience that is focused on adaptability; at the same time, she could transition into a state of being free from want—including air. At the same time, Lee describes her as a "genuine artist," whose genius is her "capacity for understanding and trusting the improvisational nature of her will" (182). Her brilliance is borne not of intention or even intellect but of both an elemental instinct to blend in with her circumstances and creative talent. Her adaptability, even when she is not "especially charismatic, or visionary," is what touches the denizens of B-Mor: "For some reason, we want to see [her] succeed" (263). All the capabilities of a bourgeois liberal subject fall to the wayside when confronting the increasingly dystopic direction of human society; Fan's ability to adapt to circumstances, regardless of her ability to read them, allows her to navigate this world with a certain degree of ease.

Like Moby Dick, she is like "a creature of prey" that draws consciousness from those around her (4). The girls at Miss Cathy's and the collective "we" narrator are piqued by her story; they mold her into the subject of myth and lore. As much as they want to see her succeed, they accede to her vulnerability; she is both beast and hunted prey. What may be touching about Fan is "the enigma of her longing," "not one born of selfishness or egoism, some belief that she was scaled . . . larger or brighter than the rest" (304). Somehow, she is not ruined by the harm around her; nor does she ever bring harm to others (to the contrary, her instinct is to provide care). Her story is littered with constant disavowal and deferral: "And so she would have had to describe how she led them out of this room, out of this house, perhaps even through the secured gates of the village altogether; but of course she did not" (259). "When it must have seemed each time that all was lost again, the tethers were now released, the moorings finally dismantled, and she was floated out" (304). In her journey, she stays true to principle: "It's perhaps more laudable simply to keep heading out into the world than always tilting to leave one's mark on it" (295). Her politics, if one could call it that, might be one of harm reduction.

As a "superbly formed . . . specimen," Fan could only truly be a work of nature, like an endangered and rare animal or plant (296). Understood on this elemental level, Fan exists as a "mere cluster of cells" (52), so "were she to disappear even she might not notice the moment of demise" (53). In *OSFS*, the individual is subjected to dissolution such that the only "identities" that remain are mere cells or collectivities. To dissolve the agency of the human may be one way for the species to recover from the tragedy of the commons; if anthropogenic activity is destroying the Earth, then perhaps a climate justice politics must involve holding those human capabilities in check first.

At the same time that our global economy has transitioned from the use of coal to oil, thus from the use of a large communal workforce to one based in isolation, the collective, or "men in aggregate," has also been banished from the novel in favor of the individual (Ghosh). *OSFS* reveals the extent to which our fossil fuel economy depends on the rise of Chinese labor by centralizing a Chinese worker as its protagonist. Like the choral narrator, we identify with Fan's loss of autonomy as laborers in a global capitalist system. While many critics have commented on the flatness of the characterization and action in *OSFS*, I suggest that the novel does put forth a climate justice politics that implicates labor as one of its central components. Despite the disintegration of the "individual," B-Mor residents gain some semblance of identity through labor: "Maybe it's the laboring that gives you shape. Might the most fulfilling times be those . . . when you are able to uncover the smallest surprises and

unlikely details of some process or operation that in turn exposes your pro-
clivities and prejudices" (6)? While the job of diving is a solo one, Fan is never
truly alone at her job. In the tanks, "the fish seem to gird her and bear her
along the tank walls like a living scaffold . . . or even playfully school themselves into just her shape and become her mirror in the water" (5). Although
the labor collective of B-Mor has ultimately failed to break out of their con-
formity with the directorate's wishes, Fan's interspecies relationship with the
fish hints at other possible alliances. This scene of interspecies collaboration
and mirroring is repeated in a mural painted at Miss Cathy's house: "The
scene itself was an underwater realm . . . seven of the thick shoots [of sea-
weed] transforming into seven faceless girls, with Fan . . . being pushed by
their number to the surface" (266). This interspecies world, separate from
the cannibalistic qualities of the other collectivities in the novel, seems to me
to be one way toward a just transition. If we are to transition from an economy predicated on extraction and exploitation to one predicated on care and
stewardship, our stories must be able to imagine this transition equally on
the level of consciousness and the laboring body. *OSFS* attempts to scale the
human subject, as geophysical forces, laboring toward the process of such
energy transitions.

Finally, factory labor mediates the communal storytelling of the "we" narrator. The story of Fan, spread in a gossip-like fashion, is told through an
assemblage of workers. Fan's adventures galvanize a group of mural artists
and viewers who perceive the common experience of talking about Fan as
"something akin to sharing a long-harbored secret" (292). Like the stories
that Miss Cathy's girls tell on their murals, "the scenes were not separated
by borders or other framing but magically melded into one another . . . so
that the whole appeared to be roiling in a continuous, visceral flow" (250).
Storytelling is the engine that maintains the flow of production. Like music,
storytelling lulls and compels our bodies to take over mechanistic operations
without thought, "the sound of one's voice caretaking this turn and the next,
and allowing the full flow" (147). The dystopian nature of cli-fi elucidates the
powerlessness of human agents, and to a certain extent the inadequacy of
human subjectivity, in confronting environmental ruin. Lee's experimentation with the characterization of Fan in *OSFS* suggests we consider humans
as different types of forces that move through, act upon, and adapt to the
world—as individuals, laborers, collectivities, and ecologies. A just transition from the liberal subject whose freedom is predicated on extraction and
exploitation demands such a climate consciousness.

Notes

1. Examples of novels include Bacigalupi's *The Water Knife*, McCarthy's *The Road*, and Atwood's *Oryx and Crake*. For an example of cli-fi in film, see Emmerich's *The Day After Tomorrow*.

2. The Anthropocene is a term used to describe the most recent epoch of the Earth's history in which humans have become a geological force and human activity has significantly altered the Earth's geology and ecosystems.

3. For an account of the relationship between environmental justice and climate justice, see Schlosberg and Collins.

4. "Choking on Growth" is also the name of the *New York Times* series on China's environmental challenges that ran in 2007.

5. The destruction of the environment is often imagined through a nuclear apocalypse. The Fukushima nuclear accident of 2011 still reverberates as a major environmental disaster in the region.

6. Even though China's carbon emissions are the highest in the world as of 2021, about 22 percent of its emissions can be attributed to the production of exports. See Roberts.

7. For example, the arrival of new immigrants after the passing of the 1965 Hart-Cellar Act was credited for revitalizing a bankrupt and declining New York City in the 1970s.

8. See Sassen.

9. For an account of how B-Mor is a model minority community, see Enriquez.

10. See Kim for an argument on how Asian Americans are racialized as pets in American culture. For more on the use of parody in *OSFS*, see Carruth.

11. Rachel Lee also describes her as possessing a "biocultural creatureliness" or "molecular agency."

12. Interestingly, Miss Cathy is also described as a climate: "It was solely her storm or fine clime they were subject to, and in this regard the greatest potential disturbance was not their complement being diminished but the specter of sudden change" (*OSFS* 285).

Works Cited

Atwood, Margaret. *Oryx and Crake*. Doubleday, 2003.

Bacigalupi, Paolo. *The Water Knife*. Knopf, 2015.

Carruth, Allison. "Wily Ecologies: Comic Futures for American Environmentalism." *American Literary History*, vol. 30, no. 1, 2018, 108–33.

Chakrabarty, Dipesh. "The Climate of History: Four Theses." *Critical Inquiry*, vol. 35, 2009, 197–222.

Chakrabarty, Dipesh. "Postcolonial Studies and the Challenge of Climate Change." *New Literary History*, vol. 43, no. 1, 2012, 1–18.

Clark, Timothy. "Nature, Post Nature." *The Cambridge Companion to Literature and the Environment*, edited by Louise Westling. Cambridge UP, 2014, 75–89.

DeLoughrey, Elizabeth M. *Allegories of the Anthropocene*. Duke UP, 2019.

Emmerich, Roland, director. *The Day After Tomorrow*. 20th Century Fox, 2004.

Enriquez, Jeshua. "Crossing the Threshold of B-Mor: Instrumental Commodification and the Model Minority in Chang-Rae Lee's *On Such a Full Sea*." *Dis-Orienting Planets: Racial Representation of Asia In Science Fiction*, edited by Isiah Lavender. UP of Mississippi, 2017, 175–87.

Fan, Christopher T. "Animacy at the End of History in Chang-rae Lee's *On Such a Full Sea.*" *American Quarterly*, vol. 69, no. 3, 2017, 675–96.

Fan, Jiayang. "New America and Old China in Dystopian Novels." *VQR Online*, Spring 2014, https://www.vqronline.org/fiction-criticism/2014/04/new-america-and-old-china-dystopian-novels. Accessed 16 Aug. 2021.

Fiskio, Jane. "Apocalypse and Ecotopia: Narratives in Global Climate Change Discourse." *Race, Gender & Class*, vol. 19, no. 1–2, 2012, 12–36.

Ghosh, Amitav. *The Great Derangement: Climate Change and the Unthinkable.* U of Chicago P, 2016.

Johns-Putra, Adeline. "A New Critical Climate." *symploke*, vol. 21, nos. 1–2, 2013, 7–10.

"Just Transition: A Framework for Change." *Climate Justice Alliance*, https://climatejustice-alliance.org/just-transition/. Accessed 16 Aug. 2021.

Kaplan, E. Ann. *Climate Trauma.* Rutgers UP, 2015.

Kim, James. "Petting Asian America." *MELUS: Multi-Ethnic Literature of the US*, vol. 36, no. 1, 2011, 135–55.

Lee, Chang-rae. "The Chorus of 'We': An Interview with Chang Rae Lee." Interview by Cressida Leyshon. *New Yorker*, 6 Jan. 2014, https://www.newyorker.com/books/page-turner/the-chorus-of-we-an-interview-with-chang-rae-lee. Accessed 16 Aug. 2021.

Lee, Chang-rae. *On Such a Full Sea.* Riverhead Books, 2014.

Lee, Rachel. "Are Biocultural Creatures Posthistorical Agents?" *Theory & Event*, vol. 21, no. 2, 2018, 518–28.

Marez, Curtis. Foreword. *Racial Ecologies*, edited by Leilani Nishime and Kim D. Hester Williams. U of Washington P, 2018, ix–xiv.

McCarthy, Cormac. *The Road.* Knopf, 2006.

Mehnert, Antonia. *Climate Change Fictions: Representations of Global Warming in American Literature.* Palgrave Macmillan, 2016.

Nixon, Rob. *Slow Violence and the Environmentalism of the Poor.* Harvard UP, 2011.

Ozeki, Ruth. *A Tale for the Time Being.* Penguin, 2013.

Page, Amanda M. *Understanding Chang-rae Lee.* U of South Carolina P, 2017.

Roberts, Alli Gold. "Calculating China's Carbon Emissions from Trade." *MIT News*, 6 March 2014, https://news.mit.edu/2014/calculating-chinas-carbon-emissions-from-trade. Accessed 16 Aug. 2021.

Sassen, Saskia. "Dead Land, Dead Water." *Expulsions: Brutality and Complexity in the Global Economy.* Belknap Press of Harvard UP, 2014, 149–210.

Schlosberg, David, and Lisette B. Collins. "From Environmental to Climate Justice: Climate Change and the Discourse of Environmental Justice." *WIREs Climate Change*, vol. 5, 2014, 359–74.

Sze, Julie. *Environmental Justice in a Moment of Danger.* U of California P, 2020.

Szeman, Imre. "Literature and Energy Futures." *PMLA*, vol. 126, no. 2, 2011, 323–26.

Yaeger, Patricia. "Editor's Column: Literature in the Ages of Wood, Tallow, Coal, Whale Oil, Gasoline, Atomic Power, and Other Energy Sources." *PMLA*, vol. 126, no. 2, 2011, 305–26.

Yamashita, Karen Tei. *Tropic of Orange.* Coffee House Press, 1997.

12

Rising Like Waves

Drowning Settler Colonial Rhetoric with Aloha

Emalani Case

"We rise like a mighty wave."

PUA CASE

If you're in Hawai'i, I have a challenge for you: go to Mauna Kea, our sacred mountain. Drive over hills and winding roads. Park near Pu'uhonua o Pu'uhuluhulu, the sanctuary established for kia'i mauna,[1] or protectors of the mountain. At noon, when the sun hits the top of your head, stand quietly with the crowds gathered and be in ceremony. Turn to face the mountain when everyone else turns and notice its every groove. Clap when everyone else claps to acknowledge the prayers being lifted. Say "Eō!" and "Ea!" when everyone else does to vocalize solidarity. Feel the moment. Feel the movement. Then, when one of the leaders, Pua Case, steps out onto the road—the road that has been occupied for more than one hundred days at the time of writing[2]—watch as her long 'ehu (reddish) hair lifts and dances and listen as she chants about pillars of strength, pillars of hope, pillars of aloha. When she gets to the last line, hear her declare, "E hū e," and respond with a forceful "Hū!" She is telling you that we are rising, rising like mighty waves, and she is inviting you to rise with us. If you do this, and if you truly allow yourself to feel the lift, you will notice something shift, something rise within, and you may just be moved to know the mountain in new ways, to love it, and to protect it as we do: with everything we have.

If you aren't in Hawai'i, imagine it. Every day, three times a day, kia'i mauna gather in this way for ceremony. They honor and recognize the earth and our many deities who dwell here with us, and they pray for change, drawing on words gifted from our ancestors and written by modern composers. The chant that ends every ceremony is one that was written by my cousin, Pua. Entitled "Nā Kūkulu" (The pillars), it brings people together to face the challenges of our world with strength, with fierce commitment, and with aloha, and as she often says, it encourages us to "hū," or to "rise like a mighty wave." Stationed at the base of Mauna Kea since 13 July 2019, the kiaʻi are dedicated to preventing the construction of a Thirty Meter Telescope (TMT) near its summit. If built, the telescope being proposed by the TMT International Observatory LLC (TIO)[3] would be the largest on the island, standing 18 stories tall, occupying five acres of land, and digging two stories into the ground to position two 5,000-gallon tanks for holding human waste and chemical waste. This would require not only the devastation of a unique ecosystem but the disrespect and violent and intentional disruption of Kanaka Maoli[4] connections to the mountain. The current occupation of the area known as Puʻuhuluhulu, and the establishment of a place of safety and sanctuary there,[5] is the latest concerted effort of Mauna Kea protectors in what has been nearly a decade of legal battles, court cases, active occupations of the mountain, and constant petitioning, testifying, and speaking out against the TMT. In this context, Pua's chant is like a daily affirmation, a daily recommitment to standing as a protector and to conducting oneself in a way that respects the mauna and represents the sacredness we stand to guard.

The importance of a chant like "Nā Kūkulu" in the current movement is immeasurable. Not only does it speak directly to the movement itself, but it was also created in it and has taken on new meaning both on and off the mountain. It is both a rallying call and a response to environmental damage and destruction. In the particular context of Hawaiʻi, additionally, it is a tool for countering settler colonial attempts to stagnate our resistance, to force Indigenous peoples into small tide pools where our actions are controlled and sanctioned, and to trick us with insidious rhetoric meant to reinforce colonial dominance while subjugating Kānaka. Rather than recount the dangers we face, however, or list the challenges we live with as our planet continues to suffer the impacts of rapid environmental decline, the chant calls us to act. It challenges us to not spend time merely thinking about movements, or what *can* be done, but to get into the wave that is already rising and be a part of changing our world.

In this chapter, I will use my cousin's chant, "Nā Kūkulu," as an opportunity to investigate the current rise at Mauna Kea and how the ripples of its wave have impacted other places and peoples both in and out of Hawaiʻi.

I will also look at the chant in conjunction with a 14-page plan for Mauna Kea prepared by the former mayor of Hawai'i Island (where Mauna Kea is located), Harry Kim. Released on 30 September 2019, the "plan" represents every attempt of the settler state to normalize itself, to operate on the premise that its presence and dominance are a given and that environmental destruction and desecration for the TMT is warranted as long as it is framed as benefiting all of humanity. I have chosen to analyze this "plan" (which is not so much a plan as it is a colonial declaration of intent to harm) together with my cousin's chant—flowing back and forth between the two—because her composition provides the tools and the opportunity to expose settler logics, to dismantle them, and to act for the rights of Indigenous peoples and the rights of the earth with wisdom gifted from our ancestors. In today's climate crisis, when sea levels are rising and swallowing islands, we have to rise in consciousness, in action, and in fierce commitment to 'āina, or to every natural source that nourishes us. We do not have time to waste building a telescope to see the stars, one that has already caused so much pain and one that will cause irreparable damage. We must, instead, turn our attention to the lands and waters that need us and that are calling on us, depending on us, to rise.

We Rise

Composed on 12 April 2017, "Nā Kūkulu" not only motivates the ongoing movement to protect Mauna Kea but also honors Indigenous connections and solidarity to other islands and islanders in Oceania, to Indigenous peoples on Turtle Island,[6] and to supporters around the world. In doing so, it challenges the idea that movements for the protection of our sacred spaces are isolated. Instead, it reinforces the understanding that to protect one mountain is to motivate protection for all mountains; to protect water in one place is to advocate for protecting water in all places; and to stand for the sacred is a lifelong commitment to viewing our lands, oceans, and waters as family. In the composition, Pua calls on all of her relatives, friends, and pillars of support to come together, chanting:

E nā hoa'āina e	*Natives, the backbone of* Hawai'i[7]
E nā hoawelo like e	*Relatives of the big ocean of Kiwa*[8]
E nā hoapili e	*Relatives of the first nation of Turtle*
E nā hoaaloha e	*Islands, friends, supports from around the*
	world

Aloha ʻāina![9]

Kūkulu, e nā kūkulu ʻehā e	*Pillars, the four cardinal points*
Kūkulu!	
He mau maka koa e	*We are beloved warriors*
nā maka kāʻeo	*wearing top knots on our heads*
Eō!	
E hū e	*Rise*
Hū!	
He kū kiaʻi mauna	*A mountain guardian*[10]
Kū!	
He pōhaku kū	*A standing rock*[11]
Kūʻē!	
He ʻiliʻili kapu	*A sacred stone*
Aloha!	
He koa wai e ola	*A water protector*[12]
Ola!	
E hū e	*Rise*
Hū!	

When this chant is done on the mauna, it is repeated three times. At the end of the third time, the line "E hū e" (meaning "We rise" or "We will rise"), which is done by the caller, and the response "Hū!" (chanted by all and acting as an affirmation of what the caller has said) are also repeated three times. With each repetition, the energy builds, and chanters feel themselves lifted, knowing that they are connected not only to those standing next to them on the mountain but to all of the other people around the world who stand for similar reasons: to protect the environment, to honor it as ancestor, and to ensure that our future generations will be able to experience themselves as Indigenous *in* their places.

The end of the chant is incredibly powerful because of what it tells us, what it inspires, and what it indicates about our movement. To "hū" is to rise or swell like a wave. The word, however, has various other meanings, including "to surge or rise to the surface, as emotion," "to roar, grunt, hum, whistle," and even "to depart from the proper course" (Pūkuʻi and Elbert 83). The multiple usages of this term are worth examining because, as Kanalu Young explains, "repeated expressions of [a] word . . . in contexts that fit any of its definitions incorporated the *mana* [power] of those alternate meanings. The homonyms work together to strengthen all definitions" (33). Using the first three meanings, when we chant "Hū!" we *are* talking about rising like waves, we *are* celebrating the surge of emotion that motivates our actions, and we *are* roaring to be heard. The fourth definition, meaning to depart from a path or course, may appear negative and somewhat contradictory in this context. It may seem to suggest, for example, a departure from the goal of the kiaʻi mauna to remain steadfast in our commitment to the mountain. However, in this instance, the hū is a denial of the status quo. It is a recognition of the fact that the paths that have been proposed for us, supposedly for our benefit, have not done us well. It is a reminder that the "proper" courses planned by the settler government (which Mayor Kim's plan is emblematic of) are not the courses we are meant to follow, not if we want to save our lands, our environments, and our future from the constant onslaught of imperial destruction.

"A Way Forward"?

Mayor Kim's plan for the mountain, entitled "Maunakea, the Heart of Aloha: A Way Forward," is one of the latest attempts by TMT proponents to package the telescope in ways that seem acceptable or even desirable. The plan uses positive language, talking about the mountain as a space to work together "for the pursuit of peace and harmony" so that Mauna Kea can be "a beacon of hope and discovery for the world" (Kim).[13] What Kim's plan fails to acknowledge is that kiaʻi mauna are far too committed to the cause and far too educated to fall victim to his recycled rhetoric. Pua's chant is symbolic of this. Once you rise and know what you stand for, in other words, there can be no going back, or as Raihānia Tipoki explains, "You can't become ignorant once you've been conscientized" (Spearim). While trying to present something new, Kim relies on old arguments that Mauna Kea protectors are already aware of and already quite practiced in refuting. Therefore, if viewed in the context of Pua's chant, Kim not only may be ignoring the hū, or the rise, but may actually be so far adrift out at sea that he somehow doesn't know it's happening and has therefore been left behind.

The first line of his plan reads, "This presentation is beyond a 'yes' or a 'no' of the TMT project. This is about asking Hawaiʻi's people to come together and finding a path to go forward in a good way" (Kim 1). For kiaʻi mauna, any plan that still allows for the construction of the TMT—which is obvious in his refusal to say "no"—is not "a way forward." Furthermore, asking us to come together to find something "good" is asking us to compromise, to give in, and to allow for destruction, as if that is a real option. Kim's statements, therefore, represent a refusal to listen to the voices of the people stationed at the mauna, and the voices of people around the world, who are calling on the government to act for the environment and for our future rather than consent to endangerment. When Kim speaks of coming together, therefore, he is only speaking to those who already agree, which leaves all kiaʻi mauna out of the conversation.

The idea of coming together also speaks, albeit indirectly, to the dominant framing of the TMT controversy as one of "culture versus science." The positioning of "culture" and "science" as being somehow binary has led to kiaʻi being pegged as "backward" or afraid of "progress" and to TMT proponents as forward-thinking and innovative. This has led to the all too common assertion that "Hawaiians need to stop living in the past" (Kuwada). In his writing on Mauna Kea, Leon Noʻeau Peralto explains the genealogical connection between Kānaka Maoli and the mountain, also known as Mauna a Wākea (the child of Wākea), which speaks to the notion that Kānaka Maoli are not in the past but are extensions of it, living in the present and connected through genealogy (234). As Hawaiians, we revere Wākea as one of our oldest ancestors and understand that it was through his union with Papahānaumoku that our lands were created and that Kānaka were then born to care for it. As mauna and Kanaka are both children of Wākea and Papahānaumoku, we are "instilled, at birth, with particular kuleana [responsibilities] to each other" (234). One of these responsibilities is to protect our mountain and all environments with it. Therefore, the framing of "culture versus science" misses the point. Kiaʻi are not, and have never been, "anti-science"[14] or stuck in a bygone era. Our stance comes from the real, ongoing, and embodied relationship between Mauna Kea and Kānaka Maoli, one that must be lived out and acted upon in the present. This bond cannot, and will not, be negotiated.

Kim, however, fails to acknowledge this relationship and the fact that being anti-desecration and anti-destruction is not anti-science. Therefore, he continues to buy into the supposed divide between science and culture so that he can assume the authority to propose integration:

When respectfully integrated with a comprehensive understanding of Maunakea and Hawaiian culture, astronomy can be such a catalyst for positive and transformative changes in Hawaiʻi. Under the leadership of dreamers, innovators, and awakened community, this can be the leverage for not only Maunakea issues, but to understand and address the wrongs of the past to make us a better people and place. (Kim 1)

This statement must be unpacked to reveal its various, and quite insidious, implications. First, the only integration that is being allowed for is one that is controlled by the government. This means that aspects of culture will be chosen selectively and will be used by the settler state only as long as they are necessary in pushing colonial agendas. In the plan, this is seen in Kim's repeated use of the term "aloha," one that has been co-opted and abused by the government to sell Hawai'i as a welcoming, loving paradise, open to all. This is also apparent in the strategic hijacking of celestial navigation—something that has seen a revival and has spurred a cultural renaissance in Hawai'i and other parts of Polynesia since the 1970s—as reason to push for the construction of the telescope. Stating, "In recent years, the Hōkūle'a[15] [voyaging canoe] gave birth to a phenomenal Hawaiian cultural renaissance, re-igniting the Hawaiians' desire to discover, grow, and explore new frontiers," Kim attempts to use this history as a means of justifying astronomical research on Mauna Kea, essentially arguing that our sailing culture, which relied on observing and honoring nature and *not* on Western instruments, can be integrated harmoniously with something destructive as long as it is in the name of "discovery" (1).

"Discovery" is a dubious word for many Indigenous peoples, especially given the narratives of European "discovery" that continue to skew history in settler colonial contexts. In the fifteenth and sixteenth centuries, the Vatican passed a series of papal bulls, or Catholic laws, that essentially allowed for conquest. Borne from these laws, Tina Ngata writes, the Doctrine of Discovery "gave the monarchies of Britain and Europe the right to conquer and claim lands, and to convert or kill the native inhabitants of those lands" (13). As further explained by Roxanne Dunbar-Ortiz, "Under this legal cover for theft, Euro-American wars of conquest and settler colonialism devastated Indigenous nations and communities, ripping their territories away from them and transforming the land" (198). Kim's plan, though seemingly innocent in its supposed quest for scientific advancement and framed as benefiting all of humanity, is actually aimed at expanding territory, marking colonial possessions with the structure of a telescope, and simultaneously separating Kānaka from 'āina. The assumption that this is not only possible but also authorized is proof that the racist mentalities birthed by these ancient laws (which have never been rescinded) are so deeply entrenched that they continue to guide colonial actions at the expense of Indigenous peoples and the environments we stand to protect.

The assumptions promoted by the Doctrine of Discovery continue to manifest today, perhaps most visibly in colonial tactics for expansion and domination. Settler colonialism is based on the premise that in order for the settler to "settle" and normalize itself, it must eliminate the native. This is done, as Tim Rowse explains, "either by erasing the Indigenous presence or by determining the forms of its survival" (302). Kim's statement above must also be unpacked in this context. In his plan, Kim attempts to establish the terms of our "survival." Canoe customs can survive, for example, as long as they are integrated to allow for colonial and capitalist enterprises, like the TMT. Other customs, however, like praying on Mauna Kea, constructing altars to honor deities,[16] or revering the mountain as an ancestor, are not within the settler-sanctioned "forms" of survival because they are too challenging, or too threatening, to the settler's quest for territoriality and constant control. This is why, as Patrick Wolfe's now often quoted phrase asserts, we must understand settler colonialism as "a structure not an event" (388). It is ongoing because it has to be. It has to continue to employ eliminatory logic, in other words, as long as Indigenous peoples exist to challenge its power. Kim's plan, in this context, attempts to reinforce the structure.

In addition to the problematic usage of words like "dreamers," "innovators," and "awakened community" in his statement above—which implies that kia'i mauna are *not* any of these things—Kim suggests that the current debate regarding the TMT is an opportunity "to address the wrongs of the past to make us a better people and place" (1). These "wrongs" are strategically located in the past so that they can be perceived as complete and, in the process, so that the government can be absolved from having to take any responsibility for current and ongoing abuses against Kānaka Maoli. The mere suggestion that a thirty-meter telescope can be built on the top of a sacred mountain, however, is an assault to our Indigeneity. It is a colonial violence happening now. However, Kim assumes that recognition of the past is, as Edward Cavanagh argues, "part of a healing process that supposedly leads into a bright and guilt-free future" (17). What kia'i mauna are acutely aware of, however, is the fact that the past is not gone and behind us but is with us every day (18). Thus, there can be no reconciliation and no moving forward as a united place and people, as Kim proposes in his idealized colonial utopia, because we are still living with the impacts of colonialism and with a settler state that needs to continually support itself by eliminating the native. Our position at the base of Mauna Kea and the very existence of a chant like "Nā Kūkulu," one that necessarily calls on us to rise against settler colonial tactics, is evidence of this.

Pillars

Pua's chant calls upon us to stand as kūkulu, or pillars, firmly grounded and unshakable. What's interesting about her use of the term is its association with structure. In a house, a pillar might be necessary to hold up the ceiling. It therefore acts as reinforcement or a source of strength and support. Kūkulu, however, like most Hawaiian words, has more than one definition. It can also mean "to build, as a house; to construct, erect, establish, organize," and as seen in the chant, it can be used to refer to "nā kukulu ʻehā," or the four cardinal points or directions (Pūkuʻi and Elbert 178). Considering all of these meanings, when Pua addresses her relatives, both near and distant, her Indigenous comrades, and her supporters and friends, she urges us to kūkulu in every sense of the word. She wants us to stand as kūkulu, like pillars that can support others, and carry the weight of our movements. At the same time, she wants us to build, to organize, and to essentially dismantle colonial structures as we reinforce our own, based on Indigenous knowledge. Further, she wants us to orient ourselves in the world, knowing our place, so that we can act upon our responsibilities to the earth with confidence and conviction.

Providing us with tools for such work, Pua disperses key Hawaiian actions and perspectives throughout the chant, arranging them as response lines. After she does the solo parts, in other words, everyone around her responds with robust affirmations, each one occurring after one of her calls: aloha ʻāina, kūkulu, eō, hū, kū, kūʻē, aloha, ola, and another hū to end. As co-performers of her chant, we commit (and recommit every time we do it) to kūkulu, to build; to eō, to call out, affirming that we are here; to hū, to rise; to kū, to stand; to kūʻē, to resist; to aloha, to love with everything we have; to ola, to thrive; and to hū, to rise again. In her chant, Pua also insists that we be aloha ʻāina, or fierce protectors of ʻāina (all of our sources of sustenance), by practicing aloha ʻāina, or loving the land, the ocean, and all of our waters.[17] In this chant, there is simply no other way to be and no other way to act. Positioned after the first four lines, where she calls out to every relative and friend, the invitation to respond with "aloha ʻāina" is really an invitation to both Kānaka

Maoli and non-Hawaiians alike to recognize that we must all be propelled to protect our world together with aloha.

Central to the movement to protect Mauna Kea has been, and continues to be, aloha. Despite constant colonial misuse of "aloha," kiaʻi mauna are claiming and reclaiming it as not only one of the most profound Hawaiian concepts but one that will also lead us forward. In Kim's plan for the mountain, the directors of the Mauna Kea observatories (or the directors of the telescopes already operating on the mountain[18]) list "the necessity to build a bright future for all people in Hawaiʻi in the spirit of aloha" as one of the most essential elements in Kim's vision, even citing it as a "pillar" in his plan (13). The state of Hawaiʻi has, for many years, tried to use "aloha" against us. With "aloha" often defined too simply as "love," Kānaka Maoli are expected to act, always, in the "spirit of aloha," meaning that we are expected to accommodate not only the settler but settler colonial interests as well. On the back cover of his 14-page plan, Kim argues that Mauna Kea can be "an opportunity for the gift of aloha to be presented to the world to make us better. This is about the mountain bringing people together." Fortunately, chants like Pua's "Nā Kūkulu" reveal a deeper sense of aloha, one rooted in the land from which it sprouted.

When Pua calls for aloha ʻāina, she is demanding our fierce and ferocious love of place. In other words, she is requiring us to protect ʻāina as we would protect family. In doing so, she is reminding us that "aloha" is not easy but instead heavy, difficult, and emotional, and she is showing us that we have to be steadfast, like pillars, in order to love this way. Kim's proposal that aloha can be a "gift to the world" co-opts one of our most important values and actions and attempts to package it as something we are required to give away. As Kānaka Maoli, however, we know that aloha is not freely given. It is, instead, born, nurtured, and maintained. What the kiaʻi mauna show when they are willing to be arrested,[19] or willing to live on a road for more than one hundred days, is aloha. What they embody when they are willing to chain themselves to cattle guards to block construction crews[20] is aloha. It is a love that comes from seeing the land as ancestor and knowing that our responsibility is to protect it, always. What the settler state shows, in their refusal to see and hear us, in their denial of our rights as Indigenous peoples, and in their complete disregard of our ability to act as stewards of the land, is the exact opposite. There is no aloha in their actions. This is why chants like "Nā Kūkulu" are so important in this movement. They reinforce, day after day, the true meaning and intention of aloha so that we can easily dismantle the fabricated, commercialized, and ultimately insulting uses of it in rhetoric used in defense of the TMT.

Rising Like Waves

Since the first day kia'i mauna stationed themselves at the base of Mauna Kea, Hawai'i has witnessed an incredible rise: a rise of people, a rise in strength, a rise in resilience, and a rise in awareness. Throughout the islands, and both on and off the mauna, people are rising like waves, daring to be braver than they ever thought they could be. At Pu'uhonua o Pu'uhuluhulu, the kia'i mauna act in accordance with kapu aloha, which is a way of conducting oneself with aloha at all times. This code of conduct has since been used to guide other movements and occupations, all of them also being centered on aloha 'āina and our duty to protect the earth. In September 2019, the Save Our Sherwoods movement set up a base in Waimānalo, O'ahu, to protect an area called Hūnānāniho from the construction of a new park that would potentially threaten natural, cultural, and historic resources and disturb iwi kupuna (ancestral bones). On 26 September 2019, while calling out things like "aloha 'āina" and "kūpa'a" (stay firm), 33 kia'i were arrested for protecting Hūnānāniho (Save Our Sherwoods). That is aloha. In October 2019, the Kū Kia'i Kahuku movement set up bases in the areas of Kalaeloa and Kahuku to prevent the construction of huge industrial turbines that would threaten wildlife, that would pose potential health risks to the community, and that would be built too close to residential units to be considered safe. As of 22 October 2019, a total of 105 kia'i had been arrested for protecting their place (Gomes and Ladao). That is aloha, a kind of love that cannot be put on a page in a plan for Mauna Kea. That is a kind of love that rises, like a wave, and sweeps people into the movement. Hawai'i is witnessing a surge in protective action, in a willingness to stand and do whatever it takes to not allow our lands, waters, and oceans to be desecrated and abused. Pua's chant, ending with a final "Hū!," tells us that this is only the beginning. We are rising like mighty waves, and we can only get bigger and stronger from here. Thus, it would be best to flow with us.

Notes

1. In supporting the movement to not make one's native language appear foreign, no words in Hawaiian will be italicized.

2. This chapter was written in 2019 before COVID safety protocols meant that many of those who were based at the mountain had to return to their homes. Rather than revise the chapter to speak to the shifts in the movement since COVID, I've decided to keep it as it was originally written: as an invitation to visit (or continually revisit) in memory or in story the movement as it was then and as it may be again in the future.

3. The TIO is a nonprofit partnership between various organizations and universities from California, Japan, China, India, and Canada. All have stakes in the project.

4. Throughout the chapter I will use "Kanaka Maoli" and "Kanaka" interchagably with "Hawaiian." If refering to more than one person, I will use the plural forms, "Kānaka Maoli" and "Kānaka."

5. For more information on Puʻuhonua o Puʻuhuluhulu, see http://www.puuhuluhulu.com/

6. "Turtle Island" is the name commonly used by Native Americans and First Nations peoples to refer to North America.

7. Note that this is not a direct translation of the Hawaiian words. Instead, this is Pua's interpretation of the mele (chant) and is what was provided to kiaʻi who participated in a prayer vigil at the mountain on 13 July 2019. Not every line has an interpretation. I've chosen not to translate those lines myself but to present the chant as Pua does.

8. "Te Moana nui a Kiwa" (the great ocean of Kiwa) is a name often used by Māori in Aotearoa to refer to the Pacific Ocean.

9. When the chant is done, all of the lines with exclamation points at the end are done by everyone. The rest of the lines are most commonly done by one solo chanter who takes the lead.

10. The phrase "kū kiaʻi mauna" (stand as a protector for the mountain) has become a slogan for the movement.

11. This is a clear reference to the movement at Standing Rock against the Dakota Access Pipeline. Pua and her daughter, Hāwane Rios, both traveled to Standing Rock in 2016 to show their support for those protecting their waterways.

12. This is not only connected to the efforts to protect water at Standing Rock but also a reference to the fact that one of the motivations to protect Mauna Kea is to protect the water aquifer beneath it.

13. This language comes from the back cover of the 14-page plan.

14. For a more thorough investigation of this, see David Maile's two-part essay, "Science, Time, and Mauna a Wākea: The Thirty Meter Telescope's Capitalist-Colonialist Violence."

15. Hōkūleʻa is a double-hulled canoe that was launched in Hawaiʻi in 1976 to test non-instrumental navigation and wayfinding in Polynesia. That year, the canoe was successfully sailed to Tahiti, led by Mau Piailug, a navigator from the island of Satawal in Micronesia.

16. On 20 June 2019, a hale (Hawaiian thatched house) and two ahu (altars) were desecrated on Mauna Kea by law enforcement officers, claiming the structures "had no traditional or customary significance" (Brestovansky and Burnett).

17. "Aloha ʻāina" is both a noun and a verb. It is the action of loving, or protecting, the earth and is what we become when we do so. In the nineteenth century, this term also had political meaning and was used to refer to someone who was a patriot, or supporter, of the queen and the sovereignty of the Hawaiian Kingdom. Today, when Kānaka Maoli use

"aloha ʻāina" as a noun to refer to themselves, they are often asserting their ongoing support of the lāhui, or the Hawaiian nation, and condeming the United States' illegal occupation of our lands.

18. There are currently 13 telescopes on Mauna Kea, the first being built in 1968. All of them have been controversial, and all of them have been contested.

19. On 17 July 2019, 33 kūpuna (elders) were arrested for protecting Mauna Kea (Brestovansky).

20. On 15 July 2019, seven kiaʻi mauna chained themselves to a cattle guard on the Mauna Kea Access Road (Big Island Video News).

Works Cited

Big Island Video News. "TMT Opponents Chained to Cattle Guard on Mauna Kea Road." *Big Island Video News*, 15 July 2019, https://www.bigislandvideonews.com/2019/07/15/video-tmt-opponents-chained-to-cattle-guard-on-mauna-kea-road/

Brestovansky, Michael. "Dozens of Kupuna Arrested on Third Consecutive Day of TMT Protect." Hawaiʻi *Tribune Herald*, 18 July 2019, https://www.hawaiitribune-herald.com/2019/07/18/hawaii-news/dozens-of-kupuna-arrested-on-third-consecutive-day-of-tmt-protest/

Brestovansky, Michael, and John Burnett. "Construction of TMT Authorized; Opponents Vow to 'Fight for Our Rights.'" Hawaiʻi *Tribune Herald*, 26 Aug. 2019, https://www.hawaiitribune-herald.com/2019/06/20/hawaii-news/two-hale-removed-from-maunakea-ige-to-announce-tmt-permitting/

Cavanagh, Edward. "History, Time and the Indigenist Critique." *Arena Journal*, no. 37–38, 2012, 16–39.

Dunbar-Ortiz, Roxanne. *An Indigenous Peoples' History of the United States*. Beacon Press, 2014.

Gomes, Andrew, and Mark Ladao. "6 More Wind-Farm Protesters Arrested in Kalaeloa and Kahuku." *Star Advertiser*, 25 Oct. 2019, https://www.staradvertiser.com/2019/10/22/breaking-news/wind-farm-protesters-gather-at-kalaeloa/

Kim, Harry. "Mauna Kea, the Heart of Aloha: A Way Forward." Office of Mayor Harry Kim, County of Hawaiʻi, 1 Oct. 2019, https://hawaiicountymayor.com/2019/09/30/maunakea-a-way-forward/

Kuwada, Bryan Kamaoli. "We Live in the Future. Come Join Us." *Ke Kaupu Hehi Ale*, 3 Apr. 2015, https://hehiale.wordpress.com/2015/04/03/we-live-in-the-future-come-join-us/

Maile, David. "Science, Time, and Mauna a Wākea: The Thirty-Meter Telescope's Capitalist-Colonialist Violence, Part I." *The Red Nation*, 13 May 2015, https://therednation.org/2015/05/13/science-time-and-mauna-a-wakea-the-thirty-meter-telescopes-capitalist-colonialist-violence-an-essay-in-two-parts/

Ngata, Tina. *Kia Mau: Resisting Colonial Fictions*. Rebel Press, 2019.

Peralto, Leon Noʻeau. "Mauna a Wākea: Hānau Ka Mauna, the Piko of Our Ea." *A Nation Rising: Hawaiian Movements for Life, Land, and Sovereignty*, edited by Noelani Goodyear-Kaʻōpua, Ikaika Hussey, and Erin Kahunawaikaʻala Wright. Duke UP, 2014, 232–43.

Pūkuʻi, Mary Kawena, and Samuel H. Elbert. *Hawaiian Dictionary: Hawaiian-English, English-Hawaiian*. U of Hawaiʻi P, 1986.

Rowse, Tim. "Indigenous Heterogeneity." *Australian Historical Studies*, vol. 45, no. 3, 2014, 297–310.

Save Our Sherwoods. "33 Kiaʻi Arrested to Save Our Sherwoods." *Save Our Sherwoods: Waimānalo Mau a Mau*, 27 Sept. 2019, https://saveoursherwoods.com/2019/09/27/33-kia%ca%bbi-arrested-to-save-our-sherwoods/

Spearim, Boe. *Let's Talk—Tina Ngata & Raihania Tipoki*. 16 Oct. 2019, 989fm.com.au/category/podcasts/lets-talk/

Wolfe, Patrick. "Settler Colonialism and the Elimination of the Native." *Journal of Genocide Research*, vol. 8, no. 4, 2006, 387–409.

Young, Kanalu. *Rethinking the Native Hawaiian Past*. Garland Publishing, 1998.

13

Imperial Debris, Vibrant Matter

Plastic in the Hands of Asian American
and Kanaka Maoli Artists

Chad Shomura

Every year, up to 12 million metric tons of plastic enter the ocean, where they disintegrate, bleed toxins, and are eaten by various creatures (Jambeck et al.). The carcasses of birds and whales burst with rainbows of plastic bits. Some plastic returns to land by washing ashore or traveling from fish bellies into human bellies. Most plastic will swirl as ocean confetti for centuries. Plastic has become a prominent member of Pacific ecosystems. The Great Pacific Garbage Patch, Kamilo Beach in Hawai'i, and Henderson Island are but a few well-publicized sites: the patch is presently estimated to be twice the size of Texas; 90 percent of the 1,500-feet-long Kamilo shoreline is covered in plastic; and Henderson Island, just 14.4 square miles in area, hosts approximately 38 million pieces of plastic that weigh 18 tons.[1]

Plastic is often treated as consumer excess, environmental hazard, and philosophical problem. Environmentalists have campaigned against the use of plastic (e.g., bottles and straws). Philosophers have considered how the longevity of plastic compels meditation on large scales of space and time (e.g., Morton). Yet the relationship of plastic to race, colonialism, and empire is not often discussed even as racialized and Indigenous peoples have been associated with the qualities of plastic to disqualify them from citizenship and the body politic. Michelle Huang astutely observes that Asian Americans have been racialized through attributes of plastic: inauthentic (perpetual foreigner), endlessly pliable and yet durable (model minority), and uncontainable and swarming (yellow peril). Indigenous peoples also have been imbued with plastic qualities. Waves of Indian removal and the "logic of elimination" that defines settler colonialism have treated Indigenous peoples as elastic and disposable (Wolfe). Settler law and culture have made Indigenous peoples inauthentic by default, demanding proof of Native identity through blood quantum and circumscribed performances of tradition (Kauanui; Povinelli).

If colonialism and imperialism have been animated by dominant strands of Western thought in which culture is the site of meaning and creativity, if nature is devoid of value and purpose, and if racialized and Indigenous peoples are positioned here or there depending on sociopolitical needs, then where does plastic fit? What happens when racialized and Indigenous peoples work with the fraught substance to address empire and ecology? This chapter offers a preliminary response to these big questions by exploring Asian American and Kanaka Maoli artworks: Wiena Lin's *Disassembly Line* and *Altar/Retail Kiosk*; Maika'i Tubbs's *Under My Skin*; and Linh Huỳnh's and my *Earthly Correspondences*. These artists use the very wastes they have been racialized as in different and perhaps incommensurable ways.[2] In their work, plastic is not only an emblem of wasteful consumption and environmental upheaval. It also functions as "imperial debris," Ann Laura Stoler's term for refuse abandoned by colonists and endured by Native and racialized peoples, and as "vibrant matter," Jane Bennett's term for material things functioning as potent forces rather than passive objects. The artworks show that while plastic marks the duration and transformation of coloniality, it can also be a vital co-participant in building alternative futures from within ecological ruination.

This chapter proposes that plastic can expand and unsettle colonial orders of being that underpin the Anthropocene. Rather than distancing themselves from plastic to ascend into humanity, racialized and Indigenous peoples might rework the material despite its status as consumer waste, ecological threat, and racializing substance. Doing so may generate futures for racialized and colonized entities, both human and not.

Imperial Plastic

Plastic first enjoyed widespread use following World War II due to its utilitarian and aesthetic features. The substance proved to be durable and manipulable while also strikingly colorful and seductively smooth, if needed. Plus, it was cheap. Consumer capitalism facilitated the integration of plastic with ordinary life in many parts of the world. It can be hard to imagine a future without plastic; the material is in clothing, packaging, toys, furniture, tools, prosthetics, vehicles, electronics, buildings, weapons, protective gear, sports equipment, musical instruments, cosmetics, and medical equipment—to name just a few things (Zurkow). By 2011, 300 million tons of plastic were being annually produced and only 10 percent of it was being recycled (Taylor). Plastic does not biodegrade. It will disrupt ecosystems as it breaks down over hundreds of years.

I treat plastic as imperial debris to situate ecological ruination in the ongoing life of coloniality. According to Stoler, imperial debris is abandoned in formerly colonized regions, where its effects unfold over long stretches of time, as seen in Agent Orange in Vietnam and nuclear radiation in the South Pacific. The duration of imperial debris means that colonialism and postcolonialism are neither smoothly continuous nor sharply discontinuous. Imperial debris shows how coloniality may continue to affect sociopolitical and environmental issues even if self-determination has been achieved.

Plastic does not become imperial debris only by being discarded by colonizers. It can become imperial debris as it passes through and accumulates in Native waterways and when it arrives from abroad in once and still occupied lands. Plastic in the United States enjoys a brief life before sizable portions are whisked away to recycling centers in Indonesia, Vietnam, Thailand, Malaysia, and, until recently, China (Taylor). Unsurprisingly, these and other areas of Southeast Asia are where most plastic bids farewell to land (Jambeck et al.). The transpacific life of plastic is shaped by a global industry of waste and recycling. It is also shaped by natural forces. As plastic breaks down, it becomes more susceptible to the push and pull of animals, wind, and water. It is blown into rivers and carried out to sea, ferried hundreds of miles by pelagic currents, held captive in ocean gyres, and heaved en masse onto distant beaches.

As it travels and settles down, plastic contributes to imperialist and colonialist disruptions of Native relationships to land, water, and nonhuman life. It afflicts humans through years of chemical exposure and ingestion, especially those who live near recycling and waste sites in the Global South, and proves fatal to animals who confuse it for mouthwatering food. These effects are akin to "slow violence," Rob Nixon's term for violences that unfold incrementally and subtly, and thus cannot be tied to immediate causes and specific events. The durability of plastic means that racialized and Indigenous groups will endure its slow violence for centuries to come.

As it transforms the Pacific without an end in sight, plastic exhibits a peculiar liveliness. "The focus," Stoler thus writes of imperial debris, "is not on inert remains but on the histories they recruit and on their vital refigurations" (348). Imperial debris welcomes the insights of new materialisms, which discern an effectivity of matter that does not rely on human guidance. According to Bennett, everything is forceful. The potency of matter depends on the assemblages of which it is a part, not whether it exhibits reason, intentionality, consciousness, or even life. Plastic interweaves histories of its transformation across production, consumption, and disposal; histories of colonialism; and earthy histories of water and wind currents.

As imperial debris and vibrant matter, plastic does not reproduce but extends and transforms colonial structures. It calls for patience with a strange idea: coloniality is partly shaped anew by matter. Western modernist, colonialist parsings of life and matter hold the latter to be passive; matter might put a check on colonial projects, though humans can establish control by marshaling enough ingenuity and willpower. However, in this new materialist twist to imperial debris, matter also positively expands the reach, power, and trajectory of coloniality. Imperial debris is not a mere tool or vessel for colonial plans. It shapes coloniality even if it is not presided over by colonizers and settlers. Its effects cannot be fully intended, anticipated, or controlled. Plastic attests to the persistence and metamorphosis of coloniality and thus, as Stoler notes of imperial debris, calls for conceptual revision, attention to nonlinear temporalities, and exhumation of alternative futures. How does plastic shift the ongoing life of coloniality?

Plastic has carried a modern racist and colonialist order of being that disentangles certain humans from dehumanized peoples and nonhuman entities in order to secure mastery. "Plastic represents the promises of modernity," writes Heather Davis, "the promise of sealed, perfected, clean, smooth abundance. It encapsulates the fantasy of ridding ourselves of the dirt of the world, of decay, of malfeasance" ("Life and Death in the Anthropocene" 349). These fantasies allude to the modern subject as masterful: the malleability of plastic suggests a (racialized and gendered) triumph of mind over matter, while the durability of plastic signals a transcendence of finitude, resilience, and a capacity to shield against the muck of the earth. We might recall that hygienic fantasies of modernity are bound up with racist concerns over sanitation in encounters with the colonized (e.g., Ahuja). We might also recall Sylvia Wynter's insight that modernity is defined by the overrepresentation of white, colonialist Man for humanity, which has abjected racialized and Indigenous peoples and, one might add, nonhuman entities. The modernist rise of liberalism initiated a transvaluation of beliefs, practices, and life-worlds, the carving of the planet into zones of civilization and primitivity, the displacement and slaughter of Indigenous peoples, the enslavement of Africans and Native Americans, and the indentured servitude of Asians in the Americas (Lowe). The insatiable colonialist hunger for resources and land evinces a drive to mastery, which, according to Julietta Singh, disentangles all beings and sorts them into dominant subjects and subordinated objects (10). The widespread dissemination of plastic extends a colonialist order of being. Plastic hails us all as masterful subjects in rapid, thoughtless cycles of use and toss as though our waste cannot affect us.

Plastic reshapes discussions of the Anthropocene, the hotly debated epoch defined by the geological impact of humanity attributed to industrialization, nuclear testing, electronic wastes, and the advent of agriculture. Some people have offered "Plasticene" to underscore the planetary imprint of plastic (Reed). This sweeping notion obscures those who shoulder the burdens of plastic, such as its accumulation throughout the Pacific, the extraction and catastrophic spillage of oil, and the dumping of plastic waste across the Global South. Indigenous scholars and allies have argued that the Anthropocene is a late reverberation of colonial violence that had been isolated to Native peoples and ecosystems. As Heather Davis and Zoe Todd insist, the "logic of the Anthropocene" originates in the Western colonialist "severing of relations between humans and the soil, between plants and animals, between minerals and our bones" (770). They invoke climate scientists Simon Lewis and Mark Maslin's evidence for humanity's geological impact dating back to 1610, when global carbon dioxide levels plummeted due to the extermination of millions of Native Americans. Tying Lewis and Maslin to Wynter, Dana Luciano reminds us that colonial genocide in the Americas began in 1492 with "the spread of a humanism that has failed much of humanity, a failure to which even the Arctic ice cores can bear witness, and that in doing so has deeply damaged the planet as well." Plastic is a geological marker of colonial orders of being, but unlike ice core samples it is not a passive record. It is a vibrant residue of colonialist mastery proliferating beyond control that racialized and colonized groups in particular, human and nonhuman alike, must learn to live with. From the point of view of plastic as imperial debris, the Anthropocene is the fallout of colonialist Man's efforts to master all that he is not.

Colonial orders of being are extended by environmentalist and humanist positions that do not treat plastic as imperial debris. For example, a deep ecologist response to plastic might seek to curb its production in order to scale back human impact on the earth. However, as Davis observes, "The desire to create for ourselves pristine environments has either dangerously backfired . . . or has been dumped elsewhere, where toxicities are accumulated at unprecedented rates by racialized, feminized, and impoverished bodies" ("Imperceptibility and Accumulation" 192). For racialized and Indigenous peoples, perhaps saying "no" to plastic, by holding distance from the racialized substance and keeping apace with environmental modernity, may be a path to humanization. That response leaves intact conjunctions between race and plastic. It does not address how settler states have treated the racialized and colonized as incompetent for ecological stewardship despite centuries of living intimately and sustainably with land and water. What other relationships to plastic could there be? Can plastic unsettle colonial orders of being? Although it has been an icon of ecological ruination, might plastic lead to other futures in and beyond the Anthropocene?

The rest of this chapter explores reconfigurations of plastic by racialized and Indigenous peoples. It focuses on artworks produced for Smithsonian Asian Pacific American Center culture labs, which are pop-up museums of art, music, films, performance, and lectures that seek to build community (Smithsonian Asian Pacific American Center). Lasting several days and attended by thousands of people, each culture lab explores a theme. Wiena Lin's *Disassembly Line* and *Altar/Retail Kiosk* were made for CTRL+ALT: A Culture Lab on Imagined Futures in New York City on 11–12 November 2016. Maika'i Tubbs's *Under My Skin* and Linh Huỳnh's and my *Earthy Correspondences* were for 'Ae Kai: A Culture Lab on Convergence in Honolulu, Hawai'i, on 7–9 July 2017. Refusing the call of mastery behind plastic and negotiating their treatment as plastic objects, these artists engage plastic as imperial debris. They rework plastic from a vessel of slow violence to a vital source of relations and futures unbound from colonial orders of being.

Disassembly Line and *Altar/Retail Kiosk*

Wiena Lin's *Disassembly Line* and *Altar/Retail Kiosk* use electronic wastes to address the ecological impacts of imperial debris. Composed of plastics and metals, e-waste becomes imperial debris as it traffics across global networks of extraction, consumption, disposal, and salvage. The planned obsolescence of electronic devices and cultivated desire for the latest gadgets have accel-

Fig. 13.1. Wiena Lin, *Disassembly Line*, 2016.

erated consumption cycles, such that cell phones often enjoy the lifespan of
a pet hamster. Deathliness haunts the brief life of electronics: the dangerous
mining of rare metals in Africa, the dismal labor conditions in Asian factories
like Foxconn, and the distribution of toxic materials throughout the Global
South. Because it is often disposed of intact, does not biodegrade, and is produced in massive quantities, e-waste may compose a future strata of earth,
yet another marker of the Anthropocene (Parikka).

    Disassembly Line addresses circuits of e-waste. Visitors wear Hazmat
suits, sit around a workshop carousel, and pick apart keyboards, cell phones,
and circuit boards. The endless rotation of the conveyor belt and the longevity of plastics and metals envelope participants within the inescapability of
imperial debris. The activity shifts participants from consumers to workers
and salvagers by altering relationships with electronics that are in many hands
yet unfamiliar beyond use. *Disassembly Line* foregrounds the disposal side of
consumer electronics; closes the gap, often so wide for privileged groups in

the Global North, between human and trash; and bridges consumers in the United States and recipients of e-wastes across the Pacific. If electronics are supposed to flow into the United States and e-wastes are meant to flow out, then Lin reassembles a transpacific geography of imperial debris by bringing trash back home.

Altar/Retail Kiosk provokes a closer look at the reworking of imperial debris. It is a collection of artifacts that are at once technological and spiritual, trash and relic, dead object and vital thing. Composed of reclaimed wastes glued together by plastic resin, they gesture to plastiglomerate, or composites of rock, sand, coral, shells, and wood fused by molten plastic that may serve as a geological token of human activity (Robertson). They blur the line between commodity fetishism and animism, between the reverence afforded to technological goods and the sacredness of objects held to be alive. They may evoke outrage over slow violence, but their ornamentation evokes play and even whimsy. Lin complicates the affective reception of imperial debris, suspending moralized reactions to plastic that obscure how racialized and Indigenous peoples creatively rework waste from the Global North.

Altar/Retail Kiosk intersperses colonial orders of being with alternative relationalities. One of the pieces, *Sparkle Chicken*, is a white bucket of drumsticks, whose meat is a shiny ball of compact disc shards melded to chicken bones. The fusion of "meat" and bone binds together sharp contrasts: the synthetic and the organic, jagged lines and smooth curves, lively sparkles and dull decay. By evoking fast food and increasingly defunct analog media, *Sparkle Chicken* juxtaposes speedy consumption practices with different rates of decomposition. It also underscores the entanglement of expendable lives: nonhuman animals that are factory farmed and human consumers of fast food, especially lower-class, racialized laborers defined by "slow death" (Berlant). Finally, from the standpoint of the white bucket, the drumsticks appear as racial excess to be contained. Yet from that of the drumsticks, the bucket seems peculiar due to its lack of detail and seeming inability to hold an unwieldy assemblage of refuse. *Sparkle Chicken* evokes these incompatible viewpoints to leverage an aggregation of racialized humans and nonhumans against the colonial order of being.

Altar/Retail Kiosk emphasizes that mastery is antithetical to endurance within ecological ruination. It challenges faith in scientific innovation to solve ecological crises, for techno-utopian fantasies committed to human mastery over nature ignore a key problem of plastic: how to live within the ecological ruination induced by imperial debris. *Altar/Retail Kiosk* underscores that

Fig. 13.2. Wiena Lin, *Sparkle Chicken*, 2016.

Fig. 13.3. Untitled from *Altar/Retail Kiosk*, 2016.

racialized and colonized peoples cannot wish away this problem. For example, one talisman made of wood, circuit board, cowrie shells, string, cables, and a resin amulet recalls the repurposing of waste from the Global North into tools and toys. Endurance within ecological ruination may depend upon intimate connections between the wastes of empire (racialized humans, discarded nonhumans) that are defined by living with, not living over.

By refiguring relationships with plastic and e-wastes, *Disassembly Line* and *Altar/Retail Kiosk* point to futures defined by endurance with imperial debris. Racialized and colonized peoples can and have repurposed imperial debris to disidentify from colonialist Man, defined by mastery, bodily integrity, and bounded subjectivity. Plastic may help to reassemble dehumanized peoples and nonhuman entities; develop alternative practices, affects, and entangled embodiments; and pursue futures shaped by collaborative endurance.

Under My Skin

Kanaka Maoli artist Maikaʻi Tubbs also reclaims waste. "I think a lot about how my ancestors worked with trash," reflects Tubbs. "Until we got colonized we used everything" (Krafft). Colonialism did not only categorize types of being; it also divided beings into valuable and discardable parts, into resource and garbage. As Singh points out, mastery is "a splitting of the object that is mastered from itself" (10). These partitions are left untouched by deep ecologists who posit that scaling back human impact will restore harmony to nature as though one could address environment and empire separately. Working instead with Kanaka Maoli notions of relationality, Tubbs decolonizes usefulness by repurposing imperial debris amid colonial theft, deprivation, and ruination. He enables the materials abjected by colonial orders of being to work against those very orders.

While Lin gestures to plastic shipped overseas, Tubbs invokes the oceanic itself in *Under My Skin*. The piece is composed of plastic marine debris encased in a large, wrinkled slab of "microbial leather." Tubbs cultivated bacteria cultures that grew into sizable panels, which he left to dry out in the sun. Because bacterial and solar powers helped to shape the end product, *Under My Skin* is anti-mastery. The piece affirms the generative capacities of bacteria in conjunction with plastic. *Under My Skin* is a vivid rendition of the "plastisphere," a term for bacterial ecosystems thriving on plastic marine debris shorter than five millimeters (Zettler, Mincer, and Amaral-Zettler). The piece's appearance as a stomach references the ingestion of plastic by human and nonhuman animals and also the 2016 discovery of *Ideonella sakaiensis*, a bacterium that has evolved to metabolize polyethylene terephthalate (the material of water bottles) (Yoshida et al.).

By foregrounding entanglements of humans, bacteria, and plastic, *Under My Skin* defies colonial orders of being. What Neel Ahuja calls "bioinsecurities" associate racialized humans and microbes with each other, driving Western imperialism to quarantine them in order to protect certain (white) humans.[3] To reconfigure the sensorium of bioinsecurities, Tubbs encourages people to touch the brown, gritty microbial leather. This is intimate contact with what is under our skin. We humans carry two to three pounds of bacteria in and on our bodies and consume plastic almost every time we eat seafood or drink water (Tyree and Morrison). In an age of chemical and biological toxicity, colonialist partitions against waste, bacteria, and those humans and animals rendered as such cannot be maintained (e.g., Zahara

Fig. 13.4. Detail shot of Maikaʻi Tubbs, *Under My Skin*, 2017.

and Hird). *Under My Skin* embraces toxicity, not as affliction but as intimacy with microbes, plastic, and other waste: a queer condition made tactile in the wrinkles, folds, and textures of a rescaled microbiome that unsettles colonialist sensoria (Chen).

This sensorial shift dislodges the hold of colonialist Man through keener attunement to nonhuman worlds. While *Altar/Retail Kiosk* emphasizes human endurance, *Under My Skin* attests to the capacity of nonhumans to reclaim imperial debris for their survival. It enfolds its audience into the aquatic lifeworld of microorganisms for whom plastic is not waste but home and good food. This "submerged perspective," as Macarena Gómez-Barris might call it, disrupts the sensorium of extractive capital in which the affective range of plastic is reduced to use and toss or, in deep ecologist responses, to condemn and refuse. But what is plastic to the microbe? Evoking a kind of "alien phenomenology," Ian Bogost's term for experience turned inside out due to communion with an alien element within humanity, *Under My Skin* places people in touch with nonhuman worlds beyond colonialist frames— worlds that are "out there" but also "in here."

By underscoring entanglement, toxicity, and nonhuman affect, *Under My Skin* untethers futurity from dead-end responses to the Anthropocene that advance the colonialist separation of humanity from nature. In the face of anthropogenic climate change and mass species extinction, it is easy to believe that humanity has overpowered nature; as Jedediah Purdy dramatically puts it, humans have "denaturalized nature." Such a view reifies colonialist partitions that render nature mechanical and purposeless, imbue humanity alone with freedom and supreme value, and have consequently furnished ecological damage. Tubbs offers a different view in the description for *Under My Skin*: "In a world of post-consumer waste, what counts as nature?" Plastic is not an artificial threat to a static nature but a component of nature under transformation. In this view, which intertwines with a minor strand of Western thought, nature is dynamic, self-generative, and incomplete; its exteriority is constituted not by what is human or artificial but by its own future forms.[4] This figuration diffuses the colonialist racialization of countless beings as premodern, inauthentic, and to be mastered by those who are humanized. By foregrounding a Kanaka Maoli ontology in which all beings are kin, Tubbs insists on forms of relation that have endured among colonialist orderings and that, if activated, may summon other futures (Goldberg-Hiller and Silva).

Earthy Correspondences

Earthly Correspondences engages plastic to explore possibilities for contact, connection, and care within ecological ruination. Artist and environmentalist Linh Huỳnh and I collaborated on the piece for 'Ae Kai, a culture lab in Honolulu, Hawai'i. Our installation replicated a shoreline like Kamilo Beach of which trash has become a constitutive feature. We adorned the walls with a colorful wave of marine debris from 808 Cleanups, an O'ahu beach cleanup organization. Huỳnh crafted jellyfish sculptures from discarded plastic bottles and a geological structure made of reclaimed cardboard and bottle caps. She hung up the jellyfish and "living" time capsules, which would be kept open rather than sealed and buried. I composed an ocean of over fifteen hundred plastic bottles that were bound by salvaged fishing net and buoys. I screened a slow-motion video of ocean waves over the bottles. The video and its audio were desynced to mark the unhinging of nature in the plastification of oceans.

While seeking to deepen awareness of rapid consumption and extreme wastefulness, Huỳnh and I underscore the entanglement of humans with the earth. The title *"Earthly Correspondences"* refers to our acknowledgment, shared by Lin and Tubbs, that humans, plastics, and wastes are all earthly beings. We hope that the status of earthling (Bennett, "Earthling, Now and Forever?") might activate forms of care unrestricted by colonial orders of being by race, species, and materiality; the earthling crosses boundaries between colonialist Man and his others. The title also references two epistolary activities. Huỳnh's *Honua: A Living Time Capsule* invites visitors to write messages to the earth or to write a message as if they were the earth speaking to humans. Participants deposit messages into the living time capsules, which others can peruse. Here, the earth serves as a repository of lively traces. My *Message in a Plastic Bottle* involves the sea of plastic bottles, some of which contain messages. Participants select a bottle, replace the message inside with one of their own, and return the bottle to the plastic ocean. They use the bottles as protective barriers to imaginatively preserve a message for centuries. The activity of picking and returning bottles positions visitors as wasters and salvagers, forcing confrontation with the fact that plastic can be moved around and reworked but not fully extricated or mastered.

Earthly Correspondences sensitizes participants to their reach, discernible in plastic and underwritten by the missive. Plastic may be in our hands

Fig. 13.5. Linh Huỳnh and Chad Shomura, *Earthy Correspondences*, 2017.

only as long as it takes to unwrap a candy bar, but it will linger for centuries. If our influence is extended through the duration of plastic, then our touch is felt by others across space and time. *Earthy Correspondences* foregrounds this connectedness. In the epistolary activities, one can receive a message only because someone else wrote it. Messages are deposited without guarantee of reception and without knowledge of their potential effects. Even if we never meet, we are present to each other through what we leave behind, whether it be trash or a message. This stranger intimacy could play a vital role in our lives. It binds together what precedes and follows us, whether human or not, whether alive or not. *Earthly Correspondences* invites reflection on how imperial debris will impact those in the future and how the spatiotemporal scale of care has been likewise expanded.

Earthly Correspondences emphasizes that we share a planet. Plastic can separate and contain, as Davis points out, but it may also forge powerful connections ("Life and Death in the Anthropocene" 348). *Earthly Correspondences* repurposes plastic from imperial debris into connective tissue between earthlings across space and time. Rather than offering a cleanup effort to restore the natural world, it immerses participants in a nature reconfigured by imperial debris. It teases out relations, futures, and forms of care undefined by colonialist orders of being.

Archives of Plastic Futures

Anna Tsing writes, "We are stuck with the problem of living despite economic and ecological ruination. Neither tales of progress nor of ruin tell us how to think about collaborative survival" (19). Imperial debris underscores the racialized and colonialist dimensions of this problem. Just as imperial debris expands and intensifies ecological ruination, so too, if reworked, can it develop alternative relations and futures. What might be learned from Asian American and Kanaka Maoli artists who have used plastic to address empire and environment?

Ecological ruination can be confronted without striving for subjectivity and bodily integrity defined by colonialist separation, enclosure, and a ranking of being by race, species, and materiality. Rather than trying to contain or jettison imperial debris, we might explore all that falls to the wayside of colonialist Man. We might identify as part of nature rather than separate from it. We might take up imperial debris as a problematic though inescapable ally as we strive to mitigate its slow violence. We might refuse positions of mastery long wielded against us. We might develop relations and modes of endurance that leave us transformed. We might grow vigilant for the metamorphosis of coloniality. We might develop a sense of connection across space and time. We might calibrate our range of care to the life of imperial debris.

"Our Plastic Age confronts the issue of duration," writes Bernadette Bensaude-Vincent. "While the manufacture of plastics destroys the archives of life on the earth, its waste will constitute the archives of the twentieth century and beyond" (24). While plastic entails the persistence of coloniality and its damage, imperial debris is not destined to only spread slow violence. It can be creatively incorporated into new forms of collaborative endurance, and that may be one way to deposit care into archives of the future that are presently in the making.

Notes

Many thanks to the editors and reviewers, whose suggestions helped to improve this essay.

1. I thank Yi-Ting Chang for bringing Henderson Island to my attention.

2. Space constraints here do not allow much discussion of the differences between Asian American and Kanaka Maoli engagements with plastic. I want to honor the incommensurability between Asian American and Kanaka Maoli positions that, in my estimation, chiefly arises over issues of land and sovereignty. Hence, I do not use "decolonial" as an umbrella term for these artworks even though they align in collective opposition to colonial orders of being.

3. Similarly, Rachel Lee has asked "whether one can act white toward people of color but not act white toward microbes; and vice versa, whether one can act white toward microbes, but not act white toward people of color" (238).

4. Examples include Spinoza's notion of *natura naturans*, Kant's brief gesture to "anomalous creatures" in his teleological judgment, Thoreau's concept of "the wild," William Connolly's "immanent naturalism," and Jane Bennett's "vital materialism."

Works Cited

Bennett, Jane. "Earthling, Now and Forever?" *Making the Geologic Now: Responses to Material Conditions of Contemporary Life*, edited by Elizabeth Ellsworth and Jamie Kruse. punctum books, 2013, 244–46.

Bennett, Jane. *Vibrant Matter: A Political Ecology of Things*. Duke UP, 2010.

Bensaude-Vincent, Bernadette. "Plastics, Materials and Dreams of Dematerialization." *Accumulation: The Material Politics of Plastic*, edited by Jennifer Gabrys, Gay Hawkins, and Mike Michael. Routledge, 2013, 17–29.

Berlant, Lauren. "Slow Death (Sovereignty, Obesity, Lateral Agency)." *Critical Inquiry*, vol. 33, no. 4, 2007, 754–80.

Bogost, Ian. *Alien Phenomenology, or What It's Like to Be a Thing*. U of Minnesota P, 2012.

Chen, Mel Y. *Animacies: Biopolitics, Racial Mattering, and Queer Affect*. Duke UP, 2012.

Connolly, William E. *A World of Becoming*. Duke UP, 2011.

Davis, Heather. "Imperceptibility and Accumulation: Political Strategies of Plastic." *Camera Obscura*, vol. 31, no. 2, 2016, 187–93.

Davis, Heather. "Life and Death in the Anthropocene: A Short History of Plastic." *Art in the Anthropocene: Encounters among Aesthetics, Politics, Environments and Epistemologies*, edited by Heather Davis and Etienne Turpin. Open Humanities Press, 2015, 347–58.

Davis, Heather, and Zoe Todd. "On the Importance of a Date, or Decolonizing the Anthropocene." *ACME: An International Journal for Critical Geographies*, vol. 16, no. 4, 2017, 761–80.

Goldberg-Hiller, Jonathan, and Noenoe Silva. "Sharks and Pigs: Animating Hawaiian Sovereignty against the Anthropological Machine." *South Atlantic Quarterly*, vol. 110, no. 2, 2011, 429–46.

Gómez-Barris, Macarena. *The Extractive Zone: Social Ecologies and Decolonial Perspectives*. Duke UP, 2017.

Huang, Michelle N. "Ecologies of Entanglement in the Great Pacific Garbage Patch." *Journal of Asian American Studies*, vol. 20, no. 1, 2017, 95–117.

Jambeck, Jenna R., et al. "Plastic Waste Inputs from Land into the Ocean." *Science*, vol. 347, no. 6223, 2015, 768–71.

Kant, Immanuel. *A Critique of Judgment*. Translated by Werner S. Pluhar. Hackett Publishing, 1987.

Kauanui, J. Kēhaulani. *Hawaiian Blood: Colonialism and the Politics of Sovereignty and Indigeneity*. Duke UP, 2008.

Krafft, Saskia. "Maikaʻi Tubbs and the MAD Artist Studios." *Bmore Art*, 29 Jan. 2016, www.bmoreart.com/2016/01/maikai-tubbs-and-the-mad-artist-studios.html. Accessed 18 Mar. 2018.

Lee, Rachel C. *The Exquisite Corpse of Asian America: Biopolitics, Biosociality, and Posthuman Ecologies*. NYU Press, 2014.

Lewis, Simon L., and Mark A. Maslin. "Defining the Anthropocene." *Nature: International Journal of Science*, vol. 519, 2015, 171–80.

Lowe, Lisa. *The Intimacies of Four Continents*. Duke UP, 2015.

Luciano, Dana. "The Inhuman Anthropocene." *Avidly*, 23 Mar. 2015, avidly.lareviewofbooks.org/2015/03/22/the-inhuman-anthropocene/. Accessed 23 Mar. 2015.

Morton, Timothy. *Hyperobjects: Philosophy and Ecology after the End of the World*. U of Minnesota P, 2013.

Nixon, Rob. *Slow Violence and the Environmentalism of the Poor*. Harvard UP, 2011.

Parikka, Jussi. "The Geology of Media." *The Atlantic*, 11 Oct. 2013, www.theatlantic.com/technology/archive/2013/10/the-geology-of-media/280523/. Accessed 11 Oct. 2013.

Povinelli, Elizabeth A. *The Cunning of Recognition: Indigenous Alterities and the Making of Australian Multiculturalism*. Duke UP, 2002.

Purdy, Jedediah. "The New Nature." *Boston Review*, 11 Jan. 2016, bostonreview.net/forum/jedediah-purdy-new-nature. Accessed 13 Jan. 2018.

Reed, Christina. "Plastic Age: How It's Reshaping Rocks, Oceans and Life." *New Scientist*, 28 Jan. 2015, www.newscientist.com/article/mg22530060-200-plastic-age-how-its-reshaping-rocks-oceans-and-life/. Accessed 29 June 2018.

Robertson, Kirsty. "Plastiglomerate." *e-flux*, vol. 78, 2016, www.e-flux.com/journal/78/82878/plastiglomerate/. Accessed 27 Apr. 2018.

Singh, Julietta. *Unthinking Mastery: Dehumanism and Decolonial Entanglements*. Duke UP, 2018.

Smithsonian Asian Pacific American Center. "The Culture Lab Manifesto." *Poetry Foundation*, 5 July 2017, www.poetryfoundation.org/poetrymagazine/articles/142894/culture-lab-manifesto. Accessed 5 July 2017.

Spinoza, Baruch. *Ethics: Treatise on the Emendation of the Intellect and Selected Letters*. Translated by Samuel Shirley. Hackett Publishing, 1992.

Stoler, Ann Laura. *Duress: Imperial Durabilities in Our Times*. Duke UP, 2016.

Taylor, Michael. "Southeast Asian Plastic Recyclers Hope to Clean Up after China Ban." *Reuters*, 15 Jan. 2018, www.reuters.com/article/us-asia-environment-waste-plastic/southeast-asian-plastic-recyclers-hope-to-clean-up-after-china-ban-idUSKBN1F504K. Accessed 29 June 2018.

Thoreau, Henry David. *Walden and Other Writings.* Edited by Brooks Atkinson. Modern Library, 1992.

Tsing, Anna Lowenhaupt. *The Mushroom at the End of the World: On the Possibility of Life in Capitalist Ruins.* Harvard UP, 2015.

Tyree, Chris, and Dan Morrison. "Invisibles: The Plastic Inside Us." *Orb Media*, orbmedia. org/stories/Invisibles_plastics. Accessed 18 Mar. 2018.

Wolfe, Patrick. "Settler Colonialism and the Elimination of the Native." *Journal of Genocide Research*, vol. 8, no. 4, 2006, 387–409.

Wynter, Sylvia. "Unsettling the Coloniality of Being/Power/Truth/Freedom: Towards the Human, After Man, Its Overrepresentation—An Argument." *CR: The New Centennial Review*, vol. 3, no. 3, 2003, 257–337.

Yoshida, Shosuke, et al. "A Bacterium That Degrades and Assimilates Poly(ethylene Terephthalate)." *Science*, vol. 351, no. 6278, 2016, 1196–99.

Zahara, Alexander R. D., and Myra J. Hird. "Raven, Dog, Human: Inhuman Colonialism and Unsettling Cosmologies." *Environmental Humanities*, vol. 7, 2015, 169–90.

Zettler, Erik R., Tracy J. Mincer, and Linda A. Amaral-Zettler. "Life in the 'Plastisphere': Microbial Communities on Plastic Marine Debris." *Environmental Science and Technology*, vol. 47, no. 13, 2013, 7137–46.

Zurkow, Marin. *The Petroleum Manga: A Project by Marina Zurkow.* punctum books, 2014.

AFTERWORD

"A New Way beyond the Darkness"

Priscilla Wald

"Perhaps a new spirit is rising among us," Martin Luther King Jr. intoned to the more than four thousand people assembled in and around New York City's Riverside Church on 4 April 1967, to hear the civil rights leader denounce U.S. involvement in the war in Vietnam. "If it is," he continued, "let us trace its movement well and pray that our own inner being may be sensitive to its guidance, for we are deeply in need of a new way beyond the darkness that seems so close around us." It was at long last, as the publicity for the speech had advertised, "A Time to Break Silence" and urge the U.S. government to move "Beyond Vietnam."[1]

Remarkable in many ways, the speech helped to bring the civil rights and anti-war movements into greater alignment by showing the connections between U.S. involvement in Vietnam and domestic racism. King was a formidable spokesperson—the most widely recognized face of the civil rights movement—and he had been urged by many of his allies and warned by governmental officials not to venture into "politics" beyond the issue of civil rights. There was too much at stake in the movement, his allies cautioned, to alienate the U.S. mainstream and especially the president, Lyndon B. Johnson, a powerful if tenuous ally.[2] Despite a growing anti-war sentiment, public support of the war was still strong in 1965.

King had not in fact been silent in that opposition. The congregation at the Ebenezer Baptist Church, where he had been ordained and eventually served as co-pastor with his father, had heard it laced throughout his sermons for several years. As president of the Southern Christian Leadership Conference, however, he represented an organization whose majority did not want to draw attention from the civil rights movement. Ultimately, however,

King could no longer resist the pressure of his religious as well as his political convictions, and in 1966 he committed to speak at New York's Riverside
Church, sponsored by the Clergy and Laymen Concerned About Vietnam, a
group of which he was a member.

A young activist who had come to Atlanta to represent the Mennonite
Service Committee in the civil rights movement had listened to King's sermons, and he connected especially with the preacher's anti-war message.
Vincent Harding quickly became a trusted friend of King and an ally in the
movement before returning to the Chicago area in 1964, where he completed
his PhD in history. In 1965, he was summoned back to Atlanta to chair the
History and Sociology Department of Spelman College. Sensing the historical momentousness of the war and U.S. involvement in Vietnam, he prepared
for his new role by schooling himself about that history. As the deep connections among the war, U.S. racism, and the legacy of colonialism became
increasingly clear to him, he realized they were not separate issues and sent a
letter to the Southern Christian Leadership Convention urging the organization to take a strong public stand against the war. Although King agreed, the
issue caused considerable controversy in the organization. When King finally
made the decision to speak at Riverside Church, however, and realized his
travel schedule would not permit him to devote the time such a speech would
require, he enlisted Harding's help in drafting it.[3]

For Harding, the war was not only unjust; it was also a "new form of
colonialism," as a February 1967 speech that served as a basis for the Riverside
speech put it.[4] But the strategy of decolonization, as the historian Simeon
Man has shown, was paradoxical: a war fought "in the name of antiracism
and anticolonialism" (12) facilitated the expression of both in new terms.[5]
It was central to the development of strategies in which "state and military
officials made sense of the unruly aftermaths of global decolonization, and . . .
sought to impose order upon a disorderly world, by engineering and con-
trolling the movements of people" (14). The war brought the countries the
United States claimed to be "liberating" into a "global economy" in which
they were "accessible to free markets and free trade" (8) and, in the process,
dashed "the dreams of anti-colonial liberation . . . and the struggles to imagine
a new humanity that came in its wake" (10).

Recognizing that war in a variety of (often obscured) forms—in effect,
total war—was quickly becoming the new reality in the United States, Harding and King sought to intervene. An early version of the speech, "The Casualties of the War in Vietnam," which King delivered in February 1967 to a

thousand-person audience at the Nation Institute in Los Angeles, enumerated the losses.[6] In addition to the horrific and tragically unnecessary loss of life, he lamented, the nation was suffering casualties of "principles and values" ranging from the programmatic damage to the UN Charter and the Great Society to the more abstract erosion of self-determination and dissent, in the name of which the U.S. involvement in Vietnam was justified, as well as the humility of the nation. Ultimately, the war represented a threat to the very "survival of mankind." Such were the casualties of colonialism in all of its forms.

The speech "Beyond Vietnam" intensified the message; profound geopolitical transformations were underway, and the United States urgently had to "undergo a radical revolution of values" if it were "to get on the right side of the world revolution." The speech inducts listeners into that revolution as it gradually unfolds the connections between U.S. racism and the colonial war. It begins with explicit connections: how the war has siphoned funding from the anti-poverty programs of the Great Society; how it is being fought disproportionately by the poor, especially "the black young men" who find themselves fighting and dying "to guarantee liberties in Southeast Asia which they had not found in southwest Georgia and East Harlem"; and, finally, how it displays the hypocrisy of a government that condemns the violence of inner-city protests while using "massive doses of violence to solve its problems, to bring about the changes it wanted."

The speech then pivots to the manifestation of that violence and hypocrisy in a historical account that shades subtly but powerfully into the imagined perspective of "the people who have been living under the curse of war for almost three decades" and who watch as this "new form of colonialism," in the name of "liberation," not only exploits their resources but also deliberately destroys them:

> They watch as we poison their water, as we kill a million acres of their crops. They must weep as the bulldozers roar through their areas preparing to destroy the precious trees. They wander into the hospitals, with at least twenty casualties from American firepower for one "Vietcong"-inflicted injury. So far we may have killed a million of them—mostly children. They wander into the towns and see thousands of the children, homeless, without clothes, running in packs on the streets like animals. They see the children, degraded by our soldiers as they beg for food. They see the children selling their sisters to our soldiers, soliciting for their mothers.

They "must weep" because that is surely what "we" would do in their place, but the "must" is also a reminder of the distinction: "we" are not watching the imminent destruction of our livelihood and can only imagine the magnitude of anger and despair. It is, however, incumbent upon us to take that empathic step, which should result in our seeing in the "we" our participation in the destruction, and to realize that if we are not protesting against the war, "we" are supporting it.

A "true revolution of values" entails a radical change in perspective. It allows "Vietnam" to appear as "but a symptom of a far deeper malady within the American spirit" and a "pattern" of U.S. global domination to emerge in the persons of "military 'advisors'" in obeisance to "the giant triplets of racism, materialism, and militarism." It makes it possible to look "with righteous indignation . . . across the seas and see individual capitalists in the West investing huge sums of money in Asia, Africa and South America, only to take the profits out with no concern for the social betterment of the countries." It makes it clear that "this business of burning human beings with napalm, of filling our nation's homes with orphans and widows, of injecting poisonous drugs of hate into veins of people normally humane, of sending men home from dark and bloody battlefields physically handicapped and psychologically deranged, cannot be reconciled with wisdom, justice, and love." And it makes it impossible to see otherwise—and to look away. In the process, the passage also performs a metamorphosis, as it subtly drops the national identifier ("our nation's") to describe the effects of war on combatants and blurs the distinction among them. War is negatively transformative, and a "true revolution of values" will show the metamorphic power of total war.

As it conjoins the anti-racism of the civil rights movement with opposition to the colonial war, "Beyond Vietnam" offers an analysis of what would come to be called structural racism, on a global scale. And it offers the environment as the blasted ground that bears its scars: "Now there is little left to build on—save bitterness. Soon the only solid physical foundations remaining will be found at our military bases and in the concrete of the concentration camps we call fortified hamlets. The peasants may well wonder if we plan to build our new Vietnam on such grounds as these?"

The Martinican poet and politician Aimé Césaire made environmental devastation and its consequences a signal feature of his magnificent 1939 anti-colonial long poem, *Notebook of a Return to a Native Land* (*Cahiers d'un retour au pays natal*). Dismayed by the state in which he finds his natal island, the homecoming poet carries "a river of turtle doves and savanna clover . . .

forever in [his] depths height-deep . . . as a guard against" the tragic ravages of colonialism that has bequeathed upon a once paradisal setting "the putre-fying force of crepuscular surroundings, surveyed night and day by a vene-real sun. . . . the hungry Antilles . . . pitted with smallpox, . . . dynamited by alcohol, stranded in the mud of this bay . . . an aged poverty rotting under the sun, silently; an aged silence, bursting with tepid pustules, the awful futility of our raison d'être."[7] The poem catalogs the devastation but offers a hopeful path for recovery rooted in an all-encompassing program of decolonization, including an entire rethinking of colonial knowledge, from geography and geopolitics to history and culture. Such environmental destruction is the result not only of resource exploitation but also of the effort to tame the col-onists and their land that is the watchword of colonialism. As a friend and mentee of Césaire, the theorist of decolonization Frantz Fanon, explained, the colonizer's view of both the land and the culture of the colonized as dan-gerous is "why we must put the DDT which destroys parasites, the bearers of disease, on the same level as the Christian religion, which wages war on embryonic heresies and instincts, and on evil as yet unborn."[8]

Chemicals such as DDT intrinsically evoked warfare as well, as the biol-ogist Rachel Carson had shown in her influential 1962 work, *Silent Spring*; chemicals developed for both world wars, she explained, had turned out to be effective insecticides and pesticides that revolutionized everything from industrial agriculture to home gardening. But, she warned, they came with devastating consequences for the environment and long-term human health, lasting into future generations. In Vietnam, the military reversed the pro-cess, turning those agricultural developments back into deliberate weapons of war with a program of "herbicidal warfare." Operation Ranch Hand was specifically designed to destroy the livelihoods and hiding places of "enemy troops" with weapons such as the notorious Agent Orange, with no regard, as "Beyond Vietnam" stresses, for the indiscriminate impact on Vietnamese noncombatants and their descendants. Reviled as King was by the main-stream U.S. media and political establishment following the speech, "Beyond Vietnam" effectively and influentially tied civil rights to the anti-war move-ment as manifestations of a "new form of colonialism" in which resource extraction and other forms of exploitation are compounded by environmen-tal destruction as a deliberate strategy of war.

The historian David Zierler documents the emergence of a movement among anti-war scientists, led by the Yale biologist Arthur Galston, who coined the word "ecocide" to protest the massive short- and long-term destruction of herbicidal warfare, which they sought to prevent. Zierler attributes their ultimate success to the movement's dovetailing with two big geopolitical transformations: the shift in foreign policy away from an almost exclusive focus on anti-communism and the recognition of humanity's impact on the environment as "global in scope and a threat to international peace and even human survival."[9] In "Beyond Vietnam," environmental devastation, a literal weapon of war, vividly manifests Fanon's indictment of colonialism as a form of total war—not just on humans but on all living things.

The "true revolution of values" for which "Beyond Vietnam" calls is central to the project of *Empire and Environment*. Both the artists and writers who are the subjects of the chapters and the contributing authors themselves grapple with the ever-changing forms of colonialism that make it so elusive, facilitating the perpetuation of its structures and effects. In so doing, they train attention on what Ann Laura Stoler—whose work weaves throughout this volume—calls "the *connective tissue* that continues to bind human potentials to degraded environments, and degraded personhoods to the material refuse of imperial projects—to the spaces redefined, to the soils turned toxic, to the relations severed between people and people, and between people and things."[10]

It is hard to imagine a better indication of the timeliness and urgency of *Empire and Environment* than the pandemic that exploded while the book was underway—or a better illustration of the consequences of the "connective tissue" and the "ecological ruination" it perpetuates. There is often a momentary clarity that accompanies a crisis—literally, a turning point—and perhaps the experience of living through the COVID-19 pandemic might impart a sharpened view of ourselves in historical context. Perhaps we might see the pandemic—as Harding and King saw Vietnam—as a symptom, the expression of geopolitical and environmental consequences of total war (the "new form of colonialism") that offer fertile ground for local outbreaks and the conditions that turn them into global pandemics: "the violence," as detailed in the introduction to *Empire and Environment*, "of forced alienation of humans from the natural world (animals, plants, organisms, lands, and seas) and also of humans (colonizers, white settlers, and men) from other humans (Indigenous peoples, subaltern populations, and women)."

The contributions in this volume invite us to "disentrance," as Rina Garcia Chua puts it in the title of her chapter, "the rot of colonialism": to see how that forced alienation is masked and with what consequences. To see that rot is to recognize "ecocidal violence" not only in the "tepid pustules" of Césaire's Antilles but also in the anti-Asian violence that proliferated during the pandemic both rhetorically and physically. That recognition can help us understand how normalized formulations such as the naming of "Asian Hantaan virus" or "Seoul virus" and its description as "another unwelcome immigrant" can turn human beings into embodiments of viral threats.[11] And how the more deliberately inflammatory racist slurs emanating from a presidential podium—"Wuhan Flu," "Kung Flu," "China Virus"—manifest and sustain "colonial rot." They make visible how common parlance—such as "We are at war with the virus"—is in fact a dangerous expression of total war.

In 2000, the Nobel prize–winning microbiologist Joshua Lederberg warned of the imminent danger of not learning to live more effectively with our microbes. Cautioning of the need for "new strategies and tactics," he advises, "our most sophisticated leap would be to drop the Manichean view of microbes—'We good; they evil'"—and replace it with "a more ecologically informed metaphor, which includes the germs'-eye view of infection."[12] While his reference point is the human body as biome, *Empire and Environment* offers a planetary analogue in which a more ecologically informed discourse might envision the interdependent human relations as well as those between humans and other living organisms in ways that stress cooperation rather than competition as a more just, equitable, and responsible way of inhabiting the planet and, indeed, as the sine qua non of human and planetary survival.

Empire and Environment, however, does more than identify the problem. Among the most remarkable features of this work is the emphasis on creative ways to move forward. The chapters and the artists and writers they take as their subjects urge neither a return to an Edenic past nor a denial of the damage we cannot undo. Rather, the volume ends with a challenge to "take up imperial debris as a problematic though inescapable ally as we strive to mitigate its slow violence" and "develop relations and modes of endurance that leave us transformed." The volume insists on the possibilities for that metamorphosis at least partly through art and other creative forms of expression.

The imagination of this volume as well as its hard-headed realism is exemplified, in Chad Shomura's final chapter, by art that imagines how even one of the most ambiguous as well as virulent metonymies of "ecological ruination," plastic, "can be creatively incorporated into new forms of collaborative endurance . . . that may be one way to deposit care into archives of the future that are presently in the making." The visionary project *Empire and Environment* advocates—and models—is as hopeful as it is urgent at a time when we are, perhaps more than we have ever been, "deeply in need of a new way beyond the darkness that seems so close around us."

Notes

1. Martin Luther King, "Beyond Vietnam: A Time to Break Silence," speech delivered 4 April 1967, https://www.americanrhetoric.com/speeches/mlkatimetobreaksilence.htm. Further references to the speech are to this site.

2. See Vincent Harding, *Martin Luther King: The Inconvenient Hero* (Orbis Books, 2000 [1996]); Benjamin Hedin, "Martin Luther King, Jr.'s Searing Antiwar Speech, Fifty Years Later," *New Yorker*, 3 Apr. 2017; Benjamin Hedin, *In Search of the Movement: The Struggle for Civil Rights Then and Now* (City Lights Books, 2015); and Taylor Branch, *At Canaan's Edge: America in the King Years, 1965–68* (Simon and Schuster, 2006).

3. Harding recounts his journey and role in drafting the speech in "Vietnam, Afghanistan, and Iran," chapter 9 of his *Martin Luther King*. The speech was a collaborative editorial process through which multiple drafts circulated among friends and Southern Christian Leadership Conference members with varying views on the tone the speech should take. On this process, see also Hedin, "Martin Luther King, Jr.'s Searing Antiwar Speech" and *In Search of the Movement*; and Branch, *At Canaan's Edge*.

4. King delivered "The Casualties of the War in Vietnam" on 25 February 1967 at the Nation Institute in Los Angeles, https://investigatinghistory.ashp.cuny.edu/module11D.php. All references to the speech are to this site.

5. Simeon Man, *Soldiering through Empire: Race and the Making of the Decolonizing Pacific* (U of California P, 2018).

6. Hedin, "Martin Luther King, Jr.'s Searing Antiwar Speech."

7. Aimé Césaire, *Notebook of a Return to a Native Land*, in *The Collected Poetry of Aimé Césaire*, translated by Clayton Eshelman and Annette Smith (U of California P, 1983), 32–85, quote on 33.

8. Frantz Fanon, *The Wretched of the Earth*, translated by Constance Farrington (Grove Press, 1963), 42.

9. David Zierler, *The Invention of Ecocide: Agent Orange, Vietnam, and the Scientists Who Changed the Way We Think about the Environment* (U of Georgia P, 2011), 4.

10. Ann Laura Stoler, "The Rot Remains: From Ruins to Ruination," *Imperial Debris: On Ruins and Ruination*, edited by Ann Laura Stoler (Duke UP, 2013), 1–35, quote on 7–8.

11. Barbara J. Culliton, "Emerging Viruses, Emerging Threat," *Science*, vol. 247, no. 4940, 1990, 279–80, quote on 279.

12. Joshua Lederberg, "Infectious History," *Science*, vol. 288, no. 5464, 14 Apr. 2000, 287–93, quote on 292–93.

CONTRIBUTORS

Editors

Heidi Amin-Hong is Assistant Professor of English at the University of California, Santa Barbara. She received her PhD in American Studies and Ethnicity from the University of Southern California. Her current project tracks ecological collapse as the material legacy of multiple forms of empire, militarism, and global capitalism in Southeast Asia and the Pacific. Her scholarship on Asian diasporic cultures, militarism, and climate displacement has been published in *Verge: Studies of Global Asias* and *ISLE: Interdisciplinary Studies in Literature and Environment*.

Rina Garcia Chua is currently a Jack and Doris Shadbolt Fellow in the Humanities at Simon Fraser University and she received her PhD in Interdisciplinary Studies from the University of British Columbia Okanagan. She is the editor of the first anthology of Philippine ecopoetry, *Sustaining the Archipelago* (University of Santo Tomas Publishing House, 2018), which was nominated for a Philippine National Book Award for Best Anthology in English. Rina is also the diversity co-officer for the Association for the Study of Literature and the Environment (ASLE), and poetry editor of *Tiger Moth Review* and *The Goose: A Journal of Arts, Environment, and Culture in Canada*.

Jeffrey Santa Ana is Associate Professor of English and affiliated faculty in Asian and Asian American Studies and Women's, Gender, and Sexuality Studies at Stony Brook University. He is the author of *Racial Feelings: Asian America in a Capitalist Culture of Emotion*. He has published articles on Asian American and Asian diasporic literatures in book volumes and journals, including *Signs*, *positions*, and *Journal of Asian American Studies*. He is currently working on a book titled "Transpacific Ecological Imagination: Envisioning the Decolonial Anthropocene."

Zhou Xiaojing is Professor of English and the Laurence Meredith Professor in the Humanities at the University of the Pacific. She is the author of four books—*Migrant Ecologies: Zheng Xiaoqiong's "Women Migrant Workers"*; *Cities of Others: Reimagining Urban Spaces in Asian American Literature*; *Ethics and Poetics of Alterity in Asian American Poetry*; and *Elizabeth Bishop: Rebel "in Shades and Shadows"*—and coeditor with Samina Najmin of the critical anthology *Form and Transformation in Asian American Literature*. Her current book project is entitled "Counter-Memory of the 'Frontier': Settler Colonialism and Japanese American Incarceration Camps."

Contributors

Emalani Case is Lecturer in Pacific Studies at Victoria University of Wellington. As a Hawaiian woman, scholar, activist, writer, and dancer, she is deeply engaged in issues of Indigenous rights and representation, colonialism and decolonization, and environmental and social justice. Her first book, *Everything Ancient Was Once New: Indigenous Persistence from* Hawaiʻi *to Kahiki*, was published in 2021. She is from Waimea, Hawaiʻi.

Ti-Han Chang is Lecturer in Asia Pacific Studies at the University of Central Lancashire. Her research focuses on contemporary ecoliterature in Taiwan and its implication in the Asia Pacific region. She is particularly interested in postcolonial ecocriticism, which draws her attention to topics such as non-human agency, borders and nations, climate change, and migration. At her home institute, she serves as the deputy head at the Centre of Austronesian Studies (COAST), and further contributes her research works through the Northern Institute of Taiwan Studies (NorITS) and the Centre for Migration, Diaspora and Exile (MIDEX). Externally, she serves as the treasurer and board member of the Francophone Association of Taiwan Studies (AFET) and has recently been elected as a board member of the European Association of Taiwan Studies (EATS). Since 2019, she has engaged with multiple research projects that investigate the Pacific climate migrants and the narratives of the displaced. Apart from her journal publications on Taiwanese ecoliterature, she also contributes online articles on more general environmental and literature topics for *The Conversation* and *Taiwan Insights*.

Emily Cheng is Associate Professor of English at Montclair State University in New Jersey. She received her PhD in Literature and Cultural Studies from the University of California at San Diego. Her research appears in journals in American Studies, Ethnic Studies, and Women's and Gender Studies such as *Western American Literature, Comparative American Studies, Frontiers: A Journal of Women's Studies,* and the *Journal of Asian American Studies.*

Kathleen (Kat) Cruz Gutierrez is Assistant Professor of Southeast Asian and Philippine History at the University of California, Santa Cruz. A specialist of colonial botany, Kat also writes on Philippine *materia medica,* weaving and dyeing technologies, and the plant humanities. Her research and writing have been supported by the Social Science Research Council, the Fulbright-Hays program of the U.S. Department of Education, California Humanities, the Oak Spring Garden Foundation, and the Andrew W. Mellon Foundation through the Humanities Institute of the New York Botanical Garden. In addition to her Philippines-based work, she is the co-PI of the project Watsonville is in the Heart, a community-generated public history initiative to preserve the stories of the first generation of Filipino farmworkers in California's Pajaro Valley.

Macarena Gómez-Barris is a scholar and writer working at the intersections of art, environment, feminist-cuir politics, and decolonial theory and praxis. She is the author of four books: *Where Memory Dwells: Culture and State Violence in Chile* (2009), *The Extractive Zone: Social Ecologies and Decolonial Perspectives* (2017), *Beyond the Pink Tide: Art and Political Undercurrents in the Américas* (2018), and *Towards a Sociology of a Trace* (2010, with Herman Gray). She is completing a new book on what she terms the "colonial Anthropocene," *At the Sea's Edge: Liquidity Beyond Colonial Extinction* (forthcoming, Duke University Press, 2022).

Rebecca H. Hogue teaches at Harvard University, where she is Lecturer on History & Literature and Studies of Women, Gender, and Sexuality. She is coeditor, along with Craig Santos Perez, of a forthcoming anthology on environmental relations in Oceania and the Pacific Islands. Her work has appeared in *Modern Fiction Studies,* the *Journal of Transnational American Studies, Amerasia,* and is forthcoming in *Critical Ethnic Studies.* She is currently working on a book entitled, "Nuclear Archipelagos."

Amy Lee works at the San Francisco Department of Public Health's Center for Learning and Innovation and teaches at UC Berkeley's Fall Program for Freshmen. She is also a campaign researcher at Asian Immigrant Women Advocates and a member of the Anti-Eviction Mapping Project. Her research interests include global China, transpacific literary and cultural studies, ethnic and postcolonial literatures, and Asian film and television studies. She has published articles on Hong Kong television, diasporic media geographies and global Chinatown, and the work of Hong Kong independent filmmaker Evans Chan.

John Charles Ryan is Adjunct Associate Professor at Southern Cross University, Australia, and Adjunct Senior Research Fellow at the Nulungu Institute, Notre Dame University, Australia. His research focuses on Aboriginal Australian literature, Southeast Asian ecocriticism, environmental humanities, ecopoetics, and critical plant studies. His recent work includes *Introduction to the Environmental Humanities* (2021, authored with J. Andrew Hubbell), *The Mind of Plants: Narratives of Vegetal Intelligence* (2021, edited with Monica Gagliano and Patrícia Vieira), and *Nationalism in India: Texts and Contexts* (2021, edited with Debajyoti Biswas).

Chitra Sankaran received her PhD from the University of London and is Deputy Head of Department and Chair of Literature in the Department of English Language and Literature at the National University of Singapore. Her areas of research interests are South and Southeast Asian fiction, postcolonial theory, feminism, and ecocriticism. Her publications include three monographs, ten edited volumes, book chapters, and research articles in international research journals such as *ISLE, Journal of Commonwealth Literature, ARIEL, Theatre Research International,* and *Australian Feminist Studies.* Her recent monograph, *Women, Subalterns and Ecologies in South and Southeast Asian Women's Fiction* (2021), was published by the University of Georgia Press. Her coauthored volume, *Revenge of Gaia: Contemporary Ecofictions from Vietnam* (2021), was published by Penguin Random House. She is the founding and current president of the Association for the Study of Literature and Environment in ASEAN and the chief editor for the *Journal of Southeast Asian Ecocriticism.*

Craig Santos Perez is a native Chamoru from the Pacific Island of Guåhan (Guam). He is the coeditor of six anthologies and the author of five poetry books and the monograph, *Navigating Chamoru Poetry: Indigeneity, Aesthetics, and Decolonization* (2022). He is Professor in the English department, and an affiliate faculty with the Center for Pacific Islands Studies and the Indigenous Politics Program, at the University of Hawai'i at Mānoa.

Chad Shomura is Assistant Professor of Ethnic Studies at the University of Colorado, Denver. His research interests include affect, biopower, new materialism, race, and ecology. His recent publications are in *American Quarterly*, *Oxford Encyclopedia of Asian American Literature and Culture*, and *Contemporary Political Theory*. His current book project, "A Life Otherwise," examines minor assemblies of life that upset the good life.

Priscilla Wald is the R. Florence Brinkley Distinguished Chair of English at Duke University; author of *Contagious: Cultures, Carriers, and the Outbreak Narrative* (2008) and *Constituting Americans: Cultural Anxiety and Narrative Form* (1995); and coeditor, with Matthew Taylor, of *American Literature* and, with David Kazanjian and Elizabeth McHenry, of the NYU Press book series America in the Long Nineteenth Century. She also codirects the First Book Institute with Sean Goudie at Penn State University. She is working on a monograph entitled "Human Being after Genocide."

INDEX

Note: Page numbers in italics refer to figures.